fourth edition

Intercultural Competence
Interpersonal Communication across Cultures

Myron W. Lustig
San Diego State University

Jolene Koester
California State University, Northridge

Allyn and Bacon

Boston   New York   San Francisco
Mexico City   Montreal   Toronto   London   Madrid   Munich   Paris
Hong Kong   Singapore   Tokyo   Cape Town   Sydney

Editor in Chief: *Karen Hanson*
Vice President, Executive Editor: *Karon Bowers*
Senior Development Editor: *Ellen Darion*
Editorial Assistant: *Jennifer Trebby*
Marketing Manager: *Mandee Eckersley*
Editorial Production Administrator: *Susan Brown*
Editorial–Production Service: *Matrix Productions Inc.*
Composition and Prepress Buyer: *Linda Cox*
Manufacturing Buyer: *JoAnne Sweeney*
Cover Administrator: *Linda Knowles*
Interior Designer: *Glenna Collett*
Photo Researcher: *Kate Cook*
Illustrations: *Glenna Collett*
Electronic Composition: *Publishers' Design and Production Services, Inc.*

For related titles and support materials, visit our online catalog at www.ablongman.com.

Between the time Website information is gathered and then published, it is not unusual for some sites to have closed. Also, the transcription of URLs can result in unintended typographical errors. The publisher would appreciate notification where these occur so that they may be corrected in subsequent editions.

Library of Congress Cataloging-in-Publication Data

Lustig, Myron W.
    Intercultural competence : interpersonal communication across cultures / by Myron W.
Lustig and Jolene Koester. — 4th ed.
      p. cm.
    Includes bibliographical references and indexes.
    ISBN 0-321-08177-3
    1. Intercultural communication.   2. Communicative competence—United States.
  3. Interpersonal communication—United States. I. Koester, Jolene. II. Title.

HM1211 .L87 2003
303.48′2—dc21   2002018692

Printed in the United States of America
10 9 8 7 6 5 4 3   06 05 04

Contents

Preface   ix

Credits   xiv

part one   *Communication and Intercultural Competence*   *1*

1   **Introduction to Intercultural Competence**   2

The Imperative for Intercultural Competence   4
    The International Imperative for Intercultural Competence   5
    The Domestic Imperative for Intercultural Competence   6
Communication   9
    Defining Communication   9
    Characteristics of Communication   10
    Interpersonal Communication   10
The Challenge of Communicating in an Intercultural World   19
Summary   23
For Discussion   23
For Further Reading   24

2   **Culture and Intercultural Communication**   25

Culture   25
    Defining Culture for the Study of Communication   25
    Culture and Related Terms   31
    Why Cultures Differ   34
Intercultural Communication   44
    Examples of Intercultural Interactions   45
    Similarities and Differences between Communicators   48

Definition of Intercultural Communication   50
Intercultural Communication and Related Terms   51
Summary   53
For Discussion   54
For Further Reading   54

3   Intercultural Communication Competence   55

The United States as an Intercultural Community   55
Metaphors of U.S. Cultural Diversity   56
What Do You Call Someone from the United States of America?   60
Cultural Groups in the United States   61
Competence and Intercultural Communication   64
Intracultural Communication Competence   64
The Components of Intercultural Competence   65
Basic Tools for Improving Intercultural Competence   72
The BASICs of Intercultural Competence   72
Description, Interpretation, and Evaluation   76
Summary   80
For Discussion   81
For Further Reading   81

part two   *Cultural Differences in Communication   83*

4   Cultural Patterns and Communication: Foundations   84

Defining Cultural Patterns   85
Components of Cultural Patterns   87
Beliefs   87
Values   88
Norms   91
Characteristics of Cultural Patterns   91
The Functions of Cultural Patterns   91
An Overview of Cultural Patterns   93
Cultural Patterns and Intercultural Competence   105
Summary   108
For Discussion   108
For Further Reading   109

5   Cultural Patterns and Communication: Taxonomies   110

Taxonomies of Cultural Patterns   110
Hall's High- and Low-Context Cultural Patterns   111
Hofstede's Cultural Patterns   115
Confucian Cultural Values   132

Cultural Taxonomies and Intercultural Competence   135
Summary   137
For Discussion   137
For Further Reading   138

6   **Cultural Identity, Cultural Biases, and Intercultural Contact   139**

Cultural Identity   140
    The Nature of Identity   140
    The Formation of Cultural Identity   142
    Characteristics of Cultural Identity   144
Cultural Biases   145
    Social Categorizing   147
    Ethnocentrism   148
    Stereotyping   151
    Prejudice   154
    Discrimination   156
    Racism   157
Intercultural Contact   161
    Dominance and Subordination between Groups   161
    Attitudes among Cultural Members   162
    Outcomes of Intercultural Contact   163
Becoming an Interculturally Competent Communicator   170
Identity, Biases, Contact, and Intercultural Competence   171
Summary   172
For Discussion   173
For Further Reading   173

part **three** *Coding Intercultural Communication   175*

7   Nonverbal Intercultural Communication   176

Definition of Nonverbal Codes   176
    Characteristics of Nonverbal Codes   178
    Relationship of Nonverbal to Verbal Communication   178
Cultural Universals in Nonverbal Communication   179
Cultural Variations in Nonverbal Communication   180
Nonverbal Messages in Intercultural Communication   182
    Body Movements   183
    Space   187
    Touch   190
    Time   192
    Voice   195
    Other Nonverbal Code Systems   197
Synchrony of Nonverbal Communication Codes   198

Nonverbal Communication and Intercultural Competence   199
Summary   201
For Discussion   201
For Further Reading   202

8   Verbal Intercultural Communication   203

The Power of Language in Intercultural Communication   203
Definition of Verbal Codes   205
    The Features of Language   206
    Rule Systems in Verbal Codes   208
    Interpretation and Intercultural Communication   213
Language, Thought, Culture, and Intercultural Communication   217
    The Sapir–Whorf Hypothesis of Linguistic Relativity   217
    Language and Intercultural Communication   224
Verbal Codes and Intercultural Competence   233
Summary   236
For Discussion   236
For Further Reading   237

9   The Effects of Code Usage in Intercultural Communication   238

Preferences in the Organization of Verbal Codes   239
    Organizational Preferences in the Use of U.S. English   239
    Organizational Preferences in Other Languages and Cultures   242
Cultural Variations in Persuasion   243
    Persuasion in Intercultural Encounters   243
    Cultural Differences in What Is Acceptable as Evidence   245
    Cultural Differences in What Is Considered Reasonable   246
    Cultural Differences in Styles of Persuasion   249
Cultural Variations in the Structure of Conversations   253
    Value of Talk and Silence   253
    Rules for Conversations   255
Effects of Code Usage on Intercultural Competence   258
Summary   259
For Discussion   260
For Further Reading   260

part four *Communication in Intercultural Relationships*   261

10   Intercultural Competence in Interpersonal Relationships   262

Cultural Variations in Interpersonal Relationships   262
    Types of Interpersonal Relationships   262

Dimensions of Interpersonal Relationships   270
Dynamics of Interpersonal Relationships   273
The Maintenance of Face in Interpersonal Relationships   274
Types of Face Needs   275
Facework and Interpersonal Communication   277
Facework and Intercultural Communication   279
Improving Intercultural Relationships   280
Learning about People from Other Cultures   280
Sharing Oneself with People from Other Cultures   284
Handling Differences in Intercultural Relationships   287
Interpersonal Relationships and Intercultural Competence   290
Summary   290
For Discussion   291
For Further Reading   291

11 **Episodes, Contexts, and Intercultural Interactions   292**

Social Episodes in Intercultural Relationships   292
The Nature of Social Episodes   292
Components of Social Episodes   294
Contexts for Intercultural Communication   301
The Health Care Context   301
The Educational Context   307
The Business Context   314
Episodes, Contexts, and Intercultural Competence   324
Summary   325
For Discussion   325
For Further Reading   325

12 **The Potential for Intercultural Competence   327**

The Ethics of Intercultural Competence   328
When in Rome . . .   329
Are Cultural Values Relative or Universal?   331
Do the Ends Justify the Means?   331
Ethics—Your Choices   332
The Perils and Prospects for Intercultural Competence   333
Impact of National and International Events on Intercultural
Communication   333
Forces That Pull Us Together and Apart   337
Summary   340
Concluding Remarks   340
For Discussion   341
For Further Reading   341

Resources   343

Intercultural Films   343
Online Resources   344

Notes   347

Author Index   374

Subject Index   379

Preface

The twenty-first century is upon us, and competence in intercultural communication has become an absolute necessity. In both your private and public lives, in all of your personal and professional endeavors, it is imperative that you learn to communicate with people whose cultural heritage makes them vastly different from you. This book is intended to help you accomplish that goal.

Features of This Text

The perspective we offer in this text differs from that of similar books in several important ways. We provide a healthy blend of the practical and the theoretical, of the concrete and the abstract, in order to make the ideas and issues salient and meaningful.

First, we recognize that intercultural communicators need specific suggestions and examples about what they should know, how they should interpret their feelings, and how they ought to behave in order to be competent in a given interaction. Beginning students, in particular, need material at the concrete end of the ladder of abstraction. Consequently, we have chosen an easy and conversational style and have linked the presentation of theories with numerous illustrative examples. The Culture Connections boxes, for instance, which are so useful to students, are designed to allow class discussions that emphasize the affective dimension of intercultural competence. The new Try This activities let students actively apply the theories they read about, both to their own experiences and to the world around them. Also new to the fourth edition, For Discussion questions and For Further Reading suggestions engage and challenge students, helping them to develop their own intercultural communication skills.

Second, we are aware of the importance of current and accurate descriptions of intercultural communication theories and their supporting research, which provide powerful ways of viewing and understanding intercultural communication phenomena. This edition includes new or updated information on communication, cultural values, cultural biases, theories of adaptation, Ebonics, cultural differences in persuasive logics, intercultural conflict, and contexts for intercultural communication. In light of the events since September 11, 2001, we also discuss the perils and prospects for intercultural communication in a global world. We have also incorporated ideas from literally hundreds of new sources across a wide spectrum of inquiry. These sources form a solid bibliography for those interested in pursuing specific topics in greater depth. As we have in the past, however, we have chosen to maintain the text's readability by placing the citations at the end of the book, where they are unobtrusive but available to interested readers.

Third, we recognize the significance and importance of cultural patterns, which provide the underlying set of assumptions for cultural and intercultural communication. The focus on cultural patterns as the lens through which all interactions are interpreted is thoroughly explored in Chapters 4 and 5, and the themes of these two chapters permeate the concepts developed in all subsequent chapters. New to this edition, for instance, is a substantial updating of Hofstede's work on cultural patterns.

Fourth, we include topics not normally emphasized in intercultural communication textbooks. The work on cultural identity and the role of cultural biases has been revised, as has the section on communication contexts. Although it is standard fare for most texts to consider verbal and nonverbal code systems, we provide a careful elaboration of the nature of differing logical systems, or preferred reasoning patterns, and the consequences for intercultural communication when the expectations for the language in use are not widely shared. Similarly, drawing heavily on the available information about interpersonal communication, we explore the dynamic processes of establishing and developing a relationship between culturally different individuals, including an elaboration of issues related to "face" in interpersonal relationships.

Fifth, we provide a discussion of important ethical and social issues for intercultural communicators. Ethical issues are often inadequately considered as one learns about intercultural communication; yet, in our view, they are crucial because intercultural competence requires a delicate balancing act on the tightrope between moral certainty and cultural relativism. Consistent with this ethical orientation, we as authors are aware of and wish to acknowledge the cultural perspective that we bring to its writing.

Acknowledgment of Cultural Ancestry

At various points in our writing, we were amazed at how subtly but thoroughly our own cultural experiences had permeated the text. Lest anyone believe that our presentation of relevant theories, examples, and practical suggestions is without the distortion of culture, we would like to describe our own cultural heritage. That heritage shapes our understanding of intercultural communication, and it affects what we know, how we feel, and what we do when we communicate with others.

Our cultural ancestry is European, and our own cultural experiences are predominantly those that we refer to in this book as European American. Both our family backgrounds and the communities in which we were raised have influenced and reinforced our cultural perspectives. The European American cultural experience is the one we know best, simply because it is who we are. Many of our ideas and examples about intercultural communication, therefore, draw on our own cultural experiences.

We have tried, however, to increase the number and range of other cultural voices through the ideas and examples that we provide. These voices and the lessons and illustrations they offer represent our colleagues, our friends, and, most important, our students.

Importance of Voices from Other Cultures

Although we have attempted to include a wide range of domestic and international cultural groups, inevitably we have shortchanged some simply because we do not have sufficient knowledge, either through direct experience or through secondary accounts, of all cultures. Our errors and omissions are not meant to exclude or discount. Rather, they represent the limits of our own intercultural communication experiences. We hope that you, as a reader with a cultural voice of your own, will participate with us in a dialogue that allows us to improve this text over a period of time. Readers of previous editions were generous with their suggestions for improvement, and we are very grateful to them for these comments. We ask that you continue this dialogue by providing us with your feedback and responses. Send us examples that illustrate the principles discussed in the text. Be willing to provide a cultural perspective that differs from our own and from those of our colleagues, friends, and students. Our commitment now and in future editions of this book is to describe a variety of cultural voices with accuracy and sensitivity. We ask for your help in accomplishing that objective.

Issues in the Use of Cultural Examples

Some of the examples in the following pages may include references to a culture to which you belong or with which you have had substantial experiences, and our example may not match your personal knowledge. As you will discover in the opening chapters of the book, both your own experiences and the example we recount could be accurate. One of the tensions we felt in writing this book was in making statements that are broad enough to provide reasonably accurate generalizations but specific and tentative enough to avoid false claims of universal applicability to all individuals in a given culture.

We have struggled as well with issues of fairness, sensitivity, representativeness, and inclusiveness. Indeed, we have had innumerable discussions with our colleagues across the country—colleagues who, like ourselves, are committed to making the United States and U.S. colleges and universities into truly multicultural institutions—and we have sought their advice about appropriate ways to reflect the value of cultural diversity in our writing. We have responded to their suggestions, and we appreciate the added measure of quality that these cultural voices supply.

Text Organization

Our goal in this book is to provide ideas and information that can help you to achieve competence in intercultural communication. Part One, "Communication and Intercultural Competence," orients you to the central ideas that underlie this book. Chapter 1 begins with a discussion of the international and domestic imperatives for attaining intercultural competence. We also define and discuss the nature of communication generally and interpersonal communication specifically. In Chapter 2, we introduce the notion of culture and explain why cultures differ. Our focus then turns to intercultural communication, and we distinguish that form of communication from others. As our concern in this book is with interpersonal communication among people from different cultures, an understanding of these key concepts is critical. Chapter 3 begins with a focus on the United States as an intercultural community, as we address the delicate but important issue of how to characterize its cultural mix and the members of its cultural groups. We then lay the groundwork for our continuing discussion of intercultural competence by explaining what competence is, what its components are, and how people can achieve it when they communicate with others. The chapter also focuses on two communication tools that could help people to improve their intercultural competence.

Part Two, "Cultural Differences in Communication," is devoted to an analysis of the fundamental ways that cultures vary. Chapter 4 provides a general overview of the ways in which cultures differ, and it emphasizes the importance of cultural patterns in differentiating among communication styles. This chapter also examines the structural features that are similar across all cultures. Chapter 5 offers two taxonomies that can be used to understand systematic differences in the ways in which people from various cultures think and communicate. Chapter 6 underscores the importance of cultural identity and the consequences of biases within intercultural communication.

In Part Three, "Coding Intercultural Communication," we turn our attention to nonverbal and verbal messages, which are central to the communication process. Chapter 7 discusses the effects of cultural differences on nonverbal codes, as the accurate coding and decoding of nonverbal symbols is vital in intercultural communication. Chapter 8 examines the coding of verbal languages and the influences of linguistic and cultural differences on attempts to communicate interculturally. Chapter 9 investigates the effects or consequences of the cultural differences in coding systems on face-to-face intercultural interactions. Of particular interest are those experiences involving participants who were taught to use different languages and organizational schemes.

Part Four, "Communication in Intercultural Relationships," emphasizes the associations that form among people as a result of their shared communication experiences. Chapter 10 looks at the all-important issues related to the development and maintenance of interpersonal relationships among people from different cultures. Chapter 11 highlights the processes by which communication events are grouped into episodes and interpreted within such contexts as health care, education, and business. Finally, Chapter 12 highlights the ethical choices individuals must face when engaged in interpersonal communication across cultures. The chapter concludes with some remarks about the problems, possibilities, and opportunities for life in our contemporary intercultural world.

A Note to Instructors

Accompanying the text are an Instructor's Manual Test Bank and Computerized Test Bank, which are available to instructors who adopt the text for their courses. Please contact your Allyn and Bacon representative for these materials. They provide pedagogical suggestions and instructional activities to enhance students' learning of course materials.

Also available from Allyn and Bacon is our companion reader, *Among US: Essays on Identity, Belonging, and Intercultural Competence.*

Teaching a course in intercultural communication is one of the most exciting assignments available. It is difficult to convey in writing the level of involvement, commitment, and interest displayed by typical students in such courses. These students are the reason that teaching intercultural communication is, quite simply, so exhilarating and rewarding.

Acknowledgments

Many people have assisted us, and we would like to thank them for their help. Reviewers who contributed detailed comments for this edition include Randy Dillon, Southwest Missouri State University; Lynda Dee Dixon, Bowling Green State University; David Lapakko, Augsburg College; Nanette Potee, Northeastern Illinois University; Fredric Wild, Jr., Lycoming College; and Fay Yokomizo Akindes, University of Wisconsin, Parkside. We are also indebted to the students and faculty at our respective institutions, to our colleagues in the communication discipline, and to many people throughout higher education who have willingly shared their ideas and cultural voices with us.

Intercultural Competence was first published in 1993. This fourth edition, then, constitutes the book's tenth anniversary. We are very grateful for the many indications, during the past decade, that intercultural communication has become an increasingly vital and essential component of many universities' curricula. While we harbor no illusions that our influence was anything but minor, it is nevertheless gratifying to have been a "strong voice in the chorus" for these positive changes. We are also pleased by this book's influence on the communication discipline, both in its standardization of terminology—the increasingly popular phrase "U.S. Americans," for example, was coined in the first edition—and in the topics now commonly addressed in intercultural communication courses. In addition, we want to thank you, the reader, for your many favorable responses to earlier editions of *Intercultural Competence;* an even bigger thank-you goes to those whose insightful criticisms have spurred vital improvements.

Finally, we would like to acknowledge each other's encouragement and support throughout the writing of this book. It has truly been a collaborative effort. We also want to acknowledge a shared responsibility for any remaining errors, omissions, oversights, mistakes, and misstatements that may exist despite our best efforts and intentions to correct them.

Myron W. Lustig
Jolene Koester

Credits

Text

Lists adapted from Dean Barnlund, *Public and Private Self in Japan and the United States: Communication styles of two cultures*, Intercultural Press, 1975. Reprinted with permission of Intercultural Press, Inc., Yarmouth, ME.

Excerpt from "Should my Tribal Past Shape Delia's Future?" by Dympna-Ugwu-Oju, *Newsweek*, Inc. (December 4, 2000). All rights reserved. Reprinted by permission.

Excerpt from *The Sweeter the Juice* by Shirlee Taylor Haizlip. Reprinted with the permission of Simon & Schuster, Inc. Copyright © 1994 by Shirlee Taylor Haizlip.

Myron W. Lustig, "Culture's Core," *Western Journal of Communication*, 60(4) Fall 1996) 415-416.

Excerpt from *Living Overseas: A Book of Preparations* by Ted Ward, pp. 95-96 and 107-109. Reprinted with the permission of The Free Press, a Division of Simon & Schuster, Inc. Copyright © 1984 by The Free Press.

Excerpt from Laurent A. Parks Daloz, Cheryl H. Keen, James P. Keen, and Sharon Daloz Parks, *Common Fire: Lives of Commitment in a Complex World* (Boston: Beacon Press, 1996) 63, 64.

Excerpt from "Getting to Know About You and Me" by Chana Schoenberger from *Newsweek*, (September 20, 1993:8) © 1993 Newsweek, Inc. All rights reserved. Reprinted by permission.

Excerpt from *Peripheral Visions: Learning Along the Way* by Mary Catherine Bateson, (New York:HarperCollins, 1994), 9-10.

Excerpt from "We and They" from *Rudyard Kipling's Verse: Definitive Edition* by Rudyard Kipling, (Garden City, NY: Doubleday, 1940) 768-769.

Excerpt from "Value Priorities and Social Desirability: Much Substance, Some Style" by Shalom H. Schwartz, Markku Verkasalo, Avishai Antonovsky, and Lilach Sagiv, *British Journal of Social Psychology, 36*, 1997, 7.

Excerpts from *Native Stranger* by Eddy L. Harris. Reprinted by permission of Sterling Lord Literistic, Inc. Copyright 1991 by Eddy L. Harris.

Reuse of "Playing the Name Game" from *Newsweek*, November 20, 1995, p. 81, from *Newsweek*, November 20, © 1995 Newsweek, Inc. All rights reserved. Reprinted by permission.

Reuse of an excerpt from "Selena Country" from *Newsweek*, October 23, 1995, p. 79.

From *Newsweek*, October 23, © 1995 Newsweek, Inc. All rights reserved. Reprinted by permission.

Reuse of an excerpt from *Black Leopard* by Steven Voien, from *Black Leopard* by Steven Voien. Copyright © 1996 by Steven Voien. Used by permission of Alfred A. Knopf, a division of Random House, Inc.

Excerpts from *Wouldn't Take Nothing For My Journey Now.* New York: Random House, 1993)33.

Excerpt from *The Ukimwi Road: From Kenya to Zimbabwe.* (New York: Riverhead Books, 1995) 68-69.

Excerpt from "Monterrey: Confronting the Future" by Michael Parfit from *National Geographic*, August 1996.

Reuse of an excerpt from "Labels Blur in mixed-race U.S.: Golfer challenges traditional distinctions" by David Barton, *The Sacramento Bee*, 4/24/97. Copyright © 1997 by The Sacramento Bee. Reprinted by permission.

Reuse of table from "Groupings on Hofstede's Four Dimensions" based on data reported in *Cultures and Organi-*

by The Associated Press. Reprinted with permission of The Associated Press.

Table 7.1 "Contrasts in Intercultural Negotiations" and Table 7.2, "Establishing Rapport" from *Multicultural Management 2000: Essential Cultural Insights for Global Business Success* by Farid Elashmawi and Philip R. Harris, Gulf Publishing Co., pp. 196, 198. Reprinted with permission of Butterworth-Heineman.

Excerpt from *Testing the Limits of Tolerance as Cultures-* "Does Freedom Mean Accepting Rituals That Repel the West?" by Barbara Crossette, *The New York Times*, March 6, 1999, A15.

Excerpt from "Diversity Issues in the Workplace" by Frances E. Kendall from *Valuing Diversity: New Tools for a New Reality* by Griggs et al. Copyright " 1995 by The McGraw-Hill Companies, Inc. Reprinted by permission of The McGraw-Hill Companies.

Excerpts from "Social Time: The Heartbeat of Culture" by R. Levine and E. Wolff, *Psychology Today*, March, 1985. Reprinted with permission from *Psychology Today Magazine*, Copyright " 1985 Sussex Publishers, Inc.

Reuse of the figure "Conference Table Seating Arrangements for Japanese Business Negotiations" from "Using Cultural Skills for Cooperative Advantage in Japan" by Richard H. Reeves-Ellington from *Human Organization*, 52 (1993): 209. Reproduced from Human Organization with the permission of the Society for Applied Anthropology.

Photos

p. 3: David Young-Wolff/PhotoEdit;
p. 6: David Silverman/Getty Images, Inc.;
p. 8: Left Lane Productions/CORBIS;
p. 9: Joseph Sohm/CORBIS;
p. 13: Gary Conner/PhotoEdit;
p. 22: Bill Bachmann/PhotoEdit;
p. 27: Michael Newman/PhotoEdit;
p. 29: left: Dorothi Littell Greco/The Image Works;
p. 29: right: Myrleen Ferguson/PhotoEdit;
p. 35: © Myron W. Lustig and Jolene Koester
p. 37: James Shaffer/PhotoEdit;
p. 39: © Myron W. Lustig and Jolene Koester
p. 40: Michael Newman/PhotoEdit;
p. 42: Gary Conner/PhotoEdit;
p. 51: Spencer Grant/PhotoEdit;
p. 57: Cleo Photography/PhotoEdit;
p. 60: Goodsmith/The Image Works;
p. 63: David Young-Wolff/PhotoEdit;
p. 68: Michael Newman/PhotoEdit;
p. 74: Peter Byron/PhotoEdit;
p. 85: left: Andy Sacks/Getty Images Inc .;
p. 85: right: Bill Aron/PhotoEdit;
p. 88: Paula Bronstein/Getty Images, Inc.;
p. 95: M. Greenlar/The Image Works;
p. 102: David Hiser/Getty Images Inc;
p. 106: David Young-Wolff/PhotoEdit;
p. 115: Michael Newman/PhotoEdit;
p. 124: Courtesy of Rock the Vote;
p. 130: John Moore/The Image Works;
p. 134: Robert Brenner/PhotoEdit;
p. 136: Michael Newman/PhotoEdit;
p. 141: Lawrence Migdale/Lawrence Migdale/Pix;
p. 143: David Young-Wolff/PhotoEdit;
p. 146: Michael Newman/PhotoEdit;
p. 150, both: Hulton Archive/Getty Images Inc.;

p. 155: Jonathan Nourok/Getty Images Inc.;
p. 157: © Myron W. Lustig and Jolene Koester
p. 159: A. Ramey/PhotoEdit;
p. 168: RNT Productions/CORBIS;
p. 180: Bruce Ayres/Getty Images Inc.;
p. 184: Tony Freeman/PhotoEdit;
p. 186: Burbank/The Image Works;
p. 190: Tim Page/CORBIS;
p. 199: Mary Kate Denny/PhotoEdit;
p. 206: PhotoDisc, Inc.;
p. 210: © Myron W. Lustig and Jolene Koester
p. 214: Michael Dwyer/Stock Boston;
p. 218: L. Goodsmith/The Image Works;
p. 226: © Myron W. Lustig and Jolene Koester
p. 228: Robert Brenner/PhotoEdit;
p. 235: Novastock/PhotoEdit;
p. 240: David Young-Wolff/PhotoEdit;
p. 252: Jeff Greenberg/PhotoEdit;
p. 256: Will Hart/PhotoEdit;
p. 265: Esbin-Anderson/The Image Works;
p. 267: Michael Newman/PhotoEdit;
p. 269: Suzanne Arms/The Image Works;
p. 281: Bill Bachmann/PhotoEdit;
p. 288: Michael Newman/PhotoEdit;
p. 296: David R. Frazier Photolibrary, Inc.;
p. 302: Spencer Grant/PhotoEdit;
p. 306: Joel Gordon/Joel Gordon Photography;
p. 309: Bob Kramer/Stock Boston;
p. 311: Will Hart;
p. 315: Don Bosler/Getty Images Inc.;
p. 317: Frank Herholdt/Getty Images Inc.;
p. 329: Bill Aron/PhotoEdit;
p. 338: Jeff Greenberg/PhotoEdit;
p. 339: Library of Congress.

part one

Communication and Intercultural Competence

chapter **1** Introduction to Intercultural Competence

chapter **2** Culture and Intercultural Communication

chapter **3** Intercultural Communication Competence

Introduction to Intercultural Competence

The Imperative for Intercultural Competence
The International Imperative for Intercultural Competence
The Domestic Imperative for Intercultural Competence
Communication

Defining Communication
Characteristics of Communication
Interpersonal Communication
The Challenge of Communicating in an Intercultural World
Summary

We live in remarkable times. All around us, there is a heightened emphasis on culture and a corresponding interplay of forces that both encourage and discourage accommodation and understanding among different people.

Consider the enormous changes that have occurred recently in the coalitions and alliances forged among members of vastly different cultural groups: the formation of the European Economic Community, the implementation of the North American Free Trade Agreement, the expansion of ASEAN (Association of Southeast Asian Nations) to include more countries in the region, and the optimistic signs in South Africa, South America, and elsewhere. These changes are only a few of the many we could name, and they redirect our attention to the problems and possibilities inherent in all attempts at communication among people from different cultures.

A counterweight to these trends toward unification and accommodation, however, has been equally powerful emphases on cultural uniqueness. The importance of maintaining one's cultural identity—and therefore the need to preserve, protect, and defend one's culturally shared values—often creates a rising tide of emotion that promotes fear and distrust while encouraging cultural autonomy and independence. This emotional tide, whose beneficial elements increase people's sense of pride and help to anchor a people in time and place, can also be a furious and unbridled force of destruction. Witness the recent problems in Cambodia, Rwanda, Bosnia, the former Yugoslavia, and Central Asia; in each instance, cultures clash over the right to control resources and ideologies. Yet as Catharine R. Stimpson has said of these clashes, the refusal to live peaceably in pluralistic societies [has been] one of the bloodiest problems—nationally and internationally—of the 20th century. No wizard, no fairy godmother is going to make this problem disappear. And I retain a pluralist's stubborn, utopian hope that people can talk about, through, across, and around their differences and that these exchanges will help us live together justly.[1]

These are remarkable times, also, because this heightened emphasis on culture is accompanied by a multitude of opportunities to interact with people from different cultural backgrounds. In virtually every facet of life—in work, play, school, and family—communication with others is marked by cultural differences. Both internationally and domestically, competent intercultural communication has become a necessity. The cultural mix challenges each of us to improve intercultural communication.

Our purpose in writing this book is to provide the conceptual tools for understanding how cultural differences can affect interpersonal communication. We also offer some practical suggestions concerning the adjustments necessary to achieve competence when dealing with cultural differences. We begin by examining the imperative to achieve intercultural communication competence.

An intercultural family plans a trip. Tourism is a major international industry, bringing people from many world cultures into contact with each other.

The Imperative for Intercultural Competence

Marshall McLuhan coined the term *global village* to describe the consequences of the mass media's ability to bring events from the far reaches of the globe into people's homes, thus shrinking the world. Communication technologies now make it possible to establish virtually instantaneous telephone connections with people in other countries. Modern transportation systems also contribute to the creation of the global village. Instead of the challenge posed in the film *Around the World in 80 Days,* astronauts now circumnavigate the globe in eighty minutes. A visit to major cities such as New York, Los Angeles, Mexico City, London, Nairobi, Istanbul, Hong Kong, or Tokyo, with their multicultural populations, demonstrates that movement of people from one country and culture to another has become commonplace. The need to understand the role of culture in interpersonal communication is growing. Internationally and domestically, in business, in education, in health care, and in personal lives, competence in managing intercultural differences in interpersonal communication is expected.

CULTURE *connections*

If the world was a village of 1000 people,

In the village would be:

607 Asians

132 Africans

120 Europeans

 79 North Americans

 57 South Americans

  5 Australians/Oceanians

There would be:

330 Christians (175 Catholics, 56 Protestants, 99 Others)

193 Muslims

134 Hindus

 64 Chinese Folk Religionists

 59 Buddhists

 67 Other Religions

153 Atheists or Nonreligious

—Bureau of the Census
The World Almanac and Book of Facts 2001

The International Imperative for Intercultural Competence

The mass media allow people in the United States and throughout the world to have daily glimpses of the events and lives of people in other countries and cultures. The superficiality of this media exposure belies the significant interdependencies that now link the United States politically, economically, socially, and interpersonally with other countries. The political and economic effectiveness of the United States in the global arena depends on individual and collective abilities to communicate competently with people from other cultures. To date, however, U.S. businesspeople who were sent overseas by U.S.-based multinational corporations have not fared as well as their European and Asian counterparts; an estimated 20 to 50 percent of these personnel return home early from their international assignments, often because they were ill prepared for their experiences.[2] As the President's Commission on Foreign Languages and International Studies has said,

> Nothing less is at stake than the nation's security. At a time when the resurgent forces of nationalism and of ethnic and linguistic consciousness so directly affect global realities, the United States requires far more reliable capabilities to communicate with its allies, analyze the behaviors of potential adversaries, and earn the trust and sympathies of the uncommitted. Yet, there is a widening gap between these needs and the American competence to understand and deal successfully in a world in flux.[3]

The political connections of the United States to other countries are matched by the global interdependence that characterizes U.S. economic relationships. For instance, U.S. international trade has more than doubled every decade since 1960, and it now totals over $2.5 trillion annually, or fifty times what it was just forty years ago.

The economic growth and stability of the United States are now inextricably linked to world business partners. For instance, if Asian or European financial markets stumble, overseas sales of U.S. goods will decline. International investors, seeking a "safe haven" for their excess cash, will be drawn to U.S. dollars; as they exchange their local

CULTURE *connections*

The casual *we* for most of us does not include the 50 percent hungry, the 60 percent in shantytowns, and the 70 percent illiterate. Most of us construct our *we* without including *them.* Thinking of the world close up, as if it were a village of one thousand people, forces us to confront what we mean when we say "we." . . .

. . . How often does our *we* come to include people of other faiths, other nations, other races? How often does our *we* link rather than divide? Our relation with the "other" may move, as Smith puts it, through a number of phases. First we talk *about* them—an objective "other." Then perhaps we talk *to* them, or more personally, we talk to you. Developing a real dialogue, we talk *with* you. And finally, we all talk with one another about us, all of us. This is the crucial stage to which our . . . dialogue must take us if we are to be up to the task of creating communication adequate for an interdependent world.

—*Diana L. Eck*

The international imperative for intercultural competence is exemplified by U.S. Secretary of State Colin Powell, who is using earphones to listen to a simultaneous interpretation of a speech.

currencies for dollars, the desirability and therefore the purchasing power of the dollar rises relative to other currencies. While international goods are thus cheaper with a strong dollar (fueling domestic consumer spending), U.S. goods cost more to sell in international markets (causing sales volume of domestic goods to weaken).

Diplomatic and economic links are reinforced by the ease with which people can now travel to other countries. Over 50 million U.S. residents travel abroad annually. United States high school and university students work, study, and travel overseas in increasing numbers. Likewise, citizens of other countries are also visiting the United States in record-setting numbers.

The vision of interdependence among cultural groups throughout the world has led Robert Shuter to declare that "culture is the single most important global communication issue" that we face.[4] Shuter's argument is also supported by the need for intercultural communication competence that characterizes the U.S. domestic scene.

The Domestic Imperative for Intercultural Competence

Nowhere is the imperative to improve intercultural communication competence stronger than within the borders of the United States. Indeed, in a recent national poll, 71 percent of respondents thought that cultural diversity in the United States was a major reason why America has been successful during the past century.[5]

The United States—and the world as a whole—is currently in the midst of what is perhaps the largest and most extensive wave of cultural mixing in recorded history.

> In the [middle of the] 21st century—and that's not far off—racial and ethnic groups in the U.S. will outnumber whites for the first time. The browning of America will alter everything in society from politics and education to industry, values, and culture.[6]

Recent census figures provide a glimpse into the shape of the changing demographics of the U.S. population. In the 1990s, growth in the Latino, African American, and Asian American populations accounted for nearly two-thirds of the nation's increase.[7] Currently, the U.S. population is 70.1 percent European American, 12.7 percent Latino, 12.5 percent African American, 3.8 percent Asian American, and 0.9 percent Native American.[8] While the U.S. population as a whole, and all cultural groups residing within the United States, is expected to increase in size during the next fifty years, the rates of growth are not uniform. By 2025, for example, the European American population is expected to decline to about 62 percent of the total, the Latino population should increase to 18 percent, the African American population will likely grow at the national average and will remain at about 13 percent of the total population, Asian American groups will increase to more than 6 percent of the U.S. population, and Native American groups are expected to maintain an estimated 1 percent of the U.S. population. If current trends continue, by 2050 the European Americans will comprise slightly more than half of the U.S. population.[9]

Perhaps after talking with other family members, describe your own cultural background and indicate how you think it affects your communication with others (both people from the same culture as you and those from other cultures).

Although changes in population diversity are most pronounced in Sun Belt states, census figures indicate that such cultural diversification is a nationwide phenomenon. Between 2000 and 2010, Vermont's Asian population is projected to grow by 80 percent, Arizona's by 52 percent, and Delaware's by 56 percent. Similarly, Latino growth is expected to exceed 40 percent in such states as Vermont, Alabama, Idaho, California, New Hampshire, and Wyoming.[10] In New Mexico, over 42 percent of the population is now Latino, and the Latino population doubled during the 1990s in Arkansas, Georgia, Nevada, and North Carolina.[11] African Americans constitute over 61 percent of the District of Columbia's population, and they constitute about 30 percent of the population in the states of Alabama, Georgia, Louisiana, Maryland, Mississippi, and South Carolina.[12] There already are "minority majorities"—populations of African Americans, Native Americans, Pacific Islanders, Latinos, and Asian Americans that, when combined, outnumber the European American population—in cities such as Laredo, Miami, Gary, Birmingham, Detroit, Washington, Oakland, Atlanta, San Antonio, Cleveland, Dallas, Los Angeles, Chicago, Baltimore, Houston, New York, Memphis, San Francisco, Fresno, and San Jose.[13]

Much of the U.S. population shift can be attributed to immigration. In 1999, about 26.4 million people—or nearly 10 percent of the U.S. population—were immigrants. This is the highest percentage of immigrants since 1930, but it is about 50 percent lower than the peak immigration years of 1890 through 1910[14] and about the same as it was in 1850, the first year the Census Bureau asked people for their place of birth.[15]

What distinguishes the current wave of immigrants from those of the early 1900s, however, is the country of origin. In 1900, the proportion of European immigrants to the United States was 86 percent; by 1970, Europeans still comprised 62 percent of the immigrant population. By 1997, however, only 16 percent of immigrants to the United States were European.[16] Conversely, in 1970 only 19 percent of the foreign-born U.S. population was from Latin America, and 9 percent was from Asia. By 1997, more than half of the immigrants to the United States came from Latin America, while another 27 percent came from Asia.[17]

Recent data clearly show that the United States is now a multicultural society. Nearly 32 million people in the United States—about one in eight—speak a language other than English at home.[18] Of children in urban public schools, one-third speak a first language other than English.[19] Recent government projections also suggest that the U.S. population will likely increase from 262 million in 1997 to 394 million by 2050, an increase of 50 percent but one demographers consider to be among the most sluggish growth rates in U.S. history. A continuing boom of Latinos and Asian Americans will lead the increase.[20] Latinos have replaced African Americans as the second largest cultural group in the United States. By 2050, the U.S. population will likely be 52.8 percent European American, 24.5 percent Latino, 13.6 percent African American, 8.2 percent Asian American, and 1.0 percent Native American.[21] As Antonia Pantoja and Wilhelmina Perry note,

> The complete picture is one of change where large numbers of non-European immigrants from Africa, Asia, South and Central America, and the Caribbean will constitute majorities in many major cities. These immigrants will contribute to existing social movements. Many of these new immigrants are skilled workers and professionals, and these qualities will be highly valued in a changing United States economy. They come from countries with a history of democratic civil struggles and political revolutions. They arrive with a strong sense of cultural and ethnic identity within their intact family and social networks and strong ties to their home countries. At the same time they have a strong determination to achieve their goals, and they do not intend to abandon or relinquish their culture as the price for their success.[22]

The consequences of this "browning of America" can be seen in every major cultural and social institution. Many U.S. schools can now be characterized as "Classrooms of Babel."[23] In the Los Angeles Unified School District, for example, more than one hundred different languages are spoken.[24] Indeed, 25 percent of schools in the greater Los Angeles area have at least ten different languages spoken by students not fluent in English, and fifteen different first languages are each used by more than 1,000 students.[25] Five million children of immigrants entered U.S. public school systems during the 1990s[26]; one-third of the students in U.S. schools come from nonwhite and Latino groups.[27] Nonwhites and Latinos already make up a majority of high school graduates in Hawaii, New Mexico, the District of Columbia, California, and Mississippi.[28]

Institutions of higher education are certainly not exempt from the forces that have transformed the United States into a multicultural society. The enrollment of "minority-group" college students is over 30 percent in twelve states, exceeds 20 percent in twenty-two states, and is above 10 percent in thirty-nine of them.[29]

The workplace also reflects increasing cultural diversity. Latinos and Latinas are opening businesses at a faster pace than any other cultural group in the United States. In recent years, the number of Latina-owned businesses grew by 300 percent, their

Modern technology facilitates the work of an intercultural team that must interact across international boundaries.

workforce surged 487 percent, and sales increased 534 percent. African American businesses also continue to grow; black-owned businesses employ more than 345 thousand people and generate $32.2 billion in sales. In sum, professional success and personal satisfaction will increasingly depend on the ability to communicate competently with people from other cultures.

Communication

To understand intercultural communication events, you must first study the more general processes involved in all human communication transactions. All communication events, including intercultural ones, are made up of a set of basic characteristics. Once these characteristics are known, they can be applied to intercultural interactions in order to analyze the unique ways in which intercultural communication differs from other forms of communication.

Defining Communication

The term *communication* has been used in many ways for varied, and often inconsistent, purposes.[30] For example, Frank Dance identified 15 different conceptual components for the term,[31] and Dance and Carl Larson listed 126 different definitions for *communication*.[32] Like all terms or ideas, we chose our specific definition because of its usefulness in explaining the thoughts and ideas we wish to convey. Consequently, our definition is not the "right" one, nor is it somehow "more correct" than the others.

The United States is a nation comprised of many cultural groups. These immigrants have just become new citizens of the U.S.

Indeed, as you might expect, our definition is actually very similar to many others with which you may be familiar. However, the definition we have selected is most useful for our purpose of helping you to achieve interpersonal competence when communicating in the intercultural setting.

> Communication is *a symbolic, interpretive, transactional, contextual process in which people create shared meanings.*

To understand what this definition means, we will explore its implications for the study of intercultural communication.

Characteristics of Communication

Six characteristics of our definition of communication require further elaboration. Our definition asserts that communication is symbolic, interpretive, transactional, contextual, a process, and involves shared meanings. Let's examine each of these characteristics more closely.

Communication Is Symbolic   Symbols are central to the communication process because they represent the shared meanings that are communicated. A *symbol* is a word, action, or object that stands for or represents a unit of meaning. *Meaning,* in turn, is a perception, thought, or feeling that a person experiences and might want to communicate to others. These meaning-ful experiences could include sensations resulting from a room's temperature, thoughts about a teacher in a particular course, or feelings of happiness or anger because of what someone said. However, the private meanings within a person cannot be shared directly with others. They can become shared and understood only when they are interpreted as a message. A *message,* then, refers to the "package" of symbols used to create shared meanings. For example, the words in this book are symbols that, taken together, form the message that we, the authors, want to communicate to you.

People's behaviors are frequently interpreted symbolically, as an external representation of feelings, emotions, and internal states. To many people in the United States, for example, raising an arm with the hand extended and moving the hand and arm up and down symbolize saying goodbye. Flags can symbolize a country, and most of the world's religions have symbols that are associated with their beliefs.

There is an important characteristic of symbols that might not be obvious to you but that nevertheless affects your ability to be a competent participant in intercultural communication: symbols vary in their degree of arbitrariness. That is, the relationships between symbols and their referents can vary in the extent to which they are fixed or arbitrary.

Some symbol systems, such as verbal languages and a special class of nonverbal symbols called *emblems,* are completely unrelated to their referents except by common agreement among a group of people to refer to things in a particular way. (Emblems are discussed more fully in Chapter 7.) There is nothing peacelike, for instance, in the peace symbol, which is a nonverbal emblem that can be displayed by extending the index and middle fingers upward from a clenched fist. The same symbol was used by Winston Churchill to indicate victory, and to many people in South American countries it is regarded as an obscene gesture. Similarly, there is nothing booklike in the object you are holding as you read these words. We call the object a book not because there is anything inherent in the object that suggests "book" but simply because, by common agreement among users of English, we have agreed to do so. Those who speak other languages have other symbols, which are equally arbitrary, to refer to the same referents.

It is quite possible for a community of language users to agree to refer to some objects by using symbols that differ from the common ones. For example, the people in a class (perhaps even your class) could decide to change the symbols and refer to the teacher as a *door,* the students as *cows,* the blackboard as a *pancake,* the classroom as a *bar,* and the desks as *pineapples.* A description of the classroom with these new and arbitrarily assigned symbols might read as follows: "When the cows entered the bar, they sat down at their pineapples, and the door began to write on the pancake." Though the sentence sounds strange (and perhaps quite humorous), if everyone consistently referred to the objects in the same way, the meaning that would be created in using these symbols would soon become widely shared.

Provide a demographic profile of the multicultural characteristics of the people in your community. You might want to look at local data from the U.S. Census Bureau at www.census.gov to accomplish this.

For many symbol systems, such as most nonverbal and visual ones, the relationship between the symbols and their referents is much less arbitrary than that of verbal languages. Such symbols as a growling stomach when hungry, a child's tears when sad, or a portrait that details a person's facial features are all so intrinsically associated with their referents that the range of expected meanings is very restricted. However, these types of symbols are useful precisely because much less knowledge of a specific language and culture is required to understand them. Thus, international traffic symbols, which consist of easily understood pictures, are frequently used in place of words to instruct drivers who might otherwise be a major hazard. Yet even with these traffic symbols, which are designed specifically to be understood easily, it cannot be assumed that everyone will automatically interpret the symbols in a identical fashion.

Communication Is Interpretive   Messages do not have to be consciously or purposefully created with the specific intention of communicating a certain set of meanings for others to be able to make sense of the symbols forming the message. Rather, communication is always an interpretive process. Whenever people communicate, they must interpret the symbolic behaviors of others and assign significance to some of those behaviors in order to create a meaningful account of the others' actions. This idea suggests that each person in a communication transaction may not necessarily interpret the messages in exactly the same way. Indeed, during episodes involving intercultural communication the likelihood is high that people will interpret the meaning of messages differently.

Many people incorrectly use the word *communication* to represent an acceptable level of similarity or agreement in their conversations. They might use the phrase "I really could communicate with her" when they have had a very pleasant conversation in which the other person expressed a similar point of view, or they might say "I just can't communicate with him any more" when disagreements exist. These errors confuse two very different outcomes of the communication process.

The first outcome of communication is that the participants *understand* what the others are trying to communicate. Understanding means that the participants have imposed similar or shared interpretations about what the messages actually mean. Indeed, without some degree of understanding between the participants, it would be inaccurate

CULTURE *connections*

When we walk into Barb Immermann's house, we see a gallery of her grandchildren's photographs crowding the mantelpiece of her rural Iowa home. Three of Barb's children chose to marry people from other countries, and the diversity of their families is reflected in these pictures. Even at a glance, we can see the panoply of visual differences: hair blonde and straight to jet black and curly; eyes brown, blue, green. It is because of these faces that we have come here. We thought it remarkable that a woman living in the rural heartland of the country, by reputation among the most homogeneous of places, would have such a thoroughly intercultural family.

—*Jessie Carroll Grearson and Lauren B. Smith*

U.S. Americans are as varied as the landscape. Here a group of college students, who represent several different cultures, have a friendly conversation.

to claim that communication has even occurred. Thus, failed attempts at communication, such as when an accident victim calls for help and no one is nearby to hear, are not actually communication.

The second outcome is reaching *agreement* on the particular issues that have been discussed. Agreement means that each participant not only understands the other's interpretations but also holds a view that is similar. However, although understanding is a necessary ingredient to say that communication has occurred, agreement is not a requirement of communication. It is possible, and often quite likely, that people will understand one another's position or ideas yet not agree with them. For instance, two people who differ in their basic beliefs about religion or politics can still communicate about their personal preferences in a meaningful and fulfilling way without necessarily expecting the other person to agree.

It should be obvious that complete accuracy in interpreting the meanings that are shared by people is rare, if not impossible. Such a level of accuracy would require symbols to be understood by the participants in *exactly* the same way. Further, even if complete understanding was possible in a given instance, it would be impossible to verify that the meanings that were created for the symbols were identical in the minds of all participants.

Our stipulation that communication requires understanding does not imply that because completely accurate interpretations are impossible, communication is also impossible. Rather, we need to recognize that there are different levels or degrees of understanding. Communication requires a degree of understanding sufficient to accomplish the purposes of the participants, which can vary from one experience to another. For example, it may or may not be communication if a man, who is dressed in unfamiliar clothes and who is obviously from another culture, walks up to you and, after bowing, utters some sounds that seem like they could be language but whose meaning is unknown to you. If his purpose is merely to provide you with a ritualistic greeting and, recognizing this, you return his bow, then relative to the purposes of the participants we would say that the two of you have created shared meanings for your behaviors and consequently communication has occurred. However, if he is asking you for directions and you merely return his bow without even recognizing his intended goal, then shared meanings do not exist and communication has not occurred relative to the task at hand.

Communication Is Transactional   To suggest that communication is transactional implies that all participants in the communication process work together to create and sustain the meanings that develop. A transactional view holds that communicators are simultaneously sending and receiving messages at every instant that they are involved in conversations.

The earliest views of the communication process were *actional.* An actional view held that communication was a linear, one-way flow of ideas and information and that the focus of this view was primarily on information transmission, or what the sender should do to structure a message that would achieve a desired result. As Figure 1.1 indicates, the earliest actional models did not even include the receivers of the messages. Later actional models added a receiver at the end of the message arrow, but those who held this view were still not very concerned with the receiver's characteristics.[33]

Actional views of the communication process are not very useful in the study of intercultural communication, for two very important reasons. First, the underlying assumption of the actional view is that the sender's goal is to persuade the receiver. The sender is not really interested in understanding others, being sensitive to cultural differences, or developing better interpersonal relationships; rather, the focus is on telling and selling. Second, actional views of communication assume that the receivers of messages are somehow inferior to the senders, with little ability to become involved in or to influence the communication process. In this view, those who create the messages should merely manipulate the receivers.

The limitations of the actional view led to the development of the *interactional* view of the communication process. Whereas the former emphasizes transmission of the message, the latter emphasizes interpretation. The interactional view explicitly includes the receiver in the communication process, and it recognizes that the receivers provide the senders with ongoing responses, called *feedback,* about how the messages are received.[34] As Figure 1.2 indicates, the focus of this view is still primarily sender-oriented. The model

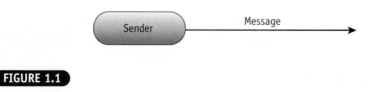

FIGURE 1.1

An actional view of communication.

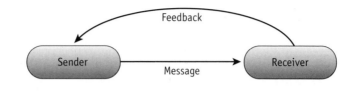

FIGURE 1.2

An interaction view of communication.

merely recognizes that senders must continually adapt their messages to the changing perceptions of the receivers to be most effective in influencing them. The implied goal of the interactional view of communication is to influence and control the receiver.

Like actional views, interactional views of the communication process are not very useful in the study of intercultural communication. The goal of the sender is still one of influencing others rather than being culturally sensitive and thereby improving intercultural relationships. The receivers, in the interactional view, need to be understood only insofar as that understanding is necessary to manipulate them more effectively. A final criticism of the interactional view is that it is not really a model of true interaction. Rather, it suggests a sequence of action–reaction behaviors in which messages are exchanged between a sender and a receiver, who perhaps alternate in these roles. Absent from the interactional view is any sense that the participants co-produce and co-interpret the messages that are communicated.

The limitations of the actional and interactional views have led to the development of the *transactional* view, which emphasizes the construction or shared creation of messages and meanings. The transactional view differs from the earlier views in two ways. First, it recognizes that the goal of communication is not merely to influence and persuade others but also to improve one's knowledge, to seek understanding, to develop agreements, and to negotiate shared meanings. Second, it recognizes that at any given instant, no one is just sending or just receiving messages, and therefore there are no such entities as pure senders or pure receivers. Nor does it make sense to describe a single message as being the exclusive one at any selected moment. Rather, all participants are simultaneously interpreting multiple messages at all moments. These messages include not only the meaning of the words that are said but also the meaning conveyed by the tone of voice, the types of gestures, the frequency of body movements, the motion of the eyes, the distances between people, the formality of the language, the seating arrangements, the clothing worn, the length of pauses, the words unsaid, and much more. Thus, as Figure 1.3 indicates, in the transactional view it is impossible to describe one person as exclusively the sender and the other as exclusively the receiver.

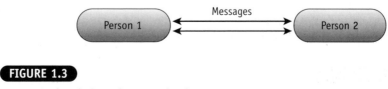

FIGURE 1.3

An transactional view of communication.

Communication Is Contextual   All communication takes place within a setting or situation called a context. By context we mean the place where people meet, the social purpose for being together, and the nature of the relationship. Thus the context includes the physical, social, and interpersonal settings within which messages are exchanged.

The Physical Context   The physical context includes the actual location of the interactants: indoors or outdoors, crowded or quiet, public or private, close together or far apart, warm or cold, bright or dark. The physical context influences the communication process in many obvious ways. Dean Barnlund captures its importance: "The streets of Calcutta, the avenues of Brazilia, the Left Bank of Paris, the gardens of Kyoto, the slums of Chicago, and the canyons of lower Manhattan provide dramatically different backgrounds for human interaction."[35] An afternoon conversation at a crowded sidewalk café and an evening of candlelight dining in a private salon will differ in the kinds of topics that are covered and in the interpretations that are made about the meanings of certain phrases or glances. As Donald Klopf so poignantly illustrates, knowledge of the physical context often provides important information about the meanings that are intended and the kinds of communication that are possible:

> I wanted to see her one more time before leaving Hong Kong. So I called her at work and she agreed to lunch. Near her office was a traditional *dim sum* restaurant. Sounded good to me; *dim sum* literally means "to touch the heart" and she had done that to me. What a mistake! Noisy?! The place was bedlam. The waitresses shouted out their wares—some sixty to seventy *dim sum* choices. We shared a table with a couple of tourists who griped about the food, and everything else. Crowded, every steno around must have decided on a *yam cha* meal today. Words of endearment didn't seem appropriate there. "Let's go next door to the Lau Ling Bar," I suggested, "for our black tea." Quiet and refined, it was the proper site to touch the heart, and I think I did.[36]

The Social Context   The social context refers to the widely shared expectations people have about the kinds of interactions that normally should occur given different kinds of social events. Of course we realize that communication at funerals differs from that at a party; the social context of a classroom makes us expect certain forms of communication that differ from those at a soccer game. However, there is often a great deal of

CULTURE *connections*

American Beats Kwan

MSNBC's erroneous headline after Tara Lipinski beat Michelle Kwan for the women's gold medal in figure skating during the 1998 Winter Olympics. Both women are U.S. Americans.

difficulty in understanding the social contexts for communication events that involve other cultures, as the common expectations about what behaviors are preferred or prohibited may be very different. For instance, before a funeral in Ireland, an all-night celebration called a wake is sometimes held. Such festive behaviors, which are appropriate to the social context of an Irish funeral, would be completely inappropriate where the social context dictates that alternative behaviors are more fitting.

The Interpersonal Context   The interpersonal context refers to the expectations people have about the behaviors of others as a result of differences in the relationships between them. Communication between teachers and students, even outside the classroom context, differs from communication between close friends. Communication among friends differs from communication among acquaintances, co-workers, or family members. As people get to know each other and develop shared experiences, the nature of their interpersonal relationships is altered. This change in the interpersonal context is accompanied by alterations in the kinds of messages created and in the interpretations made about the meanings of the messages exchanged. As we suggested about physical and social contexts, people behave differently from one interpersonal context to another. The meanings assigned to particular behaviors can differ dramatically as different definitions of the context are imposed. As John Condon says about differences in male–female relationships in the United States and Mexico,

> There are meanings to be read into settings and situations which must be learned if one is to avoid misunderstandings and even unpleasant experiences. A boss who invites his secretary out for a drink after work may or may not have ulterior motives in either country. However, the assumption that this was a romantic overture would be far more common in Mexico City than in New York or Los Angeles.[37]

Communication Is a Process   People, relationships, activities, objects, and experiences can be described either in static terms or as part of a dynamic process. Viewing communication in static terms suggests that it is fixed and unchanging, whereas viewing it as a process implies that things are changing, moving, developing, and evolving. A process is a sequence of many distinct but interrelated steps. To understand communication as a process, it is necessary to know how it can change over time.

Like the old adage "You can't stand in the same stream twice," communication events are unique, as seemingly identical experiences can take on vastly different meanings at different stages of the process. This stream of events, which involves both past experiences and future expectations, is always moving and changing. Thus, the very same message may be interpreted very differently when said at different stages of the communication process.

Communication Involves Shared Meanings   The interpretive and transactional nature of communication suggests that correct meanings are not just "out there" to be discovered. Rather, meanings are created and shared by groups of people as they participate in the ordinary and everyday activities that form the context for common interpretations. Our focus, therefore, must be on the ways that people attempt to "make sense" of their common experiences in the world.

Interpersonal Communication

Definitions, as we have said, are chosen because they are useful for conveying the thoughts, ideas, and distinctions that one wishes to explain.

> *Interpersonal communication is a form of communication that involves a small number of individuals who are interacting exclusively with one another and who therefore have the ability both to adapt their messages specifically for those others and to obtain immediate interpretations from them.*

Each of the four characteristics of this definition will now be discussed.

A Small Number of People   To a certain degree, all communication could be called interpersonal, as it occurs between (*inter*) two or more people. However, we think it useful and practical to differentiate those relationships that involve a relatively small number of people—such as couples, families, friends, work groups, and even classroom groups—from those involving much larger numbers of people—such as public rallies or massive television audiences. Unlike other forms of communication, interpersonal communication involves person-to-person interactions. In addition, the perception that a social bond has developed between the interactants, however tenuous and temporary it may seem, is also much more likely.

People Interacting Exclusively with One Another   Unlike public speaking or mass media communication events, in which messages are sent to large, undifferentiated, and heterogeneous audiences, interpersonal communication typically involves clearly identified participants who are able to select those with whom they interact. In addition, when people interact directly with one another, they may use many sensory channels to convey information. Such details as looks, grunts, touches, postures, nods, smells, voice changes, and other specific behaviors are all available for observation and interpretation.

CULTURE *connections*

What does it mean, for example, to speak of "Africa"—a landmass that appears, in purely cartographic terms, to be a "natural" area? Cultural geography provides a different perspective, linking people across great physical divides, while dividing much closer neighbors. The "Black Atlantic," for example, conjoins the western hemisphere diaspora and West Africa, including southern Nigeria, while northern Nigeria looks culturally toward the desert, the Sahel, and the Islamic world to the north. We are also reminded that we find "Africa" in New York City, where Senegalese cloth traders and Ethiopian perfume vendors ply their wares on Harlem street corners, and return to their countries blending the cultures they know and experience. And "Africa" is in the rich and diverse musical and religious traditions of Brazil, Haiti, or Jamaica. Finally, one cannot think clearly about "the African economy" without analyzing World Bank policies made in Washington.

—*Toby Alice Volkman*

CULTURE *connections*

Many Americans are not who they think they are; hundreds of thousands of white people in America are not "white." Some know it; others don't. Ten thousand people each year cross the visible and invisible color line and become "white." If a new sociological method of determining race were devised, equal numbers of black people might no longer be black. What happened in my family and many others like it calls into question the concept of color as a means of self-definition.

Genes and chromosomes from Africa, Europe, and a pristine America commingled and created me. I have been called Egyptian, Italian, Jewish, French, Iranian, Armenian, Syrian, Spanish, Portuguese, and Greek. I have also been called black and Peola and nigger and high yellow and bright. I am an American anomaly. I am an American ideal. I am the American nightmare. I am the Martin Luther King dream. I am the new America.

—*Shirley Taylor Haizlip*

Adapted to Specific Others   Because interpersonal communication involves a small number of people who can speak exclusively to one another, it is possible for the participants to assess what is being understood and how the messages are being interpreted. Since many of the messages are designed to evoke a particular effect in other people, the messages can be adapted to fit the specific people for whom they are intended.

Immediate Interpretations   In interpersonal communication, in contrast to books or newspapers, the interpretation of messages can occur essentially simultaneously with their creation. The swift and instantaneous adaptations that people can make as a consequence of these immediate interpretations can permit a subtle and ongoing adjustment to the setting and the other participants.

The Challenge of Communicating in an Intercultural World

As inhabitants of the twenty-first century, you no longer have a choice about whether to live and communicate in a world of many cultures. The forces that bring people from other cultures into your life are dynamic, potent, and ever present. What does this great cultural mixing mean as you strive for success, satisfaction, well-being, and feelings of involvement and attachment to families, communities, organizations, and nations? What role can competent intercultural communication play in addressing the stereotypes and prejudices likely to be present?

In each of the settings in which you conduct your lives—in work, school, the neighborhood, personal relationships, and the family—intercultural competence is crucial. Economic success increasingly depends on the ability to display competent communication behaviors with individuals from other cultures, even if the work is within the national boundaries of the United States. Corporations also bring people from one country to another, so within the workforce of most nations there are representatives from

In your class, find someone who fits each description and get her or his signature. Try to find a different person for each description.

Knows how to use chopsticks   _____

Has been in more countries
than you have   _____

Has purchased a Eurail pass   _____

Has parents who speak a
second language at home   _____

Pronounces words differently
than you do   _____

Knows where Kuala Lumpur is   _____

Considers this school a
foreign culture   _____

Drives an imported car   _____

Has been in cars where
traffic moves on the left
side of the road   _____

Knows where Morocco is   _____

Is wearing some clothing
not made in the USA   _____

Likes to eat sushi   _____

Has studied Spanish   _____

Has a relative from a
different culture   _____

Has watched TV soap operas
in a language other
than English   _____

Was born in another country   _____

Knows what time it is right
now in Paris   _____

Has a good friend from a
culture other than his or
her own   _____

Has a pen pal from another
culture   _____

Has eaten couscous   _____

CULTURE *connections*

What sets worlds in motion is the interplay of differences, their attractions and repulsions. Life is plurality, death is uniformity. By suppressing differences and peculiarities, by eliminating civilizations and cultures, progress weakens life and favors death. The ideal of a single civilization for everyone, implicit in the cult of progress and technique, impoverishes and mutilates us. Every view of the world that becomes extinct, every culture that disappears, diminishes a possibility of life.

—*Octavio Paz*

cultures throughout the world. The citizenry itself includes many individuals who are strongly identified with a particular culture. Thus, it is no longer safe to assume that clients, customers, business partners, and co-workers will have similar cultural views about what is important and appropriate.

Diversity in languages and cultures has become a prominent influence within elementary schools, high schools, colleges, and universities. This mixture affects students' learning and interpersonal relationships. Teachers' interactions with students, parents' interactions with teachers, and students' interactions with other students are all mediated by the kinds of linguistic and cultural differences we describe in this book. Inevitably, cultural differences in communication affect the ability of everyone involved in the educational process to achieve their educational goals.

Personal satisfaction, too, will increasingly depend on the ability to communicate competently with people from other cultures. Neighbors may speak different first languages, have different values, and celebrate different customs. As Dwight Conquergood says, "cities throughout the United States have become sites of extraordinary diversity."[38] Families are also becoming more culturally diverse, as marriages and adoptions contribute to the cultural mix.[39] The challenge of the twenty-first century is to understand and to appreciate cultural differences and to translate that understanding into competent interpersonal communication.

There are some obvious consequences to living in an intercultural world. It will inevitably introduce doubt about others' expectations and will reduce the certainty that specific behaviors, routines, and rituals mean the same things to everyone. Renato Rosaldo, who believes that encounters with "difference" are now an inherent and inescapable part of modern urban life, provides a personal anecdote to illustrate alternative cultural responses to common, everyday experiences.

I grew up speaking Spanish to my father and English to my mother. Consider the cultural pertinence of my father's response, during the late 1950s, to having taken our dog, Chico, to the veterinarian. Born and raised in Mexico, my father arrived home with Chico in a mood midway between pain and amusement. Tears of laughter streamed down his cheeks until, finally, he mumbled something like, "What will these North Americans think of next?" He explained that when he entered the veterinarian's office a nurse in white had greeted him at the door, sat him down, pulled out a form, and asked,

"What's the patient's name?" In my dad's view, no Mexican would ever come so close to confusing a dog with a person. To him, it was unthinkable that a clinic for dogs could ever resemble one for people with its nurses in white and its forms for the "patient."[40]

Cultural mixing implies that people will not always feel completely comfortable as they attempt to communicate in another language or as they try to talk with individuals who are not proficient in theirs. Their sense of "rights" and "wrongs" will be threatened when challenged by the actions of those with an alternative cultural framework. Many people will need to live in two or more cultures concurrently, shifting from one to another as they go from home to school, from work to play, and from the neighborhood to the shopping mall.

The tensions inherent in creating successful intercultural communities and nations are obvious. Examples abound that underscore how difficult it is for groups of culturally different individuals to live, work, and play together harmoniously. The consequences of failing to create a harmonious intercultural society are also obvious—human suffering, hatred passed on from one generation to another, disruptions in people's lives, and unnecessary conflicts that sap people's creative talents and energies and that siphon off scarce resources from other important societal needs.

There are no simple prescriptions or pat answers that can guarantee competent intercultural communication in all settings. Nor has anyone discovered how to eliminate

The challenge of communicating in an intercultural world occurs in our families, homes, work settings, schools, and neighborhoods.

the destructive consequences of prejudice and racism. Nevertheless, the joys and benefits of embracing an intercultural world are many. As the world is transformed into a place where cultural boundaries cease to be impenetrable barriers, differences among people become reasons to celebrate and share rather than to fear and harm. The opportunities to understand, experience, and benefit from unfamiliar ways are unprecedented. You are—we are all—twenty-first-century pioneers on an incredible voyage, a new kind of pilgrim on a new frontier.

Summary

The chapter began with descriptions of the international and domestic imperatives for achieving intercultural communication competence. Throughout your lifetime, you will probably engage in many types of intercultural encounters. The chapter next provides a general analysis of the human communication process and discusses the topics of communication and interpersonal communication. These topics are of central importance to an understanding of intercultural communication, as they form the foundation for all of our subsequent ideas about the nature of intercultural transactions.

We defined communication as a symbolic, interpretive, transactional, contextual process in which people create shared meanings. Each of the characteristics of communication included in the definition was considered in turn. The role of symbols, which are the words, actions, or objects that stand for or represent units of meaning, was discussed. The consequences of the interpretation of symbols by both senders and receivers of messages on the outcomes of communication were explored. We also described the transactional nature of communication as involving the mutual influence of all individuals on communicative outcomes, so that every person simultaneously creates and interprets meanings and messages. The physical, social, and interpersonal contexts that bound each message were explained. Finally, we described communication as a process, an always-changing flow of interpretations.

We then narrowed our focus to the study of interpersonal communication, which we defined as a form of communication that involves a small number of people who can interact exclusively with one another and who therefore have the ability both to adapt their messages specifically for those others and to obtain immediate interpretations from them. Again, each of the important characteristics of interpersonal communication contained in this definition was considered.

Living in an intercultural world provides numerous challenges and opportunities, as your success and well-being increasingly depend on your ability to behave competently in intercultural encounters. In Chapter 2 we consider two concepts that are central to this book—culture and intercultural communication.

For Discussion

1. What are some of the implications for a U.S. workforce in which, for the first time, European American males will be in the minority?
2. What does it mean to say that communication is "a symbolic, interpretive, transactional, contextual process in which people create shared meanings"?

For Further Reading

Larry L. Barker and Deborah A. Gaut, *Communication,* 8th ed. (Boston: Allyn and Bacon, 2001). Excellent background for students who have not previously studied the human communication process.

Joseph A. DeVito, *The Interpersonal Communication Reader* (Boston: Allyn and Bacon, 2001). Provides insights into the special characteristics that influence interpersonal communication.

Ronald Takaki, *A Different Mirror: A History of Multicultural America* (Boston: Little, Brown, 1993). Redefines the United States from a nation with only a European American history to one that, from its very beginning, has been a racially and culturally diverse country.

Ronald Takaki (ed.), *From Different Shores: Perspectives on Race and Ethnicity in America,* 2nd ed. (New York: Oxford University Press, 1994). Essays in this volume are written from a sociological and historical perspective and look at the differences and similarities in the experiences of various racial, ethnic, and gender groups that make up the "pattern" of race and ethnicity in the United States.

Sarah Trenholm, *Thinking through Communication: An Introduction to the Study of Human Communication,* 3rd ed. (Boston: Allyn and Bacon, 2001). Another excellent introduction to the study of human communication that will be particularly useful to the beginning student of communication.

U.S. Census Bureau, www.census.gov. This Web site is a veritable treasure trove of statistical information about the multicultural character of the population of the United States of America.

For additional information about intercultural films and about Web sites on specific cultures, turn to the Resources section at the back of this book.

chapter 2

Culture and Intercultural Communication

Culture
Defining Culture for the Study
   of Communication
Culture and Related Terms
Why Cultures Differ
Intercultural Communication
Examples of Intercultural Interactions

Similarities and Differences
   between Communicators
Definition of Intercultural
   Communication
Intercultural Communication
   and Related Terms
Summary

This book is about interpersonal communication between people from different cultures. Our goal is to explain how you can achieve interpersonal competence in interactions that involve intercultural communication. This chapter provides a general understanding of culture and intercultural communication. It also includes a discussion about why one culture differs from another. Chapter 3 will continue the discussion by exploring the nature of intercultural communication competence.

Culture

Definitions of *culture* are numerous. In 1952 Alfred L. Kroeber and Clyde Kluckhohn published a book with over two hundred pages devoted to different definitions of the term.[1] Since then, many other scholars have offered additional definitions and approaches.

Our concern in this book is with the link between culture and communication. Consequently, our definition of *culture* is one that allows us to investigate how culture contributes to human symbolic processes.

Defining Culture for the Study of Communication

Our goal in presenting a particular definition of *culture* is to explain the important link between culture and communication. However, we emphasize that the way we define culture is not the "right" or "best" way. Rather, it is a definition that is useful for our

CULTURE *connections*

Culture's Core

I recall now, so very clearly,
as evening clings like tapestry,
a distant time when I was small
and loved to creep along the wall
toward the circle cast by light
where elders talked, among themselves, into the night.

They filled the room with stirring tales, as I—
in my pajamas with the little feet—would lie
behind the outsized chair, hair pressed to rug,
listening invisibly, 'til wakened by the hug
of arms that cradled me 'round knee and head
and placed me back in sagging bed.

They told their stories,
one by one, of hardships suffered, and of glories—
times endured, evils feared,
stunning triumphs engineered
by luck, effort, patience, cunning,
and those who saved themselves by running.

I remember, too, the sagas told
about the turning points in growing old
amidst the tempests once withstood,
and tender details of first kisses, which were good
for waves of jokes and laughter
that I scarcely understood 'til after
I had aged, and learned of love affairs,
and private things that people do in pairs.

So now, like sages who have been and done,
who've told their tales of favors lost and won,
I primp my heirs with stories from my youth
of the vainglorious pursuits of truth,
justice, and the 'Merican way,
'til a still small voice can guide, I pray,
the journey forth where only they may go,
toward a promised land, which I will never know.

Thus repeats the simple lore
of passion, pleasure, pain, and pride
that marks us all, deep down inside,
as humans with a common core.

—*Myron W. Lustig*

The beliefs, values, and norms of our culture are learned. Families are often a major setting in which these cultural patterns are acquired.

purpose of helping you to understand the crucial link between culture and communication as you set out to improve your intercultural competence.

> *Culture* is *a learned set of shared interpretations about beliefs, values, and norms, which affect the behaviors of a relatively large group of people.*

Culture Is Learned   Humans are not born with the genetic imprint of a particular culture. Instead, people learn about their culture through interactions with parents, other family members, friends, and even strangers who are part of the culture. Later in this chapter we explain why some cultures are so different from others. For now, we want to describe the general process by which people learn their culture.

Culture is learned from the people you interact with as you are socialized. Watching how adults react and talk to new babies is an excellent way to see the actual symbolic transmission of culture among people. Two babies born at exactly the same time in two parts of the globe may be taught to respond to physical and social stimuli in very different ways. For example, some babies are taught to smile at strangers, whereas others are taught to smile only in very specific circumstances. In the United States, most children are asked from a very early age to make decisions about what they want to do and what they prefer; in many other cultures, a parent would never ask a child what she or he wants to do but would simply tell the child what to do.

CULTURE *connections*

I'm a member of the Ibo tribe of Nigeria, and although I've lived in the United States most of my adult life, my consciousness remains fixed on the time and place of my up-bringing. On the surface, I'm as American as everyone else. My husband, who was also raised in Nigeria, and I are both professionals. We live in the suburbs and go to PTA meetings. In my private life, my Iboness—the customs that rigidly dictate how the men and women of my tribe live their lives—continues to influence the choices I make. I see these American and Ibo aspects of my life as distinct; I separate them perfectly, and there are no blurrings. Except for maybe one: Delia.

When I left Nigeria at 18, I had no doubts about who and what I was. I was a woman. I was *only* a woman.

All my life my mother told me that a woman takes as much in life as she's given; if she's educated, it's only so that she can better cater to her husband and children. When I was Delia's age, I knew with absolute certainty that I would marry the Ibo man my family approved for me and bear his children. I understood that receiving a good education and being comfortable in both the Western and the traditional worlds would raise the bride price my prospective husband would pay my family. My role was to be a great asset to my husband, no matter what business he was engaged in.

I understood all of that clearly; I was, after all, raised within the context of child brides, polygamy, clitorectomies and arranged marriages. But then I married and had my own daughter, and all my certainty, all my resolve to maintain my Ibo beliefs, collapsed in a big heap at my feet.

First, my daughter's ties to Ibo womanhood are only as strong as the link—meaning me. Therein lies the problem. I haven't been half the teacher to my daughter that my mother was to me.

I've struggled daily with how best to raise my daughter. Every decision involving Delia is a tug of war between Ibo and American traditions. I've vacillated between trying to turn her into the kind of woman her grandmothers would be proud of and letting her be the modern, independent woman she wants to be. Each time Delia scores an academic or athletic victory, I start to applaud her, but my cheers get stuck in my throat as I hear both her grandmothers' voices warning, "She's only a woman." I know in my heart that her achievements will not matter to her relatives; they will judge her by the kind of man she marries, and the children—preferably male—that she bears.

At 18, Delia knows very little about the rules that govern the lives of Ibo women. She knows just enough about housekeeping to survive. She will most likely not consider my feelings in choosing her spouse. She is not the selflessly loyal daughter that I was to my mother.

I wonder about the implications for people like me, women from traditional cultures raising American-born daughters. Should we limit their opportunities to keep them loyal to our beliefs and our pasts, or should we encourage our daughters to avail themselves of all experiences, even at the risk of rejecting who and what we are?

Maybe what I feel is what parents all over the world feel: that I could have done a better job of instilling my beliefs in my child. Now, it's too late.

Or perhaps I've always known that Delia is her own person with her own life to lead.

Delia called the other night from Princeton. She's coming home soon, and I'm infected by her excitement. But I wonder: will I know the young woman who steps off the plane?

—Dympna Ugwu-Oju

Culture is also taught by the explanations people receive for the natural and human events around them. Parents tell children that a certain person is a good boy because _____. People from different cultures would complete the blank in contrasting ways. The people with whom the children interact will praise and encourage particular kinds of behaviors (such as crying or not crying, being quiet or being talkative). Certainly there are variations in what a child is taught from family to family in any given culture. However, our interest is not in these variations but in the similarities across most or all families that form the basis of a culture. Because our specific interest is in the relationship between culture and interpersonal communication, we focus on how cultures provide their members with a set of interpretations that they then use as filters to make sense of messages and experiences.

Culture Is a Set of Shared Interpretations   Shared interpretations establish the very important link between communication and culture. Cultures exist in the minds

By teaching and explaining to their children, parents help them to develop a common set of meanings and expectations.

of people, not in external or tangible objects or behaviors. Integral to our discussion of communication is an emphasis on symbols as the means by which all communication takes place. The meanings of symbols exist in the minds of the individual communicators; when those symbolic ideas are shared with others, they form the basis for culture. Not all of an individual's symbolic ideas are necessarily shared with other people, and some symbols will be shared only with a few. A culture can form only if symbolic ideas are shared with a relatively large group of people.

Culture Involves Beliefs, Values, and Norms   The shared symbol systems that form the basis of culture represent ideas about beliefs, values, and norms. Because of their importance in understanding the ways in which cultures vary and their role in improving intercultural communication competence, the first section of Chapter 4 is devoted to their detailed explanation. For now, it is enough to know that beliefs refer to the basic understanding of a group of people about what the world is like or what is true or false. Values refer to what a group of people defines as good and bad or what it regards as important. Norms refer to rules for appropriate behavior, which provide the expectations people have of one another and of themselves.

Describe one belief, one value, and one norm that you hold that is also held by the "typical" member of your culture. Describe how each of these affects your communication with parents or other elders.

Culture Affects Behavior   If culture were located solely in the minds of people, we could only speculate about what a culture is, since it is impossible for one person to see into the mind of another. However, these shared interpretations about beliefs, values, and norms affect the *behaviors* of large groups of people. In other words, the shared interpretations that characterize a culture give people guidelines about what things mean, what is important, and what should or should not be done. Thus, culture establishes predictability in human interactions. Cultural differences are evident in the varying ways in which people conduct their everyday activities, as people "perform" their culture in their behavioral routines.

Within a given geographical area, people who interact with one another over time will form social bonds that help to stabilize their interactions and patterns of behavior. The stable patterns become the basis for making the predictions and forming expectations about others.

Culture Involves Large Groups of People   We differentiate between smaller groups of individuals, who may engage in interpersonal communication, and larger groups of people more traditionally associated with cultures. For example, if you work every day with the same group of people and you regularly see and talk to them, you will undoubtedly begin to develop shared perceptions and experiences that will affect the way you communicate. Although some people might want to use the term *culture* to refer to the bonds that develop among the people in a small group, we prefer to distinguish between the broad-based, culturally shared beliefs, values, and norms that people bring to their interactions and the unique expectations and experiences that arise as a result

CULTURE *connections*

Joseph Campbell has said that the myths of every culture provide answers to four questions: (1) Who am I? (2) Who are we? (3) What is the nature of the world in which we live? and (4) What is the nature of the answers to these questions?

---

of particular interpersonal relationships that develop. Consequently, we will restrict the use of the term *culture* to much larger, societal levels of organization.

Culture is also often used to refer to other types of large groups of people. Mary Jane Collier and Milt Thomas, for example, assert that the term "can refer to ethnicity, gender, profession, or any other symbol system that is bounded and salient to individuals."[2] Our definition does not exclude groups such as women, the deaf, gays and lesbians, and others identified by Collier and Thomas. However, our emphasis is primarily on culture in its more traditional forms, which Collier and Thomas refer to as ethnicity.

Culture and Related Terms

Terms such as *nation, race,* and *ethnic group* are often used synonymously with the term *culture. Subculture* and *coculture* are other terms that are sometimes used in talking about groups of people. There are important distinctions, however, between these terms and the groups of people to which they might refer.

Nation   In our everyday language, people commonly treat *culture* and *nation* as equivalent terms. They are not. *Nation* is a political term referring to a government and a set of formal and legal mechanisms that regulate the political behavior of its people. These regulations often encompass such aspects of a people as how leaders are chosen, by what rules the leaders must govern, the laws of banking and currency, the means to establish military groups, and the rules by which a legal system is conducted. Foreign policies, for instance, are determined by a nation and not by a culture. The culture, or cultures, that exist within the boundaries of a nation-state certainly influence the regulations that a nation develops, but the term *culture* is not synonymous with *nation.* Although one cultural group predominates in some nations, most nations contain multiple cultures within their boundaries.

The United States is an excellent example of a nation that has several major cultural groups living within its geographical boundaries; European Americans, African Americans, Native Americans, Latinos, and various Asian American cultures are all represented in the United States. All the members of these different cultural groups are citizens of the nation of the United States.

Even the nation of Japan, often regarded as so homogeneous that the word *Japanese* is commonly used to refer both to the nation and to the culture, is actually multicultural. Though the Yamato Japanese culture overwhelmingly predominates within the nation of Japan, there are other cultures living there. These groups include the Ainu, an indigenous group with their own culture, religion, and language; other cultures that have lived in Japan for many generations and originate mainly from Okinawa, Korea, and China; and more recent immigrants also living there.[3]

Race   *Race* commonly refers to certain physical similarities, such as skin color or eye shape, that are shared by a group of people and are used to mark or separate them from others. Contrary to popular notions, however, race is not primarily a biological term; it is a political and societal one that was invented to justify economic and social distinctions. In the United States, for example, various non-Anglo-Saxon and non-Nordic cultural groups that would now be regarded as predominantly "white"—European Jews and people from such places as Ireland, Italy, Poland, and other eastern and southern European locales—were initially derided as being racial "mongrels" and therefore nonwhite.[4] Conversely, Latinos who were classified as "white" through the 1960 census are now regarded by the United States as "not-quite whites, as in Hispanic whites."[5] Similarly, the U.S. Census Bureau has changed the racial classification of various Asian American groups from white to Asian. Thus, one's "race" is best understood as a social and legal construction.[6]

Though racial categories are inexact as a classification system, it is generally agreed that *race* is a more all-encompassing term than either *culture* or *nation*. Not all Caucasian people, for example, are part of the same culture or nation. Many western European countries principally include people from the Caucasian race. Similarly, among Caucasian people there are definite differences in culture. Consider the cultural differences among the primarily Caucasian countries of Great Britain, Norway, and Germany to understand the distinction between culture and race.

Sometimes race and culture do seem to work hand in hand to create visible and important distinctions among groups within a larger society; and sometimes race plays a part in establishing separate cultural groups. An excellent example of the interplay of culture and race is in the history of African American people in the United States. Although race may have been used initially to set African Americans apart from Caucasian U.S. Americans, African American culture provides a strong and unique source

CULTURE *connections*

It was the first day of a sociology graduate course on race and students were going around the table introducing themselves and their areas of interest. When it was my turn, I stated my name and described my interest in the racial identity development of multiracial people and how such identities might affect our current notions of race. The professor, who, during my introduction, repeated my last name in perfect Spanish commented, "Oh, so you're jumping on the multiracial bandwagon!" to which I replied, "Well actually I was born on it."

—*Diana Alvarado*

of identity to members of the black race in the United States. Scholars now acknowledge that African American culture, with its roots in traditional African cultures, is separate and unique and has developed its own set of cultural patterns. Although a person from Nigeria and an African American are both from the same race, they are from distinct cultures. Similarly, not all black U.S. Americans are part of the African American culture, since many have a primary cultural identification with cultures in the Caribbean, South America, or Africa.

Race can, however, form the basis for prejudicial communication that can be a major obstacle to intercultural communication. Categorization of people by race in the United States, for example, has been the basis of systematic discrimination and oppression of people of color. We will explore the impact of racism more fully in Chapter 6.

Ethnicity   *Ethnic group* is another term often used interchangeably with culture. *Ethnicity* is actually a term that is used to refer to a wide variety of groups who might share a language, historical origins, religion, nation-state, or cultural system. The nature of the relationship of a group's ethnicity to its culture will vary greatly depending on a number of other important characteristics. For example, many people in the United States still maintain an allegiance to the ethnic group of their ancestors who emigrated from other nations and cultures. It is quite common for people to say they are German or Greek or Armenian when the ethnicity indicated by the label refers to ancestry and perhaps some customs and practices that originated with the named ethnic group. Realistically, many of these individuals now are typical members of the European American culture. In other cases, the identification of ethnicity may coincide more completely with culture. In the former Yugoslavia, for example, there are at least three major ethnic groups—Slovenians, Croatians, and Serbians—each with its own language and distinct culture, who were forced into one nation-state following World

CULTURE *connections*

As a woman with some Cherokee ancestors on my father's side and a blonde, blue-eyed daughter, I find it impossible to pin down the meaning of ethnicity. It's an especially delicate business here in the Southwest, where so many of us boil in one pot without much melting. We're never allowed to forget we are foreign bodies in the eyes of our neighbors. The annual Winter Holiday Concert at Camille's school features a bright patchwork of languages and rituals, each of which must be learned by a different subset of kids, the others having known it since they could talk. It sounds idyllic, but then spend half an hour on the playground and you're also likely to come away with a whole new vocabulary of racial slurs. On the playground no one's counting the strengths of your character, nor the woman your great-grandfather married, unless her genes have dyed your hair and fixed your features. It's the fact on your passport that gets you in. Faces that set us apart, in separate houses.

—*Barbara Kingsolver*

War II. It is also possible for members of an ethnic group to be part of many different cultures and/or nations. For instance, Jewish people share a common ethnic identification, even though they belong to widely varying cultures and are citizens of many different nations.

Subculture and Co-culture   *Subculture* is also a term sometimes used to refer to racial and ethnic minority groups that share both a common nation-state with other cultures and some aspects of the larger culture. Often, for example, African Americans, Arab Americans, Asian Americans, Native Americans, Latinos, and other groups are referred to as subcultures within the United States. The term, however, has connotations that we find problematic, because it suggests subordination to the larger European American culture. Similarly, the term *co-culture* is occasionally employed in an effort to avoid the implication of a hierarchical relationship between the European American culture and these other important cultural groups that form the mosaic of the United States. This term, too, is problematic for us. *Co-culture* suggests, for instance, that there is a single overarching culture in the United States, implicitly giving undue prominence to the European American cultural group. In our shrinking and interdependent world, most cultures must coexist alongside other cultures. We prefer to regard African Americans, Arab Americans, Chinese Americans, Native Americans, Latinos, and similar groups of people as cultures in their own right. When used to refer to cultural groups within a nation, therefore, the term *co-culture* strikes us as redundant. When used to refer to one's identity as a member of various groups based on occupation, hobbies, interests, and the like, *co-culture* seems less precise to us than such alternative terms as *lifestyle* or *social group*. Chapter 6 elaborates on this distinction between one's cultural and social identities.

Why Cultures Differ

Cultures look, think, and communicate as they do because of the need to accommodate and adapt to the pressures and forces that influence the culture as a whole. Members of a culture seldom notice these forces because they usually exert a steady and continuous effect on everyone. Few people pay attention to the subtleties of commonplace events and circumstances. Instead, they remain oblivious to the powerful forces that create and maintain cultural differences. This tendency has led Gustav Ichheiser to declare that "nothing evades our attention as persistently as that which is taken for granted."[7]

In this section we ask you to explore with us the taken-for-granted forces that create and maintain cultural differences. Our goal is to explain *why* one culture differs from another. As you read, consider your own culture and compare it to one that is very different or foreign to you. Why are they different? Why aren't all cultures alike? Why do cultures develop certain characteristics? Why do cultures communicate as they do? Why are they changing?

Forces That Maintain Cultural Differences   Cultural differences are created and sustained by a complex set of the forces that are deeply embedded within the culture's members. We have selected six forces that help to generate cultural differences, including a culture's history, ecology, technology, biology, institutional networks, and interpersonal communication patterns. Of course, this list is by no means exhaustive.

Consider these forces as representing factors with the potential to influence the ways in which cultures develop and maintain their differences yet change over time.

History   The unique experiences that have become part of a culture's collective wisdom constitute its *history*. Wars, inheritance rules, religious practices, economic consequences, prior events, legislative acts, and the allocation of power to specific individuals are all historical developments that contribute to cultural differences.

In the United States, for instance, historical forces that have affected the development and maintenance of cultures include the economic depression of 1929 and the fear of hyperinflation in 1979; the lessons learned in waging wars and making peace with Germany, Japan, Korea, Vietnam, Iraq, and Somalia; the bread lines and the gas lines; the deaths of John F. Kennedy, Martin Luther King, Jr., John Lennon, the *Challenger* astronauts, Selena, Tupac Shakur, and Aaliyah; and the horrific events of September 11, 2001, when terrorists killed thousands of people at the World Trade Center and the Pentagon. All of these events have had profound effects on the ways in which U.S. Americans view themselves and their country. You have undoubtedly heard parents or other elders describe historical events as significantly influencing them and the lives of everyone in their generation. Descriptions of such events are transmitted across

The Parthenon, at the Acropolis in Athens, Greece, has become a symbol of the important historical influence that the Greek culture has had on many other Western cultures.

CULTURE *connections*

The first time I saw coconut-skating I was so sure it was a joke that I laughed out loud. The scowl that came back was enough to tell me that I had completely misunderstood the situation. In the Philippines a maid tends to be all business, especially when working for Americans.

But there she was, barefooted as usual, with half of a coconut shell under each broad foot, systematically skating around the room. So help me, *skating.*

If this performance wasn't for my amusement or hers (and her face said it wasn't), then she had gone out of her head. It wasn't the first time, nor the last, that my working hypothesis was that a certain local person was at least a part-time lunatic.

I backed out and strolled down the hall, trying to look cool and calm.

"Ismelda . . . Ismelda is skating in the living room," I said to Mary, who didn't even look up from the desk where she was typing.

"Yes, this is Thursday, isn't it." . . .

"She skates only on Thursdays? That's nice," I said as I beat an awkward retreat from Mary's little study room.

"Oh, you mean *why* is she skating—right?" Mary called after me.

"Yes, I guess that's the major question," I replied.

Mary, who had done part of her prefield orientation training in one of my workshops, decided to give me a dose of my own medicine: "Go out there and watch her skate; then come back and tell me what you see." And so I did.

Her typewriter clicked on, scarcely missing a beat, until I exclaimed from the living room hallway, "I've got it!"

"Well, good for you; you're never too old to learn." Mary's voice had just enough sarcasm in it to call me up short on how I must sound to others. And while the typing went on I stood there admiring nature's own polish for hardwood floors, coconut oil, being applied by a very effective Southeast Asian method.

—*Ted Ward*

---

generations and form the shared knowledge that guides a culture's collective actions. As David McCullough says of such events and experiences, "You have to know what people have been through to understand what people want and what they don't want. That's the nub of it. And what people have been through is what we call history."[8]

Ecology   The external environment in which the culture lives is the culture's ecology. It includes such physical forces as the overall climate, the changing weather patterns, the prevailing land and water formations, and the availability or unavailability of certain foods and other raw materials.

There is a considerable amount of evidence to demonstrate that ecological conditions affect a culture's formation and functioning in many important and often subtle ways. Often, the effects of the culture's ecology remain hidden to the members of a culture because the climate and environment are a pervasive and constant force. For example, the development and survival of cultures living in cold-weather climates demand an adaptation that often takes the form of an increased need for technology, industry, urbanization, tolerance for ambiguity, and social mobility.[9] High levels of involvement and closer physical distances in communication characterize cultures that develop in warm climates. High-contact cultures tend to be located in such warm-weather climates as the Middle East, the Mediterranean region, Indonesia, and Latin America, whereas low-contact cultures are found in cooler climates such as Scandinavia, northern Europe, England, portions of North America, and Japan.[10]

In the United States, differences in climate are related to variations in self-perceptions and interaction patterns. Compared to residents in the warmer areas of the South, for instance, those living in the colder areas of the northern United States tend to be less verbally dramatic, less socially isolated, less authoritarian in their communication style, more tolerant of ambiguity, more likely to avoid touching others in social situations, and lower in feelings of self-importance or self-worth.[11] Surviving a harsh cold-weather climate apparently requires that people act in a more constrained and organized fashion, maintain flexibility to deal with an ambiguous and unpredictable environment, cooperate with others to stave off the wind and the weather, and recognize how puny humans are when compared to such powerful forces as ice storms and snow drifts.

Another important aspect of the ecological environment is the predominant geographical and geological features. For instance, an abundant water supply shapes the economy of a region and certainly influences the day-to-day lifestyles of people. If water is a scarce commodity, a culture must give a major portion of its efforts to locating and providing an item that is essential to human life. Energy expended to maintain

The climate of a culture, along with other forces of cultural change, produces unique cultural characteristics. Here, a major flood in Davenport, Iowa, required people to make adaptations in order to survive.

a water supply is not available for other forms of accomplishment. Likewise, the shape and contour of the land, along with the strategic location of a culture in relation to other people and places, can alter the mobility, outlook, and frequency of contact with others. Natural resources such as coal, tin, wood, ivory, silver, gold, spices, precious stones, agricultural products, and domesticated animals all contribute to the ecological forces that help to create differences among cultures.

Technology   The inventions that a culture has created or borrowed are the culture's *technology,* which includes such items as tools, weapons, hydraulic techniques, navigational aids, paper clips, barbed wire, stirrups, and microchips. Changes in the available technology can radically alter the balance of forces that maintain a culture. For instance, the invention of barbed wire allowed the U.S. American West to be fenced in, causing range wars and, ultimately, the end of free-roaming herds of cattle.[12] Similarly, stirrups permitted the Mongols to sweep across Asia, because they allowed riders to control their horses while fighting with their hands.

How have telephones changed the way people communicate? If you are a frequent phone user, do not use the phone for one week and keep track of the adaptations and compensations you make. (You can substitute e-mail use or similar technologies if you use them frequently.)

You have undoubtedly experienced the relationship of technology to culture. Can you remember when most U.S. American homes did not have a microwave oven? Two generations before microwave ovens became common, most homes also did not have refrigerators and freezers, relying instead on daily trips to the butcher and the baker, and on regular visits from the milkman and the iceman to keep foods from spoiling. Think about how a family's food preparation has changed in the United States. Grocery stores now stock very different food products because of the prevalence of refrigerators and microwave ovens; entirely new industries have developed as well (as shown by the many freezer-to-microwave dishes).

An example of a technological change with even greater consequences is the microchip, which has led to the creation of computers, video games, handheld calculators, and "smart" machines that are capable of adapting to changing circumstances. The corresponding revolution in the storage, processing, production, and transmission of printed words (such as this textbook) because of the computer has led to a society in which there is an abundance of information.

One special form of technology that has had a major influence on cultures around the world is the media. The media allow human beings to extend sensory capabilities to communicate across time and long distances with duplicate messages. Thus, media are any technologies that extend the ability to communicate beyond the limits of face-to-face encounters. Traditional media, such as books, newspapers, magazines, telegraph, telephone, photography, radio, phonograph, and television, have had a major influence in shaping cultures. The new media technologies, such as satellites, cassettes, videotape, videotext, cable television, videodisk, cellular phones, computers, and the internet, further extend the capabilities of the traditional media.

Media are responsible for introducing ideas from one culture to another rapidly, in a matter of a few weeks or less. The latest designs from a Paris fashion show can be faxed to Hong Kong manufacturers within minutes of their display in France, and accurate copies of the clothing can be ready for sale in the United States within a very short time.

Especially relevant is the way in which media technologies influence people's perceptions about other cultures. How do *I Love Lucy* reruns, beamed by satellite to Jakarta, influence the way Indonesians try to communicate with someone from the United States?[13] In what ways do U.S. action-adventure films, in which many of the characters commit acts of violence to resolve interpersonal disagreements, affect the expectations of people from Brazil when they visit the United States? To what extent do media programs accurately reflect a culture and its members? Media-generated stereotypes have important consequences for the processes and outcomes of intercultural communication.

Biology   The inherited characteristics that cultural members share are the result of *biology,* as people with a common ancestry have similar genetic compositions. These hereditary differences often arise as an adaptation to environmental forces, and they are evident in the biological attributes often referred to as *race.* Depending on how finely you wish to make distinctions, there are anywhere from three to hundreds of human races. Biologists are quick to point out, however, that there is far more genetic diversity within each race than there is among races, as humans have had both the means and the motive to mate with others across the entire spectrum of human genetic differences. This makes race an arbitrary but sometimes useful term.[14]

Although it is undeniable that genetic variations among humans exist, it is equally clear that biology cannot explain all or even most of the differences among cultures. For example, the evidence from studies that have been conducted in the United States on differences in intelligence suggests that most of the variation in intelligence quotient

Harnessing the energy of animals has been a major labor-saving technology throughout the world. These Cambodian men use a a water buffalo and a plow to till the field.

(IQ) scores is unrelated to cultural differences. Studies of interracial adoption, for instance, reveal that educational and economic advantages, along with the prebirth intrauterine environment, are the critical factors in determining children's IQ scores.[15] The data therefore suggest that although hereditary differences certainly exist, most of the distinctions among human groups result from cultural learning or environmental causes rather than from genetic or biological forces. As Michael Winkelman suggests, "biology provides the basis for acquiring capacities, while culture provides those specific skills as related to specific tasks and behaviors."[16]

Readily observable biological differences among groups of people have been amply documented, particularly for external features such as body shape, skin color, and other physical attributes. These visible differences among cultures are often used to define racial boundaries, though they can be affected by climate and other external constraints and are therefore not reliable measures of racial makeup. Better indicants of genetic group distinctions, according to scientists who study their origins and changes, are the inherited single-gene characteristics such as differences in blood types, ear wax, and the prevalence of wisdom teeth. Type B blood, for instance, is common among Asian and African races, whereas Rh-negative blood is relatively common among Europeans but rare among other races; Africans and Europeans have soft, sticky ear wax, whereas Japanese and many Native American groups have dry, crumbly earwax; and many Asians lack the third molars, or wisdom teeth, whereas about 15 percent of Europeans and almost all West Africans have them.[17] Of course, racial distinctions such as these are not what is intended by those who differentiate among individuals based on their physical or "racial" characteristics.

The technology of the computer, along with the internet, are dramatically changing how people acquire information about the world. This engineer is running tests for the Space Shuttle program.

A complicating factor in making racial distinctions is that virtually all human populations are of mixed genetic origins. One theory about human biological differences holds that all humans can trace their ancestry back to the genes of a single African woman who lived between 166,000 and 249,000 years ago. An analysis of differences in the mitochondrial DNA of 189 people, 121 of whom were from Africa, was used to estimate the degree of relationship among people.[18] Mitochondrial DNA, which is found in every living cell, is passed along substantially unchanged from a mother to her children.

Because there are no "pure" races, membership in a particular racial category is less a matter of biology, genetics, and inherited characteristics than it is a matter of politics, social definitions, and personal preferences.[19] Experts have estimated, for instance, that about 25 percent of the genes of African Americans come from white ancestors, and numerous African Americans have Native American ancestry as well. Conversely, up to 5 percent of the genes of European Americans come from black ancestors.[20]

Unfortunately, most studies that claim to associate differences in people's biological race with innate IQ differences do not measure the degree to which genetic heritages come from particular racial stocks.[21] Instead, social definitions of race, which assess people's cultural rather than biological identities, are used by researchers to draw conclusions about innate biological differences. Since culture is learned rather than inherited, any obtained differences in these studies are likely the result of lived experiences and intellectual opportunities, rather than of inherited genetic differences.

However, the lack of a biological basis for racial distinctions does not mean that race is unimportant. Rather, race should be understood as a sociological term that refers to people who are believed by themselves or by others to constitute a group of people who share common physical attributes.

Racial differences are often used as the defining features to include some individuals in a particular group while excluding others. Interestingly, U.S. census data, and often social pressures, require individuals to include themselves in only one of the available racial categories, despite ample evidence that many people are of mixed race and have multiple ethnic identities. Thus a woman whose mother is a black Latino and whose father is a third-generation Korean American is often expected to disavow some parts of her heritage while identifying with other parts. Difficulties with the census classification system can be seen in the data on the Native American population, which seemingly quadrupled from 1960 to 1990. From 1980 to 1990 alone, the Native American population increased 118 percent in Alabama and 78 percent in New Jersey. As these increases are not related to "natural" causes such as fertility rates and immigration patterns, demographers have concluded that a newfound pride and an increasing sense of cultural awareness have led many people to so identify themselves on census forms.[22] Indeed, had the film *Dances with Wolves* been released before the census in April 1990, rather than at the end of that year, the number of Native Americans would undoubtedly have been even higher. In the decade since *Dances with Wolves* was released, census data suggest that the Native American population increased by 110 percent.

Institutional Networks   *Institutional networks* are the formal organizations in societies that structure activities for large numbers of people. These include government, education, religion, work, professional associations, and even social organizations.

The importance of government as an organizing force is acknowledged by the emphasis placed in secondary schools on the different types of government systems around the globe. Because their form of government influences how people think about the world, this institutional network plays an important role in shaping culture.

The importance of institutional networks is also illustrated by the variability in the ways that people have developed to display spirituality, practice religion, and confront our common mortality. Indeed, religious practices are probably as old as humankind. Even 50,000 years ago, Neanderthal tribes in western Asia buried their dead with food, weapons, and fire charcoal, which were to be used in the next life.

Religion is an important institutional network that binds people to one another and helps to maintain cultural bonds. However, the manner in which various religions organize and connect people differs widely. In countries that practice Christianity or Judaism, people who are deeply involved in the practice of a religion usually belong to a church or synagogue. The congregation is the primary means of affiliation, and religious services are attended at the same place each time. As people become more involved in religious practices, they meet others and join organizations in the congregation, such as men's and women's clubs, Bible study, youth organizations, and Sunday school. Through the institutional network of the church or synagogue, religious beliefs connect people to one another and reinforce the ideas that initially led them to join.

Religious organizations in non-Christian cultures are defined very differently, and the ways they organize and connect people to one another are also very different. In India, for example, Hindu temples are seemingly everywhere. Some are very small and simple, whereas others are grand and elaborate. The idea of a stable congregation hold-

Buddhists pray together at a temple. The practice of religion provides important institutional networks in most cultures.

ing regularly scheduled services, as is done in the religious practices of Christianity and Judaism, is unknown. People may develop a level of comfort and affiliation with a particular temple, but they don't "join the congregation" and attend prayer meetings. They simply worship in whatever temple and at whatever time they deem appropriate.

Interpersonal Communication Patterns   The face-to-face verbal and nonverbal coding systems that cultures develop to convey meanings and intentions are called *interpersonal communication patterns*. These patterns include links among parents, siblings, peers, teachers, relatives, neighbors, employers, authority figures, and other social contacts.

Differences in interpersonal communication patterns both cause and result from cultural differences. Verbal communication systems, or languages, give each culture a common set of categories and distinctions with which to organize perceptions. These common categories are used to sort objects and ideas and to give meaning to shared experiences. Nonverbal communication systems provide information about the meanings associated with the use of space, time, touch, and gestures. They help to define the boundaries between members and nonmembers of a culture.

Interpersonal communication patterns are also important in maintaining the structure of a culture because they are the means through which a culture transmits its beliefs and practices from one generation to another. The primary agents for conveying these basic tenets are usually parents, but the entire network of interpersonal relationships provides unrelenting messages about the preferred ways of thinking, feeling, perceiving, and acting in relation to problems with which the culture must cope. For instance, when a major storm causes death and the destruction of valuable property, the explanations given can shape the future of the culture. An explanation that says "God is punishing the people because they have disobeyed" shapes a different perception of the relationship among humans, nature, and spirituality than an explanation that says "Disasters such as this one happen because of tornadoes and storms that are unrelated to human actions."

Cultures organize and assign a level of importance to their interpersonal communication patterns in various ways, and the level of importance assigned in turn influences other aspects of the culture. Ideas concerning such basic interpersonal relationships as *family* and *friend* often differ because of unique cultural expectations about the obligations and privileges that should be granted to a particular network of people. In the United States, for instance, college students consider it appropriate to live hundreds of miles from home if doing so will allow them to pursue the best education. Many Mexican college students, however, have refused similar educational opportunities because in Mexico one's family relationships are often more important than individual achievement. In the Republic of Korea, family members are so closely tied to one another in a hierarchy based on age and gender that the oldest male relative typically has the final say on such important matters as where to attend school, what profession to pursue, and whom to marry.

Because an understanding of cultural differences in interpersonal communication patterns is so crucial to becoming interculturally competent, it is a central feature of this book. Subsequent chapters will focus specifically on the importance of interpersonal communication patterns and will consider more general issues about the nature of interpersonal communication among cultures.

The Interrelatedness of Cultural Forces   Although we have discussed the forces that influence the creation and development of cultural patterns as if each operated independently of all the others, we do wish to emphasize that they are all interrelated. Each force affects and is affected by all of the others. Each works in conjunction with the others by pushing and pulling on the members of a culture to create a vector of constraints that alters the cultural patterns.

Changes in a culture's institutions or traditions cause its members to alter their behaviors in some way. These alterations, in turn, foster additional adjustments to the institutions or traditions in a continual process of adaptation and accommodation. Thus, nomadic herders change the land by plowing fields, and the plowed fields change the herders by making them remain in one place to farm. The ready availability of food allows towns and villages to become large cities, but cities require other technological improvements in roads and irrigation systems in order to sustain their increased size. Technological changes require corresponding institutional changes as more complex social structures are needed to organize and coordinate joint activities.

As an example of the interrelationship among these powerful forces, consider the effects of population, religion, resource availability, and life expectancy on the formation of certain cultural values and practices in Ireland and India during the late nineteenth century.[23] In Ireland, the population was large relative to the available food, and severe food shortages were common. Therefore, there was a pressing need to reduce the size of the population. Because the Irish were predominantly Catholic, artificial methods of birth control were unacceptable. Given the negative cultural value associated with birth control and the problems of overpopulation and lack of food, a cultural practice evolved that women did not marry before the age of about thirty. The population was reduced, of course, by the delay in marriages. India, at about that same time, also had harsh economic conditions, but the average life expectancy was about twenty-eight years, and nearly half of the children died before age five. Given that reality, a cultural value evolved that the preferred age for an Indian woman to marry was around twelve or thirteen. That way, all childbearing years were available for procreation, thus increasing the chances for the survival of the culture.

Cultural adaptations and accommodations, however extreme, are rarely made consciously. Rather, cultures attempt to adjust to their unique configuration of forces by altering the shared and often unquestioned cultural assumptions that guide their thoughts and actions.

Intercultural Communication

A simple way to define the term *intercultural communication* is to use the definition of *communication* that was provided in the previous chapter and insert the phrase "from different cultures." This addition would yield the following definition:

> Intercultural communication is *a symbolic process in which people from different cultures create shared meanings.*

This definition, although accurate, is difficult to apply. In the following examples we describe several situations and ask you to analyze them with this definition in mind.

CULTURE *connections*

A sense of tribe is deeply embedded in the human soul. All of us are appropriately dependent upon and interdependent with networks of belonging. Grounded in the quest for survival and security, millennia of human existence in bands and tribes have fundamentally shaped our attitudes and behaviors as a species. . . . So we use the word "tribe" with caution, as a metaphor to acknowledge an aspect of human evolution at the core of our social identity. Our prosperity as social beings is woven by patterns of kinship, mutual assistance, and affection. Despite individualism's triumph, the industrial revolution, the power of nation states and international corporations, nothing has finally erased the human need to belong, to share an identity with others whom we recognize as "like me" and "one of us."

—*Laurent A. Parks Daloz, Cheryl H. Keen, James P. Keen, and Sharon Daloz Parks*

Our intention in the discussion that follows is to give you a more sophisticated understanding of the term *intercultural communication* by exploring more fully the meaning of the phrase "people from different cultures."

Examples of Intercultural Interactions

Read the description of each interaction and think carefully about the questions that follow. Decide whether you think the communication between the people involved is or is not intercultural. Our answers to these questions are provided in the subsequent discussion.

Example 1

Dele is from Nigeria and Anibal is from Argentina. Both young men complete secondary education in their own countries and then come to the United States to study. They study at the same university, live in the same dormitory their first year on campus, and choose agriculture as their major. Eventually, they become roommates, participate in many of the same activities for international students, and have many classes together. After completing their bachelor's degrees, they enroll in the same graduate program. After four more years in the United States, each returns to his home country and takes a position in the country's Agricultural Ministry. In letters to each other, both comment on the difficulties that they are experiencing in working with farmers from their own country.

Questions for Example 1

▶ When they first begin their studies in the United States, is the communication between Dele and Anibal intercultural communication?

▶ When they complete their studies in the United States, is the communication between Dele and Anibal intercultural communication?

▶ After they return to their home countries, is the communication between each man and the farmers with whom they work intercultural communication?

Example 2

Janet grew up in a small town of about 3,500 people in western Massachusetts. She is surrounded by her immediate family, many other relatives, and lots of friends. Her parents grew up in this same town, but Janet is determined to have experiences away from her family and away from the small portion of New England that has formed the boundaries of her existence. Despite parental concerns, Janet goes to one of California's major public universities, which is located in a large urban area, and she begins her life in the West. Janet is at first excited and thrilled to be living in California, but within a very short period of time, she begins to feel very isolated. She is assigned to live in a co-educational dormitory, and she finds it disconcerting to be meeting male students as she walks down the hallway in her bathrobe. Although her fellow students seem friendly, her overtures for coffee or movies or even studying together are usually met with a smile and a statement that "It would be great, but. . . ." The superficial friendliness of most of the people she meets starts to annoy her, and Janet becomes bad-tempered and irritable.

Questions for Example 2

▶ Is the culture of Massachusetts sufficiently different from that of California to characterize Janet's communication with her fellow students as intercultural?

▶ Would Janet have had the same kinds of feelings and reactions if she had moved into a coeducational dormitory at a university in urban Massachusetts?

Example 3

Even though Andy Wong's parents immigrated to the United States from Taiwan before he was born, they still speak Chinese at home and expect Andy and his brothers and sisters to behave like proper Chinese children. Because Andy is the eldest child, his parents have additional expectations for him. Andy loves his parents very much, but he finds their expectations difficult to fulfill. He thinks he speaks respectfully to his mother when he tells her that he is going out with his friends after dinner, but his parents tell him he is being disrespectful. The family reaches a major crisis when Andy announces that he is going to go to a college that has a good studio arts program, rather than pursue the solid science background his parents want him to have in preparation for medical school.

Question for Example 3

▶ Is Andy's communication with his parents intercultural, either because Andy is very U.S. American and his parents are Chinese or because parents and children have different cultures?

Example 4

Jane Martin works for a U.S. company that has a major branch in South Korea. Although Jane is fairly young, her boss has asked her to travel to Seoul to teach her Korean counterparts a new internal auditing system. Despite Jane's lack of linguistic skill in Korean (she speaks no Korean) and little experience in another country (she has spent a week in London and a week in Paris on holiday), she is confident that she will be successful in teaching the Korean employees the new system. She has won high praise for her training skills in the United States, and the company promises to provide her with a good interpreter. "After all," Jane thinks, "we're all part of the same company—we do the same kinds of work with the same kinds of corporate regulations and expectations. Besides, Koreans are probably familiar with U.S. Americans."

Questions for Example 4

▶ Is Jane's communication with South Koreans intercultural, or does working for the same corporation mean that Jane and her South Korean counterparts share a common culture?
▶ Is Jane's age a factor in communication with her Korean counterparts?
▶ Would you answer the previous questions any differently if Jane's company were sending her to the branch office in England rather than to the one in South Korea?

Example 5

Angela enjoys watching soap operas on television. In fact, she's a real soap opera fanatic; she reads *Soap Opera Digest* for the summaries of the episodes, arranges her day to be able to watch her favorite shows, and uses her videocassette recorder to tape the ones she must miss. One afternoon, as Angela switches through the cable channels looking for her regular program, she stops at a channel with a program in Spanish that she immediately recognizes as a soap opera. Fascinated, Angela watches the entire program and believes that, despite having no knowledge of Spanish, she has followed the plot line accurately.

Questions for Example 5

▶ Do you accept Angela's assessment that she understood the Spanish soap opera because soap opera plots are all similar?
▶ Can intercultural communication take place even if those communicating do not share a common language?

Example 6

John has worked for the same company, based in Minneapolis, Minnesota, for the six years since his graduation from college. A recent promotion means that John has to move to his company's branch office in Milwaukee, Wisconsin. John faces difficulties almost immediately after beginning work in Milwaukee.

His boss has a much different management style than the one with which John is familiar. His new job responsibilities require some knowledge and sophistication in areas in which John is not an expert. After several months on the job, John is feeling fairly beleaguered and is beginning to lose confidence in his abilities.

Question for Example 6

▶ Is John's communication with his boss intercultural communication?

Each of these examples represents a likely communication event in today's world. It is very probable that two people from different countries will spend an extended period of time in a third country, as Dele and Anibal have. It is also very likely that these two people will, over time, form relationships that create a shared set of experiences. Moving from one part of a country to another is a commonplace occurrence, whether the goal is to attend a university, as Janet did, or to advance professionally, as John did. Immigration of people from one country to another also occurs frequently, producing communication problems typical of those experienced by U.S.-born-and-raised Andy with his Chinese-born-and-identified parents. The significance of the global marketplace means that work often takes people to countries around the world, as companies like Jane's become increasingly multinational. With the advent of modern communication technologies, many more people will be able to select television programs, films, music, radio shows, and computerized messages that are arranged in verbal and non-verbal codes different from their own. Angela's experience with the Spanish soap opera will be repeatable almost everywhere. But are these examples, all of which involve communication, also examples of intercultural communication? Do any of them clearly *not* involve intercultural communication? In the next sections we attempt to provide answers to these questions.

Similarities and Differences between Communicators

By applying the definition of intercultural communication given at the beginning of the chapter, it would be relatively simple to categorize each example. You would go through the examples and make a bipolar choice—either yes or no—based on whether the people in the examples were from different cultures. Thus, you would probably decide that the communication between Anibal and Dele was intercultural when they arrived in the United States. It would be much more difficult to judge their communication after they completed their studies. Perhaps you would decide that their communication with people from their own country following their return home was not intercultural, or perhaps you would say that it was. Similarly, you might be convinced that California is indeed a different culture from Massachusetts, or you might argue vehemently that it is not. Most likely you would decide that Jane's communication with her Korean counterparts was intercultural, even though they undoubtedly did share some common expectations about work performance because the same company employed them. Had her company decided to send Jane to England instead of to Korea, her communication with her English coworkers would have been similarly intercultural. Yet you might feel a bit uncomfortable, as we are, with the idea of putting U.S.–Korean communication into the same category as U.S.–English communication.

The difficulties encountered in a simple yes-or-no decision lead us to suggest an alternative way of thinking about intercultural communication. What is missing is an answer to three questions that emerge from the preceding examples:

1. What differences among groups of people constitute cultural differences?
2. How extensive are those differences?
3. How does extended communication change the effects of cultural differences?

This last question suggests the possibility that initially one's interactions could be very intercultural, but subsequent communication events could make the relationship far less intercultural.

To demonstrate the importance of these questions, we would like you to take the examples presented earlier and arrange them in order from most intercultural to least intercultural.[24] Use a continuum like the one shown in Figure 2.1.

Thus, you will be identifying the degree of interculturalness in each interaction and, in effect, you will be creating an "interculturalness" scale. It should even be possible to make distinctions among those communication situations that are placed in the middle, with some closer and some farther from the most intercultural end. When you place the examples on a continuum, they might look something like Figure 2.2.

We suspect that the continuum you have created is very similar to ours. Where we might disagree is on how we ordered the examples placed near the middle.

The next important issue for understanding the definition of intercultural communication concerns the characteristics present in the encounters. What is it about the people, the communication, the situation, or some combination of those factors that increases the likelihood that the communication will be intercultural?

What varies and changes across the examples is the degree of similarity or the amount of difference between the interactants. For instance, Anibal (from Argentina) and Dele (from Nigeria) are very different when they first come to study in the United States. Each speaks English, but as a second language to Spanish and Yoruba, respectively; their facility with English is initially weak, and they are uncomfortable with it. In addition, their values, social customs, gestures, perceptions of attractiveness, and expectations about personal space and how friendships are established differ. Initially, Anibal and Dele are culturally very different, or heterogeneous, and their communication should certainly be placed near the "most intercultural" end of the continuum. However, after eight years in the United States, having studied the same academic subjects, shared many of the same friends, and participated in many common experiences, their communication with each other does not have the same degree of interculturalness as it did initially. Certainly, each still retains part of his own cultural heritage and point of

Most intercultural	Least intercultural

FIGURE 2.1

A continuum of interculturalness.

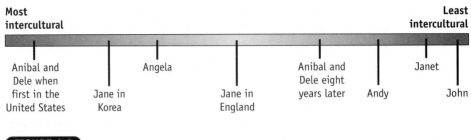

| Most intercultural | | | | | | | | Least intercultural |

Anibal and Dele when first in the United States; Jane in Korea; Angela; Jane in England; Anibal and Dele eight years later; Andy; Janet; John

FIGURE 2.2

A continuum of interculturalness, with examples.

view, but the two men have also created an important set of common understandings between themselves that is not grounded in their respective cultural frameworks.

Janet, in contrast, was placed near the "least intercultural" end of the continuum because of the degree of similarity, or homogeneity, she shares with Californians. They speak the same language, and their values, gestures, social perceptions, and expectations about relationships are all similar. Certainly, Californians use slang and jargon with which Janet is not familiar, but they speak, read, and study in English. And certainly, Californians, particularly urban Californians, seem to place importance on different things than Janet does. She also thinks it unusual and a bit uncomfortable to be sharing a living space with men she does not even know. Nevertheless, the magnitude of these differences is relatively small.

There are learned differences among groups of people that are associated with their culture, such as cultural patterns, verbal and nonverbal codes, relationship rules and roles, and social perceptions. When such important differences are relatively large, they lead to dissimilar interpretations about the meanings of the messages that are created, and they therefore indicate that people are from different cultures. Thus,

> *People are from different cultures whenever the degree of difference between them is sufficiently large and important that it creates dissimilar interpretations and expectations about what are regarded as competent communication behaviors.*

Definition of Intercultural Communication

Previous definitions have described the central terms *communication* and *culture*. By combining the meanings of these terms with the ideas suggested in our discussion

CULTURE *connections*

I wanted my children to have the best combination: American circumstances and Chinese character. How could I know that these two things do not mix?

—*Amy Tan*

about the degrees of difference that can occur among people from dissimilar cultures, we offer the following definition of intercultural communication:

> *Intercultural communication* occurs *when large and important cultural differences create dissimilar interpretations and expectations about how to communicate competently.*

The degree to which individuals differ is the degree to which there is intercultural-ness in a given instance of communication. Situations in which the individuals are very different from one another are most intercultural, whereas those in which the individuals are very similar to one another are least intercultural.

Intercultural Communication and Related Terms

The relationship between culture and communication is important to many disciplines. Consequently, many terms have been used to describe the various ways in which the study of culture and communication intersect: *cross-cultural communication, international communication, intracultural communication, interethnic communication,* and *interracial communication.* The differences among these terms can be confusing, so we would like to relate them to the focus of study in this book.[25]

Intercultural communication occurs when large and important cultural differences create dissimilar interpretations and expectations about how to communicate competently.

Intracultural Communication   The term *intercultural,* used to describe the end points of the continuum, denotes the presence of at least two individuals who are culturally different from each other on such important attributes as their value orientations, preferred communication codes, role expectations, and perceived rules of social relationships. We would now like to relabel the "least intercultural" end of the continuum, which is used to refer to communication between culturally similar individuals, as *intracultural.* John's communication with his new boss in Milwaukee is intracultural. Janet's communication with her fellow students in California is more intracultural than intercultural. Both *intercultural* and *intracultural* are comparative terms. That is, each refers to differences in the magnitude and importance of expectations that people have about what constitutes competent communication behaviors.

Interethnic and Interracial Communication   Just as *race* and *ethnic group* are terms commonly used to refer to cultures, *interethnic* and *interracial communication* are two labels commonly used as substitutes for *intercultural communication.* Usually, these terms are used to explain differences in communication between members of racial and ethnic groups who are all members of the same nation-state. For example, communication between African Americans and European Americans is often referred to as interracial communication. The large numbers of people of Latino origin who work and live with people of European ancestry produce communication characterized as interethnic. Sometimes the terms are also used to refer to communication between people from various ethnic or racial groups who are not part of the same nation but live in specific geographic areas. Although it may be useful in some circumstances to use the terms *interethnic* and *interracial,* we believe these types of communication are most usefully categorized as subsets of intercultural communication.

Describe five interactions in which you have been an active participant and which you would regard as intercultural experiences. Place these five communication experiences on a continuum based on their interculturalness.

Both ethnicity and race contribute to the perceived effects of cultural differences on communication, which moves that communication toward the "most intercultural" end of the continuum. We will therefore rely on the broader term of *intercultural communication* when discussing, explaining, and offering suggestions for increasing your degree of competence in interactions that involve people from other races and ethnic groups. In Chapter 6, however, when considering particular cultural biases, we will give special attention to the painful and negative consequences of racism.

Cross-Cultural Communication   The term *cross-cultural* is typically used to refer to the study of a particular idea or concept within many cultures. The goal of such investigations is to conduct a series of intracultural analyses in order to compare one culture to another on the attributes of interest. For example, someone interested in studying the marriage rituals in many cultures would be considered a cross-cultural researcher. Scholars who study self-disclosure patterns, child-rearing practices, or educational methods as they exist in many different cultures are doing cross-cultural comparisons. Whereas intercultural communication involves interactions among people from different cultures, cross-cultural communication involves a comparison of interactions among people from the same culture to those from another culture. While cross-

CULTURE *connections*

Chinese-Americans, when you try to understand what things in you are Chinese, how do you separate what is peculiar to childhood, to poverty, insanities, one family, your mothers who marked your growing with stories, from what is Chinese? What is Chinese tradition and what is the movies?

—*Maxine Hong Kingston*

cultural comparisons are very useful for understanding cultural differences, our principle interest is in using these cross-cultural comparisons to understand intercultural communication competence.

International Communication   *International communication* refers to interactions among people from different nations. Scholars who compare and analyze nations' media usage also use this term. Certainly, communication among people from different countries is likely to be intercultural communication, but that is not always true, as illustrated by the example of Anibal and Dele after eight years together in the United States. As we suggested with the terms *interracial* and *interethnic communication,* we prefer to focus on *intercultural communication.*

Summary

Our goal in this chapter has been to provide an understanding of some of the key concepts underlying the study of intercultural competence. We began with a discussion of the concept of culture. From the many available approaches to defining culture, we selected one that emphasizes the close relationship between culture and communication. We defined culture as a learned set of shared perceptions about beliefs, values, and norms, which affect the behaviors of a relatively large group of people. We emphasized that people are not born with a culture but learn it through their interactions with others. Our definition located culture in the minds of people, and in the shared ideas that can be understood by their effects on behavior. We distinguished between culture and other groups to which people belong by suggesting that culture occurs only when beliefs, values, and norms affect large groups of people. We next made some important distinctions among terms such as *culture, nation, race, ethnic group,* and *subculture.*

We also explored some of the reasons that cultures differ. The shared experiences remembered by cultural members, or a culture's history, were considered first. In the United States, for instance, the lesson of the country's historical experiences affects U.S. Americans' views of their government's relationships with other countries. The ways in which a culture's unique ecology profoundly alters the collective actions of its people were then illustrated. Next we discussed the biological or genetic forces affecting cultures. Genetic variations among people are only a small source of cultural differences. We also explained the role of the formal organizations of a culture, the institutional networks such as government, religion, work organizations, and other social organizations. These institutional networks organize groups of individuals and provide the regulations by which the culture functions as a collective. The undisputed effects of technology on a culture were explored next. Technological differences promote vast changes in the ways cultures choose to function. Finally, interpersonal communication patterns, the means by which cultural patterns are transmitted from one generation to another, were considered. These interpersonal communication patterns include the links a culture emphasizes among parents, siblings, peers, teachers, relatives, neighbors, authority figures, and other social contacts. The reciprocal relationship among these forces suggests the inevitability and constancy of accommodations and changes that characterize all cultures.

The chapter concludes with a discussion of a topic that is central to this book: intercultural communication. We began with several examples, which were followed by an exploration of issues related to similarities and differences among communicators that produce intercultural communication. Finally, after providing our definition of intercultural communication, we differentiated between that term and related terms, including *intracultural, interethnic, interracial, cross-cultural,* and *international* communication. In Chapter 3 we consider an additional concept that is the focal point of this book—intercultural communication competence.

For Discussion

1. What differences are there between the view that "people are born into a culture" versus the opinion that "one becomes a member of a culture through a process of learning"?
2. In the United States, what is the relationship among the following terms: *nation, race, culture,* and *co-culture*?
3. What historical events have had a dramatic impact on the development of your culture? Have cultural traditions and behaviors changed as a result of these developments?
4. Which current technologies do you think affect and change your culture? How so?
5. What links are there between intercultural communication and interpersonal communication?

For Further Reading

A. L. Kroeber and Clyde Kluckhohn, *Culture: A Critical Review of Concepts and Definitions* (Cambridge, MA: The Museum, 1952). A classic work providing hundreds of definitions of culture by scholars across many disciplines.

Myron W. Lustig and Jolene Koester (eds.), *AmongUS: Essays on Identity, Belonging, and Intercultural Competence* (New York: Longman, 2000). This collection includes many essays, written in the first person, that document the emotions and experiences of people living in a multicultural world.

Craig Storti, *The Art of Crossing Cultures,* 2nd ed. (Yarmouth, ME: Intercultural Press, 2001). A straightforward guide to managing one's thinking and emotions as one spends substantial time living in another culture.

For additional information about intercultural films and about Web sites on specific cultures, turn to the Resources section at the back of this book.

chapter 3

Intercultural Communication Competence

The United States as an Intercultural Community
Metaphors of U.S. Cultural Diversity
What Do You Call Someone from the United States of America?
Cultural Groups in the United States
Competence And Intercultural Communication

Intracultural Communication Competence
The Components of Intercultural Competence
Basic Tools for Improving Intercultural Competence
The BASICs of Intercultural Competence
Description, Interpretation, and Evaluation
Summary

When does communication become intercultural communication? What distinguishes intercultural communication from communication that is not intercultural? What does it mean to be a competent intercultural communicator? In Chapters 1 and 2 we defined the terms *communication, culture,* and *intercultural communication.* In this chapter we first discuss the multicultural nature of the United States, where intercultural competence is essential. Then we focus our attention on the components and characteristics of intercultural communication competence. Our purpose is to establish boundaries and common understandings about this central idea.

The United States as an Intercultural Community

A set of complicated issues underlies our discussion in Chapter 1 about the domestic and international imperatives for intercultural communication. Stated most simply, these issues focus on what it means to be an American and on decisions about how to refer to the various cultural groups that reside within the borders of the United States. In the following sections, we first examine the implications of four metaphors that have been used to describe U.S. cultural diversity. Next, we analyze the question of what to call someone from the United States. Finally, we describe the difficult choices we faced in selecting labels to refer to the domestic cultures within the United States.

CULTURE *connections*

Because we are the people of an idea and not of blood or soil, American nationality often is a deeply felt ambiguity. Because we are a nation of immigrants, ethnicity and individual identity co-mingle here in uniquely American ways.

The hyphen we choose to embed in our self-description—Irish American, Mexican American, African American—does not simply designate a familial origin. For many of us, it is the pivot on which we balance delicate questions of acceptance and rejection, pain and pride, assimilation and self-assertion. . . .

—*Tim Rutten*

Metaphors of U.S. Cultural Diversity

Many cultural groups live within the borders of the United States. When people talk about the blend of U.S. cultural groups, their ideas are often condensed into a few key words or phrases. These summary images, called *metaphors,* imply both descriptions of what is and, less obviously, prescriptions of what should be. Though we will have much more to say in subsequent chapters about the effects of language and labeling on the intercultural communication process, we would like to focus now on four metaphors that have been used to describe the cultural mix within the United States: a melting pot, a set of tributaries, a tapestry, and a garden salad.

The Melting Pot Metaphor   Perhaps the oldest metaphor for describing multiple cultures in the United States is the melting pot.[1] America, according to this image, is like a huge crucible, a container that can withstand extremely high temperatures and can therefore be used to melt, mix, and ultimately fuse together metals or other substances. This image was the dominant way to represent the ideal blending of cultural groups at a time when the hardened steel that was forged in the great blast furnaces of Pittsburgh helped to make the United States into an industrial power. According to this view, immigrants from many cultures came to the United States to work, live, mix, and blend together into one great assimilated culture that is stronger and better than the unique individual cultures of which it is composed.

Dynamic as the melting pot metaphor has been in the United States, it has never been an accurate description. The tendency for diverse cultures to melt together and assimilate their unique heritages into a single cultural entity has never really existed. Rather, the many cultural groups within the United States have continuously adapted to one another as they accommodated and perhaps adopted some of the practices and preferences of other groups while maintaining their own unique and distinctive heritages.

The Tributaries Metaphor   A currently popular metaphor for describing the mix of cultures in the United States is that of tributaries or tributary streams. America, according to this image, is like a huge cultural watershed, providing numerous paths in

Intercultural communication occurs when there are significant differences among the communicators. What do you suppose are the consequences of these differences for the family shown here?

which the many tributary cultures can flow. The tributaries maintain their unique identities as they surge toward their common destination. This view is useful and compelling. Unlike the melting pot metaphor, which implies that all cultures in the United States ought to be blended to overcome their individual weaknesses, the tributary image seems to suggest that it is acceptable and desirable for cultural groups to maintain their unique identities. However, when the metaphor of tributaries is examined closely, there are objections to some of its implications.

Tributary streams are small, secondary creeks that ultimately flow into a common stream, where they combine to form a major river. Our difficulty with this notion rests in the hidden assumption that the cultural groups will ultimately and inevitably blend together into a single, common current. Indeed, there are far fewer examples of cultures that have totally assimilated into mainstream U.S. culture than there are instances of cultures that have remained unique. Further, the idea of tributaries blending together to form one main stream suggests that the tributaries are somehow subordinate to or less important than the mighty river into which they flow.

The Tapestry Metaphor   A tapestry is a decorative cloth made up of many strands of thread. The threads are woven together into an artistic design that may be pleasing to some but not to others. Each thread is akin to a person, and groups of similar threads are analogous to a culture. Of course, the types of threads differ in many ways; their thickness, smoothness, color, texture, and strength may vary. The threads can range from gossamer strands to inch-thick yarn, from soft silk to coarse burlap, from pastel hues to fluorescent radiance, and from fragile spider webs to steel cables. The weaving process itself can vary from one location to another within the overall tapestry. Here, a wide swatch of a single type of thread may be used; there, many threads might be interwoven with many others, so no single thread is distinguished; and elsewhere, the threads may have been grouped together into small but distinguishable clumps.

   Although the metaphor of a tapestry has much to commend it, the image is not flawless. After all, a tapestry is rather static and unchangeable. One does not typically unstring a bolt of cloth, for instance, only to reassemble the threads elsewhere in a different configuration. Cultural groups in the United States are more fluid than the tapestry metaphor might imply; migrations, immigrations, and mortality patterns all alter the cultural landscape. Despite its limitations, however, we find this metaphor preferable to the previous two.

The Garden Salad Metaphor   Like a garden salad made up of many distinct ingredients that are being tossed continuously, some see the United States as made up of a complex array of distinct cultures that are blended into a unique, and one hopes tasteful, mixture. Substitute one ingredient for another, or even change how much of each ingredient is present, and the entire flavor of the salad may be changed. Mix the salad differently and the look and feel will also differ. A salad contains a blend of ingredients, and it provides a unique combination of tints, textures, and tastes that tempt the palate.

> Create your own metaphor of cultural diversity in the United States. How can you accurately depict the many cultures in the United States? What metaphor might capture this diversity most succinctly?

   Like the other metaphors, the garden salad is not without its flaws. In contrast to the tapestry image, which implies that the United States is too fixed and unchanging, a garden salad suggests an absence of firmness and stability. A typical garden salad has no fixed arrangement; it is always in a state of flux. Cultural groups in the United States, however, are not always moving, mixing, and mingling with the speed and alacrity that the metaphor would suggest. Nevertheless, we recommend this metaphor, and that of the tapestry, as the two images that are likely to be most useful in characterizing the diversity of cultural groups in the United States. In addition, we encourage you to invent your own metaphors.

CULTURE *connections*

Fish Cheeks

I fell in love with the minister's son the winter I turned 14. He was not Chinese, but as white as Mary in the manger. For Christmas I prayed for this blond-haired boy, Robert, and a slim new American nose.

When I found out that my parents had invited the minister's family over for Christmas Eve dinner, I cried. What would Robert think of our shabby *Chinese* Christmas? What would he think of our noisy *Chinese* relatives who lacked proper American manners? What terrible disappointment would he feel upon seeing not a roast turkey and sweet potatoes but *Chinese* food?

On Christmas Eve I saw that my mother had outdone herself in creating a strange menu. She was pulling black veins out of the backs of prawns. The kitchen was littered with appalling mounds of raw food: a slimy rock cod with bulging fish eyes that pleaded not to be thrown in a pan of hot oil. Tofu, which looked like stacked wedges of rubber white sponges. A bowl soaking dried fungus back to life. A plate of squid, their backs crisscrossed with knife markings so they resembled bicycle tires.

And then they arrived—the minister's family and all my relatives in a clamor of doorbells and rumpled Christmas packages. Robert grunted hello, and I pretended he was not worthy of existence.

Dinner threw me deeper in despair. My relatives licked the ends of their chopsticks and reached across the table, dipping them into the dozen or so plates of food. Robert and his family waited patiently for platters to be passed to them. My relatives murmured with pleasure when my mother brought out the whole steamed fish. Robert grimaced. Then my father poked his chopsticks just below the fish eye and plucked out the soft meat. "Amy, your favorite," he said, offering me the tender fish cheek. I wanted to disappear.

At the end of the meal my father leaned back and belched loudly, thanking my mother for her fine cooking. "It's a polite Chinese custom to show you are satisfied," explained my father to our astonished guests. Robert was looking down at his plate with a reddened face. The minister managed to muster up a quiet burp. I was stunned into silence for the rest of the night.

After everyone had gone, my mother said to me, "You want to be the same as American girl on the outside." She handed me an early gift. It was a miniskirt in beige tweed. "But inside you must always be Chinese. You must be proud to be different. Your only shame is to have shame."

And even though I didn't agree with her then, I knew that she understood how much I had suffered during the evening's dinner. It wasn't until many years later—long after I had gotten over my crush on Robert—that I was able to appreciate fully her lesson and the true purpose behind our particular menu. For Christmas Eve that year, she had chosen all my favorite foods.

—*Amy Tan*

What Do You Call Someone from the United States of America?

Many people who live in the United States of America prefer to call themselves American. However, people from Brazil, Argentina, Guatemala, Mexico, and many other Central and South American countries also consider themselves American, as they are all part of the continents known collectively as the Americas. Indeed, people from these countries consider the choice of *American* for those from the United States to be imperialistic and insulting. They resent the implication that they are less central or less important.

An alternative choice for a name, which is frequently selected by those who are trying to be more sensitive to cultural differences, is *North American. North American* is the English translation of the Spanish label that is commonly used by people from many Central and South American countries to refer to people from the United States, and the name is widely regarded as far less insulting and imperialistic. However, this label still has the potential for creating friction and causing misunderstanding. *North American* refers to an entire continent, and people from Mexico and Canada are, strictly speaking, also North Americans. Indeed, conversations with Canadians and Mexicans have confirmed for us that *North American* is not the ideal term.

One possibility that is often overlooked is to refer to people from the United States as *United Statians* or *United Staters*. These labels have the obvious advantage of being unambiguous, as they specifically identify people from a single country. Realistically, however, these are not labels that citizens of the United States would regard as comfortable and appropriate, and we agree that they are artificial and unlikely to be widely used.

Our preference is the label *U.S. Americans*. This referent retains the word *American* but narrows its scope to refer only to those from the United States. The term retains the advantages of a name that is specific enough to be accurate, yet it does not resort to a form of address that people would be unlikely to use and would regard as odd.

Cultural Groups in the United States

It is also important to select terms that adequately and sensitively identify the variety of cultural groups that make up the U.S. citizenry. As the population of the United States becomes increasingly more varied culturally, it is extremely urgent that we find ways to refer to these cultures with terms that accurately express their differences but avoid negative connotations and evaluations.

Some of the terms used in the past have negative associations, and we, as authors, have struggled to find more appropriate alternatives. For example, earlier writings about intercultural communication often referred to the culture associated with white U.S. Americans as either the "dominant" culture or the "majority" culture. The term *dominant* usually suggested the economic and political power of white U.S. America, referring to the control of important sources of institutional and economic power. The term often conveyed a negative meaning to members of other cultural groups, as it suggested that white U.S. Americans were somehow better or superior. It also implied that people from nondominant cultures were somehow subordinate or inferior to the dominant group. As more and more cultural groups have gained political and economic power in the United States, *dominant* no longer accurately reflects the current reality.

An alternative label for white U.S. Americans was *majority culture*. This term was intended to reflect a numerical statement that the majority of U.S. Americans are from a particular cultural group. Majority was often coupled with the term *minority,* which also had negative connotations for many members of other cultural groups: it suggested to some people that they were not regarded as important or significant as members of the majority. In addition, as previously suggested, nonwhite cultural groups now make up a sufficient proportion of the total population, so white U.S. Americans no longer constitute an absolute majority in many places. Thus, we prefer to avoid such emotionally charged words as *majority, minority, dominant, nondominant,* and *subordinate* when we discuss the cultural groups residing in the United States.

We have also elected not to use the term *white* or *Caucasian* in all subsequent discussions about a specific cultural group of U.S. Americans. *White* and *Caucasian* refer to a particular race. As suggested in Chapter 2, a racial category does not necessarily identify and distinguish a particular culture. Although many members of this group prefer to use the term *white,*[2] we think it is less useful in this book on inter*cultural* communication to refer to a cultural group in the United States by a term that denotes race. Consequently, because their common cultural heritage is predominantly European, we have chosen to describe white U.S. cultural members as European Americans.

Many black Americans prefer to be identified by a term that distinguishes them by their common cultural characteristics rather than by their racial attributes. *African American* recognizes the effects of traditional African cultural patterns on U.S. Americans of African heritage, and it acknowledges that African American cultural patterns are distinct from those of European Americans. Because it denotes a cultural rather than a racial distinction, we will use the latter term in this book.

Another set of terms is usually applied to those residents of the United States whose surname is Spanish. *Hispanic, Chicano, Mexican American,* and *Latino* are often used interchangeably, but the distinctions between the terms can be quite important.[3] *Hispanic* derives from the dominant influences of Spain and the Spanish language, but many shy away from this term because it tends to homogenize all groups of people who have Spanish surnames and who use the Spanish language. *Chicano* (or *Chicana*) refers to the "multiple-heritage experience of Mexicans in the United States" and speaks to a political and social consciousness of the Mexican American.[4] Specific terms such as *Mexican American* or *Cuban American* are preferred by those who wish to acknowledge their cultural roots in a particular national heritage while simultaneously emphasizing their pride in being U.S. Americans.[5] Finally, *Latino* (or *Latina*) is a cultural and linguistic term that includes "all groups in the Americas that share the Spanish language, culture, and traditions."[6] As Earl Shorris notes, "language defines the group, provides it with history and home; language should also determine its name—Latino."[7] Because *Latino* and *Latina* suggest cultural distinctions, we will use them in this book.

Terms routinely used to describe members of other cultural groups include *Native American, Arab American, Asian American,* and *Pacific Islander.* Each of these labels, as well as those previously described, obscures the rich variety of cultures that the single term represents. For instance, many tribal nations can be included under the term *Native American,* and members of those groups prefer a specific reference to their culture (e.g., Chippewa, Sioux, Navajo, Choctaw, Cherokee, and Inuit). Similarly, *Asian American* is a global term that can refer to Japanese Americans, Chinese Americans, Malaysian Americans, Korean Americans, and people from many other cultures that geographically originated in the part of the world loosely referred to as Asia. Even

CULTURE *connections*

The other day, I eavesdropped on a conversation between several U.S.-born Latinos who asked a fellow student whether she, who was born in Guatemala but raised half of her life in the United States, considered herself "Latina" or "American" or "what?"

The rather bookish student smiled and, without blinking, told her schoolmates, "I'm Mayan." She then uttered a few phrases in her native Kanjobal dialect. "Wow, that's cool!" one of the students responded. . . .

Rather than simply teach students about "Latinos," "African Americans," "Asians," "Native Americans" or other broad and often meaningless categories of people, we must prepare today's students for the new global realities. To do this, we must both know more about and also transcend ethnic identity. . . .

The current historical moment requires that we break up what currently passes for ethno-racial categories, ideas that box in our thinking and our institutions. Our children cannot afford to lose the valuable knowledge available right in front of them in this most global of cities and countries.

—*Roberto Lovato*

European American obscures differences among those whose heritage may be English, French, Italian, or German. Our use of these overly broad terms is not meant to deny the importance of cultural distinctions but to allow for an economy of words. We will use the broader, more inclusive, and less precise terms when making a generalization that describes a commonality among these cultures. When using examples that are limited to a particular culture, we will use the more specific nomenclature.

Notice that there are some inherent difficulties in our choices of cultural terms to refer to U.S. Americans. If precision were our only criterion, we would want to make many further distinctions. But we are also aware of the need for economy and the force of common usage. Although it is not our intent to advocate terms that ignore or harm particular cultural groups, we do prefer a vocabulary that is easily understood, commonly used, and positively regarded. Please remember, however, that the term preferred by specific individuals is an important reflection of the way they perceive themselves. Michael Hecht and Sidney Ribeau, for example, found differences in the expressed identities of individuals who defined themselves as "black" versus "black American."[8] Similarly, a "Chicana" defines herself differently from someone who labels herself a "Mexican American."

Competence and Intercultural Communication

Competent interpersonal communication is a worthy and often elusive goal. Interpersonal competence in intercultural interactions is an even more difficult objective to achieve, because cultural differences create dissimilar meanings and expectations that require even greater levels of communication skill. We base our understanding of intercultural competence on the work of scholars who have studied communicative com-

In this traditional wedding ceremony, this couple celebrate their cultural traditions with relatives and friends.

petence from a primarily intracultural perspective and on the conclusions of other scholars who have studied intercultural competence.

The study of intercultural competence has been motivated primarily by practical concerns. Businesses, government agencies, and educational institutions want to select people for intercultural assignments who will be successful. Lack of intercultural competence means failed business ventures, government projects that have not achieved their objectives, and unsuccessful learning experiences for students.

Intracultural Communication Competence

Although there is still some disagreement among communication scholars about how best to conceptualize and measure communication competence, there is increasing agreement about certain of its fundamental characteristics.[9] In our discussion we draw heavily on the work of Brian Spitzberg and his colleagues. The following definition of communication competence illustrates the key components of their approach:

> Competent communication is interaction that is perceived as effective in fulfilling certain rewarding objectives in a way that is also appropriate to the context in which the interaction occurs.[10]

This definition provides guidance for understanding communicative and intercultural competence in several ways. A key word is *perceived* because it means that competence is best determined by the people who are interacting with each other. In other words, communicative competence is a social judgment about how well a person interacts with others. That competence involves a social perception suggests that it will always be specific to the context and interpersonal relationship within which it occurs. Therefore, whereas judgments of competence are influenced by an assessment of an individual's personal characteristics, they cannot be wholly determined by them, because competence involves an interaction between people.

Competent interpersonal communication results in behaviors that are regarded as *appropriate.* That is, the actions of the communicators fit the expectations and demands of the situation. Appropriate communication means that people use the symbols they are expected to use in a given context.

Competent interpersonal communication also results in behaviors that are *effective* in achieving desired personal outcomes. Satisfaction in a relationship or the accomplishment of a specific task-related goal is an example of an outcome people might want to achieve through their communication with others.

Thus, communication competence is a social judgment that people make about others. The judgment depends on the context, the relationship between the interactants, the goals or objectives that the interactants want to achieve, and the specific verbal and nonverbal messages that are used to accomplish those goals.

The Components of Intercultural Competence

Our central concern in this book is improving your intercultural competence, and the ideas presented here are the key to doing so. In the remaining chapters, we will return to the concepts that follow to suggest ways to improve your ability.

A word of caution is necessary before we begin, however. We cannot write a prescription guaranteed to ensure competence in intercultural communication. The complexity of human communication in general, and intercultural communication in particular, denies the possibility of a quick fix. There is not necessarily only one way to be competent in your intercultural interactions. Even within the context of a specific person and specific setting, there may be several paths to competent interaction. The goal here is to understand the many ways that a person can behave in an interculturally competent manner.

> Identify someone you know whom you regard as a competent communicator. Describe the reasons why you believe she or he is competent. How does this person compare to the textbook definition of competence?

The remaining portion of this chapter provides a description of the characteristics of people, what they bring to the intercultural communication situation, and the nature of the communication itself, all of which increase the possibility of competence in intercultural communication. Subsequent chapters build on this discussion by offering guidelines for achieving competence. The summary of previous research suggests that competent intercultural communication is contextual; it produces behaviors that are both appropriate and effective; and it requires sufficient knowledge, suitable motivations, and skilled actions. Let's examine each of these components.

Context   Intercultural competence is *contextual.* An impression or judgment that a person is interculturally competent is made with respect to both a specific relational context and a particular situational context. Competence is not independent of the relationships and situations within which communication occurs.

Thus, competence is not an individual attribute; rather, it is a characteristic of the association between individuals.[11] It is possible, therefore, for someone to be perceived as highly competent in one set of intercultural interactions and only moderately competent in another. For example, a Canadian woman living with a family in India might establish competent relationships with the female family members but be unable to relate well to the male members.

Judgments of intercultural competence also depend on cultural expectations about the permitted behaviors that characterize the settings or situations within which people communicate. The settings help to define and limit the range of behaviors that are regarded as acceptable. Consequently, the same set of behaviors may be perceived as very competent in one cultural setting and much less competent in another. As an obvious example that competence is situationally determined, consider what might happen when two people who come from very different cultural backgrounds are involved in a close business relationship. Whereas one person might want to use highly personalized nicknames and touching behaviors in public, the other person might regard such visible displays as unwarranted and therefore incompetent.

Many previous attempts to describe intercultural competence have erroneously focused on the traits or individual characteristics that make a person competent. Thus in the past, individuals have been selected for particular intercultural assignments based solely on such personality attributes as authoritarianism, empathy, self-esteem, and world-mindedness. Because intercultural competence is contextual, these trait approaches have been unsuccessful in identifying competent intercultural communicators. Although specific personality traits might allow a person to be more or less competent on particular occasions, there is no prescriptive set of characteristics that inevitably guarantees competence in all intercultural relationships and situations.

Appropriateness and Effectiveness   Both interpersonal competence and intercultural competence require behaviors that are appropriate and effective. By *appropriate* we mean those behaviors that are regarded as proper and suitable given the expectations generated by a given culture, the constraints of the specific situation, and the nature of the relationship between the interactants. By *effective* we mean those behaviors that lead to the achievement of desired outcomes. The following example illustrates this important distinction between appropriateness and effectiveness.

> Brian Holtz is a U.S. businessperson assigned by his company to manage its office in Thailand. Mr. Thani, a valued assistant manager in the Bangkok office, has recently been arriving late for work. Holtz has to decide what to do about this problem. After carefully thinking about his options, he decides there are four possible strategies:
>
> 1. Go privately to Mr. Thani, ask him why he has been arriving late, and tell him that he needs to come to work on time.
> 2. Ignore the problem.
> 3. Publicly reprimand Mr. Thani the next time he is late.
> 4. In a private discussion, suggest that he is seeking Mr. Thani's assistance in dealing with employees in the company who regularly arrive late for work, and solicit his suggestions about what should be done.

CULTURE *connections*

Calling attention to the idea that their ways are not your ways is the right of your host. You are the outsider. Your calling attention to differences, even in little things, can create awkwardness, sometimes tension or embarrassment. But if *they* call attention to differences, it will usually be in the form of a compliment—especially if your host should come across with the *big* one: "Most Americans don't do it the way we do—you're different." It can be fun to hear this, especially in reference to something no one ever told you—something you noticed and figured out for yourself.

My first experience with the *mandi* of Indonesia was of this sort. As it turned out, there was no one to observe, but there were plenty of clues all around. My host had handed me a towel and invited me to "cool off . . . take as long as you want." He pointed outside to a little shed attached to the house. I nodded and headed for the shed. Inside I found a waist-high cubic concrete tub filled with water, a pair of hooks high on one wall, and a floor covered with wooden slats and slightly tilted toward a low spot where a sizable drain hole was covered with a small square of metal screening. Now what?

Was I supposed to get in that tub? In spite of the extremely hot and sultry weather, I didn't relish the idea of climbing into such a large tub of unheated water. Furthermore, whoever had installed the pipe (yes, there was only one) had positioned the faucet almost directly over the center of the tub. How could you get in and out with that thing in the middle? I was confused and not at all comfortable, so I did what uncomfortable, confused people do—I found a scapegoat: stupid Indonesian plumbers. And, as usual, that helped in no way whatsoever—except to remind me that "stupid locals" is an outsider's cover-up for his or her own ignorance.

So I looked around some more. This time two more things came into view: there was a plastic sauce pan with a long handle. Could it be an oversize dipper? And a small plastic box was perched on a crosspiece of the wall frame some distance from the tub. What was in it? Aha! soap; but why so far from the tub?

While all this observing and thinking was going on I got out of my clothes. Although I wasn't sure what to do next, I didn't imagine that Indonesians could keep as clean and neat as they do by daily face-washing. And with my pants in hand, I looked for a place to put them. The hooks high on the wall! Indonesians come in fairly short sizes, so I wondered at the height of the hooks. But, unlike my long-legged problem in many an American bathroom, the cuffs weren't going to get wet here, I thought. And then it began to fall into place.

Standing right there on the slatted floor was where my "shower" was to take place. The dipper was my shower, the tub was my ample reservoir, and the faucet was to refill the reservoir when I was through. At least all those ideas fit together.

It seemed to be a reasonable set of hypotheses. If I could just confirm any one part of it, I'd give it a try. The reservoir idea—why not just work directly from the faucet? I turned it. A trickle. More turns. Still a trickle. Never could you shower with that little flow. But over time, it would accumulate in the reservoir and you could have plenty to shower with. Further, as the cold tap water stood in the tub it would be warmed to a more pleasant temperature.

Fingers in the water. Right. Exactly the temperature to refresh without inducing a heart attack on this steamy day.

Here we go. The dipper. A half-cup down the left arm. A bit of soap. The water ran to the floor-slats and headed across to the drain. Aha! The open-air plumbing does work, after all. A little more water this time, and again.

Suddenly a childhood reading experience flashed into mind. Was it Kipling in India? Stevenson on his visits to Polynesia? I had read them all. (Childhood reading and my Great Aunt Mabel had got me into all of this in the first place.) I recalled the writer singing at the top of his voice as he splashed (yes, that was the word), splashed, and "threw water everywhere" (yes!). So I tried it. First the singing, then the splashing. And a bit more of each until the whole household could hear that I had found one of the profound pleasures of Indonesia, the *mandi*.

In the process I discovered why the clothes hooks are high on the wall. When the celebration of elemental values of life came to an end, I rebuttoned the not-too-wet essentials and emerged. My host was grinning from ear to ear.

You've used a *mandi* before, I gather," he said with a slight bow.

"No, but it doesn't take me long to learn."

"I should have explained it to you, but I didn't know if you needed me to."

Here's an important point: I could have asked. Perhaps I should have asked. Indeed, I would have asked if it had remained a mystery after I had taken a good look. But I didn't need to, and even if I had done something fundamentally wrong—even had I climbed bodily into the tub and displaced two hundred pounds of water, my host would have accepted it. I was an outsider. My ways were not his ways. But he wouldn't have been quite so delighted that I could enjoy *his* ways even without being told.

And then came the reward: "Did you turn on the faucet when you finished?" he asked.

"Yes," I replied. "It likely will take thirty minutes or so to replace what I used from the tub."

"Yes, about that. I'll turn it off after awhile. Do you know you are the first American ever to visit us who knew to leave the water running?" And his smile became even warmer.

—*Ted Ward*

Holtz's first strategy would be effective, as it would probably accomplish his objective of getting Mr. Thani to arrive at work more promptly. However, given the expectations of the Thai culture, which are that one person never directly criticizes another, such behavior would be very inappropriate. Conversely, Holtz's second strategy would be appropriate but not effective, as there would probably be no change in Mr. Thani's behavior. The third option would be neither appropriate nor effective because public humiliation might force Mr. Thani, a valuable employee, to resign. The fourth option, which is the best choice, is both appropriate and effective. By using an indirect means

Two Korean businessmen simultaneously bow, shake hands, and exchange business cards. Intercultural competence requires an understanding of the appropriate and effective behaviors that are required in a given setting.

to communicate his concerns, Mr. Thani will be able to "save face" while Holtz accomplishes his strategic goals.

Knowledge, Motivations, and Actions   Intercultural competence requires sufficient knowledge, suitable motivations, and skilled actions. Each of these components alone is insufficient to achieve intercultural competence.

Knowledge   Knowledge refers to the cognitive information you need to have about the people, the context, and the norms of appropriateness that operate in a specific culture. Without such knowledge, it is unlikely that you will interpret correctly the meanings of other people's messages, nor will you be able to select behaviors that are appropriate and that allow you to achieve your objectives. Consequently, you will not be able to determine what the appropriate and effective behaviors are in a particular context.

The kinds of knowledge that are important include culture-general and culture-specific information. The former provides insights into the intercultural communication process abstractly and can therefore be a very powerful tool in making sense of cultural practices, regardless of the cultures involved. For example, the knowledge that cultures differ widely in their preferred patterns (or rules) of interaction should help to sensitize you to the need to be aware of these important differences. This book is an excellent example of a source for culture-general knowledge. Knowledge about interpersonal communication and the many ways in which culture influences the communication process is very useful in understanding actual intercultural interactions.

Intercultural competence also depends on culture-specific information, which is used to understand a particular culture. Such knowledge should include information about the forces that maintain the culture's uniqueness (see Chapter 2) and facts about the cultural patterns that predominate (see Chapters 4 and 5). The type of intercultural encounter will also suggest other kinds of culture-specific information that might be useful. Exchange students might want to seek out information about the educational system in the host country. Businesspeople may need essential information about the cultural dynamics of doing business in a specific country or with people from their own country who are members of different cultural groups. Tourists would benefit from guidebooks that provide information about obtaining lodging, transportation, food, shopping, and entertainment.

An additional—and crucial—form of culture-specific knowledge involves information about the specific customs that govern interpersonal communication in the culture. For example, before traveling to Southeast Asia, it would be very useful to know that many Southeast Asian cultures regard a display of the soles of the feet as very offensive. This small bit of information can be filed away for later recall when travelers visit temples and attempt to remove their shoes. The imperative to learn about other cultures is equally strong for those cultures with which you interact on a daily basis. Culture-specific knowledge about the rules and customs of the multiple cultures that make up the cultural landscape of the United States is essential information if you are to be interculturally competent.

Often overlooked is knowledge of one's own cultural system. Yet the ability to attain intercultural competence may be very closely linked to this kind of knowledge. Knowledge about your own culture will help you to understand another culture. Fathi Yousef has even suggested that the best way to train businesspeople who must deal with cultural differences might be to teach them about the characteristics of their own culture rather than those of others.[12] The idea behind this admonition is that if people are able to understand how and why they interpret events and experiences, it is more likely that they would be able to select alternative interpretations and behaviors that are more appropriate and effective when interacting in another culture.

Motivations   Motivations include the overall set of emotional associations that people have as they anticipate and actually communicate interculturally. As with knowledge, different aspects of the emotional terrain contribute to the achievement of intercultural competence. Human emotional reactions include both feelings and intentions.

Feelings refer to the emotional or affective states that you experience when communicating with someone from a different culture. Feelings are not thoughts, though

people often confuse the two; rather, feelings are your emotional and physiological reactions to thoughts and experiences. Feelings of happiness, sadness, eagerness, anger,
tension, surprise, confusion, relaxation, and joy are among the many emotions that can
accompany the intercultural communication experience. Feelings involve your general
sensitivity to other cultures and your attitudes toward the specific culture and individuals with whom you must interact. How would you characterize your general motivation toward other cultures? Are you excited by the thought of talking with someone
from a culture that is different from yours? Or are you anxious at the prospect? Do you
think your culture is superior to other cultures? Are you even willing to entertain the
idea that another culture's ways of doing various life activities might be as good as, or
even better than, your culture's ways? Some people simply do not want to be confronted with things that differ from what they are used to. The different sights, sounds,
and smells of another culture are often enough to send them running back to the safety
of a hotel room. Eagerness and a willingness to experience some uncertainty is a necessary part of your motivation to achieve intercultural competence.

CULTURE *connections*

This summer I was one of 20 teens who spent five weeks at the University of Wisconsin
at Superior studying acid rain with a National Science Foundation Young Scholars program. . . . It was amazing, given the variety of backgrounds, to see the ignorance of some
of the smartest young scholars on the subject of other religions.

On the first day, one girl mentioned that she had nine brothers and sisters. "Oh, are
you Mormon?" asked another girl, who I knew was a Mormon herself. The first girl,
shocked, replied, "No, I dress normal!" She thought Mormon was the same as Mennon-
ite, and the only thing she knew about either religion was that Mennonites don't, in her
opinion, "dress normal."

My friends, ever curious about [my] Judaism, asked me about everything from our
basic theology to food preferences. . . .

Nobody was deliberately rude or anti-Semitic, but I got the feeling that I was representing the entire Jewish people through my actions. I realized that many of my friends
would go back to their small towns thinking that all Jews like Dairy Queen Blizzards and
grilled cheese sandwiches. After all, that was true of all the Jews they knew (in most cases,
me and the only other Jewish young scholar, period). . . .

Ignorance was the problem I faced this summer. By itself, ignorance is not always a
problem, but it leads to misunderstandings, prejudice, and hatred. Many of today's problems involve hatred. If there weren't so much ignorance about other people's
backgrounds, would people still hate others as badly as they do now? Maybe so, but at
least that hatred would be based on facts and not flawed beliefs.

—*Chana Schoenberger*

Intentions are what guide your choices in a particular intercultural interaction. Your intentions are the goals, plans, objectives, and desires that focus and direct your behavior. Intentions are often affected by the stereotypes you have of people from other cultures because stereotypes reduce the number of choices and interpretations you are willing to consider. For instance, if you begin an intercultural interaction having already formed a negative judgment of the other person's culture, it will be very difficult for you to develop accurate interpretations of the behaviors that you observe. Intentions toward the specific interaction partner also must be positive. If your intentions are positive, accurate, and reciprocated by the people with whom you are interacting, your intercultural competence will likely be enhanced.

Actions   Finally, actions refer to the actual performance of those behaviors that are regarded as appropriate and effective. Thus, you can have the necessary information, be motivated by the appropriate feelings and intentions, and still lack the behavioral skills necessary to achieve competence. For example, students from other cultures who enroll in basic public speaking classes often have an excellent understanding of the theory of speech construction. In addition, they have a positive attitude toward learning U.S. speaking skills; they want to do well and are willing to work hard in preparation. Unfortunately, their speaking skills sometimes make it difficult for them to execute the delivery of a speech with the level of skill and precision that they would like.[13]

Basic Tools for Improving Intercultural Competence

In the preceding section we suggested that intercultural competence means using your knowledge, motivation, and skills to deal appropriately and effectively with cultural differences. We now offer two tools to assist you in becoming more interculturally competent. These tools can help you improve your interpersonal interactions and will facilitate the development of intercultural relationships.

The BASICs of Intercultural Competence

The Behavioral Assessment Scale for Intercultural Competence (BASIC), developed by Jolene Koester and Margaret Olebe,[14] is based on work done originally by Brent Ruben and his colleagues.[15] A very simple idea provides the key to understanding how to use these BASIC skills: what you actually do, rather than your internalized attitudes or your projections of what you might do, is what others use to determine whether you are interculturally competent. The BASIC skills are a tool for examining people's communication behaviors—yourself included—and in so doing provides a guide to the very basics of intercultural competence.

Eight categories of communication behavior are described in the BASIC instrument, each of which contributes to the achievement of intercultural competence. As each of the categories is described, mentally assess your own ability to communicate. Do you display the behaviors necessary to achieve intercultural competence? From what you now know about intercultural communication, what kinds of changes might make your behavior more appropriate and effective?

Before we describe each of the BASIC skills, we would like to emphasize that the BASIC descriptions of behaviors are culture-general. That is, most cultures use the

Use the BASIC dimensions to evaluate your behaviors when interacting with someone from a culture other than your own. What does this evaluation reveal about your intercultural interactions?

types of behaviors that are described to make judgments of competence about themselves and others. But within each culture there may be, and in all likelihood will be, different ways of exhibiting these behaviors. For example, actions that show respect for others, and the ability to maintain conversations and manage communicative interactions, are necessary in all cultures for someone to be judged as competent. However, the way each culture teaches its members to exhibit these actions is culture-specific. Even among the various cultural groups that live in the United States, the rules for taking turns in a conversation vary widely. The eight types of communication behaviors are each discussed and are summarized in Table 3.1.

Display of Respect   Although the need to display respect for others is a culture-general concept, within every culture there are specific ways to show respect and specific expectations about those to whom respect should be shown. What constitutes respect in one culture, then, will not necessarily be so regarded in another culture.

Respect is shown through both verbal and nonverbal symbols. Language that can be interpreted as expressing concern, interest, and an understanding of others will often convey respect, as will formality in language, including the use of titles, the absence of jargon, and an increased attention to politeness rituals. Nonverbal displays of respect include showing attentiveness through the position of the body, facial expressions, and the use of eye contact in prescribed ways. A tone of voice that conveys interest in the other person is another vehicle by which respect is shown. The action of displaying respect increases the likelihood of a judgment of competence.

Orientation to Knowledge   Orientation to knowledge refers to the terms people use to explain themselves and the world around them. A competent orientation to knowledge occurs when people's actions demonstrate that all experiences and interpretations are individual and personal rather than universally shared by others.

TABLE 3.1   BASIC Dimensions of Intercultural Competence

Display of Respect	The ability to show respect and positive regard for another person
Orientation to Knowledge	The terms people use to explain themselves and the world around them
Empathy	The capacity to behave as though you understand the world as others do
Interaction Management	Skill in regulating conversations
Task Role Behavior	Behaviors that involve the initiation of ideas related to group problem-solving activities
Relational Role Behavior	Behaviors associated with interpersonal harmony and mediation
Tolerance for Ambiguity	The ability to react to new and ambiguous situations with little visible discomfort
Interaction Posture	The ability to respond to others in descriptive, nonevaluative, and nonjudgmental ways

Many actions exhibit people's orientation to knowledge, including the specific words that are used. Among European Americans, for instance, declarative statements that express personal attitudes or opinions as if they were facts, and an absence of qualifiers or modifiers, would show an ineffective orientation to knowledge:

- "New Yorkers must be crazy to live in that city."
- "Parisians are rude and unfriendly."
- "The custom of arranged marriages is barbaric."
- "Every person wants to succeed—it's human nature."

In contrast, a competent intercultural communicator acknowledges a personal orientation to knowledge, as illustrated in the following examples:

- "I find New York a very difficult place to visit and would not want to live there."
- "Many of the people I interacted with when visiting Paris were not friendly or courteous to me."
- "I would not want my parents to arrange my marriage for me."
- "I want to succeed at what I do, and I think most people do."

At least some of the time, all people have an orientation to knowledge that is not conducive to intercultural competence. In learning a culture, people develop beliefs about the "rightness" of a particular way of seeing events, behaviors, and people. It is actually very natural to think, and then to behave, as if your personal knowledge and experiences are universal. Intercultural competence, however, requires an ability to move beyond the perspective of your cultural framework.

Empathy   Individuals who are able to communicate an awareness of another person's thoughts, feelings, and experiences are regarded as more competent in intercultural interactions. Alternatively, those who lack empathy, and who therefore indicate little or no awareness of even the most obvious feelings and thoughts of others, will not be perceived as competent. Empathetic behaviors include verbal statements that identify the experiences of others and nonverbal codes that are complementary to the moods and thoughts of others.

CULTURE *connections*

The new *mestiza* copes by developing a tolerance for contradictions, a tolerance for ambiguity. She learns to be an Indian in Mexican culture, to be Mexican from an Anglo point of view. She learns to juggle cultures. She has a plural personality, she operates in a pluralistic mode—nothing is thrust out, the good, the bad and the ugly, nothing rejected, nothing abandoned. Not only does she sustain contradictions, she turns the ambivalence into something else.

—Gloria Anzaldúa

Learning about other cultures is a necessary prerequisite to achieving intercultural competence.

It is necessary to make an important distinction here. Empathy does not mean "putting yourself in the shoes of another." It is both physically and psychologically impossible to do so. However, it is possible for people to be sufficiently interested and aware of others that they appear to be putting themselves in others' shoes. The skill we are describing here is the capacity to *behave as if one understands the world as others do.* Of course, empathy is not just responding to the tears and smiles of others, which may, in fact, mean something very different than your cultural interpretations would suggest. Although empathy does involve responding to the emotional context of another person's experiences, tears and smiles are often poor indicators of emotional states.

Interaction Management   Some individuals are skilled at starting and ending interactions among participants and at taking turns and maintaining a discussion. These management skills are important because through them all participants in an interaction are able to speak and contribute appropriately. In contrast, dominating a conversation or being nonresponsive to the interaction is detrimental to competence. Continuing to engage people in conversation long after they have begun to display signs of disinterest and boredom or ending conversations abruptly may also pose problems. Interaction management skills require knowing how to indicate turn taking both verbally and nonverbally.

Task Role Behavior   Because intercultural communication often takes place where individuals are focused on work-related purposes, appropriate task-related role behaviors are very important. Task role behaviors are those that contribute to the group's problem-solving activities, for example, initiating new ideas, requesting further information or facts, seeking clarification of group tasks, evaluating the suggestions of others, and keeping a group on task. The difficulty in this important category is the display of culturally appropriate behaviors. The key is to recognize the strong link to a culture's underlying patterns and to be willing to acknowledge that tasks are accomplished by cultures in multiple ways. Task behaviors are so intimately entwined with cultural expectations about activity and work that it is often difficult to respond appropriately to task expectations that differ from one's own. What one culture defines as a social activity, another may define as a task. For example, socializing at a restaurant or a bar may be seen as a necessary prelude to conducting a business negotiation. Sometimes that socializing is expected to occur over many hours or days, which surprises and dismays many European Americans, who believe that "doing business" is separate from socializing.

Relational Role Behavior   Relational role behaviors concern efforts to build or maintain personal relationships with group members. These behaviors may include verbal and nonverbal messages that demonstrate support for others and that help to solidify feelings of participation. Examples of competent relational role behaviors include harmonizing and mediating conflicts between group members, encouraging participation from others, general displays of interest, and a willingness to compromise one's position for the sake of others.

Tolerance for Ambiguity   Tolerance for ambiguity concerns a person's responses to new, uncertain, and unpredictable intercultural encounters. Some people react to new situations with greater comfort than do others. Some are extremely nervous, highly frustrated, or even hostile toward the new situations and those who may be present in them. Those who do not tolerate ambiguity well may respond to new and unpredictable situations with hostility, anger, shouting, sarcasm, withdrawal, or abruptness.

Others view new situations as a challenge; they seem to do well whenever the unexpected or unpredictable occurs, and they quickly adapt to the demands of changing

CULTURE *connections*

Ambiguity is the warp of life, not something to be eliminated. Learning to savor the vertigo of doing without answers or making do with fragmentary ones opens up the pleasures of recognizing and playing with pattern, finding coherence within complexity, sharing within multiplicity. Improvisation and new learning are not private processes; they are shared with others at every age. The multiple layers of attention involved cannot safely be brushed aside or subordinated to the completion of tasks. We are called to join in a dance whose steps must be learned along the way, so it is important to attend and respond. Even in uncertainty, we are responsible for our steps.

—*Mary Catherine Bateson*

environments. Competent intercultural communicators are able to cope with the nervousness and frustrations that accompany new or unclear situations, and they are able to adapt quickly to changing demands.

Interaction Posture   Interaction posture refers to the ability to respond to others in a way that is descriptive, nonevaluative, and nonjudgmental. Although the specific verbal and nonverbal messages that express judgments and evaluations can vary from culture to culture, the importance of selecting messages that do not convey evaluative judgments is paramount. Statements based on clear judgments of rights and wrongs indicate a closed or predetermined framework of attitudes, beliefs, and values, and they are used by the evaluative, and less competent, intercultural communicator. Nonevaluative and nonjudgmental actions are characterized by verbal and nonverbal messages based on descriptions rather than on interpretations or evaluations.

Description, Interpretation, and Evaluation

We have approached the study of intercultural competence by looking at the elements of culture that affect interpersonal communication. There is, however, a tool that allows people to control the meanings they attribute to the verbal and nonverbal symbols used by others. The tool is based on the differences in how people think about, and then verbally speak about, the people with whom they interact and the events in which they participate.

The interaction tool is called *description, interpretation,* and *evaluation*. It starts with the assumption that, when most people process the information around them, they use a kind of mental shorthand. Because people are taught what symbols mean, they are not very aware of the information they use to form their interpretations. In other words, when people see, hear, and in other ways receive information from the world around them, they generally form interpretations and evaluations of it without being aware of the specific sensory information they have perceived. For example, students and teachers alike often comment about the sterile, institutional character of many of the classrooms at universities. Rarely do these conversations detail the specific perceptual information on which that interpretation is based. Rarely does someone say, for instance, "This room is about twenty by forty feet in size, the walls are painted a cream color, there is no artwork on the walls, it is lit by eight fluorescent bulbs, and the floors are cream-colored tiles with multiple pieces of dirt." Yet when students and professors say that their classroom is "sterile, institutional-looking, and unattractive," most people who have spent a great deal of time in such rooms have a fairly accurate image of the classroom. Similarly, if a friend is walking toward you, you might say, "Hi! What's wrong? You look really tired and upset." That kind of comment is considered normal, but if you said instead, "Hi! Your shoulders are drooping, you're not standing up straight, and you are walking much slower than usual," it would be considered strange. In both examples, the statements considered to be normal are really interpretations and evaluations of sensory information the individual has processed.

The skill we are introducing trains you to distinguish among statements of description, interpretation, and evaluation. These statements can be made about all characteristics, events, persons, or objects. A statement of description details the specific perceptual cues and information a person has received, without judgments or inter-

CULTURE *connections*

We and They

Father, Mother, and Me,
   Sister and Auntie say
All the people like us are We,
   And everyone else is They.
And They live over the sea,
   While We live over the way,
But—would you believe it?—They look upon We
   As only a sort of They!
All good people agree,
   And all good people say,
All nice people, like Us, are We
   And everyone else is They:
But if you cross over the sea,
   Instead of over the way,
You may end by (think of it!) looking on We
   As only a sort of They!

—Rudyard Kipling

---

pretations—in other words, without being distorted by opinion. A statement of interpretation provides a conjecture or hypothesis about what the perceptual information might mean. A statement of evaluation indicates an emotional or affective judgment about the information.

Often, the interpretations people make of perceptual information are very closely linked to their personal evaluation of that information. Any description can have many different interpretations; but because most people think in a mental shorthand, they are generally aware of only the interpretation that immediately comes to mind, which they use to explain the event. For example, teachers occasionally have students who arrive late to class. A statement of description about a particular student engaging in this behavior might be as follows:

> Think of a recent instance when someone's behavior annoyed or offended you. Using the D-I-E framework, write descriptive, interpretive, and evaluative statements about that event. Are there alternative interpretations and evaluations that emerge as you do this?

▶ Kathryn arrived ten minutes after the start of the class.
▶ Kathryn also arrived late each of the previous times the class has met.

Statements of interpretation, which are designed to explain Kathryn's behavior, might include some of the following:

- ◗ Kathryn doesn't care very much about this particular class.
- ◗ Kathryn is always late for everything.
- ◗ Kathryn has a job on the other side of campus and is scheduled to work until ten minutes before this class. The person who should relieve her has been late, thus not allowing Kathryn to leave to be on time for class.
- ◗ Kathryn is new on campus this semester and is misinformed about the starting time for the class.

For each interpretation, the evaluation can vary. If the interpretation is "Kathryn doesn't care very much about this class," different professors will have differing evaluations:

- ◗ I am really offended by that attitude.
- ◗ I like a student who chooses to be enthusiastic only about classes she really likes.

The interpretation a person selects to explain something like Kathryn's behavior influences the evaluation that is made of that behavior. In people's everyday interactions, distinctions are rarely made among description, interpretation, and evaluation. Consequently, people deal with their interpretations and evaluations as if these were actually what they saw, heard, and experienced.

The purpose of making descriptive statements when you are communicating interculturally is that they allow you to identify the sensory information that forms the basis of your interpretations and evaluations. Descriptive statements also allow you to consider alternative hypotheses or interpretations. Interpretations, although highly personal, are very much affected by underlying cultural patterns. Sometimes when you engage in intercultural communication with specific persons or groups of people for an extended period of time, you will be able to test the various interpretations of behavior that you are considering. By testing the alternative interpretations, it is also possible to forestall the evaluations that can negatively affect your interactions. Consider the following situation, and notice how differences among description, interpretation, and evaluation affect John's intercultural competence:

> John Richardson has been sent by his U.S.-based insurance company to discuss, and possibly to sell, his company's products with an Argentinean company that has expressed great interest in them. His secretary has set up four appointments with key company officials. John arrives promptly at his first appointment, identifies himself to the receptionist, and is asked to be seated. Some thirty minutes later he is ushered into the office of the company official, who has one of his employees in the office with whom he is discussing another issue. John is brought into the office of his second appointment within a shorter period of time, but the conversation is constantly disrupted by telephone calls and drop-in visits from others. At the end of the day, John is very discouraged; he calls the home office and says, "This is a waste of time; these guys aren't interested in our products at all! I was left cooling my heels in their waiting rooms. They couldn't even give me their attention when I got in to see them. There were constant interruptions. I really tried to control myself, but I've had it. I'm getting on a plane and coming back tomorrow."

John would be better off if he approached this culturally puzzling behavior by separating his descriptions, interpretations, and evaluations. By doing so, he might choose very different actions for himself. Descriptive statements might include the following:

- My appointments started anywhere from fifteen to thirty minutes later than the time I scheduled them.
- The people with whom I had appointments also talked to other company employees when I was in their offices.
- The people with whom I had appointments accepted telephone calls when I was in their offices.

Interpretations of this sensory information might include the following:

- Company officials were not interested in talking with me or in buying my company's products.
- Company officials had rescheduled my appointments for a different time, but they neglected to tell my secretary about the change.
- In Argentina, attitudes toward time are very different from those in the United States; although appointments are scheduled for particular times, no one expects that people will be available at precisely that time.
- In Argentina it is an accepted norm of interaction between people who have appointments with each other to allow others to come into the room, either in person or by telephone, to ask their questions or to make their comments.

Contrast the difference between your own culture and the culture of those in the picture. Use the skill of Description, Interpretation, and Evaluation to understand this family eating their mid-day meal in Mauritania. How difficult would it be for you to communicate competently in this setting?

These interpretations suggest very different evaluations of John's experiences. His frustration with the lack of punctuality and the lack of exclusive focus on him and his ideas may still be a problem even if he selects the correct cultural interpretation, which is that in Argentina time is structured and valued very differently than it is in the United States. But by considering other interpretations, John's evaluations and his actions will be more functional, as he might say the following:

▶ I don't like waiting around and not meeting according to the schedule I had set, but maybe I can still make this important sale.

▶ Some of the people here are sure interesting and I am enjoying meeting so many more people than just the four with whom I had scheduled appointments.

The tool of description, interpretation, and evaluation increases your choices for understanding, responding positively to, and behaving appropriately with people from different cultures. The simplicity of the tool makes it available in any set of circumstances and may allow the intercultural communicator to suspend judgment long enough to understand the symbols used by the culture involved.

Summary

The United States is an intercultural community, and four metaphors—melting pots, tributaries, tapestries, and garden salads—were next introduced to describe its diversity. We suggested that the term *U.S. American* should be used to characterize someone from the United States, but noted that a variety of terms are used to refer to the nation's cultural groups. The goal is to find ways to refer to cultural groups that reflect their differences accurately while avoiding negative connotations and evaluations.

This chapter next focused on intercultural communication competence. We began by explaining *intra*cultural communication competence, which was followed by an examination of *inter*cultural competence. Three components of intercultural competence were discussed, including the interpersonal and situational contexts within which the communication occurs; the degree of appropriateness and effectiveness in the interaction; and the importance of knowledge, motivations, and actions.

Two tools were provided to improve intercultural competence. The first is the culture-general Behavioral Assessment Scale for Intercultural Competence (BASIC), which includes the ability to display respect, a recognition that knowledge is personal rather than universal, an empathic sense about the experiences of others that results in behaviors appropriate to those experiences, the ability to manage interactions with others, skills in enacting appropriate task and relational role behaviors, the capacity to tolerate uncertainty without anxiety, and a nonevaluative posture toward the beliefs and actions of others. Within each culture there will be culturally specific ways of behaving that are used to demonstrate these competencies. The second tool is the ability to distinguish among the techniques of description, interpretation, and evaluation. This tool encourages communicators to describe the sensory information they receive and then to construct alternative evaluations about their perceptions by making correspondingly different interpretations.

For Discussion

1. What do you think about using the terms *United Statians, United Staters, North Americans,* or *U.S. Americans* to refer to people in the United States? What alternative phrases might accurately and sensitively be used to refer to people from the United States?
2. What do we lose, and what do we gain, by using general terms such as *Asian American* and *Native American* when referring to cultural groups in the United States?
3. What does it mean to say that communication competence is a social judgment that people make about others?
4. Why is it impossible to "put yourself in someone else's shoes"?
5. What three BASIC skills would you argue are most important for developing intercultural communication competence?
6. How would you describe your own interaction posture?

For Further Reading

Nina Boyd Krebs, *Edgewalkers: Defusing Cultural Boundaries on the New Frontier* (Liberty Corner, NJ: New Horizon Press, 1999). Replete with examples of individuals living with a multicultural identity in the United States and the issues they face as they navigate familial, friendship, and professional obligations.

Ge Gao and Stella Ting-Toomey, *Communicating Effectively with the Chinese* (Thousand Oaks, CA: Sage, 1998). An example of a culture-specific approach in the development of intercultural competence. For those interested in specific ways in which communication between a Chinese person and a non-Chinese person will be influenced by their differing cultural backgrounds.

Myron W. Lustig and Jolene Koester (eds.), *AmongUS: Essays on Identity, Belonging, and Intercultural Competence* (New York: Longman, 2000). This collection of essays is written in the first person and documents the emotions and experiences of people living in a multicultural world.

Sherwyn P. Morreale, Brian H. Spitzberg, and J. Kevin Barge, *Human Communication: Motivation, Knowledge, & Skills* (Belmont, CA: Wadsworth, 2001). A basic communication textbook that also provides an intellectual foundation for understanding interpersonal communication competence.

Richard L. Wiseman, "Intercultural Communication Competence," *Handbook of International and Intercultural Communication,* 2nd ed., ed. William B. Gudykunst and Bella Mody (Thousand Oaks, CA: Sage, 2002) 207–224. An up-to-date summary of theoretical and methodological approaches to the identification of intercultural communication competence.

Richard L. Wiseman and Jolene Koester (eds.), *Intercultural Communication Competence* (Newbury Park, CA: Sage, 1993). A comprehensive state-of-the-art summary of research, theory, and methods used in understanding various approaches to intercultural competence.

For additional information about intercultural films and about Web sites on specific cultures, turn to the Resources section at the back of this book.

part two

Cultural Differences in Communication

chapter 4   Cultural Patterns and Communication: Foundations

chapter 5   Cultural Patterns and Communication: Taxonomies

chapter 6   Cultural Identity, Cultural Biases, and Intercultural Communication

Cultural Patterns and Communication: Foundations

Defining Cultural Patterns
Components of Cultural Patterns
Beliefs
Values
Norms

Characteristics of Cultural Patterns
The Functions of Cultural Patterns
An Overview of Cultural Patterns
Cultural Patterns and Intercultural Competence
Summary

If you have had even limited contact with people from other cultures, you know that they differ in both obvious and subtle ways. An obvious cultural difference is in the food people eat, such as the ubiquitous hamburger, the U.S. offering to the world's palate. We identify pasta with Italy, stuffed grape leaves with Greece and Turkey, sushi with Japan, curry with India and Southeast Asia, and kimchee with Korea.

Another obvious difference between cultures is the clothing people wear. Walk down the streets near United Nations Plaza in New York City or in diplomatic areas of Washington, D.C., and you will see men wearing colorful African dashikis, women in graceful and flowing Indian saris, and men from Middle Eastern cultures with long robes and headdresses.

Other cultural differences are more subtle and become apparent only after more extensive exposure. This chapter and the next are about those subtle, less visible differences that are taken for granted within a culture. In defining culture we called the effects of these subtle differences *shared perceptions*. Shared perceptions lead to actions that are regarded as appropriate and effective behaviors within a culture. They are therefore very important, and they result from the culture's collective assumptions about what the world is, shared judgments about what it should be, and widely held expectations about how people should behave. We are going to call these unseen but shared expectations *cultural patterns*. Cultural patterns cannot be seen, heard, tasted, or experienced because they exist only in the minds of people. Cultural patterns are made up of people's beliefs, values, and norms, and they provide a way of thinking about the world and orienting oneself to it. In other words, cultural patterns may be seen as mental programming that predisposes people to comprehend the world in a particular way.

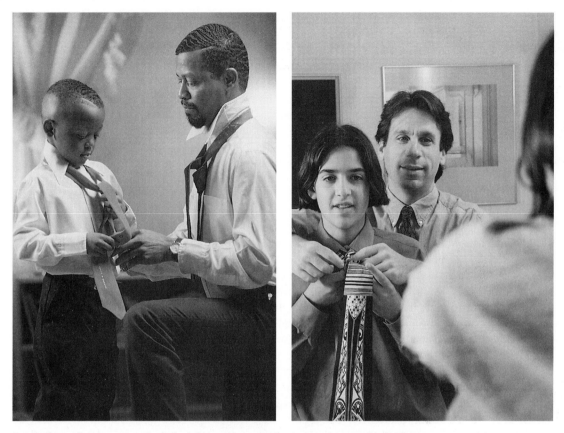

People from all cultures teach their children the norms for proper dress and behavior.

It is extremely important that you understand differences in cultural patterns if you wish to develop competence in intercultural communication. Cultural patterns are the basis for interpreting the symbols used in communication. If the cultural patterns between people are sufficiently different, the symbols used in communicating will be interpreted differently and may be misunderstood—unless people are aware that no common set of behaviors is universally interpreted in the same way nor regarded with the same degree of favorability.

Defining Cultural Patterns

Shared beliefs, values, and norms that are stable over time and that lead to roughly similar behaviors across similar situations are known as cultural patterns. These cultural patterns affect perceptions of competence. Despite their importance in the development and maintenance of cultures, they can be seen, heard, and experienced only indirectly. However, the consequences of cultural patterns—shared interpretations that are evident in what people say and do—are readily observable. Cultural patterns are inside people, in their minds. They provide a way of thinking about the world, of orienting oneself to it. Therefore, cultural patterns are shared mental programs that govern specific behavior choices.

Cultural patterns provide the basic set of standards that guide thought and action. Some aspects of this mental programming are, of course, unique to each individual. Even within a culture, no two people are programmed identically, and these distinctive personality differences separate the members of a culture. In comparisons across cultures, some mental programs are essentially universal. A mother's concern for her newborn infant, for example, reflects a biological program that exists across all known cultures and is part of our common human experience.

In addition to those portions of our mental programs that are unique or universally held, there are those that are widely shared only by members of a particular group or culture. These collective programs can be understood only in the context of a particular culture, and they include such areas as the preferred degree of social equality, the importance of group harmony, the degree to which emotional displays are permitted, the value ascribed to assertiveness, and the like.

Cultural patterns are not so much consciously taught as unconsciously experienced as a by-product of day-to-day activities. Most core assumptions are programmed at a very early age and are reinforced continuously. Saudi Arabians, for example, are taught to admire courage, patience, honor, and group harmony. European Americans are trained to admire achievement, practicality, material comfort, freedom, and individuality.

Because of their importance in shaping judgments about intercultural competence, we will discuss cultural patterns in great detail through several approaches. We emphasize both what is similar about all cultural patterns and what is different among them.

CULTURE *connections*

What becomes clear to us early in our conversation, however, is the central importance of family in Fiji. The very interconnectedness that makes it so hard to trace the branches of Violette's family tree is at the heart of the Fijian family's character. "It's a Polynesian culture, so we have more of an extended family than the United States does, and we're not as mobile. It's smaller. Fiji is not very big, only a little bigger than Hawaii, so extended family is very important. I am my nieces' and nephews' other mother, and the language reflects that. Either you are 'big mother' or 'small mother.' Because I am older than my sister, I am 'big mother.' When the families are together, I don't hesitate to discipline my nephew and my niece. And vice versa." . . .

Fijians share property in much the same way they share family members; the Fijian system of land ownership is communal. "In Fiji, you do not own a piece of land or have a title to it." The combination of extended family and communal property, we learn, ensures a community-based identity, more "we" than "I," a system that emphasizes sharing and cooperation over competition, respect and love for family and friends far above individuality, independence, or personal achievement.

—*Jessie Carroll Grearson and Lauren H. Smith*

We begin by describing the basic components of all cultural patterns: beliefs, values, and norms. We then turn to characteristics of cultural patterns. Chapter 5 presents three systematic approaches, or taxonomies, to describe the ways in which cultures differ.

Components of Cultural Patterns

In Chapter 2 we offered a definition of culture as a learned set of shared perceptions about beliefs, values, and norms. At that point, however, we left these three key terms undefined. We now explain in some detail the nature of beliefs, values, and norms, the components of cultural patterns.

Beliefs

A belief is an idea that people assume to be true about the world. Beliefs, therefore, are a set of learned interpretations that form the basis for cultural members to decide what is and what is not logical and correct.

Beliefs can range from ideas that are central to a person's sense of self to those that are more peripheral. Central beliefs include the culture's fundamental teachings about what reality is and expectations about how the world works. Less central, but also important, are beliefs based on or derived from the teachings of those regarded as authorities. Parents, teachers, and other important elders transmit the culture's assumptions about the nature of the physical and interpersonal world. Peripheral beliefs refer to matters of personal taste. They contribute to each person's unique configuration of ideas and expectations within the larger cultural matrix.[1]

Identify the most obvious characteristics of your culture. Then try to identify the more subtle characteristics of your culture. How likely are people from other cultures to understand these "obvious" and "subtle" cultural characteristics?

Discussing culturally shared beliefs is difficult because people are usually not conscious of them. Culturally shared beliefs are so fundamental to assumptions about what the world is like and how the world operates that they are typically unnoticed. We hope you will come to realize through this discussion of cultural beliefs that much of what you consider to be reality may, in fact, not be reality to people from other cultures. What you consider to be the important "givens" about the world, such as the nature of people and their relationships with one another, are based on your culturally shared beliefs, which have been transmitted to and learned by you and are not a description of some invariant, unchanging characteristic of the world.

A well-known example of a widely shared belief dates back to the time when Europeans believed that the earth was flat. That is, people "knew" that the earth was flat. Most people now "know" (believe) that the earth is basically round and would scoff at any suggestion that it is flat.

Another example of a belief for many European Americans is that in "reality" there is a separation between the physical and spiritual worlds. If a teacher one day started kicking the doorsill at the front of the room, the students might begin to worry about the teacher's mental health. The students would probably not be concerned about the doorsill itself, nor would they be alarmed about the spirits who might reside there. Of course, you and they "know" that there are no spirits in doorsills. But people from

Thailand and elsewhere "know" that spirits do indeed reside in inanimate objects such as doorsills, which is why doorsills should always be stepped over rather than on. In addition to their concern about the teacher, therefore, people from other cultures might conceivably worry about upsetting the spirits who dwell in the doorsill.

Members of the European American culture see humans as separate from nature. Based on this set of beliefs about the world, European Americans have set out to control nature. From the viewpoint of the typical European American, a person who believes, as the typical Indian woman does, that she "catches colds and fevers from evil spirits that lurk in trees"[2] would be seen as strange. European Americans "know" that people do not become ill from spirits that live in trees. Yet in the Indian culture, people "know" that human illness is caused by such spirits.

Values

Cultures differ not only in their beliefs but also in what they value. *Values* involve what a culture regards as good or bad, right or wrong, fair or unfair, just or unjust, beautiful or ugly, clean or dirty, valuable or worthless, appropriate or inappropriate, and kind or cruel.[3] Because values are the *desired* characteristics or goals of a culture, a culture's values do not necessarily describe its *actual* behaviors and characteristics. However, values are often offered as the explanation for the way in which people communicate.

Shalom Schwartz describes the range of values that cultures can have.[4] Based on extensive research in over forty-nine countries, he has concluded that there are ten universal value types that could serve as guiding principles or central goals within a culture. These value types are provided in Table 4.1. Schwartz also suggests that the ten value

Thai Muslim men attend a prayer for peace the week before the start of Ramadan. Prayer is an activity that reflects aspects of a person's culture.

TABLE 4.1 Schwartz's Value Types

Value Type	Characteristics	Representative Values
Power	Social status and prestige, control or dominance over people and resources	Social power, wealth, authority
Achievement	Personal success through demonstrating competence according to social standards	Successful, capable, ambitious, influential
Hedonism	Pleasure or sensuous gratification for oneself	Pleasure, enjoying life
Stimulation	Excitement, novelty, and challenge in life	Daring, a varied life, an exciting life
Self-direction	Independence in thought and action—choosing, creating, and exploring	Creativity, freedom, curious, independent, choosing own goals
Universalism	Understanding, appreciation, tolerance, and protection for the welfare of all people and for nature	Social justice, world at peace, broadminded, equality, wisdom, unity with nature, a world of beauty, protecting the environment
Security	Safety, harmony, and stability of society, of relationships, and of the self	Family security, national security, social order, reciprocation of favors, clean
Benevolence	Preservation and enhancement of the welfare of people with whom one is in frequent personal contact	Helpful, forgiving, honest, loyal, true friendship
Tradition	Respect, commitment, and acceptance of the customs and ideas that one's culture and religion impose on the self	Accepting my portion in life, devout, respect for tradition, humble, moderate
Conformity	Restraint of actions, inclinations, and impulses likely to upset or harm others and violate social expectations or norms	Obedient, self-discipline, politeness, honoring parents and elders

Source: Shalom H. Schwartz, Markku Verkasalo, Avishai Antonovsky, and Lilach Sagiv, "Value Priorities and Social Desirability: Much Substance, Some Style," *British Journal of Social Psychology 36*(1997): 7.

types can be arrayed into two basic dimensions that organize and provide a consistent structure for the relationships among the value types. These two dimensions are represented in Figure 4.1. Complementary value types are located in close proximity to one another, while opposing value types are found across from one another. Thus, for instance, cultures that value Tradition and Conformity are also likely to value Security and Benevolence but not Self-Direction and Stimulation.

From culture to culture, values differ in their valence and intensity. *Valence* refers to whether the value is seen as positive or negative. *Intensity* indicates the strength or importance of the value, or the degree to which the culture identifies the value as significant. For example, in some U.S. American cultures, the value of respect for elders is negatively valenced and held with a modest degree of intensity. Many U.S. Americans value youth rather than old age. In Korea, Japan, and Mexico, however, respect for elders is a positively valenced value, and it is very intensely held. It would be possible after studying any particular culture to determine its most important values and each value's valence and intensity.

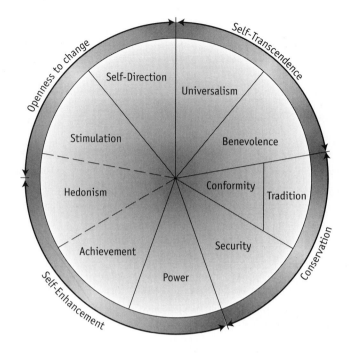

FIGURE 4.1

Relationships among Schwartz's value types.

Source: Shalom H. Schwartz, Markku Verkasalo, Avishai Antonovskys, and Lilach Sagiv, "Value Priorities and Social Desirability: Much Substance, Some Style," *British Journal of Social Pscyhology, 36* (1997) 8.

CULTURE *connections*

Senegal lay before me, the beginning of the road into the heart of Africa. My mind looked only forward. . . .

The earth was not quite sand, separated from the desert by this river, but the dryness continued. The ground was not quite dirt, either, but fragile and brittle dust.

But the rains will one day come. When they do, the land will flower green and fertile. The earth will become mud and hold in place for a time. The world once again will seem abundant, but only for a time so short and so delicate that when the land dries again under the sun, the memories of bounty will be faint and the fertile time will seem as distant as a dream. . . .

I asked when the rainy season usually begins. The answers were vague, uncertain, as if to say: *We don't really remember. And what does it matter anyway?* "The rains will come when it's time for them to come," I was told. And the people will wait for them. If the rains don't come this year, they will come next year, or they will come the year after, or maybe the year after that. And the people will be here waiting.

—*Eddy L. Harris*

Norms

The outward manifestations of beliefs and values are *norms,* which are socially shared expectations of appropriate behaviors. When a person's behaviors violate the culture's norms, social sanctions are usually imposed. Norms, like values, can vary within a culture in terms of their importance and intensity. Unlike values, however, norms can change over a period of time, whereas beliefs and values are much more enduring.

Norms exist for a wide variety of behaviors and include typical social routines. For example, the greeting behaviors of people within a culture are governed by norms. Similarly, good manners in a variety of situations are based on norms. Social routines exist to guide people's interactions at public functions and indicate how to engage in conversation, what to talk about, and how to disengage from the conversation. All these actions are based on norms for expected communication behaviors.

Norms are the surface characteristics that emerge from a culture's beliefs and values. Because norms are evident through behaviors, they can be readily observed. People are expected to behave according to their culture's norms, and they therefore come to see their own norms as the "right" way of communicating. Norms, then, are linked to beliefs and values to form the patterns of a culture.

Characteristics of Cultural Patterns

In this section we describe a set of similarities underlying all cultural patterns. In so doing, we draw heavily on the work of Kluckhohn and Strodtbeck and their theory of value orientations. Next we elaborate on those ideas to provide a general overview of cultural patterns.

The Functions of Cultural Patterns

Florence Kluckhohn and Fred Strodtbeck wanted to make sense of the work of cultural anthropologists who for many years had described systematic variations both between and within cultures. That is, cultures clearly differed from one another, but within every culture there were individuals who varied from the cultural patterns most often

CULTURE *connections*

Spirit is an invisible force made visible in all life. In many African religions there is the belief that all things are inhabited by spirits which must be appeased and to which one can appeal. So, for example, when a master drummer prepares to carve a new drum, he approaches the selected tree and speaks to the spirit residing there. In his prayer he describes himself, his experience, and his expertise; then he explains his intent. He assures the spirit that he will remain grateful for the gift of the tree and that he will use the drum only for honorable purposes.

—*Maya Angelou*

associated with it.[5] To explain both these cultural-level and individual-level differences, Kluckhohn and Strodtbeck offered four conclusions about the functions of cultural patterns that apply to all cultures:

1. People in all cultures face common human problems for which they must find solutions.
2. The range of alternative solutions to a culture's problems is limited.
3. Within a given culture, there will be preferred solutions, which most people within the culture will select, but there will also be people who will choose other solutions.
4. Over time, the preferred solutions shape the culture's basic assumptions about beliefs, values, and norms—the cultural patterns.

The first conclusion, that all cultures face similar problems, is not just about everyday concerns such as "Do I have enough money to get through the month?" or "Will my parent overcome a serious illness?" Rather, the problems involve relationships with others and with the world. Kluckhohn and Strodtbeck describe five problems or orientations that each culture must address:

1. What is the human orientation to activity?
2. What is the relationship of humans to each other?
3. What is the nature of human beings?
4. What is the relationship of humans to the natural world?
5. What is the orientation of humans to time?

Each culture, in its own unique way, must provide answers to these questions in order to develop a coherent and consistent interpretation of the world. We will return to these questions, in modified form, in our discussion of cultural patterns.

Kluckhohn and Strodtbeck's second conclusion is that a culture's possible responses to these universal human problems are limited, as cultures must select their solutions from a range of available alternatives. Thus, a culture's orientation to the importance and value of activity can range from passive acceptance of the world (a "being" orientation), a preference for a gradual transformation of the human condition (a "being-in-becoming" orientation), or more direct intervention (a "doing" orientation). A culture's solution to how it should organize itself to deal with interpersonal relationships can vary along a continuum from hierarchical social organization ("linearity") to group identification ("collaterality" or collectivism) to individual autonomy ("individualism"). The available alternatives to the problem "What is the nature of human beings?" can range from "Humans are evil" to "Humans are a mixture of good and evil" to "Humans are good." A culture's response to the preferred relationship of humans to the natural world can range from a belief that "People are subjugated by nature" to "People live in harmony with nature" to "People master nature." Finally, the culture's preferred time orientation can emphasize events and experiences from the past, the present, or the future. Table 4.2 summarizes the Kluckhohn and Strodtbeck value orientation theory.

Kluckhohn and Strodtbeck's third conclusion is their answer to an apparent contradiction that scholars found when studying cultures. They argued that within any culture, a preferred set of solutions will be chosen by most people. However, not all people from a culture will make exactly the same set of choices, and, in fact, some people from

TABLE 4.2   Kluckhohn and Strodtbeck's Value Orientations

Orientation	Postulated Range of Variations		
Activity	Being	Being-in-becoming	Doing
Relationships	Linearity	Collaterality	Individualism
Human nature	Evil	Mixture of good and evil	Good
People–nature	Subjugation to nature	Harmony with nature	Mastery over nature
Time	Past	Present	Future

Source: Adapted from Florence R. Kluckhohn and Fred Strodtbeck, *Variations in Value Orientations* (Evanston, IL: Row, Peterson, 1960).

each culture will select other alternatives. For example, most people who are part of European American culture have a "doing" orientation, a veneration for the future, a belief in control over nature, a preference for individualism, and a belief that people are basically good and changeable. But clearly not everyone identified with the European American culture shares all of these beliefs.

Kluckhohn and Strodtbeck's fourth conclusion explains how cultural patterns develop and are sustained. A problem that is regularly solved in a similar way creates an underlying premise or expectation about the preferred or appropriate way to accomplish a specific goal. Such preferences, chosen unconsciously, implicitly define the shared meanings of the culture. Over time, certain behaviors to solve particular problems become preferred, others permitted, and still others prohibited.

Kluckhohn and Strodtbeck's ideas have been very influential among intercultural communication scholars, and they form the foundation for our understanding of cultural patterns. In the following section, we extend their work to explain, in a general way, the variations in beliefs, values, and norms that are typically associated with cultural patterns. Chapter 5 extends this overview to focus on specific conceptual taxonomies that can be used to understand cultural differences.

An Overview of Cultural Patterns

Members of a culture generally have a preferred set of responses to the world. Imagine that for each experience, there is a range of possible responses from which a culture selects its preferred response. In this section we draw upon the ideas of Edward Stewart, Milton Bennett, John Condon, and Fathi Yousef, which extend the thoughts of Kluckhohn and Strodtbeck, in order to describe these alternative responses.[6] In so doing, we will compare and contrast the cultural patterns of different cultural groups and suggest their implications for the process of interpersonal communication. Comparing the patterns of different cultures can sometimes be tricky because a feature of one culture, when compared to another culture, may appear very different than it would when compared to a third culture. Kluckhohn and Strodtbeck's cultural orientations are

TRY THIS

A friend of yours has been critical of you to a mutual friend. How do you respond to the first friend the next time you see her or him?

especially useful because they describe a broad range of cultural patterns against which a particular culture can be understood.

The five major elements in Kluckhohn and Strodtbeck's description of cultural patterns address the manner in which a culture orients itself to activities, social relations, the self, the world, and the passage of time. Note that there are strong linkages among the various elements. As you read the descriptions in the sections that follow, try to recognize the preferred patterns of your culture. Also, focus on your own beliefs, values, and norms, as they may differ in certain respects from your culture's predominant pattern.

Activity Orientation   An activity orientation defines how the people of a culture view human actions and the expression of self through activities. This orientation provides answers to questions such as the following:

▶ Is it important to be engaged in activities in order to be a "good" member of one's culture?
▶ Can and should people change the circumstances of their lives?
▶ Is work very different from play?
▶ Which is more important, work or play?
▶ Is life a series of problems to be solved or simply a collection of events to be experienced?

To define their activity orientation, cultures usually choose a point on the being–becoming–doing continuum. "Being" is an activity orientation that values inaction and an acceptance of the status quo. African American and Greek cultures are usually regarded as "being" cultures. Another characterization of this orientation is a belief that all events are determined by fate and are therefore inevitable. Hindus from India often espouse this view.

A "becoming" orientation sees humans as evolving and changing; people with this orientation, including Native Americans and most South Americans, are predisposed to think of ways to change themselves as a means of changing the world.

"Doing" is the dominant characteristic of European Americans, who rarely question the assumption that it is important to get things done. Thus, European Americans ask, "What do you do?" When they first meet someone, a common greeting is "Hi! How are you doing?" and Monday morning conversations between coworkers often center on what each person "did" over the weekend. Similarly, young children are asked what they want to be when they grow up (though what is actually meant is "What do you want to do when you grow up?"), and cultural heroes are those who do things. The "doing" culture is often the striving culture, in which people seek to change and control what is happening to them. The common adage "Where there's a will there's a way" captures the essence of this cultural pattern. When faced with adversity, for example, European Americans encourage one another to fight on, to work hard, and not to give up.

How a person measures success is also related to the activity orientation. In cultures with a "doing" orientation, activity is evaluated by scrutinizing a tangible product or by evaluating some observable action directed at others. In other words, activity should have a purpose or a goal. In the "being" and "becoming" cultures, activity is not

Cultures with a "being" orientation value contemplative behaviors. In Thailand, all men are encouraged to serve as Buddhist monks, at least a short period of time. This Thai woman greets one of them.

necessarily connected to external products or actions; the contemplative monk or the great thinker is most valued. Thus the process of striving toward the goal is sometimes far more important than accomplishing it.

In "doing" cultures, work is seen as a separate activity from play and an end in itself. In the "being" and "becoming" cultures, work is a means to an end, and there is no clear-cut separation between work and play. For these individuals, social life spills over into their work life. When members of a "being" culture work in the environment of a "doing" culture, their behavior is often misinterpreted. A Latina employee described her conversation with a European American coworker who expressed anger that she spent so much "work" time on the telephone with family and friends. For the Latina, it was important to keep in contact with her friends and family; for the European American, only work was done at work, and one's social and personal relationships were totally separated from the working environment. In a "doing" culture, employees who spend too much time chatting with their fellow employees may be reprimanded by a supervisor. In the "being" and "becoming" cultures, those in charge fully expect their employees to mix working and socializing. Along with the activity orientation of "doing" comes a problem–solution orientation. The preferred way of dealing with a difficulty is to see it as a challenge to be met or a problem to be solved. The world is viewed as something that ought to be changed in order to solve problems rather than as something that ought to be accepted as it is, with whatever characteristics it has.

In every culture, these preferences for particular orientations to activities shape the interpersonal communication patterns that will occur. In "doing" cultures, interpersonal communication is characterized by concerns about what people do and how they solve problems. There are expectations that people should be involved in activities, that work comes before play, and that people should sacrifice in other parts of their lives in order to meet their work responsibilities. In "being" cultures, interpersonal communication is characterized by being together rather than by accomplishing specific tasks, and there is generally greater balance between work and play. Figure 4.2 summarizes the alternative cultural orientations to activities.

Social Relations Orientation   The social relations orientation describes how the people in a culture organize themselves and relate to one another. This orientation provides answers to questions such as the following:

▶ To what extent are some people in the culture considered better or superior to others?

▶ Can social superiority be obtained through birth, age, good deeds, or material achievement and success?

▶ Are formal, ritualized interaction sequences expected?

▶ In what ways does the culture's language require people to make social distinctions?

▶ What responsibilities and obligations do people have to their extended families, their neighbors, their employers or employees, and others?

A social relations orientation can range from one that emphasizes differences and social hierarchy to one that strives for equality and the absence of hierarchy. Many Eu-

---

1. How do people define activity?

   doing————————————— becoming ————————————— being

   striving ——————————————————————— fatalistic

   compulsive ————————————————————— easygoing

2. How do people evaluate activity?

   techniques ————————————————————— goals

   procedures ————————————————————— ideals

3. How do people regard and handle work?

   an end in itself————————————————— a means to other ends

   separate from play————————————————— integrated with play

   a challenge ————————————————————— a burden

   problem solving ————————————————— coping with situations

FIGURE 4.2

Activity orientations.

ropean Americans, for example, emphasize equality and evenness in their interpersonal relationships, even though certain groups have been treated in discriminatory and unequal ways. Equality as a value and belief is frequently expressed and is called on to justify people's actions. The phrase "We are all human, aren't we?" captures the essence of this cultural tenet. From within this cultural framework, distinctions based on age, gender, role, or occupation are discouraged. Conversely, other cultures, such as the Korean, emphasize status differences between individuals. Mexican American culture, drawing on its cultural roots in traditional Mexican values, also celebrates status differences and formalizes different ways of communicating with people depending on who they are and what their social characteristics happen to be.

One noticeable difference in social relations orientations is in the degree of importance a culture places on formality. In cultures that emphasize formality, people address others by appropriate titles, and highly prescriptive rules govern the interaction. Conversely, in cultures that stress equality, people believe that human relationships develop best when those involved can be informal with one another. Students from other cultures who study in the United States are usually taken aback by the seeming informality that exists between teachers and students. Many professors allow, even ask, students to call them by their first names, and students disagree with and challenge their teachers in front of the class. The quickness with which interpersonal relationships in the United States move to a first-name basis is mystifying to those from cultures where the personal form of address is used only for selected, special individuals. Many U.S. Americans who share aspects of both European American culture and another culture also express difficulty with this aspect of cultural behavior.

In cultures such as those of Japan, Korea, and China, individuals identify with only a few distinct groups, and the ties that bind people to these groups are so strong that group membership may endure for a lifetime. Examples of these relationships include nuclear and extended families, friends, neighbors, work groups, and social organizations. In contrast, European Americans typically belong to many groups throughout their lifetimes, and although the groups may be very important for a period of time, they are easily discarded when they are no longer needed. That is, voluntary and informal groups are meant to be important for brief periods of time, often serving a transitory purpose. In addition, it is accepted and even expected that European Americans often change jobs and companies. "Best friends" may only be best friends for brief periods.

Another important way in which social relations orientations can vary is how people define their social roles or their place in a culture. In some cultures, the family and the position into which a person is born determine a person's place. At the other extreme are cultures in which all people, regardless of family position, can achieve success and high status. Among African Americans and European Americans, for instance, there is a widespread belief that social and economic class should not predetermine a person's opportunities and choices. From the story of poor Abraham Lincoln, who went from a log cabin to the White House, to the Sylvester Stallone hero in the movie Rocky, who went from journeyman boxer to heavyweight champion of the world, there is a common belief that people should not be restricted by the circumstances of their birth.

Cultural patterns can also prescribe appropriate behaviors for men and women. In some cultures, very specific behaviors are expected; other cultures allow more ambiguity in the expected roles of women and men.

A culture's social relations orientation affects the style of interpersonal communication that is most preferred. Cultures may emphasize indirectness, obliqueness, and ambiguity, which is the typical pattern for Mexican Americans, or they may emphasize directness or confrontation, which is the typical European American pattern.

The European American preference for "putting your cards on the table" and "telling it like it is" presupposes a world in which it is desirable to be explicit, direct, and specific about personal reactions and ideas, even at the expense of social discomfort on the part of the person with whom one is interacting. For European Americans, good interpersonal communication skills include stating directly one's personal needs and reactions to the behaviors of others. Thus, if European Americans hear that others have complained about them, they would probably ask, "Why didn't they tell me directly if they have a problem with something that I have done?"

Contrast this approach to that of Asian cultures such as those in Japan, Korea, Thailand, and China, where saving face and maintaining interpersonal harmony are so highly valued that it would be catastrophic to confront another person directly and verbally express anger. The same values are also usually preferred in many Asian American cultures. Yet a Filipino American man describes being very discouraged and upset when, on a visit to the Philippines, he would ask people to meet him and, although it seemed to him that they had agreed verbally, subsequently they did not appear. As he says of the experience, "They would never say no; rather they would say yes or I'll try." Unfortunately, he felt as if he had been "stood up" several times, until someone explained to him that Filipinos think it is rude to turn down an invitation directly.

The tendency to be verbally explicit in face-to-face interactions is related to a preference for direct interaction rather than interaction through intermediaries. Among European Americans there is a belief that ideally people should depend only on themselves to accomplish what needs to be done. Therefore, the notion of using intermediaries to accomplish either personal or professional business goals is not widely accepted.

Although African Americans prefer indirectness and ambiguity in conversations with fellow cultural members, they do not choose to use intermediaries in these conversations. In many cultures, however, the use of intermediaries is the preferred method of conducting business or passing on information.[7] Marriages are arranged, business deals are made, homes are purchased, and other major negotiations are all conducted through third parties. These third parties soften and interpret the messages of both sides, thereby shielding the parties from direct, and therefore risky and potentially embarrassing, transactions with each other. Similarly, among many cultures from southern Africa, such as Swaziland, there is a distinct preference for the use of intermediaries to deal with negotiations and conflict situations. Consider the experience of the director of an English program in Tunisia, a culture that depends on intermediaries. One of the Tunisian teachers had been consistently late to his morning classes. Rather than calling the teacher in and directly explaining the problem, the director asked the teacher's friend about the teacher's health and happiness. The director indicated that the teacher's late arrival for class might have been a sign that something was wrong. The friend then simply indirectly conveyed the director's concern to the late teacher, who was late no more.

A culture's social relations orientation also affects the sense of social reciprocity, that is, the underlying sense of obligation and responsibility between people. Some cul-

1. How do people relate to others?

   as equals ————————————————————————— hierarchical

   informal ————————————————————————— formal

   member of many groups ————————————— member of few groups

   weak group identification ————————— strong group identification

2. How are roles defined and allocated?

   achieved ————————————————————————— ascribed

   gender roles similar ————————————— gender roles distinct

3. How do people communicate with others?

   directly ————————————————————————— indirectly

   no intermediaries ————————————————— intermediaries

4. What is the basis of social reciprocity?

   independence ——————— interdependence ——————— dependence

   autonomy ————————————————————————— obligation

FIGURE 4.3

Social relations orientations.

tures prefer independence and a minimum number of obligations and responsibilities; alternatively, other cultures accept obligations and encourage dependence. The nature of the dependence is often related to the types of status and the degree of formality that exist between the individuals. Cultures that depend on hierarchy and formality to guide their social interactions are also likely to have both a formal means for fulfilling social obligations and clearly defined norms for expressing them. Figure 4.3 summarizes the alternative cultural orientations to social relations.

Self-Orientation   Self-orientation describes how people's identities are formed, whether the culture views the self as changeable, what motivates individual actions, and the kinds of people who are valued and respected. A culture's self-orientation provides answers to questions such as the following:

- Do people believe they have their own unique identities that separate them from others?
- Does the self reside in the individual or in the groups to which the individual belongs?
- What responsibilities does the individual have to others?
- What motivates people to behave as they do?
- Is it possible to respect a person who is judged "bad" in one part of life but is successful in another part of life?

CULTURE *connections*

It astounded me that these young men could so quickly adjust to being free (if their peculiar situation may be so described) after seven months in Pollsmoor [prison]. Observing the scene over the heads of the two toddlers who had settled in my lap (small children abounded in this shack) I felt again the power with which Africans reinforce each other. Our individualism, our *self*-consciousness, cuts us off from that sort of reinforcement. We have developed other resources, other coping mechanisms—but have we become too isolated, one from another, too proudly self-reliant? Why do we need professional help—counsellors and "support groups"—to see us through divorce, bereavement, rape, bankruptcy, car-accident trauma, life after prison? Tony and Albany were getting all the help they needed from their friends.

—*Dervla Murphy*

For most European Americans, the emphasis on the individual self is so strong and so pervasive that it is almost impossible for them to comprehend a different point of view. Thus, many European Americans believe that the self is located solely within the individual and the individual is definitely separate from others. From a very young age, children are encouraged to make their own decisions. Alternatively, cultures may define who people are only through their associations with others because an individual's self-definition may not be separate from that of the larger group. Consequently, there is a heightened sense of interdependence, and what happens to the group (family, work group, or social group) happens to the person. For example, Mary Jane Collier, Sidney Ribeau, and Michael Hecht found that Mexican Americans "place a great deal of emphasis on affiliation and relational solidarity."[8] The sense of being bonded or connected to others is very important to members of this cultural group. Vietnamese Americans have a similarly strong affiliation with their families.

The significance to intercultural communication of a culture's preferences for defining the self is evident in the statement of a Latina student describing her friendship with a second-generation Italian American woman, whose family has also maintained "traditional values."

> I think we are able to communicate so well because our cultural backgrounds are very similar. I have always been family-oriented and so has she. This not only allowed us to get along, but it allowed us to bring our families into our friendship. [For instance] a rule that the two of us had to live by up to this point has been that no matter how old we may get, as long as we are living at home we must ask our parents for permission to go out.

Related to self-orientation is the culture's view of whether people are changeable. Naturally, if a culture believes that people can change, it is likely to expect that human beings will strive to be "better," as the culture defines and describes what "better" means.

The source of motivation for human behavior is also part of a culture's self-orientation. Among African Americans and European Americans, individuals are motivated to achieve external success in the form of possessions, positions, and power. Self-orientation combines with the "doing" orientation to create a set of beliefs and values that place individuals in total control of their own fate. Individuals must set their own goals and identify the means necessary to achieve them. Consequently, failure is viewed as a lack of willpower and a disinclination to give the fullest individual effort. In this cultural framework, individuals regard it as necessary to rely on themselves rather than on others.

Another distinguishing feature of the cultural definition of self is whether the culture emphasizes duties, rights, or some combination of the two. One culture that induces its members to act because it is their duty to do so is Japan. In contrast, for European Americans, the concept of duties to others is not a powerful motivator.

An additional part of self-orientation is the set of characteristics of those individuals who are valued and cherished. Cultures vary in their allegiance to the old or to the young, for example. Many cultures venerate their elders and view them as a source of wisdom and valuable life experience. Individuals in these cultures base decisions on the preferences and desires of their elders. Many Asian and Asian American cultures illustrate this preference. The value on youth typifies the European American culture, in which innovation and new ideas, rather than the wisdom of the past, are regarded as important. European Americans venerate the upstart, the innovator, and the person who tries something new. Figure 4.4 summarizes the alternative cultural orientations to the self.

1. How should people form their identities?

   by themselves ———————————————————— with others

2. How changeable is the self?

   changeable ———————————————————— unchangeable

   self-realization stressed ——————— self-realization not stressed

3. What is the source of motivation for the self?

   reliance on self ——————————————— reliance on others

   rights ———————————————————————— duties

4. What kind of person is valued and respected?

   young ——————————————————————————— aged

   vigorous ————————————————————————— wise

   innovative —————————————————————— prominent

   material attributes ————————— spiritual attributes

FIGURE 4.4

Self-orientations.

A Mexican woman lights a candle during the annual "Day of the Dead" celebration. In many cultures, memorial services are held to honor those who have died.

World Orientation   Cultural patterns also tell people how to locate themselves in relation to the spiritual world, nature, and other living things. A world orientation provides answers to questions such as the following:

- Are human beings intrinsically good or evil?
- Are humans different from other animals and plants?
- Are people in control of, subjugated by, or living in harmony with the forces of nature?
- Do spirits of the dead inhabit and affect the human world?

In the African and African American worldview, human beings live in an interactive state with the natural and spiritual world. Daniel and Smitherman describe a fundamental tenet of the traditional African worldview as that of "a dynamic, hierarchical unity between God, man, and nature, with God serving as the head of the hierarchy."[9] In this view of the relationship between the spiritual and material world, humans are an integral part of nature. Thus, in the African and African American worldview, "One becomes a 'living witness' when he aligns himself with the forces of nature and instead of being a proselytized 'true believer' strives to live in harmony with the universe."[10] Native

American groups, as well, clearly have a view of humans as living in harmony with nature.[11] Latino culture places a great value on spirituality but views humans as being subjugated to nature, with little power to control circumstances that influence their lives.[12]

Most European Americans view humans as separate and distinct from nature and other forms of life. Because of the supremacy of the individual and the presumed uniqueness of each person, most European Americans regard nature as something to be manipulated and controlled in order to make human life better. Excellent examples of this cultural belief can be found in news reports whenever a natural disaster occurs in the United States. For instance, when a large earthquake hit the Los Angeles area in January, 1994, and many people were killed when an apartment building and freeways collapsed, political leaders from California were outraged that the state's buildings and bridges could be unsafe. The assumption in these pronouncements was that the consequences of natural forces such as earthquakes could have been prevented simply by using better technology and by reinforcing the structures to withstand the forces of nature.

This position is also associated with a belief that disease, poverty, and adversity can be overcome in order to achieve health and wealth. In this cultural framework the "natural" part of the human experience—illness, loss, even death—can be overcome, or at least postponed, by selecting the right courses of action and having the right kinds of attitudes.

The spiritual and physical worlds can be viewed as distinct or as one. Among European Americans there is generally a clear understanding that the physical world, of which humans are a part, is separate from the spiritual world. If people believe in a spiritual world, it exists apart from the everyday places where people live, work, and play. Individuals who say they are psychic or who are mind readers are viewed with suspicion and curiosity. Those who have seen ghosts are questioned in an effort to find a more "logical" and "rational" explanation. In other cultural frameworks, however, it is "logical" and "rational" for spirits to live in both animate and inanimate objects.[13] Alternatives in cultural orientations to the world are summarized in Figure 4.5.

1. What is the nature of humans in relation to the world?

   separate from nature ————————————— integral part of nature

   humans modify nature ————————————— humans adapt to nature

   health natural ————————————————— disease natural

   wealth expected ————————————————— poverty expected

2. What is the world like?

   spiritual–physical dichotomy ——————— spiritual–physical unity

   empirically understood ———————————— magically understood

   technically controlled —————————————— spiritually controlled

FIGURE 4.5

World orientations.

Time Orientation   The final aspect of cultural patterns concerns how people con-ceptualize time. This orientation provides answers to questions such as the following:

- How should time be valued and understood?
- Is time a scarce resource or is it unlimited?
- Is the desirable pace of life fast or slow?
- Is time linear or cyclical?

Some cultures choose to describe the future as most important, others emphasize the present, and still others emphasize the past. In Japanese and Chinese cultures the anniversary of the death of a loved one is celebrated, illustrating the value these cultures place on the past. In contrast, Native Americans and Latinos are present-oriented. European Americans, of course, are future-oriented.

Most European Americans view time as a scarce and valuable commodity akin to money or other economic investments. They strive to "save time," "make time," "spend time," and "gain time." Events during a day are dictated by a schedule of activities, pre-cisely defined and differentiated. Most cultures in Latin America bring an entirely different orientation to time, responding to individuals and circumstances rather than following a scheduled plan for the day. Time is viewed within this cultural frame as endless and ongoing.

A culture's time orientation also suggests the pace of life. The fast, hectic pace of European Americans, governed by clocks, appointments, and schedules, has become so commonly accepted that it is almost a cliché. The pace of life in cultures such as India, Kenya, and Argentina and among African Americans is less hectic, more relaxed, and more comfortably paced. In African American culture, for example, orientations to time are driven less by a need to "get things done" and conform to external demands than by a sense of participation in events that create their own rhythm. As Jack Daniel and Geneva Smitherman suggest about time in African American culture,

> Being on time has to do with participating in the fulfillment of an activity that is vital to the sustenance of a basic rhythm, rather than with appearing on the scene at, say, "twelve o'clock sharp." The key is not to be "on time" but "in time."[14]

CULTURE *connections*

Diane and Blong met, as it happens, on the Fourth of July 1997 at one in the morning, "just after the fireworks." Diane can be as exact about times and dates as her husband is hypothetical and vague—apparently the Hmong do not pay much attention to dates and do not keep birth records, which makes tracing events in Blong's eventful life difficult. "But she remembers everything," Blong comments indulgently about Diane's precision, as though making room for a somewhat odd American obsession.

—*Jessie Carroll Grearson and Lauren B. Smith*

1. How do people define time?

   future ——————————————— present ——————————————— past

   precisely measurable ————————————————— undifferentiated

   linear ——————————————————————— cyclical

2. How do people value time?

   scarce resource ——————————————————— unlimited

   fast pace ——————————————————— slow pace

FIGURE 4.6

Time orientations.

Alternatives in cultural orientations to time are summarized in Figure 4.6. In Chapter 7, the discussion of nonverbal communication codes also considers the influence of a culture's orientation toward time on aspects of communication.

A culture's underlying patterns consist of orientations to activity, social relations, the self, the world, and time. The interdependence among these aspects of culture is obvious from the preceding discussion. Kluckhohn and Strodtbeck provide a way to understand, rather than to judge, different cultural predispositions, and it demonstrates that there are different ways of defining the "real," "good," and "correct" ways to behave.

Cultural Patterns and Intercultural Competence

There is a strong relationship between the foundations of cultural patterns and intercultural competence. Remember that intercultural competence depends on knowledge, motivation, and actions, which occur in specific contexts with messages that are both appropriate and effective.

The patterns of a culture create the filter through which all verbal and nonverbal symbols are interpreted. Because all cultures have distinct beliefs, values, and norms, symbols do not have universal interpretations, nor will the interpretations have the same degree of favorability. Judgments of competence are strongly influenced by the underlying patterns of a person's cultural background. In every intercultural interaction, a cultural pattern that is different from one's own may be used to interpret one's messages. Every intercultural interaction, then, can be viewed as a puzzle or a mystery that needs to be solved.

How individuals define the relational context is always related to the mental programming that cultures provide. One person's definition of the relationship (e.g., friend) may not match that of the person with whom he or she interacts (e.g., fellow student), causing radically different expectations and interpretations of behaviors.

In solving the intercultural puzzle, it is critical to remember another valuable insight from Kluckhohn and Strodtbeck's foundational work. Although a culture (the

The significance of appointments, being "on time," and time efficiency varies across cultures.

collectivity of people) will make preferred choices about beliefs, values, and norms, not all cultural members will necessarily share all of those preferred choices, nor will they share them with the same degree of intensity. The immediate consequence of this conclusion for the development of intercultural competence is that every person represents the cultural group with which he or she identifies, but to a greater or lesser degree. A cultural pattern may be the preferred choice of most cultural members, but what can accurately be described for the culture in general cannot necessarily be assumed to be true for a specific individual. In simple terms, this principle translates into an important guideline for the development of intercultural competence: even though you may have culture-specific information, you can never assume that every person from that culture matches the profile of the typical cultural member.

Because cultural patterns describe what people perceive as their reality, what they view as desirable, and how they should behave, there are repercussions for the motivational component of intercultural competence. Recall that communicators' feelings in intercultural interactions affect their ability to be open to alternative interpretations. Yet if cultural patterns predispose people to a particular definition of what is real, good, and right, reactions to others as unreal, bad, or wrong may create psychological distance between interactants. When confronting a set of beliefs, values, and norms that

CULTURE *connections*

There's something deeply satisfying about being on your own reservation, something more than nationalism, more than security. It's a feeling of survival, of being a link in an improbable continuity. It's a responsibility fulfilled, an important promise kept, a preference for what seems less than what the outside world offers but in fact is more than imagined. Those fond of make-believe noble savages are devoted to the notion that there is a mystical quality at the root of the relationship between Indians and the land, but they misunderstand. Land is the opposite of magic: it's real, solid, firm. Land is legacy, it enables and supports life, it's both a source and a destination. Land is rocks, hidden roots, dirt, and buried bones, very personal and simultaneously communal. And if it's not yours by right of blood and memory, you always enter for the first time as a trespasser.

—*Michael Dorris*

are inconsistent with their own, many people will evaluate them negatively. Strong emotional reactions are often predictable; after all, these variations from other cultures challenge the basic view people have of their world. Nevertheless, other cultures' ways of believing and their preferred values are not crazy or wrong, just different.

Cultural patterns form the basis for what is considered to be communicatively appropriate and effective. Examples that illustrate how beliefs, values, and norms set the boundaries of appropriateness and effectiveness include such instances as speaking your mind, in contrast to being quiet; defending yourself against a criticism, in contrast to accepting it; confronting another person about a problem rather than indirectly letting her or him know of the concern; and emphasizing the differences in status in relationships, in contrast to emphasizing commonality. Simply knowing what is appropriate and what has worked to accomplish your personal objectives in your own culture may not, and in all likelihood will not, have similar results when you interact with culturally different others. Intercultural competence usually requires alternative choices for actions.

What cultural characteristics are embedded in the following list of proverbs?

- The person who stands alone excites our imagination.
- There should be equality for everyone, because we are all human beings.
- The purpose of our existence is not to attain happiness but to be worthy of it.
- The person who has achieved success has lived well, laughed often, and loved much.
- A well-raised child is one who does not have to be told twice to do something.
- Let us eat, drink, and be merry, for tomorrow we may die.
- A rich life requires constant activity, the use of one's muscles, and openness to adventure.
- Friendship should only go so far in working (business) relationships.
- To lay down your life for a friend—this is the summit of a good life.
- We are all born to love; it is the principle of existence and its only true end.
- The past is dead; there are new worlds to conquer; the world belongs to the future.

Consequently, we recommend that before acting, you should contemplate, draw on your culture-specific knowledge, and make behavioral choices that are appropriate for interacting with members of the other culture.

The patterns of a culture shape, but do not determine, the mental programming of its people. Because cultural patterns define how people see and define reality, they are a powerful emotional force in competent intercultural interaction.

Summary

This chapter began the discussion about cultural patterns, which are invisible differences that characterize cultures. Beliefs, values, and norms are the ingredients of cultural patterns. Beliefs are ideas that people assume to be true about the world. Values are the desired characteristics of a culture. Norms, the final component of cultural patterns, are socially shared expectations of appropriate behaviors.

Cultural patterns are shared among a group of people, and they form the foundation for maintenance of cultures. They are stable over relatively long periods of time, and they lead most members of a culture to behave in roughly similar ways when they encounter similar situations.

Florence Kluckhohn and Fred Strodtbeck suggest that each culture selects a preferred set of choices to address common human issues. While not all people in the culture make exactly the same choices, the preferred solutions define the shared meanings of the culture.

Cultural patterns focus on the way cultures orient themselves to activities, social relations, the self, the world, and time. The activity orientation defines how people express themselves through activities and locate themselves on the being–becoming–doing continuum. The social relations orientation describes the preferred forms of interpersonal relationships within a culture. The self-orientation indicates the culture's conception of how people understand who they are in relation to others. The world orientation locates a culture in the physical and spiritual worlds. The time orientation directs a culture to value the past, present, or future.

For Discussion

1. How might individuals from *doing, being,* and *becoming* cultures engage in conflict in the workplace, in school, or in interpersonal relationships?
2. One person comes from a culture that believes "We're all humans, aren't we?" Another person comes from a culture that says "Status is everything." What might occur as these two individuals try to communicate with each other?
3. *Truth* or *lie, just* or *unjust, right* or *wrong,* and *good* or *bad* are all common human judgments of the actions of others. How does your awareness of cultural patterns affect your understanding of each of these sets of terms?
4. Using the five dimensions of cultural patterns described in this chapter, describe how you think each is displayed in your own culture.

For Further Reading

Elisabeth Bumiller, *May You Be the Mother of a Hundred Sons: A Journey among the Women of India* (New York: Fawcett Columbine, 1991). A journalistic exploration of the impact of cultural beliefs, values, and norms on the perspectives and desires of women living in India.

Martin J. Gannon and Associates, *Understanding Global Cultures: Metaphorical Journeys through 23 Nations,* 2nd ed. (Thousand Oaks, CA: Sage, 2001) An excellent guide to understanding the worldviews and perspectives of many cultures throughout the world.

Edward C. Stewart and Milton J. Bennett, *American Cultural Patterns,* rev. ed. (Yarmouth, ME: Intercultural Press, 1991) Provides a detailed description of European American cultural patterns, as well as some potential contrasts to the patterns of other cultures.

Esther Wanning, *Culture Shock! USA* (Singapore: Times Books International, 1991). Written for those unfamiliar with European American culture, this book provides an interesting "outsiders" view of the dominant cultural patterns in the United States.

For additional information about intercultural films and about Web sites on specific cultures, turn to the Resources section at the back of this book.

Cultural Patterns and Communication: Taxonomies

Taxonomies of Cultural Patterns
Hall's High- and Low-Context Cultural
   Patterns
Hofstede's Cultural Patterns

Confucian Cultural Values
**Cultural Taxonomies and Intercultural
   Competence**
Summary

$\mathbf{I}$n the previous chapter, we provided an overview of the patterns that underlie all cultures. We described the nature of cultural patterns and the importance of beliefs, values, and norms in helping cultures to cope with problems. We now focus on specific conceptual taxonomies that are useful for understanding cultural differences.

We have chosen two different but related taxonomies to describe variations in cultural patterns. The first was developed by Edward Hall, who noted that cultures differ in the extent to which their primary message patterns are high context or low context. The second describes the ideas of Geert Hofstede, who identifies five dimensions along which cultures vary and provides a statistical profile of how and to what degree cultures actually differ from one another.

Taxonomies of Cultural Patterns

As you read the descriptions of cultural patterns by Hall and Hofstede, we caution you to remember three points. First, there is nothing sacred about these approaches and the internal categories they employ. Each approach takes the whole of cultural patterns (beliefs, values, and norms) and divides them in different ways.

Second, the parts of each of the systems are interrelated. We begin the description of each system at an arbitrarily chosen point, presupposing other parts of the system that have not yet been described. Cultural patterns are understandable not in isolation but as a unique whole.

Finally, individual members of a culture may vary greatly from the pattern that is typical of that culture. Therefore, as you study these approaches to cultural patterns, we encourage you to make some judgments about how your own culture fits into the pat-

CULTURE *connections*

Monterrey is wealthier than many Mexican towns. . . . Two of the characteristics of Mexico—family values and willingness to work—plus Monterrey's relative closeness to the border have made a powerful force for development. . . . The family is an example of one of the vital differences between the United States and Mexico: throughout the spectrum of commerce, work and family still mingle intimately.

Chief executives are linked by blood rather than professional background, and work is conducted on a much more personal level. "You don't get right down to business," said an American who has worked for [Mexican] charitable organizations. "First you socialize, they get to know you, they ask about your family. After dinner they put out a bottle of Chivas Regal, and you talk."

tern. Then, as you place it within the pattern, also try to discern how you, as an individual, fit into the patterns described. Similarly, as you learn about other cultural patterns, please remember that a specific person may or may not be a typical representative of that culture. As you study your own cultural patterns and those of other cultures, you improve the knowledge component of intercultural competence.

Hall's High- and Low-Context Cultural Patterns

Edward T. Hall, whose writings about the relationship between culture and communication are well known, organizes cultures by the amount of information implied by the setting or context of the communication itself, regardless of the specific words that are spoken.[1] Hall argues that every human being is faced with so many perceptual stimuli—sights, sounds, smells, tastes, and bodily sensations—that it is impossible to pay attention to them all. Therefore, one of the functions of culture is to provide a screen between the person and all of those stimuli to indicate what perceptions to notice and how to interpret them. Hall's approach is compatible with the other approaches discussed in this chapter. Where it differs is in the importance it places on the role of context.

According to Hall, cultures differ on a continuum that ranges from high to low context. High-context cultures prefer to use high-context messages in which most of the meaning is either implied by the physical setting or presumed to be part of the individual's internalized beliefs, values, and norms; very little is provided in the coded, explicit, transmitted part of the message. Examples of high-context cultures include Japanese, African American, Mexican, and Latino. Low-context cultures prefer to use low-context messages, in which the majority of the information is vested in the explicit code. Low-context cultures include German, Swedish, European American, and English.

A simple example of high-context communication is interactions that take place in a long-term relationship between two people who are often able to interpret even the slightest gesture or the briefest comment. The message does not need to be stated explicitly because it is carried in the shared understandings about the relationship.

A simple example of low-context communication is now experienced by more and more people as they interact with computers. For computers to "understand" a message, every statement must be precise. Many computers will not accept or respond to instructions that do not have every space, period, letter, and number in precisely the right location. The message must be overt and very explicit.

Hall's description of high- and low-context cultures is based on the idea that some cultures have a preponderance of messages that are high context, others have messages that are mostly low context, and yet others have a mixture of both. Hall also describes other characteristics of high- and low-context cultures, which reveal the beliefs, values, and norms of the cultural system. These characteristics include the use of covert or overt messages, the importance of ingroups and outgroups, and the culture's orientation to time.

Use of Covert and Overt Messages   In a high-context culture such as that of Japan, meanings are internalized and there is a large emphasis on nonverbal codes. Hall describes messages in high-context cultures as almost preprogrammed, in which very little of the interpretation of the message is left to chance because people already know that in the context of the current situation, the communicative behaviors will have a

CULTURE *connections*

Like the rest of my family, I have no idea how old I am; I can only guess. A baby who is born in my country has little guarantee of being alive one year later, so the concept of tracking birthdays does not retain the same importance. When I was a child, we lived without artificial time constructions of schedules, clocks, and calendars. Instead, we lived by the seasons and the sun, planning our moves around our need for rain, planning our day around the span of daylight available. We told time by using the sun. If my shadow was on the west side, it was morning; when it moved directly underneath me, it was noon. When my shadow crossed to the other side, it was afternoon. As the day grew longer, so did my shadow—my cue to start heading home before dark.

When we got up in the morning, we decided what we'd do that day, then did that task the best we could until we finished or the sky grew too dark for us to see. There was no such notion of getting up and having your day all planned out for you. In New York, people frequently whip out their datebooks and ask, "Are you free for lunch on the fourteenth—or what about the fifteenth?" I respond with "Why don't you call me the day before you want to meet up?" No matter how many times I write down appointments, I can't get used to the idea. When I first came to London, I was mystified by the connection between people staring at their wrist, then crying, "I've got to dash!" I felt like everyone was rushing everywhere, every action was timed. In Africa there was no hurry, no stress. African time is very, very slow, very calm. If you say, "I'll see you tomorrow around noon," that means about four or five o'clock.

—*Waris Dirie and Cathleen Miller*

specific and particular message. In low-context cultures, people look for the meaning of others' behaviors in the messages that are plainly and explicitly coded. The details of the message are expressed precisely and specifically in the words that people use as they try to communicate with others.

Another way to think about the difference between high- and low-context cultures is to imagine something with which you are very familiar, such as repairing a car, cooking, sewing, or playing a particular sport. When you talk about that activity with someone else who is very familiar with it, you will probably be less explicit and instead use a more succinct set of verbal and nonverbal messages. You will talk in a verbal shorthand that does not require you to be specific and precise about every aspect of the ideas that you are expressing, because the others will know what you mean without their specific presentation. However, if you talk to someone who does not know very much about the activity, you will have to explain more, be more precise and specific, and provide more background information.

In a high-context culture, much more is taken for granted and assumed to be shared, and consequently the overwhelming preponderance of messages are coded in such a way that they do not need to be explicitly and verbally transmitted. Instead, the demands of the situation and the shared meanings among the interactants mean that the preferred interpretation of the messages is already known.

The difference between high-context and low-context cultural styles is illustrated in a dialogue between a European American (low-context culture) and a Malaysian (high-context culture); the Malaysian's message is revealed only by implication. Both people in the dialogue teach at a community college in the United States, and the Malaysian's objective in this conversation is to have the European American drive him off campus for lunch because the Malaysian does not have a car.

> *Malaysian:* Can I ask you a question?
> *European American:* Yes, of course.
> *Malaysian:* Do you know what time it is?
> *European American:* Yes, it's two o'clock.
> *Malaysian:* Might you have a little soup left in the pot?
> *European American:* What? I don't understand.
> *Malaysian:* (becoming more explicit since the colleague is not getting the point): I will be on campus teaching until nine o'clock tonight, a very long day for any person, let alone a hungry one!
> *European American:* (finally getting the point): Would you like me to drive you to a restaurant off campus so you can have lunch?
> *Malaysian:* What a very good idea you have!

Reactions in high-context cultures are likely to be reserved, whereas reactions in low-context cultures are frequently very explicit and readily observable. It is easy to understand why this is so. In high-context cultures, an important purpose in communicating is to promote and sustain harmony among the interactants. Unconstrained reactions could threaten the face or social esteem of others. In low-context cultures, however, an important purpose in communicating is to convey exact meaning. Explicit messages help to achieve this goal. If messages need to be explicit, so will people's reactions. Even when the message is understood, a person cannot assume that the meanings are clear in the absence of verbal messages coded specifically to provide feedback.

Importance of Ingroups and Outgroups   In high-context cultures, it is very easy to determine who is a member of the group and who is not. Because so much of the meaning of messages is embedded in the rules and rituals of situations, it is easy to tell who is acting according to those norms. As there are fixed and specific expectations for behaviors, deviations are easy to detect.

Another distinction concerns the emphasis placed on the individual in contrast to the group as a source of self-identity. In a high-context culture, the commitment between people is very strong and deep, and responsibility to others takes precedence over responsibility to oneself. Loyalties to families and the members of one's social and work groups are long-lasting and unchanging. This degree of loyalty differs from that found in a low-context culture, in which the bonds between people are very fragile and the extent of involvement and commitment to long-term relationships is lower.

Orientation to Time   The final distinguishable characteristic of high- and low-context cultures is their orientation to time. In the former, time is viewed as more open, less structured, more responsive to the immediate needs of people, and less subject to external goals and constraints. In low-context cultures, time is highly organized, in part because of the additional energy required to understand the messages of others. Low-context cultures are almost forced to pay more attention to time in order to complete the work of living with others.

As Table 5.1 indicates, Edward Hall's placement of cultures onto a continuum that is anchored by preferences for high-context messages and low-context messages offers a way to understand other variations in cultural patterns. A high-context culture chooses to use covert and implicit messages that rely heavily on nonverbal code systems. In a high-context culture, the group is very important, as are traditions, and members of the ingroup are easily recognized. Time is less structured and more responsive to people's needs. Low-context cultures are characterized by the opposite attributes: messages are explicit and dependent on verbal codes, group memberships change rapidly, innovation is valued, and time is highly structured.

TABLE 5.1   Characteristics of Low- and High-Context Cultures

High-Context Cultures	Low-Context Cultures
Covert and implicit	Overt and explicit
Messages internalized	Messages plainly coded
Much nonverbal coding	Details verbalized
Reactions reserved	Reactions on the surface
Distinct ingroups and outgroups	Flexible ingroups and outgroups
Strong interpersonal bonds	Fragile interpersonal bonds
Commitment high	Commitment low
Time open and flexible	Time highly organized

Hofstede's Cultural Patterns

Geert Hofstede's impressive studies of cultural differences in value orientations offer another approach to understanding the range of cultural differences.[2] Hofstede's approach is based on the assertion that people carry mental programs or "software of the mind" that is developed during childhood and is reinforced by their culture. These mental programs contain the ideas of a culture and are expressed through its dominant values. To identify the principal values of different cultures, Hofstede surveyed over 100,000 IBM employees in seventy-one countries. IBM is a large multinational business organization. Subsequent to his original research, Hofstede and others have extended the investigations to additional countries not originally included in the IBM sample, and he has recently extended his theorizing to incorporate current research.

> Describe how you think each of Hofstede's five dimensions is displayed in your own culture.

Through theoretical reasoning and statistical analyses, Hofstede identified five dimensions along which dominant patterns of a culture can be ordered: power distance, uncertainty avoidance, individualism versus collectivism, masculinity versus femininity, and long-term versus short-term orientation to time. Recent evidence suggests that Hofstede's work provides an excellent summary of the relationships between cultural values and social behaviors.[3]

A Korean daughter and granddaughter groom their elder. An accepted principle of many cultures requires people to show respect and acknowledge social differences.

Power Distance   One of the basic concerns in all cultures, and a problem for which they all must find a solution, is the issue of human inequality. Contrary to the claim in the U.S. Declaration of Independence that "all men are created equal," all people in a culture do not have equal levels of status or social power. Depending on the culture, some people might be regarded as superior to others because of their wealth, age, gender, education, physical strength, birth order, personal achievements, family background, occupation, or a wide variety of other characteristics.

Cultures also differ in the extent to which they view such status inequalities as good or bad, right or wrong, just or unjust, and fair or unfair. That is, all cultures have particular value orientations about the appropriateness or importance of status differences and social hierarchies. Hofstede refers to these variations as the power distance

CULTURE *connections*

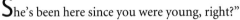

She's been here since you were young, right?"

I nodded. . . .

"So what's her name?" Lelia asked after a moment.

"I don't know."

"What?"

I told her I didn't know. That I had never known.

"What's that you call her, then?" she said. "I thought that was her name. Your father calls her that, too."

"It's not her name," I told her. "It's not her name. It's just a form of address."

It was the truth. Lelia had great trouble accepting this stunning ignorance of mine. That summer, when it seemed she was thinking about it, she would stare in wonderment at me as if I had a gaping hole blown through my head. I couldn't blame her. Americans live on a first-name basis. She didn't understand that there weren't moments in our language —the rigorous, regimental one of family and servants—when the woman's name would have naturally come out. Or why it wasn't important. At breakfast and lunch and dinner my father and I called her "Ah-juh-ma," literally *aunt,* but more akin to "ma'am," the customary address to an unrelated Korean woman. But in our context the title bore much less deference. I never heard my father speak her name in all the years she was with us.

But then he never even called my mother by her name, nor did she ever in my presence speak his. She was always and only "spouse" or "wife" or "Mother"; he was "husband" or "Father" or "Henry's father." And to this day, when someone asks what my parents' names were, I have to pause for a moment, I have to rehear them not from the memory of my own voice, my own calling to them, but through the staticky voices of their old friends phoning from the other end of the world.

"I can't believe this," Lelia cried, her long Scottish face all screwed up in the moonlight. "You've known her since you were a kid! She practically raised you."

—*Chang-rae Lee*

dimension, which reflects the degree to which the culture believes that institutional and organizational power should be distributed unequally and the decisions of the power holders should be challenged or accepted.

Hofstede has created a power distance index (PDI) to assess a culture's relative location on the power distance dimension. At one extreme are cultures of such countries as Austria, Denmark, Israel, and New Zealand. These cultures, all of which have relatively low PDIs and prefer small power distances as a cultural value, believe in the importance of minimizing social or class inequalities, questioning or challenging authority figures, reducing hierarchical organizational structures, and using power only for legitimate purposes. Conversely, cultures in the Arab countries, Guatemala, Malaysia, and the Philippines all have relatively high PDIs and prefer large power distances. They believe that each person has a rightful and protected place in the social order, that the actions of authorities should not be challenged or questioned, that hierarchy and inequality are appropriate and beneficial, and that those with social status have a right to use their power for whatever purposes and in whatever ways they deem desirable. Table 5.2 provides a numerical rating of sixty-six countries and three regions on the power distance dimension.

Predictors of Power Distance   What can account for the differences in a culture's preferred level of power distance? Surprisingly, Hofstede suggests that three factors—climate, population size, and wealth—are strongly implicated.

Climate, as measured by geographical latitude, is by far the single best predictor of a culture's power distance. Cultures of people who live in high-latitude climates far from the equator, and therefore have moderate to cold climates, tend to have low PDI scores. Cultures that exist in low-latitude climates near the equator, and therefore have tropical or subtropical climates, tend to have high PDI scores. Hofstede speculates that the relationship between climate and power distance occurs because the culture's climate requires it to invent technological solutions to the weather problems that threaten its very survival.

In colder and more extreme climates, human survival requires more protection against the hardships of nature. Consequently, survival and population growth can occur only if the culture can develop solutions that counteract the extreme forces of nature. The need for solutions to its climatic problems predisposes the culture to seek less traditional and more innovative answers to its common problems, which leads in turn to a greater need for modernization, mass literacy, independent thinking, decentralization of political power, technological innovations, and a general questioning of authority. Conversely, survival in warmer climates is far less dependent on intervention with nature. The need for technological solutions to problems is low, more traditional approaches to obstacles are preferred, formal mass education is not required for survival, and independent thinking is not as necessary. People are therefore more likely to learn from their elders, and consequently there is less questioning of authority in general.

Population size is another predictor of power distance. Generally speaking, the larger the culture, the greater the power distance is likely to be. As the size of any social group increases, it must inevitably develop additional rules and formal procedures for coping with the increased complexities that arise. In addition, large social groups will require more centralized concentrations of political power to function effectively.

TABLE 5.2   Country Ratings on the Power Distance Dimension

	Power Distance*		Power Distance*
Malaysia	204	Uruguay	7
Slovakia	204	Greece	2
Guatemala	163	South Korea	2
Panama	163	Iran	−7
Philippines	158	Taiwan	−7
Russia	154	Czech Republic	−12
Romania	140	Spain	−12
Surinam	117	Malta	−16
Mexico	99	Pakistan	−21
Venezuela	99	Japan	−25
Arab countries	94	Italy	−44
Bangladesh	94	Argentina	−48
China	94	South Africa	−48
Ecuador	85	Trinidad	−58
Indonesia	85	Hungary	−62
India	80	Jamaica	−67
West Africa	80	Estonia	−90
Yugoslavia	76	Luxembourg	−90
Singapore	66	U.S.A	−90
Bulgaria	48	Canada	−94
Morocco	48	Netherlands	−99
Vietnam	48	Australia	−108
Brazil	43	Costa Rica	−113
France	39	Germany	−113
Hong Kong	39	Great Britain	−113
Poland	39	Switzerland	−117
Colombia	34	Finland	−122
Salvador	30	Norway	−131
Turkey	30	Sweden	−131
Belgium	25	Ireland	−145
East Africa	21	New Zealand	−173
Peru	21	Denmark	−191
Thailand	21	Israel	−214
Chile	16	Austria	−223
Portugal	16		

*A large positive score means the country prefers a large power distance; a large negative score means the country prefers a small power distance. The average score is zero. Ratings are in standardized scores, with the decimal point omitted.

Source: Adapted from Geert Hofstede, *Cultures and Organizations: Software of the Mind.* (London: McGraw–Hill, 1991), 26.

Consequently, for cultures with large populations to function effectively, they must adopt a political hierarchy that is more distant, more impersonal, and less accessible than that needed by cultures with small populations. The need to concentrate political power in the hands of a few select people helps to create and reinforce a cultural norm that social hierarchy is desirable and that authorities should not be questioned or challenged.

Hofstede's third predictor of power distance is wealth. However, Hofstede suggests that it is the distribution of wealth, rather than the sheer amount of wealth, that best predicts power distance. His analyses reveal that the more unequally wealth is distributed within a culture, the greater the culture's power distance. More evenly distributed wealth is related to cultures that value education, technology, and a decentralization of political power. These attributes lead to an increased tendency to question authority and to value a small power distance. Conversely, an unequal distribution of wealth is related to a centralized political system, a decreased tendency to question the actions of authorities, and a large power distance.

Consequences of Power Distance   The consequences of the degree of power distance that a culture prefers are evident in family customs, the relationships between students and teachers, organizational practices, and in other areas of social life. Even the language systems in high-PDI cultures emphasize distinctions based on a social hierarchy.

Children raised in high-PDI cultures are expected to obey their parents without challenging or questioning them, while children raised in low-PDI cultures put less value on obedience and are taught to seek reasons or justifications for their parents' actions. Even the language of high-PDI cultures is more sensitive to hierarchical distinctions; Chinese and Korean languages, for instance, have separate terms for older brother, oldest brother, younger sister, youngest sister, and so on.

Students in high-PDI cultures are expected to comply with the wishes and requests of their teachers, and conformity is regarded very favorably. As a consequence, the curriculum in high-PDI cultures is likely to involve a great deal of rote learning, and students are discouraged from asking questions because questions might pose a threat to the teacher's authority. In low-PDI cultures, students regard their independence as very important, and they are less likely to conform to the expectations of teachers or other authorities. The educational system itself reinforces the low-PDI values by teaching students to ask questions, to solve problems creatively and uniquely, and to challenge the evidence leading to conclusions.

In the business world, managers in high-PDI cultures are likely to prefer an autocratic or centralized decision-making style, whereas subordinates in these cultures expect and want to be closely supervised. Alternatively, managers in low-PDI cultures prefer a consultative or participative decision-making style, and their subordinates expect a great deal of autonomy and independence as they do their work.

European Americans tend to have a relatively low power distance, though it is by no means exceptionally low. However, when European Americans communicate with people from cultures that value a relatively large power distance, problems related to differences in expectations are likely. For example, European American exchange students in a South American or Asian culture sometimes have difficulty adapting to a world in which people are expected to do as they are told without questioning the reasons for the requests. Conversely, exchange students visiting the United States from high-PDI cultures sometimes feel uneasy because they expect their teachers to direct and supervise their work closely, but they may also have been taught that it would be rude and impolite to ask for the kinds of information that might allow them to be more successful.

Uncertainty Avoidance A second concern of all cultures is how they will adapt to changes and cope with uncertainties. The future will always be unknown in some respects. This unpredictability and the resultant anxiety that inevitably occurs are basic in human experience.

Cultures differ in the extent to which they prefer and can tolerate ambiguity, and therefore in the means they select for coping with change. Thus, all cultures differ in their perceived need to be changeable and adaptable. Hofstede refers to these variations as the uncertainty avoidance dimension, the extent to which the culture feels threatened by ambiguous, uncertain situations and tries to avoid them by establishing more structure.

Hofstede has created an uncertainty avoidance index (UAI) to assess a culture's relative location along the uncertainty avoidance dimension. At one extreme are cultures such as those of Denmark, Jamaica, Ireland, and Singapore, all of which have relatively low UAIs. These cultures therefore have a high tolerance for uncertainty and ambiguity; they believe in minimizing the number of rules and rituals that govern social conduct and human behavior, in accepting and encouraging dissent among cultural members, in tolerating people who behave in ways that are considered socially deviant, and in taking risks and trying new things. Conversely, the cultures of Greece, Guatemala, Portugal, and Uruguay all have relatively high UAIs and prefer to avoid uncertainty as a cultural value. These cultures desire or even demand consensus about societal goals, and they do not tolerate dissent or allow deviation in the behaviors of cultural members. They try to ensure certainty and security through an extensive set of rules, regulations, and rituals. Table 5.3 provides a numerical rating of sixty-six countries and three regions on the uncertainty avoidance dimension.

CULTURE *connections*

At the center of the old Sioux society was the tiyospaye, the extended family group, the basic hunting band, which included grandparents, uncles, aunts, in-laws, and cousins. The tiyospaye was like a warm womb cradling all within it. Kids were never alone, always fussed over by not one but several mothers, watched and taught by several fathers. The real father, as a matter of fact, selected a second father, some well-thought-of relative with special skills as a hunter or medicine man, to help him bring up a boy, and such a person was called "Father" too. And the same was true for the girls. Grandparents in our tribe always held a special place for caring for the little ones, because they had more time to devote to them, when the father was out hunting, taking the mother with him to help with the skinning and butchering.

—*Mary Crow Dog*

TABLE 5.3   Country Ratings on the Uncertainty Avoidance Dimension

	*Uncertainty Avoidance**		*Uncertainty Avoidance**
Greece	191	Arab c ountries	6
Portugal	158	Morocco	6
Guatemala	145	Ecuador	1
Uruguay	141	Germany	−7
Malta	124	Thailand	−11
Russia	120	Bangladesh	−28
Belgium	115	Estonia	−28
Salvador	115	Finland	−32
Poland	111	Iran	−32
Japan	107	Switzerland	−37
Surinam	107	Trinidad	−49
Romania	98	West Africa	−53
Yugoslavia	90	Netherlands	−58
Peru	86	East Africa	−62
Argentina	82	Australia	−66
Chile	82	Slovakia	−66
Costa Rica	82	Norway	−70
France	82	New Zealand	−75
Panama	82	South Africa	−75
Spain	82	Canada	−79
Bulgaria	77	Indonesia	−79
South Korea	77	U.S.A.	−87
Turkey	77	Philippines	−96
Hungary	65	India	−113
Mexico	65	Malaysia	−129
Israel	60	Great Britain	−134
Colombia	56	Ireland	−134
Brazil	39	China	−155
Venezuela	39	Vietnam	−155
Italy	35	Hong Kong	−159
Czech Republic	31	Sweden	−159
Austria	14	Denmark	−184
Luxembourg	14	Jamaica	−227
Pakistan	14	Singapore	−248
Taiwan	10		

*A large positive score means the country prefers to avoid uncertainty; a large negative score means the country does not prefer to avoid uncertainty. The average score is zero. Ratings are in standardized scores, with the decimal point omitted.

Source: Adapted from Geert Hofstede, *Cultures and Organizations: Software of the Mind*. (London: McGraw–Hill, 1991), 113.

Predictors of Uncertainty Avoidance   Unlike the power distance dimension, there are no straightforward explanations to account for the differences in a culture's preferred level of uncertainty avoidance. In general, high-UAI cultures tend to be those that are beginning to modernize and are therefore characterized by a high rate of change. Historically, these cultures tend to have an extensive system of legislative rules and laws with which to resolve disputes, and they often embrace religions such as Catholicism and Islam, which stress absolute certainties. Conversely, low-UAI cultures tend to be advanced in their level of modernization and are therefore more stable and predictable in their rate of change. These cultures are likely to have far fewer rules and laws that govern social conduct, preferring instead to resolve disputes by negotiation or conflict. They are also more likely to adopt religions such as Buddhism and Unitarianism, which emphasize relativity.

Consequences of Uncertainty Avoidance   Cultures must cope with the need to create a world that is more certain and predictable, and they do so by inventing rules and rituals to constrain human behaviors. Because members of high-UAI cultures tend to be worried about the future, they have high levels of anxiety and are highly resistant to change. They regard the uncertainties of life as a continuous threat that must be overcome. Consequently, high-UAI cultures develop many rules to control social behaviors, and they often adopt elaborate rituals and religious practices that have a precise form or sequence.

Members of low-UAI cultures tend to live day to day, and they are more willing to accept change and take risks. Conflict and competition are natural, dissent is acceptable, deviance is not threatening, and individual achievement is regarded as beneficial. Consequently, low-UAI cultures need few rules to control social behaviors, and they are unlikely to adopt religious rituals that require precise patterns of enactment.

Differences in level of uncertainty avoidance can result in unexpected problems in intercultural communication. For instance, European Americans tend to have a moderately low level of uncertainty avoidance. When these U.S. Americans communicate with someone from a high-UAI culture such as Japan or France, they are likely to be seen as too nonconforming and unconventional, and they may view their Japanese or French counterparts as rigid and overly controlled. Conversely, when these U.S. Americans communicate with someone from an extremely low-UAI country such as Ireland or Sweden, they are likely to be viewed as too structured and uncompromising, whereas they may perceive their Irish or Swedish counterparts as too willing to accept dissent.

Individualism versus Collectivism   A third concern of all cultures involves people's relationships to the larger social groups of which they are a part. People must live and interact together for the culture to survive. In doing so, they must develop a way of relating that strikes a balance between showing concern for themselves and concern for others.

Cultures differ in the extent to which individual autonomy is regarded favorably or unfavorably. Thus, cultures vary in their tendency to encourage people to be unique and independent or conforming and interdependent. Hofstede refers to these variations as the individualism–collectivism dimension, the degree to which a culture relies on and has allegiance to the self or the group.

CULTURE *connections*

Notice how Ann Landers, in devaluing obligations to elders and one's family, provides a typical U.S. American response to an interpersonal communication dilemma.

Dear Ann: I come from a very large, middle-class, Asian family. We emigrated from Vietnam 10 years ago.

As a result of that unforgettable war, the desperation for freedom, being a refugee living in a foreign country with a different culture (Canada) and facing an uncertain future, I am mature beyond my years—yet I am treated like a child.

All my life I have been an obedient, dutiful daughter. Being the youngest girl in the family has its benefits, but there are also many drawbacks.

To explain: I am a straight-A student, but I am not allowed to have any dates even though I am now 22. I cannot go anywhere without my mother's permission. I must finish college, have a job, build a career and be what my family expects me to be. Ann, I feel like a prisoner.

Being raised in an Asian family will always assure obedient and dutiful children. My mother is very strict and domineering. I was trained to be an achiever. I am not permitted to have any close friends, male or female. Consequently, I have become a loner.

You'd be amazed how many Asian children are in this same position. Please don't suggest family counseling because that is definitely out of the question. Thank you for being a true friend in whom I can confide. Sign me . . .

Oppressed, repressed
and depressed in
Vancouver, B.C.

Dear Vancouver: With all due respect to your cultural heritage, a woman of 22 should be free to have friends, both male and female, so that she can develop culturally and emotionally as well as intellectually.

I urge you to discuss this problem with a professor at your school. Your mother's life has been a very hard one and she deserves respect, but you are entitled to a life of your own and I urge you to assert yourself.

—*Ann Landers*

Hofstede has created an individualism index (IDV) to assess a culture's relative location on the individualism–collectivism dimension. At one extreme are Australia, Belgium, the Netherlands, and the United States. Such cultures, all of which have relatively high IDVs and therefore are highly individualistic, believe that people are only supposed to take care of themselves, and perhaps their immediate families. In individualist cultures, the autonomy of the individual is paramount. Key words used to invoke this cultural pattern include independence, privacy, self, and the all-important *I*. Decisions are based on what is good for the individual, not for the group, because the person is the primary source of motivation. Similarly, a judgment about what is right or wrong can be made only from the point of view of each individual.

Such cultures as Guatemala, Indonesia, Pakistan, and West Africa all have relatively low IDVs and prefer a collectivist orientation as a cultural value. These cultures require an absolute loyalty to the group, though the relevant group might be as varied as the nuclear family, the extended family, a caste or jati (a subgrouping of a caste), or even the organization for which a person works. In collectivist cultures, decisions that juxtapose the benefits to the individual and the benefits to the group are always based on what is best for the group, and the groups to which a person belongs are the most important social units. In turn, the group is expected to look out for and take care of its individual members. Consequently, collectivist cultures believe in obligations to the group, dependence of the individual on organizations and institutions, a "we" consciousness, and an emphasis on belonging. For example, Hui-Ching Chang and G. Richard Holt emphasize that the Chinese cultural pattern of relationships is built on an other-oriented perspective. Interpersonal bonding, from this point of view, is not due solely to "honest communication" but also has its basis in obligations and expectations that are already established and ongoing.[4] Table 5.4 provides a numerical rating of sixty-six countries and three regions on the individualism–collectivism dimension.

The preeminent status of the individual and the individual's right to speak freely are central characteristics of the European American cultural pattern.

TABLE 5.4   Country Ratings on the Individualism–Collectivism Dimension

	*Individualism**		*Individualism**
U.S.A.	200	Arab countries	−22
Australia	195	Brazil	−22
Great Britain	191	Turkey	−26
Canada	154	Uruguay	−30
Hungary	154	Greece	−34
Netherlands	154	Philippines	−47
New Zealand	149	Bulgaria	−55
Italy	137	Mexico	−55
Belgium	133	Romania	−55
Denmark	129	East Africa	−67
France	116	Portugal	−67
Sweden	116	Yugoslavia	−67
Ireland	112	Malaysia	−72
Norway	108	Hong Kong	−76
Switzerland	104	Chile	−84
Germany	99	Bangladesh	−97
South Africa	91	China	−97
Finland	83	Singapore	−97
Estonia	70	Thailand	−97
Luxembourg	70	Vietnam	−97
Poland	70	West Africa	−97
Malta	66	Salvador	−101
Czech Republic	62	South Korea	−105
Austria	49	Taiwan	−109
Israel	45	Peru	−113
Slovakia	37	Trinidad	−113
Spain	33	Costa Rica	−118
India	20	Indonesia	−122
Surinam	16	Pakistan	−122
Argentina	12	Colombia	−126
Japan	12	Venezuela	−130
Morocco	12	Panama	−134
Iran	−9	Ecuador	−147
Jamaica	−17	Guatemala	−155
Russia	−17		

*A large positive score means the country prefers individualism; a large negative score means the country prefers collectivism. The average score is zero. Ratings are in standardized scores, with the decimal point omitted.

Source: Adapted from Geert Hofstede, *Cultures and Organizations: Software of the Mind.* (London: McGraw–Hill, 1991), 53.

Predictors of Individualism–Collectivism   There is a strong relationship between a culture's location on the power distance dimension and its location on the individualism–collectivism dimension. High-PDI cultures tend to be collectivistic, whereas low-PDI cultures tend to be individualistic. Consequently, there are some similarities to the power distance dimension in predicting a culture's level of individualism–collectivism.

The best predictor of individualism–collectivism is economic development; wealthy cultures tend to be individualistic, whereas poor cultures tend to be collectivistic. Though it is impossible to determine whether increased economic development leads to increased levels of individualism or vice versa, there is strong evidence to suggest that cultures become more individualistic as they become more economically advanced.

Another predictor is climate. Cultures in colder climates tend to be individualistic, whereas cultures in warmer climates tend to be collectivistic. As we suggested in the discussion of power distance, colder climates are likely to foster and support individual initiative and innovative solutions to problems, whereas warmer climates make individual achievements far less necessary.

CULTURE *connections*

Until the American Occupation in the late 1940s, the individual had had no rights in Japan; in fact, the whole notion of "rights" was a Western import. Instead, the family had always been the legal unit. The family was actually responsible and liable for the actions of its members. All that talk about not doing anything to make your family lose face was more than just Confucian morals.

Even now, if you get down to it, you aren't your own person, you're just one new line entered in the record of an entire family. The record is registered in the family's hometown, and it goes back for generations. Everything that happens in the family is recorded in detail: births, deaths, marriages. When a daughter is married off, she is removed from her parents' family register and put in a new one with the husband as the head. These documents are officially confidential, but in fact anyone in the family has access to them. Each time legal identification is required—say, when you get married or receive an inheritance—you have to go to the local government office in person and get an official copy of your family register. They'll ask you to sign for it with a certified seal bearing the family name. All very proper and correct.

Then the Americans came in and "democratized" the system. Sort of. With the introduction of voting and local taxation, it became necessary to keep closer track of people, so another layer of documentation came into being: the residence certificate. Individual but temporary. This is valid only as long as you stay at a specific current address, but it doesn't affect your permanent address, where your "real self" is considered to reside. For less official purposes like taking out a library card, all you need is the residence certificate and not the family register. For most legal purposes, though, you need both. And if you live far away, getting the family register through the proper channels can take forever.

—*Miyuki Miyabe*

Consequences of Individualism–Collectivism   Huge cultural differences can be explained by differences on the individualism–collectivism dimension. We have already noted that collectivistic cultures tend to be group-oriented. A related characteristic is that they typically impose a very large psychological distance between those who are members of their group (the ingroup) and those who are not (the outgroup). Ingroup members are required to have unquestioning loyalty, whereas outgroup members are regarded as almost inconsequential. Conversely, members of individualistic cultures do not perceive a large chasm between ingroup and outgroup members; ingroup members are not as close, but outgroup members are not as distant. Scholars such as Harry Triandis believe that the individualism–collectivism dimension is by far the most important attribute that distinguishes one culture from another.[5]

Individualist cultures train their members to speak out as a means of resolving difficulties. In classrooms, students from individualistic cultures are likely to ask questions of the teacher; students from collectivistic cultures are not. Similarly, people from individualistic cultures are more likely than those from collectivistic cultures to use confrontational strategies when dealing with interpersonal problems; those with a collectivistic orientation are likely to use avoidance, third-party intermediaries, or other face-saving techniques. Indeed, a common maxim among European Americans, who are highly individualistic, is that "the squeaky wheel gets the grease" (suggesting that one should make noises in order to be rewarded); the corresponding maxim among the Japanese, who are somewhat collectivistic, is "the nail that sticks up gets pounded" (so one should always try to blend in).

Masculinity versus Femininity   A fourth concern of all cultures, and for which they must all find solutions, pertains to the extent to which they prefer achievement and assertiveness or nurturance and social support. Hofstede refers to these variations as the masculinity–femininity dimension, though an alternative label is achievement–nurturance. This dimension indicates the degree to which a culture values such behaviors as assertiveness and the acquisition of wealth or caring for others and the quality of life.

To avoid the common trap of thinking about cultural differences as polar opposites—us versus them—focus on three cultures (your own and two others that differ from yours) and choose one aspect of these cultures (such as religion, personal space, time, status of women, individuality, silence, history, etc.) to research. That is, provide three separate cultural views of this one characteristic.

Hofstede has created a masculinity index (MAS) to assess a culture's relative location along the masculinity–femininity dimension. At one extreme are such cultures as those of Austria, Italy, Japan, and Mexico. These cultures, all of which have a relatively high MAS, believe in achievement and ambition in judging people on the basis of their performance and in the right to display the material goods that have been acquired. The people in high-MAS cultures also believe in ostentatious manliness, and very specific behaviors and products are associated with appropriate male behavior.

Low-MAS cultures, such as those of Chile, Portugal, Sweden, and Thailand, believe less in external achievements and shows of manliness and more in the importance of life choices that improve intrinsic aspects of the quality of life, such as service to others and sympathy for the unfortunate. People in these feminine cultures are also likely to prefer equality between the sexes, less prescriptive role behaviors associated with each gender, and an acceptance of nurturing roles for both women and men. Table 5.5 provides a numerical rating of sixty-six countries and three regions on the masculinity–femininity dimension.

Predictors of Masculinity–Femininity   The best predictor of masculinity–femininity is climate. Masculine cultures tend to live in warmer climates near the equator, and feminine cultures typically reside in colder climates away from the equator. As he suggested in the argument relating climate to power distance, Hofstede speculates that colder climates require more technology for the culture to survive, which in turn imposes a need for education and equality. Hofstede extends this argument to include equality between the sexes because cold-weather climates impose a need for both men and women to master a set of complex skills that make sexual inequality less functional and therefore less likely.

Consequences of Masculinity–Femininity   Members of highly masculine cultures believe that men should be assertive and women should be nurturing. Sex roles are clearly differentiated, and sexual inequality is regarded as beneficial. The reverse is true for members of highly feminine cultures: men are far less interested in achievement, sex roles are far more fluid, and equality between the sexes is the norm.

Teachers in masculine cultures praise their best students because academic performance is rewarded highly. Similarly, male students in these high-MAS cultures strive to be competitive, visible, successful, and vocationally oriented. In feminine cultures, teachers rarely praise individual achievements and academic performance because social accommodation is more highly regarded. Male students try to cooperate with one another and develop a sense of solidarity; they try to behave modestly and properly; they select subjects because they are intrinsically interesting rather than vocationally rewarding; and friendliness is much more important than brilliance.

CULTURE *connections*

"You don't understand," she said. "You think a woman feels bad if she's exchanged for cows or money. But if there's no exchange she feels worth nothing. I cost my husband *ten* cows. I had good education from Irish nuns in Mbarara. I speak English and can run a business. My father spent money on me, why give me away for nothing? Our families keep accounts of what girls cost to feed and clothe and educate, that way they can show a daughter is valuable to a young man's family. You want a healthy, educated bride—OK, you pay for it!"

—*Dervla Murphy*

TABLE 5.5   Country Ratings on the Masculinity–Femininity Dimension

	Masculinity*		Masculinity*
Slovakia	317	Brazil	−6
Japan	238	Singapore	−11
Hungary	201	Israel	−16
Austria	153	Malta	−16
Venezuela	121	Indonesia	−22
Italy	105	West Africa	−22
Switzerland	105	Taiwan	−27
Mexico	100	Turkey	−27
Ireland	95	Panama	−32
Jamaica	95	France	−38
China	84	Iran	−38
Germany	84	Peru	−43
Great Britain	84	Romania	−43
Colombia	74	Spain	−43
Philippines	74	East Africa	−48
Poland	74	Bulgaria	−53
Ecuador	68	Salvador	−53
South Africa	68	Vietnam	−53
U.S.A.	63	South Korea	−59
Australia	58	Uruguay	−64
New Zealand	42	Guatemala	−69
Trinidad	42	Surinam	−69
Czech Republic	37	Russia	−75
Greece	37	Thailand	−85
Hong Kong	37	Portugal	−101
Argentina	31	Estonia	−106
India	31	Chile	−117
Bangladesh	26	Finland	−128
Belgium	21	Costa Rica	−154
Arab countries	15	Yugoslavia	−154
Morocco	15	Denmark	−181
Canada	10	Netherlands	−191
Luxembourg	0	Norway	−223
Malaysia	0	Sweden	−239
Pakistan	0		

*A large positive score means the country prefers masculinity; a large negative score means the country prefers femininity. The average score is zero. Ratings are in standardized scores, with the decimal point omitted.

Source: Adapted from Geert Hofstede, *Cultures and Organizations: Software of the Mind*. (London: McGraw–Hill, 1991), 84.

Although Saudi Arabian women are expected to wear the abaaya while in public places, these wedding dresses are appropriate for private family gatherings.

Long-Term versus Short-Term Time Orientation   A fifth concern of all cultures relates to its orientation to time. Hofstede has acknowledged that the four previously described dimensions have a Western bias, as they were developed by scholars from Europe or the United States who necessarily brought to their work an implicit set of assumptions and categories about the types of cultural values they would likely find. His time-orientation dimension is based on the work of Michael H. Bond, a Canadian who has lived in Asia for the past thirty years and who assembled a large team of researchers from Hong Kong and Taiwan to develop and administer a Chinese Value Survey to university students around the world.[6]

The time-orientation dimension refers to a person's point of reference about life and work. Cultures that promote a long-term orientation toward life admire persistence, thriftiness, humility, a sense of shame, and status differences within interpersonal relationships. Linguistic and social distinctions between elder and younger siblings are common, deferred gratification of needs is widely accepted, and family life is guided by shared tasks. Conversely, cultures with a short-term orientation toward changing events have a deep appreciation for tradition, personal steadiness and stability, maintaining the "face" of self and others, balance or reciprocity when greeting others, giving and receiving gifts and favors, and an expectation of quick results following one's actions.[7] Table 5.6 provides a numerical rating of twenty-nine countries on the time-orientation dimension.

CULTURE *connections*

Southeast Asian refugees come from societies where modesty is praised, where a man who is truly good will never say he is good. But they now live in a society where the most successful group often is the one that stands up and states its case the loudest.

"Public relations is a new term for us. Americans are masters of the art," one leader said, asking to remain anonymous for fear of sounding brash. Unlike Americans, he said, "I don't like to see my name in the paper. I am reluctant to do interviews, unless it is my duty."

Even something as simple and essential as venturing downtown to discuss issues with City Council members remains a foreign journey, leaders admit. Until that happens there will likely not be a Southeast Asian leader known to the general public, much less a council member or county supervisor.

—*Tony Bizjak and Jeannie Wong*

TABLE 5.6 Country Ratings on the Long-Term Orientation Dimension

	Confucian Value*		Confucian Value*
China	253	Sweden	−46
Hong Kong	176	Poland	−50
Taiwan	144	Australia	−53
Japan	119	Germany	−53
Vietnam	119	New Zealand	−57
South Korea	102	U.S.A.	−60
Brazil	67	Great Britain	−74
India	52	Zimbabwe	−74
Thailand	35	Canada	−81
Hungary	14	Philippines	−96
Singapore	7	Nigeria	−106
Netherlands	−7	Czech Republic	−117
Bangladesh	−22	Pakistan	−163
Slovakia	−29		

*A large positive score means the country prefers a long-term orientation; a large negative score means the country prefers a short-term orientation. The average score is zero. Ratings are in standardized scores, with the decimal point omitted.

Source: Adapted from Geert Hofstede, *Cultures and Organizations: Software of the Mind*. (London: McGraw–Hill, 1991).

Comparing Hofstede's Five Dimensions   Each of Hofstede's five dimensions provides insights into the influence of culture on the communication process. Cultures with similar configurations on the five dimensions would likely have similar communication patterns, and cultures that are very different from one another would probably behave dissimilarly. Table 5.7 groups the countries on the basis of their similarities.

As we suggested in Chapter 4, each of Hofstede's dimensions of cultural patterns represents a universal social choice that must be made by all cultures and that is learned from the family and throughout the social institutions of a culture: in the degree to which children are encouraged to have their own desires and motivations, in the solidarity and unity expected in the family, in the role models that are presented, and throughout the range of messages that are conveyed. Hofstede's dimensions describe cultural expectations for a range of social behaviors: power distance refers to relationships with people higher or lower in rank, uncertainty avoidance to people's search for truth and certainty, individualism–collectivism to expected behaviors toward the group, masculinity–femininity to the expectations surrounding achievement and gender differences, and time orientation to people's search for virtue and lasting ideals.[8] This last dimension describes cultural patterns that are consistent with the teachings of Confucius. Because Confucian teachings are substantially different from value orientations described previously, we will examine them next in greater detail.

Confucian Cultural Values

Kong Fu Ze, who was renamed Confucius by Jesuit missionaries, was a Chinese civil servant of humble origins who lived about 2,500 years ago. An intellectual like the Greek philosopher Socrates (who lived eighty years later), Confucius was known for his wit and great wisdom. His many followers, who regularly surrounded him and recorded his teachings, provide us with what we now know of his ideas.

Confucianism is not a religion but a set of practical principles and ethical rules for daily life. Derived from what Confucius understood as the lessons of Chinese history, these ideas have long held a central place not only in China but also in Japan, Korea, and elsewhere in Asia.[9]

Key principles of Confucian teaching include the following:

1. *Social order and stability are based on unequal relationships between people.* The five basic human relationships, and the essential social virtues that correspond to each role, include leader and follower (justice and loyalty), father and son (love and closeness), husband and wife (initiative and obedience), older brother and younger brother (friendliness and reverence), and friends (mutual faithfulness). Each of these relationships, including those among friends (who differ, however slightly, in age and in other indicants of status), presumes the existence and legitimacy of a social hierarchy and the reciprocal, complementary obligations that each position in the hierarchy requires. The higher-status person in each pair must provide protection and consideration, while the lower-status person owes respect and obedience. In addition,

From the list of films in the Resources section at the end of this book, select a film about a culture other than your own. Through the actions of the characters, analyze what the film indicates about the cultural patterns of the culture that is depicted.

TABLE 5.7   Groupings on Hofstede's Dimensions

Type of Culture	Characteristics	Countries or Regions
More developed Latin	Medium to high PDI High UAI Medium to high IDV Medium MAS	Argentina, Belgium, Brazil, Italy, France, Spain
Less developed Latin	Medium to high PDI High UAI Low IDV Low to high MAS	Chile, Columbia, Peru, Costa Rica, Ecuador, Guatemala, Mexico, Panama, Portugal, Salvador, Uruguay, Venezuela
Caribbean	Low PDI Low to medium UAI Medium IDV High MAS	Jamaica
More developed Asian	Medium PDI High UAI Medium IDV High MAS	Japan
Less developed Asian	Medium to high PDI Low to medium UAI Low IDV Medium MAS	Hong Kong, India, Indonesia, Malaysia, Pakistan, Philippines, Singapore, South Korea, Taiwan, Thailand
African	Medium to high PDI Low UAI Low IDV Medium to low MAS	East Africa, West Africa
Near Eastern	Medium to high PDI Medium to high UAI Low IDV Medium MAS	Arab Countries, Greece, Iran, Turkey, Yugoslavia
Germanic	Low PDI Medium to high UAI Medium to high IDV Medium to high MAS	Austria, Germany, Israel, Switzerland
Anglo	Low PDI Low UAI High IDV High MAS	Australia, Canada, Great Britain, Ireland, New Zealand, South Africa, U.S.A.
Nordic	Low PDI Low to medium UAI High IDV Low MAS	Denmark, Finland, Netherlands, Norway, Sweden

Source: Based on data reported in Geert Hofstede, *Cultures and Organizations: Software of the Mind* (London: McGraw-Hill, 1991) 26, 53, 84, 113.

there are different norms for the degree and form of the respect or obedience that is shown, depending on whether the relationship is close or distant.

2. *The family is the prototype for all social relationships.* Like the outwardly expanding rings resulting from a pebble tossed into a lake, the virtues learned within family relationships form the central core that specifies how to interact with others in the widening circle of social relationships. Similarly, the roles regulating family relationships can be extended to include the whole town, organization, or country. As Hui-Ching Chang and G. Richard Holt explain,

> Since the family serves as the basis of the society, one relates to the outside world in the same way one relates to the family members. Even if there is no blood connection or marriage relation, Chinese are still able to follow the rules of ordering between interactants. The common rule, based on the Confucian teachings is: if the other is older than twice one's age, one must treat him like a father; if the other is older within ten years, one must treat him like one's elder brother; if the other is not older than five years, one can walk with him a minor distance to show respect. In other words, regardless of who one interacts with, one must follow the rules for ordering.[10]

Thus, a person is not an isolated individual concerned with personal gain and voluntary group membership; rather, like a proper family member, a person has obliga-

Family relationships are central to many cultures and often serve as the prototype for all social relationships. This four-generation Korean family proudly celebrates their baby's 100th day of life.

tions to seek the common good for the benefit of others, to "behave like your actions reflect on all Chinese."[11] As June Ock Yum suggests, this mutual interdependence "requires that one be affiliated with relatively small and tightly knit groups of people and have a relatively long identification with those groups."[12] From childhood onward, therefore, people are taught to make a sharp distinction between ingroup and outgroup members. Similarly, children are trained to act with restraint, to overcome their individuality, and to maintain the appearance of group harmony; a person's thoughts, however, remain free.

Harmony is sustained through the maintenance of "face," or people's sense of dignity, self-respect, and prestige. Indeed, the English word *face* is derived from the Chinese term, and losing one's social dignity is indeed akin to losing one's eyes, ears, nose, and mouth. Social relations, according to Confucius, should be conducted so that everyone's face is maintained. Thus, intermediaries are used to initiate social contacts and avoid conflicts, indirect language is used to avoid embarrassing confrontations, and formality is used to maintain a heightened sense of politeness that preserves face.

3. *Proper social behavior consists of not treating others as you would not like to be treated yourself.* This negatively phrased Golden Rule, which emphasizes benevolence toward others, does not extend as far as the Christian injunction to "Love thy enemy"; rather, Confucian teachings invoke this rule only in the context of a reciprocal relationship, where there are shared expectations about social obligations and responsibilities. This principle also refers to the kinds of people with whom others should associate; those who are upright, devoted, and learned are most desirable, while those who are fawning, flattering, and too eloquent should be avoided. Lest it seem that the burden for change and adaptation falls solely on the others with whom a person interacts, Confucius taught that a person must first learn to be sensitive to and sympathetic of others' feelings before she or he can expect to achieve harmonious relationships. Thus, a person should first examine herself or himself when problems in communication and interpersonal relationships arise. Ideally, people should learn to harmonize not only with others but with the universe as well.

4. *People should be skilled, educated, hardworking, thrifty, modest, patient, and persevering.* Teaching and learning are highly valued, moderation in all things is preferred, conspicuous consumption is frowned on, losing one's temper is unacceptable, and persistence in solving difficult problems is widely valued. Because human nature is assumed to be inherently good, it is the responsibility of each individual to train his or her moral character in these standards of behavior. The goal of such practices is to help promote a world at peace, where no one needs to govern or be governed.

Cultural Taxonomies and Intercultural Competence

The major lesson in this chapter is that cultures vary systematically in their choices about solutions to basic human problems. The taxonomies offer lenses through which cultural variations can be understood and appreciated, rather than negatively evaluated and disregarded. The categories in these taxonomies can help you to describe the fundamental aspects of cultures. As frames of reference, they provide mechanisms to understand all intercultural communication events. In any intercultural encounter,

Time management, productivity, and communication all depend upon the patterns of one's culture to define their importance.

people may be communicating from very different perceptions of what is "reality," what is "good," and what is "correct" behavior. The competent intercultural communicator must recognize that cultural variations in addressing basic human issues such as social relations, emphasis on self or group, and preferences for verbal or nonverbal code usage will always be a factor in intercultural communication.

The taxonomies allow you to use culture-specific knowledge to improve intercultural competence. First, begin by seeking out information about the cultural patterns of those individuals with whom you engage in intercultural communication. To assist your understanding of the culture, select one of the taxonomies presented and seek information that allows you to create a profile of the culture's preferred choices. Libraries are a natural starting place for this kind of knowledge. So, too, are representatives of the culture. Engage them in conversation as you try to understand their culture. Most people welcome questions from a genuinely curious person. Be systematic in your search for information by using the categories thoroughly. Think about the interrelatedness of the various aspects of the culture's patterns.

Second, study the patterns of your own culture. Because you take your beliefs, values, and norms for granted, stepping outside of your cultural patterns by researching them is very useful. You might want to describe the preferences of your own culture by using one of the taxonomies.

The third step requires only a willingness to reflect on your personal preferences. Do your beliefs, values, and norms match those of the typical person in your culture? How do your choices coincide with and differ from the general cultural description?

Finally, mentally consider your own preferences by juxtaposing them with the description of the typical person from another culture. Note the similarities and differences in beliefs, values, and norms. Can you predict where misinterpretations may occur because of contrasting assumptions about what is important and good? For example, the European American who shares the culture's preference for directness would inevitably encounter difficulties in communication with a typical member of the Japanese culture or a typical Latino cultural member. Similarly, knowing that you value informality, and usually act accordingly, can help you to monitor your expressions when communicating with someone from a culture that prefers formality. Viewing time as linear often causes problems in communication with people from cultures with other orientations to time. Interpretations of behavior as "late," "inattentive," or "disrespectful," rather than just "different," can produce alternative ways of viewing the ticking of the clock.

Summary

This chapter discusses two important taxonomies that can be used to describe cultural variations. Edward Hall placed cultures on a continuum from high context to low context. High-context cultures prefer messages in which most of the meaning is either implied by the physical setting or is presumed to be part of the individual's internalized beliefs, values, and norms; low-context cultures prefer messages in which the information is contained within the explicit code.

Geert Hofstede identified five dimensions along which dominant patterns of a culture can be ordered: power distance, uncertainty avoidance, individualism–collectivism, masculinity–femininity, and time orientation. The power distance dimension assesses the degree to which the culture believes that institutional power should be distributed equally or unequally. The uncertainty avoidance dimension describes the extent to which cultures prefer and can tolerate ambiguity and change. The individualism–collectivism dimension describes the degree to which a culture relies on and has allegiance to the self or the group. The masculinity–femininity dimension indicates the degree to which a culture values assertiveness and the acquisition of wealth or caring for others and the quality of life. The time-orientation dimension refers to a long-term versus short-term orientation toward life and work.

The ideas presented in this chapter and the previous one offer alternative lenses through which cultures can be understood and appreciated. Taken together, these two chapters provide multiple frames of reference that can be used to enhance your knowledge, motivations, and skills in intercultural communication.

For Discussion

1. What does Edward Hall mean when he refers to culture as a "screen" for its members?
2. Describe how each of Hofstede's dimensions of cultural patterns is displayed within your culture.
3. Does Hofstede's taxonomy coincide with your own intercultural experiences? Explain.
4. Consider the following two philosophical statements: "I think, therefore I am" and "I am, because we are." What do these two statements reveal about the underlying cultural values of those who use them?

5. Compare your own values to Confucian cultural values. In what ways are they the same? Different? What might this suggest about intercultural communication?

For Further Reading

Edward T. Hall, *Beyond Culture* (New York: Anchor Books, 1989). Describes, in great detail, the cultural variations among high- and low-context cultures.

Jamake Highwater, *The Primal Mind: Vision and Reality in Indian America* (New York: Harper and Row, 1981) An excellent summary of the cultural framework that is central to many of the Native American tribes in the United States.

Geert Hofstede, *Culture's Consequences: Comparing Values, Behaviors, Institutions, and Organizations across Nations,* 2nd ed. (Thousand Oaks, CA: Sage, 2001). An update to Hofstede's extensive work documenting, through extensive quantitative evidence, variations among cultures on five dimensions.

For additional information about intercultural films and about Web sites on specific cultures, turn to the Resources section at the back of this book.

chapter 6

Cultural Identity, Cultural Biases, and Intercultural Contact

Cultural Identity
The Nature of Identity
The Formation of Cultural Identity
Characteristics of Cultural Identity
Cultural Biases
Social Categorizing
Ethnocentrism
Stereotyping
Prejudice
Discrimination
Racism

Intercultural Contact
Dominance and Subordination between
    Groups
Attitudes among Cultural Members
Outcomes of Intercultural Contact
**Becoming an Interculturally
    Competent Communicator**
**Identity, Biases, Contact, and
    Intercultural Competence**
Summary

In the previous two chapters we emphasized the critical importance of cultural patterns in shaping the preferred ways to think, feel, and act in a variety of situations. An equally interesting and important question in the development of intercultural communication competence concerns how people come to identify themselves as belonging to a particular cultural group. For example, how and when does a child begin to think of herself as a Latina, Japanese American, or Japanese? When do adults who are born into one culture and living in another begin to think of their cultural identity as embracing parts of both their original culture and the later culture? Similarly, how are some people defined as "not members" of our cultural groups? How and why do groups of people from one culture develop negative attitudes and actions toward other cultural groups? Can't we all, as Rodney King so poignantly asked, just get along?

The present chapter discusses some aspects of cultural identity that can have a very large effect on intercultural communication. We begin with a discussion of cultural identity and the powerful ways in which one's self-concept as a member of a particular cultural group filters our interpretations of the world. Next we explore the nature of cultural biases, rooted in cultural identity, as we examine the effects of ethnocentrism,

CULTURE *connections*

*"W*hat was it really like, growing up in America?"

"You mean what was it really like, growing up in white America with an Asian face?"

He told me about going to school in Chinatown in New York and identifying only with white America. He hated Chinese school because he did not wish to be different from his white classmates. Gradually he realized that although he thought of himself as American he would always be a foreigner, a Chinese, to his white peers. Martin felt himself caught between two worlds. He became convinced that prejudice was inherent in human nature and was present in every society, including his own home. His parents objected strongly when he once dated a West Indian girl, calling her a *see yu gui nui* (soya-sauce female foreign devil).

—*Adeline Yen Mah*

stereotyping, prejudice, discrimination, and racism on intercultural interactions. Finally, we analyze the effects of these cultural biases on intercultural contacts.

Cultural Identity

As part of the socialization process, children learn to view themselves as members of particular groups. Children in all cultures, for example, are taught to identify with their families (even though, as Chapter 10 indicates, whom to include as part of one's "family" differs across cultures). As a child becomes a teenager and then an adult, the development of vocational and avocational interests creates new groups with which to identify. "Baseball player," "ballet dancer," or "scientist" may become important labels to describe the self.

Another feature of socialization is that people are taught about groups to which they do not belong, and they often learn that certain groups should be avoided. This tendency to identify as a member of some groups, called *ingroups,* and to distinguish these ingroups from *outgroups,* is so prevalent in human thinking that it has been described as a universal human tendency.[1]

The Nature of Identity

Related to the distinction between ingroup and outgroup membership is the concept of one's *identity* or self-concept. An individual's self-concept is built on cultural, social, and personal identities.[2]

Cultural identity refers to one's sense of belonging to a particular culture or ethnic group. It is formed in a process that results from membership in a particular culture, and it involves learning about and accepting the traditions, heritage, language, religion, ancestry, aesthetics, thinking patterns, and social structures of a culture. That is, peo-

In this multicultural family, the children will draw upon the cultures of both of their parents in forming their own cultural identities.

ple internalize the beliefs, values, and norms of their culture and identify with that culture as part of their self-concept.

Social identity develops as a consequence of memberships in particular groups within one's culture. The characteristics and concerns common to most members of such social groups shape the way individuals view their characteristics. The types of groups with which people identify can vary widely and might include perceived similarities due to age, gender, work, religion, ideology, social class, place (neighborhood, region, and nation), and common interests. For instance, those baseball players, ballet dancers, and scientists who strongly identify with their particular professions likely view themselves as "belonging" to "their" group of professionals, with whom they have similar traits and share similar concerns.

Finally, *personal identity* is based on people's unique characteristics, which may differ from those of others in their cultural and social groups. You may like cooking or chemistry, singing or sewing; you may play tennis or trombones, soccer or stereos; you may view yourself as studious or sociable, goofy or gracious; and most assuredly you have abilities, talents, quirks, and preferences that differ from those of others.

For ease and clarity, we have chosen to present aspects of a person's identity as separate categories. There is a great deal of interdependence, however, among these three aspects of identity. Characteristics of people's social identities will inevitably be linked

List the culture(s) of which you are a member. Which of your beliefs, values, and norms come from your culture(s)? Which are your personal characteristics?

to the preferences shaped by their cultural identities. Similarly, how people enact their unique interests will also be heavily influenced by their cultural identities. Thus, for example, a teenage girl's identity will likely be strongly linked to her culture's preferences for gendered role behaviors as well as to her social class and her personal characteristics and traits.

The Formation of Cultural Identity

Cultural identities often develop through a process involving three stages: unexamined cultural identity, cultural identity search, and cultural identity achievement.[3] During the *unexamined cultural identity* stage, one's cultural characteristics are taken for granted, and consequently there is little interest in exploring cultural issues. Young children, for instance, typically lack an awareness of cultural differences and the distinguishing characteristics that differentiate one culture from another. Teenagers and adults may not want to categorize themselves as belonging to any particular culture.[4] Some people may not have explored the meanings and consequences of their cultural membership but may simply have accepted preconceived ideas about it that were obtained from parents, the community, the mass media, and others. Consequently, some individuals may unquestioningly accept the prevailing stereotypes held by others and may internalize common stereotypes of their own culture and of themselves. Scholars have suggested that the cultural identities of many European Americans, in particular, have remained largely unexamined, a consequence of the power, centrality, and privilege that the European American cultural group has had in the United States.[5] As Judith Martin, Robert Krizek, Thomas Nakayama, and Lisa Bradford suggest,

> This lack of attention to white identity and self-labeling reflects the historical power held by Whites in the United States. That is, Whites as the privileged group take their identity as the norm or standard by which other groups are measured, and this identity is therefore invisible, even to the extent that many Whites do not consciously think about the profound effect being white has on their everyday lives.[6]

CULTURE *connections*

My mother is Vietnamese, and my father is African American. People have stereotypes about me. They think, she's Asian; she's smart, she doesn't need help. Or she's a black girl: she's likely to get pregnant.

—Monica Watkins, 18
  San Leandro, California

—Kristen Golden

The use of cultural artifacts in the celebration of Kwanzaa helps this African American family strengthen their cultural identity.

Cultural identity search involves a process of exploration and questioning about one's culture in order to learn more about it and to understand the implications of membership in that culture. By exploring the culture, individuals can learn about its strengths and may come to a point of acceptance both of their culture and of themselves. For some individuals, a turning point or crucial event precipitates this stage, whereas for others it just begins with a growing awareness and reinterpretation of everyday experiences. Common to this stage is an increased social and political awareness along with an increased desire to learn more about one's culture. Such learning may be characterized by an increased degree of talking with family and friends about cultural issues, independent reading of relevant sources, enrolling in appropriate courses, or increased attendance at cultural events such as festivals and museums. There may also be an emotional component to this stage, of varying intensity, which involves tension, anger, and perhaps even outrage directed toward other groups. These emotions may intensify as people become aware of and wrestle with the effects of discrimination on their present and future lives and the potential difficulties in attaining educational, career, and personal objectives.

Cultural identity achievement is characterized by a clear, confident acceptance of oneself and an internalization of one's cultural identity. Such acceptance can calmly and securely be used to guide one's future actions. People in this stage have developed ways of dealing with stereotypes and discrimination so that they do not internalize others' negative perceptions and are clear about the personal meanings of their culture. This outcome contributes to increased self-confidence and positive psychological adjustment. Table 6.1 provides sample comments from individuals in each of the three stages of cultural identity development.

Characteristics of Cultural Identity

Once formed, cultural identities provide an essential framework, organizing and interpreting our experiences of others. This is because cultural identities are central, dynamic, and multifaceted components of one's self-concept.

Cultural identities are central to a person's sense of self. Like gender and race, your culture is more "basic" because it is broadly influential and is linked to a great number of other aspects of your self-concept. These core aspects of your identity are likely to be important in most of your interactions with others. Most components of your identity,

TABLE 6.1   Stages in the Development of Cultural Identity

Stage	Sample Comments	Source of Comments
Unexamined cultural identity	"My parents tell me about where they lived, but what do I care? I've never lived there."	Mexican American Male
	"Why do I have to learn who was the first black woman to do this or that? I'm just not too interested."	African American Female
	"I don't have a culture. I'm just an American."	European American Male
Cultural identity search	"I think people should know what black people had to go through to get to where we are now."	African American Female
	"There are a lot of non-Japanese people around me and it gets pretty confusing to try and decide who I am."	Japanese American Male
	"I want to know what we do and how our culture is different from others."	Mexican American Female
Cultural identity achievement	"My culture is important and I am proud of what I am. Japanese people have so much to offer."	Japanese American Male
	"It used to be confusing to me, but it's clear now. I'm happy being black."	African American Female

Source: Adapted from Jean S. Phinney, "A Three-Stage Model of Ethnic Identity Development in Adolescence," *Ethnic Identity: Formation and Transmission among Hispanics and Other Minorities,* ed. Martha E. Bernal and George P. Knight (Albany: State University of New York Press, 1993) 61–79.

however, become important only when they are activated by specific circumstances. For many people, the experience of living in another culture or interacting with a person from a different culture triggers an awareness of their own cultural identities that they did not have before. When a component of your identity becomes conscious and important to you, or "activated," your experiences get filtered through that portion of your identity. As Fernando Delgado suggests, aspects of one's cultural identity can be activated not only by direct experiences with others but also by the media reports, by artistic portrayals that have particular cultural themes, by musical performances (such as rap music) that are identified with specific cultural groups, and by a range of other personal and mass-mediated experiences.[7] Because your cultural identity is likely to be central to your sense of self, most of your experiences are interpreted or "framed" by your cultural membership.

Because cultural identities are dynamic, your cultural identity—your sense of the culture to which you belong and who you are in light of this cultural membership—exists within a changing social context. Consequently, your identity is not static, fixed, and enduring; rather, it is dynamic and changes with your ongoing life experiences. In even the briefest encounter with people whose cultural backgrounds differ from your own, your sense of who you are *at that instant* may well be altered, at least in some small ways. Over time, as you adapt to various intercultural challenges, your cultural identity may be transformed into one that is substantially different from what it used to be.[8] The inaccurate belief that cultural identities are permanent, that "Once a Swedish American, always a Swedish American," ignores the possibility of profound changes that people may experience as a result of their intercultural contacts.

Cultural identities are also multifaceted. At any given moment, you have many "components" that make up your identity. For instance, a specific person may simultaneously view herself as a student, an employee, a friend, a woman, a southerner, a daughter, a Methodist, a baby boomer, and more. Similarly, there are typically many facets or components to your cultural identity.

Many people incorrectly assume that an individual could, or perhaps should, identify with only one cultural group. However, as Young Yun Kim suggests,

> If someone sees himself or herself, or is seen by others, as a Mexican-American, then this person's identity is [commonly] viewed to exclude all other identities. This tendency to see cultural identity in an "all-or-none" and "either-or" manner glosses over the fact that many people's identities are not locked into a single, uncompromising category, but incorporate other identities as well.[9]

Given our increasingly multicultural world, in which people from many cultures coexist and in which the United States has become a country in which individuals from many cultures live and interact, the multifaceted characteristic of cultural identity becomes even more important.[10]

Cultural Biases

In Chapter 2, we defined culture as a learned set of shared interpretations about beliefs, values, and norms that affect the behaviors of a relatively large group of people. We also pointed out that culture really exists in people's minds, but that the consequences of culture—the shared interpretations—can be seen in people's communication behaviors. Shared interpretations, which we have called cultural patterns, provide guidelines about how people should behave, and they indicate what to expect in interactions with others. In other words, a culture's shared interpretations create predictability and stability in people's lives. Cultural similarity allows people to reduce uncertainty and to know what to expect when interacting with others.

Interaction only within one's own culture produces a number of obvious benefits. Because the culture provides predictability, it reduces the threat of the unknown. When something or someone that is unknown or unpredictable enters a culture, the culture's beliefs, values, and norms tell people how to interpret and respond appropriately, thus reducing the perceived threat of the intrusion. Cultural patterns also allow for automatic responses to stimuli; in essence, cultural patterns save people time and energy.

Intercultural communication, by definition, means that people are interacting with at least one culturally different person. Consequently, the sense of security, comfort, and predictability that characterizes communication with culturally similar people is lost. The greater the degree of interculturalness, the greater the loss of predictability and certainty. Assurances about the accuracy of interpretations of verbal and nonverbal messages are lost.

Terms that are often used when communicating with culturally different people include *unknown, unpredictable, ambiguous, weird, mysterious, unexplained, exotic, unusual, unfamiliar, curious, novel, odd, outlandish,* and *strange.* As you read this list, consider how the choice of a particular word might also reflect a particular value. What characteristics, values, and knowledge allow individuals to respond more competently to the threat of dealing with cultural differences? What situations heighten the perception of threat among members of different cultural groups? To answer questions such as these, we need to explore how people make sense of information about others as they categorize or classify others in their social world.

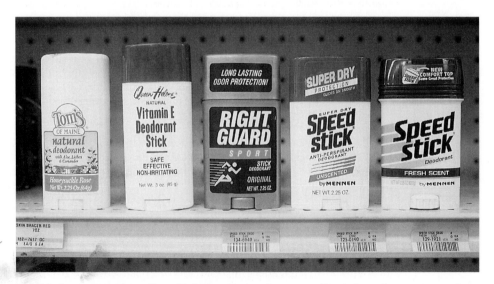

The U.S. American preoccupation with body odors can be seen on the shelves of every grocery store.

Social Categorizing

Three features in the way all humans process information about others are important to your understanding of intercultural competence. First, as cognitive psychologists have repeatedly demonstrated, people impose a pattern on their world by organizing the stimuli that bombard their senses into conceptual categories. Every waking moment, people are presented with literally hundreds of different perceptual stimuli. Therefore, it becomes necessary to simplify the information by selecting, organizing, and reducing it to less complex forms. That is, to comprehend stimuli, people organize them into categories, groupings, and patterns. As a child, you might have completed a drawing by connecting numbered dots. Emerging from the lines was the figure of an animal or a familiar toy. Even though its complete form was not drawn, it was relatively easy to identify. This kind of recognition occurs simply because human beings have a tendency to organize perceptual cues to impose meaning, usually by using familiar, previous experiences.

Second, most people tend to think that other people perceive, evaluate, and reason about the world in the same way that they do. In other words, humans assume that other people with whom they interact are like themselves. Indeed, it is quite common for people to draw on their personal experiences to understand and evaluate the motivations of others. This common human tendency is sometimes called "ethnocentrism."

Third, humans simplify the processing and organizing of information from the environment by identifying certain characteristics as belonging to certain categories of persons and events. For example, a child's experiences with several dogs that growled and snapped are likely to result in a future reaction to other dogs as if they will also growl and snap. The characteristics of particular events, persons, or objects, once experienced, are often assumed to be typical of similar events, persons, or objects. Though these assumptions are sometimes accurate, often they are not. Not all dogs necessarily

For each of the following items, indicate the extent to which you would find such a behavior or custom "quite ordinary" or "quite strange." Use the scale below for your judgments. Why did you respond the way you did?

Quite ordinary	Ordinary	Neutral	Strange	Quite strange	
1	2	3	4	5	

1. A man wearing a skirt   _____

2. A person remaining silent upon meeting someone for the first time   _____

3. Two women holding hands in a park   _____

4. A woman breastfeeding her child in public   _____

5. Talking with someone who does not look you in the eye   _____

6. A family taking a communal bath   _____

7. Praying to many gods   _____

8. Eating a formal meal without utensils   _____

CULTURE *connections*

"The problem of the 20th century is the problem of the color line," summed up W.E.B. Du Bois in 1903. How dispiriting to realize it is the problem of the 21st century as well. . . .

But in truth there are really no public discussions of race. There are discussions of affirmative action, and single parenthood, and, in the wake of human tragedies like the Diallo killing, of police training and procedures. These are discussions designed to cause the least amount of discomfort to the smallest possible number of white people. . . .

Poll after poll shows a great gap in understanding, between a white America that believes things are ever so much better and a black America that thinks that is delusional. And that gap mirrors a gap more important than numbers, between what many of us believe we believe, and the subtle assumptions that creep into our consciousness, and which we are often unwilling to admit are there. For a long time we blamed this chasm on black men and women. We who are white expected them to teach us what it was like to be them, to make us comfortable, and we complained when they did not. . . .

America is a nation riven by geographic apartheid, with precious few truly integrated neighborhoods, particularly in the suburbs. The great divide between black and white yawns wide with the distance of ignorance, and the silence of shame.

. . . The most talkative nation on earth falls silent in the face of the enormity of the failure, of being two nations across a Mason–Dixon line of incomprehension and subtle assumptions.

—*Anna Quindlen*

growl and snap at young children. Nevertheless, information processing results in a simplification of the world, so that prior experiences are used as the basis for determining both the categories and the attributes of the events. This process is called "stereotyping."

Please note that we are describing these human tendencies nonevaluatively. Their obvious advantage is that they allow people to respond efficiently to a variety of perceptual stimuli. Nevertheless, this organization and simplification can create some genuine obstacles to intercultural competence because they may lead to prejudice, discrimination, and racism.

Ethnocentrism

All cultures teach their members the "preferred" ways to respond to the world, which are often labeled as "natural" or "appropriate." Thus, people generally perceive their own experiences, which are shaped by their own cultural forces, as natural, human, and universal. This belief that the customs and practices of one's own culture are superior to those of other cultures is called *ethnocentrism*.

Cultures also train their members to use the categories of their own cultural experiences when judging the experiences of people from other cultures. Our culture tells us that the way we were taught to behave is "right" or "correct," and those who do things differently are wrong. William G. Sumner, who first introduced the concept of ethnocentrism, defined it as "the view of things in which one's own group is the center of everything, and all others are scaled and rated with reference to it."[11] Sumner illustrates how ethnocentrism works in the following example:

> When Caribs were asked whence they came, they replied, "We alone are people." "Kiowa" means real or principal people. A Laplander is a "man" or "human being." The highest praise a Greenlander has for a European visiting the island is that the European by studying virtue and good manners from the Greenlanders soon will be as good as a Greenlander. Nature peoples call themselves "men" as a rule. All others are something else, but not men. The Jews divide all mankind into themselves and Gentiles—they being the "chosen people." The Greeks and Romans called outsiders "barbarians." Arabs considered themselves as the noblest nation and all others as barbarians. Russian books and newspapers talk about its civilizing mission, and so do the books and journals of France, Germany, and the United States. Each nation now regards itself as the leader of civilization, the best, the freest, and the wisest. All others are inferior.[12]

Ethnocentrism is a learned belief in cultural superiority. Because cultures teach people what the world is "really like" and what is "good," people consequently believe that the values of their culture are natural and correct. Thus, people from other cultures who do things differently are wrong. When combined with the natural human tendency to prefer what is typically experienced, ethnocentrism produces emotional reactions to cultural differences that reduce people's willingness to understand disparate cultural messages.

Ethnocentrism tends to highlight and exaggerate cultural differences. As an interesting instance of ethnocentrism, consider beliefs about body odor. Most U.S. Americans spend large sums of money each year to rid themselves of natural body odor. They then replace their natural odors with artificial ones as they apply deodorants, bath powders, shaving lotions, perfumes, hair sprays, shampoos, mousse, gels, toothpaste, mouthwash, and breath mints. Many U.S. Americans probably believe that they do not have an odor—even after they have routinely applied most, if not all, of the artificial ones in the preceding list. Yet the same individuals will react negatively to culturally different others who do not remove natural body odors and who refuse to apply artificial ones.

Another example of ethnocentrism concerns the way in which cultures teach people to discharge mucus from the nose. Most U.S. Americans purchase boxes of tissues and strategically place them at various points in their homes, offices, and cars so that they will be available for use when blowing their noses. In countries where paper products have historically been scarce and very expensive, people blow their noses onto the ground or the street. Pay attention to your reaction as you read this last statement. Most U.S. Americans, when learning about this behavior, react with a certain amount of disgust. But think about the U.S. practice of blowing one's nose into a tissue or handkerchief, which is then placed on the desk or into a pocket or purse. Now ask yourself which is really more disgusting—carrying around tissues with dried mucus in them or blowing the mucus onto the street? Described in this way, both practices have a certain element of repugnance, but because one's culture teaches that there is one preferred way, that custom is familiar and comfortable and the practices of other cultures are seen as wrong or distasteful.

Ethnocentrism can occur along all of the dimensions of cultural patterns discussed in the previous two chapters. People from individualistic cultures, for instance, find the idea that a person's self-concept is tied to a group to be unfathomable. To most U.S. Americans, the idea of an arranged marriage seems strange at best and a confining and reprehensible limitation on personal freedom at worst.

One area of behavior that quickly reveals ethnocentrism is personal hygiene. For example, U.S. Americans like to see themselves as the cleanest people on earth. In the United States, bathrooms contain sinks, showers or bathtubs, and toilets, thus allowing the efficient use of water pipes. Given this arrangement, people bathe themselves in close proximity to the toilet, where they urinate and defecate. Described in this way, the cultural practices of the United States may seem unclean, peculiar, or even absurd. Why would people in a so-called modern society place two such contradictory functions next to each other? People from many other cultures, who consider the U.S. arrangement to be unclean and unhealthy, share that sentiment. Our point here is that what is familiar and comfortable inevitably seems the best, right, and natural way of doing things. Judgments about what is "right" or "natural" create emotional responses to cultural differences that may interfere with our ability to understand the symbols used by other cultures. For example, European Americans think it is "human nature" to orient oneself to the future and to want to improve one's material status in life. Individuals whose cultures have been influenced by alternative forces, resulting in contrary views, are often judged negatively and treated with derision.

To be a competent intercultural communicator, you must realize that you typically use the categories of your own culture to judge and interpret the behaviors of those who are culturally different from you. You must also be aware of your own emotional reactions to the sights, sounds, smells, and variations in message systems that you encounter when communicating with people from other cultures. The competent intercultural communicator does not necessarily suppress negative feelings, but ac-

The depiction of harmful stereotypes in TV shows like "The Lone Ranger" and films such as "Gone with the Wind" are common even today. Such images underscore the links between media portrayals of various cultural groups and everyday prejudices.

knowledges their existence and seeks to minimize their effect on her or his communication. If you are reacting strongly to some aspect of another culture, seek out an explanation in the ethnocentric preferences that your culture has taught you.

Stereotyping

Journalist Walter Lippmann introduced the term *stereotyping* in 1922 to refer to a selection process that is used to organize and simplify perceptions of others.[13] Stereotypes are a form of generalization about some group of people. When people stereotype others, they take a category of people and make assertions about the characteristics of all people who belong to that category. The consequence of stereotyping is that the vast degree of differences that exists among the members of any one group may not be taken into account in the interpretation of messages.

To illustrate how stereotyping works, read the following list: college professors, surfers, Marxists, Democrats, bankers, New Yorkers, Californians. Probably, as you read each of these categories, it was relatively easy for you to associate particular characteristics and traits with each group. Now imagine that a person from one of these groups walked into the room and began a conversation with you. In all likelihood you would associate the group's characteristics with that specific individual.

Your responses to this simple example illustrate what typically occurs when people are stereotyped.[14] First, someone identifies an outgroup category—"they"—whose characteristics differ from those in one's own social ingroup. Next, the perceived dissimilarities between the groups are enlarged and accentuated, thereby creating differences that are clearer and more distinct. By making sharper and more pronounced boundaries between the groups, it becomes more difficult for individuals to move from one group to another.[15] Concurrently, an evaluative component is introduced, whereby the characteristics of the outgroup are negatively judged; that is, the outgroup is regarded as wrong, inferior, or stigmatized as a result of given characteristics. Finally, the group's characteristics are attributed to all people who belong to the group, so that a specific person is not treated as a unique individual but as a typical member of a category.

Categories that are used to form stereotypes about groups of people can vary widely, and they might include the following:

▶ Regions of the world (Asians, Arabs, South Americans, Africans)
▶ Countries (Kenya, Japan, China, France, Great Britain)
▶ Regions within countries (northern Indians, southern Indians, U.S. Midwesterners, U.S. Southerners)
▶ Cities (New Yorkers, Parisians, Londoners)
▶ Cultures (English, French, Latino, Russian, Serbian, Yoruba, Mestizo, Thai, Navajo)
▶ Race (African, Caucasian)
▶ Religion (Muslim, Hindu, Buddhist, Jewish, Christian)
▶ Age (young, old, middle-aged, children, adults)
▶ Occupations (teacher, farmer, doctor, housekeeper, mechanic, architect, musician)
▶ Relational roles (mother, friend, father, sister, brother)
▶ Physical characteristics (short, tall, fat, skinny)
▶ Social class (wealthy, poor, middle class)

This list is by no means exhaustive. What it should illustrate is the enormous range of possibilities for classification and simplification. Consider your own stereotypes of people in these groups. Many may have been created by direct experience with only one or two people from a particular group. Others are probably based on second-hand information and opinions, output from the mass media, and general habits of thinking; they may even have been formed without any direct experience with individuals from the group. Yet many people are prepared to assume that their stereotypes are accurate representations of all members of specific groups.[16] Interestingly, stereotypes that are based on second-hand opinions—that is, stereotypes that are derived from the opinions of others or from the media—tend to be more extreme, less variable from one person to another, more uniformly applied to others, and more resistant to change than are stereotypes based on direct personal experiences and interactions.[17]

Stereotypes can be inaccurate in three ways.[18] First, as we have suggested, stereotypes often are assumed to apply to all or most of the members of a particular group or category, resulting in a tendency to ignore differences among the individual members of the group. This type of stereotyping error is called the *outgroup homogeneity effect* and results in a tendency to regard all members of a particular group as much more similar to one another than they actually are.[19] Arab Americans, for instance, complain that other U.S. Americans often hold undifferentiated stereotypes about members of their culture. Albert Mokhiber laments that

> [i]f there's problem in Libya we're all Libyans. If the problem is in Lebanon we're all Lebanese. If it happens to be Iran, which is not an Arab country, we're all Iranians. Conversely, Iranians were picked on during the Gulf War as being Arabs. Including one fellow who called in who was a Polynesian Jew. But he looked like what an Arab should look like, and he felt the wrath of anti-Arab discrimination. Nobody's really free from this. The old civil rights adage says that as long as the rights of one are in danger, we're all in danger. I think we need to break out of our ethnic ghetto mentality, all of us, from various backgrounds, and realize that we're in this stew together.[20]

A second form of stereotype inaccuracy occurs when the group average, as suggested by the stereotype, is simply wrong or inappropriately exaggerated. This type of inaccuracy occurs, for instance, when Germans are stereotypically regarded as being very efficient, or perhaps very rigid, when they may actually be less efficient or less rigid than the exaggerated perception of them would warrant.

A third form of stereotype inaccuracy occurs when the degree of error and exaggeration differs for positive and negative attributes. For instance, imagine that you have stereotyped a culture as being very efficient (a positive attribute) but also very rigid and inflexible in their business relationships (a negative attribute). If you tend to overestimate the prevalence and importance of the culture's positive characteristics, such as its degree of efficiency,

Make a list of the stereotypes that you think others hold about your culture. In your view, how accurate are they generally? To what extent are the stereotypes correct for you?

while simultaneously ignoring or underestimating its rigidity and other negative characteristics, you would have a "positive valence inaccuracy." Conversely, a "negative valence inaccuracy" occurs if you exaggerate the negative attributes while ignoring or devaluing its positive ones. This latter condition, often called *prejudice,* will be discussed in greater detail below.

The problems associated with using stereotyping as a means of understanding individuals is best illustrated by identifying the groups to which you belong. Think about the characteristics that might be stereotypically assigned to those groups. Determine whether the characteristics apply to you or to others in your group. Some of them may be accurate descriptions; many, however, will be totally inaccurate, and you would resent being thought of in that way. Stereotypes distort or hide the individual. Ultimately, people may become blind to the actual characteristics of the group because not all stereotypes are accurate. Most are based on relatively minimal experiences with particular individuals.

Stereotype inaccuracy can lead to errors in interpretations and expectations about the behaviors of others. Interpretation errors occur because stereotypes are used not only to categorize specific individuals and events but also to judge them. That is, one potentially harmful consequence of stereotypes is that they provide inaccurate labels for a group of people, which are then used to interpret subsequent ambiguous events and experiences involving members of those groups. As Ziva Kunda and Bonnie Sherman-Williams note,

> Consider, for example, the unambiguous act of failing a test. Ethnic stereotypes may lead perceivers to attribute such failure to laziness if the actor is Asian but to low ability if the actor is Black. Thus stereotypes will affect judgments of the targets' ability even if subjects base these judgments only on the act, because the stereotypes will determine the meaning of the act.[21]

Because stereotypes are sometimes applied indiscriminately to members of a particular culture or social group, they can also lead to errors in one's expectations about the future behaviors of others. Stereotypes provide the bases for estimating, often inaccurately, what members of the stereotyped group are likely to do. Most disturbingly, stereotypes will likely persist even when members of the stereotyped group repeatedly behave in ways that disconfirm them. Once a stereotype has taken hold, members of the stereotyped group who behave in nonstereotypical ways will be expected to compensate in their future actions in order to "make up for" their atypical behavior. Even when some individuals from a stereotyped group repeatedly deviate from expectations, they may be regarded as exceptions or as atypical members of their group. Indeed, stereotypes may remain intact, or may even be strengthened, in the face of disconfirming experiences; those who hold the stereotypes often expect that the other members of the stereotyped social group will be even *more* likely to behave as the stereotype predicts, in order to "balance out" or compensate for the "unusual" instances that they experienced. That is, stereotypes encourage people to expect future behaviors that compensate for perceived inconsistencies and thus allow people to anticipate future events in a way that makes it unnecessary to revise their deeply held beliefs and values.[22]

The process underlying stereotyping is absolutely essential for human beings to function. Some categorization is necessary and normal. Indeed, there is survival value in the ability to make accurate generalizations about others, and stereotypes function as mental "energy-saving devices" to help make those generalizations efficiently.[23] However, stereotypes may also promote prejudice and discrimination directed toward members of cultures other than one's own. Intercultural competence requires an ability to move beyond stereotypes and to respond to the individual. Previous experiences should be used only as guidelines or suggested interpretations rather than as hard-and-fast categories. Judee Burgoon, Charles Berger, and Vincent Waldron suggest that mindfulness—that is, paying conscious attention to the nature and basis of one's stereotypes—can help to reduce stereotype inaccuracies and thereby decrease intercultural misunderstandings.[24]

Prejudice

Prejudice refers to negative attitudes toward other people that are based on faulty and inflexible stereotypes. Prejudiced attitudes include irrational feelings of dislike and even hatred for certain groups, biased perceptions and beliefs about the group members that are not based on direct experiences and first-hand knowledge, and a readiness to behave in negative and unjust ways toward members of the group. Gordon Allport, who first focused scholarly attention on prejudice, argued that prejudiced people ignore evidence that is inconsistent with their biased viewpoint, or they distort the evidence to fit their prejudices.[25]

The strong link between prejudice and stereotypes should be obvious. Prejudiced thinking is dependent on stereotypes and is a fairly normal phenomenon.[26] To be prejudiced toward a group of people sometimes makes it easier to respond to them. We are not condoning prejudice or the hostile and violent actions that may occur as a result of prejudice. We are suggesting that prejudice is a universal psychological process; all people have a propensity for prejudice toward others who are unlike themselves. For individuals to move beyond prejudicial attitudes and for societies to avoid basing social structures on their prejudices about groups of people, it is critical to recognize the prevalence of prejudicial thinking.

What functions does prejudice serve? We have already suggested that the thought process underlying prejudice includes the need to organize and simplify the world. Richard Brislin describes four additional benefits, or what he calls functions, of prejudice.[27] First, he suggests that prejudice satisfies a *utilitarian* or adjustment function. Displaying certain kinds of prejudice means that people receive rewards and avoid punishments. For example, if you express prejudicial statements about certain people, other people may like you more. It is also easier to simply dislike and be prejudiced toward members of other groups because they can then be dismissed without going through the effort necessary to adjust to them. Another function that prejudice serves is an *ego-defensive* one; it protects self-esteem.[28] If others say or do things that are inconsistent with the images we hold of ourselves, our sense of self may be deeply threatened, and we may try to maintain our self-esteem by scorning the sources of the message. So, for example, people who are unsuccessful in business may feel threatened by groups whose members are successful. Prejudice may function to protect one's self-image by denigrating or devaluing those who might make us feel less worthy.[29] Still another advantage of prejudicial attitudes is the *value-expressive* function. If people believe that their group has certain qualities that are unique, valuable, good, or in some way special, their prejudicial attitudes toward others is a way of expressing those values. Finally, Brislin describes the *knowledge function* as prejudicial attitudes that people hold because of their need to have the world neatly organized and boxed into categories.

The language of stereotyping and prejudice is subtle but powerful. Notice the important difference between labeling someone as an "undocumented immigrant" versus an "illegal alien."

This function takes the normal human proclivity to organize the world to an extreme. The rigid application of categories and the prejudicial attitudes assigned to certain behaviors and beliefs provide security and increase predictability. Obviously, these functions cannot be neatly applied to all instances of prejudice. Nor are people usually aware of the specific reasons for their prejudices. For each person, prejudicial attitudes may serve several functions.

CULTURE *connections*

Dawoud remembers an incident in fourth grade when one of the little girls got her lunch stolen, and he looked up to find the teacher singling him out. He saw her cold stare and her accusatory finger waving in his face, and he felt baffled and confused. "I was innocent, I didn't even get the connection. 'Me?' I stammered. 'Are you talking to *me*?" asked Dawoud in a sweat. Yes, she meant *him,* and he was to go down to the guidance office immediately. He was the culprit. There was no doubt in her mind. Dawoud rose up from his seat, walked the long march to the door amid the quiet stares of his classmates, and dutifully took himself to the guidance office, where the counselor interpreted his "acting out" as some kind of "mental problem" and gave him some "weird" tests "putting square pegs in round holes." In Dawoud's memory this is one story among many. "I'd get singled out. Much of the time I was in a conflicted state. There were strange things going on, but what do you say? I couldn't name what was happening, and I couldn't find the words or the courage to ask."

The following year, in fifth grade, he remembers that the class was writing a group play about Colonial America, and the play was to be written in verse. Dawoud loved the assignment and he leapt right into the middle of the work. "I *loved* writing poetry. It was a breeze for me. So I started knocking this stuff out." The teacher was gratified by the way her class pulled off the assignment so quickly and with such apparent ease and mature collaboration. She inquired of everyone how they had been so incredibly productive, and the children all pointed to Dawoud, who smiled back shyly. "I remember," says Dawoud with hurt in his eyes, "how her expression changed in that moment. The raised eyebrow, the amazement, the surprise." She must have applauded his inspired work and thanked him for his contribution. But the only thing that Dawoud can remember is her utter bafflement and *his* inner confusion. "The teacher was unable to reconcile my brightness with her stereotype of me. How could this black boy produce this verse? She seemed *tormented* by this. It was always this way in elementary school. At the same moment I'd receive these great commendations, and be sent off to the guidance counselor."

—*Sara Lawrence-Lightfoot*

Discrimination

Whereas *prejudice* refers to people's attitudes or mental representations, the term *discrimination* refers to the behavioral manifestations of that prejudice. Thus discrimination can be thought of as prejudice "in action."

Discrimination can occur in many forms. From the extremes of segregation and apartheid to biases in the availability of housing, employment, education, economic resources, personal safety, and legal protections, discrimination represents unequal treatment of certain individuals solely because of their membership in a particular group.

Teun van Dijk has conducted a series of studies of people's everyday conversations as they discussed different racial and cultural groups. Van Dijk concludes that when individuals make prejudicial comments, tell jokes that belittle and dehumanize others, and share negative stereotypes about others, they are establishing and legitimizing the existence of their prejudices and are laying the "communication groundwork" that will make it acceptable for people to perform discriminatory acts.[30]

Often, biases and displays of discrimination are motivated not by direct hostility toward some other group but merely by a strong preference for, and loyalty to, one's own culture.[31] Thus, the formation of one's cultural identity, which we discussed earlier in this chapter, can sometimes lead to hostility, hate, and discrimination directed against nonmembers of that culture.

Racism

One obstacle to intercultural competence to which we want to give special attention is racism. Because racism often plays such a major role in the communication that occurs between people of different races or ethnic groups, it is particularly important to understand how and why it occurs.

The word *racism* itself can evoke very powerful emotional reactions, especially for those who have felt the oppression and exploitation that stems from racist attitudes and behaviors. For members of the African American, Asian American, Native American, and Latino cultures, racism has created a social history shaped by prejudice and discrimination.[32] For individual members of these groups, racism has resulted in the pain of oppression. To those who are members of cultural groups that have had the power to oppress and exploit others, the term *racism* often evokes equally powerful thoughts and emotional reactions that deny responsibility for and participation in racist acts and thinking. In this section, we want to introduce some ideas about racism that illuminate the reactions of both those who have received racist communication and those who are seen as exhibiting it.

Robert Blauner has described racism as a tendency to categorize people who are culturally different in terms of their physical traits, such as skin color, hair color and texture, facial structure, and eye shape.[33] Dalmas Taylor offers a related approach that

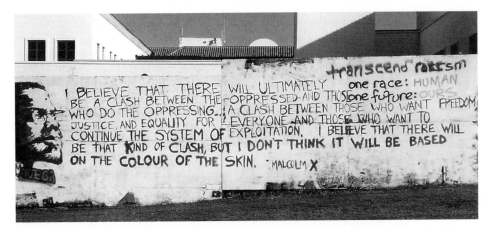

Racism is a force with which both individuals and social systems must grapple.

focuses on the behavioral components of racism. Taylor defines racism as the cumulative effects of individuals, institutions, and cultures that result in the oppression of ethnic minorities.[34] Taylor's approach is useful in that it recognizes that racism can occur at three distinct levels: individual, institutional, and cultural.

At the individual level, racism is conceptually very similar to prejudice. Individual racism involves beliefs, attitudes, and behaviors of a given person toward people of a different racial group.[35] Specific European Americans, for example, who believe that African Americans are somehow inferior, exemplify individual racism. Positive contact and interaction between members of the two groups can sometimes change these attitudes. Yet as the preceding discussion of prejudice suggests, people with prejudicial beliefs about others often distort new information to fit their original prejudices.

At the institutional level, racism is the exclusion of certain people from equal participation in the society's institutions solely because of their race.[36] Institutional racism is built into such social structures as the government, schools, the media, and industry practices. It leads to certain patterns of behaviors and responses to specific racial or cultural groups that allow those groups to be systematically exploited and oppressed. For example, institutional racism has precluded both Jews and African Americans from attending certain public schools and universities, and at times it has restricted their participation in particular professions.[37] Repeated instances of institutional racism, which commonly appear in the popular media, can be especially difficult to overcome. By focusing on some topics or characteristics and not on others, the media often "prime" people's attention and thereby influence the interpretations and evaluations one makes of others. Such biased portrayals can be particularly salient when the media provide people's primary or only knowledge of particular cultures and their members. Consider, for example, Elizabeth Bird's insightful analysis of the ways in which Native Americans are marginalized by the popular media's portrayal of their sexuality:

> The representations we see are structured in predictable, gendered ways. Women are faceless, rather sexless squaws in minor roles, or sexy exotic princesses or maidens who desire White men. Men are either handsome young warriors, who desire White women, or safe sexless wise elders, who dispense ancient wisdom. Nowhere, in this iconography, do the male and female images meet. The world where American Indian men and women love, laugh, and couple *together* lurks far away in the shadows. These days, representations of American Indians are more accurate, in terms of costume, cultural detail, and the like than in the 1950s, when White actors darkened their skins to play American Indians. As far as suggesting an authentic, subjective American Indian experience, though, there has been little progress.[38]

As Bird concludes of such portrayals, "the lovely princess and American Indian lover of the 1990s may be more benign images than the squaw or the crazed savage, but they are equally unreal, and ultimately, equally dehumanizing."[39]

At the cultural level, racism denies the existence of the culture of a particular group,[40] for example, the denial that African Americans represent a unique and distinct culture that is separate from both European American culture and all African cultures. Cultural racism also involves the rejection by one group of the beliefs and values of another, such as the "negative evaluations by whites of black cultural values."[41]

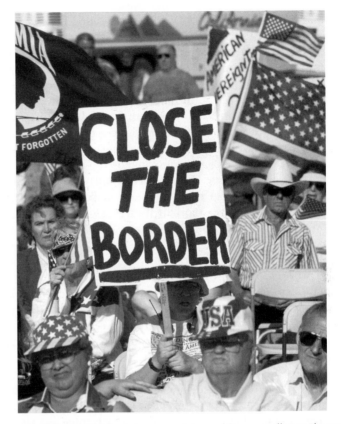

Racism is a potent and destructive force in any society, and it occurs all over the world. These European Americans are demonstrating against the current US immigration policies.

Though racism is often used synonymously with *prejudice* and *discrimination,* the social attributes that distinguish it from these other terms are oppression and power. Oppression refers to "the systematic, institutionalized mistreatment of one group of people by another."[42] Thus racism is the tendency by groups in control of institutional and cultural power to use it to keep members of groups who do not have access to the same kinds of power at a disadvantage. Racism oppresses entire groups of people, making it very difficult, and sometimes virtually impossible, for their members to have access to political, economic, and social power.[43]

Forms of racism vary in intensity and degree of expression, with some forms far more dangerous and detrimental to society than others. The most extreme form of racism is *old-fashioned racism.* Here, members of one group openly display obviously bigoted views about those from another group. Judgments of superiority and inferiority are commonplace in this kind of racism, and there is a dehumanizing quality to it. African Americans and other cultural groups in the United States have often experienced this form of racism from other U.S. Americans.

Symbolic racism, which is sometimes called *modern racism,* is currently prevalent in the United States. In symbolic racism, members of a group with political and economic power believe that members of some other group threaten their traditional values, such as individualism and self-reliance. Fears that the outgroup will achieve economic or social success, with a simultaneous loss of economic or social status by the ingroup, typify this form of racism. In many parts of the United States, for instance, this type of racism has been directed toward Asians and Asian Americans who are accused of being too "pushy" because they have achieved economic success. Similarly, symbolic racism includes the expression of feelings that members of cultures such as African Americans and Mexican Americans are moving too fast in seeking social change, are too demanding of equality and social justice, are not playing by the "rules" established in previous generations, and simply do not deserve all that they have recently gained. Paradoxically, while symbolic racists typically do not feel personally threatened by the successes of other cultures, they fear for their core values and the continued maintenance of their political and economic power.[44]

Tokenism as a form of racism occurs when individuals do not perceive themselves as prejudiced because they make small concessions to, while holding basically negative attitudes toward, members of the other group. Tokenism is the practice of reverse discrimination, in which people go out of their way to favor a few members of another group in order to maintain their own self-concepts as individuals who believe in equality for all. While such behaviors may increase a person's esteem, they may also decrease the possibilities for more meaningful contributions to intercultural unity and progress.

Aversive racism, like tokenism, occurs when individuals who highly value fairness and equality among all racial and cultural groups nevertheless have negative beliefs and feelings about members of a particular race, often as a result of childhood socialization experiences. Individuals with such conflicting feelings may restrain their overt racist behaviors, but they may also avoid close contact with members of the other group and may express their underlying negative attitudes subtly, in ways that appear rational and that can be justified on the basis of some factor other than race or culture. Thus the negativity of aversive racists "is more likely to be manifested in discomfort, uneasiness, fear, or avoidance of minorities rather than overt hostility."[45] An individual at work, for instance, may be polite but distant to a co-worker from another culture but may avoid that person at a party they both happen to attend.

Genuine likes and dislikes may also operate as a form of racism. The cultural practices of some groups of people can form the basis for a prejudicial attitude simply because the group displays behaviors that another group does not like. For example, individuals from cultures that are predominantly vegetarian may develop negative attitudes toward those who belong to cultures that eat meat.

Finally, the least alarming form of racism, and certainly one that everyone has experienced, is based on the *degree of unfamiliarity* with members of other groups. Simply responding to unfamiliar people may create negative attitudes because of a lack of experience with the characteristics of their group. The others may look, smell, talk, or act differently, all of which can be a source of discomfort and can form the basis for racist or prejudicial attitudes.

Intercultural Contact

Many people believe that creating the opportunity for personal contact fosters positive attitudes toward members of other groups. Indeed, this assumption provides the rationale for numerous international exchange programs for high school and college students. There are also international "sister city" programs, wherein a U.S. city pairs itself with a city in another country and encourages the residents of both cities to visit with and stay in one another's homes. Sometimes, of course, intercultural contact does overcome the obstacles of cultural distance, and positive attitudes between those involved do result.

Unfortunately, there is a great deal of historical and contemporary evidence to suggest that contact between members of different cultures does not always lead to good feelings. In fact, under many circumstances such contact only reinforces negative attitudes or may even change a neutral attitude into a negative one. For instance, tourists in other countries are sometimes repelled by the inhabitants, and immigrants to the United States have not always been accepted by the communities into which they have settled. In some communities and among some people, there is still much prejudice and negative feeling between European Americans and African Americans. The factors that lead to cordial and courteous interactions among people from different cultural groups are very complicated. One factor, that of access to and control of institutional and economic power, strongly influences attitudes between members of different cultures.

Dominance and Subordination between Groups

Not all groups within a nation or region or on the same continent have equal access to sources of institutional and economic power. When cultures share the same political, geographic, and economic landscapes, some form of a status hierarchy often develops. Groups of people who are distinguished by their religious, political, cultural, or ethnic identity often struggle among themselves for dominance and control of the available economic and political resources.

CULTURE *connections*

"I'm Kate Shugak," she said. "I met your wife at church this morning."

"Kate Shugak?" She nodded. "Any relation to Ekaterina Shugak?" She nodded again. He took in the color of her skin and the epicanthic folds of her eyes, she the slant of his cheekbones and the thick, straight black hair. He didn't say, "Aleut?" and she didn't say, "Athabaskan?" but they both relaxed a little, the way people of color always do when the door closes after the last white person has left the room.

—*Dana Stabenow*

Recent examples of these "culture clashes" include the events in Eastern Europe. Yugoslavia, for instance, was a country that was held together for decades by a strong and repressive dictator. Now the country is in a virtual civil war because the Serbians and Croatians, which are the major cultural groups in that region, have historically felt animosity toward each other and are unable to work cooperatively to maintain a nation-state. Similarly, the loss of control by the Soviet Union's central government, coupled with economic hardships and political turmoil, has resulted in outbreaks of violence between members of cultural groups sharing the same territory within the former USSR. In the United States, racial tensions between African Americans and European Americans have resulted in numerous incidents. Immigrants from various parts of the world have experienced open hostility, and sometimes violent reactions, from people who live in areas where they have settled. When these kinds of competitive tensions characterize the political and economic setting in which individuals from differing cultures interact, intercultural communication is obviously affected.

A cultural group that has primary access to institutional and economic power is often characterized as *dominant* or as the *majority*. As we indicated in Chapter 1, we find these terms imprecise when describing cultural groups in the United States. Now, however, we choose to use the term *dominant* to refer to institutional and economic power.

Scholars have given considerable attention to the influence of dominant and subordinate group membership on interpersonal and intercultural communication processes.[46] The results of their investigations suggest that there is a very interesting set of relationships among the factors that affect these interactions. For instance, members of dominant cultures will often devalue the language styles of subordinate cultural members and judge the "correctness" of their use of preferred speech patterns. In some cases, members of subordinate cultures will try to accommodate or adapt their speech to that of the dominant culture. In other circumstances, they will very deliberately emphasize their group's unique speech characteristics when they are in the presence of people from the dominant culture.

As we will discuss in the next chapter, special forms of language are often used to signal identification among members of the subordinate group and to indicate a lack of submission to the dominant group. Similarly, members of the dominant group are likely to retain the special characteristics of their language, including preferences for certain words, accents, and linguistic patterns, and may therefore devalue the linguistic patterns of others. For example, there are instances in which European Americans have devalued the use of Black Standard English.[47]

Attitudes among Cultural Members

Our focus in this section is on the attitudes that form among members of cultures that have frequent contact with one another. In his classic study, Amir describes four conditions that are likely to lead to positive attitudes as a result of intercultural communication: (1) There is support from the top; that is, a person who is in charge, or who is recognized as an authority, organizes and supports the intercultural contact. (2) Those involved have a personal stake in the outcome, so the interactions are regarded as personal rather than casual. (3) The intercultural contacts are pleasing and pleasant. (4) All parties benefit from the contact; that is, members of both cultures have common goals or view the interaction as allowing them to achieve their own individual goals.[48]

Recent investigations suggest that four additional factors also affect attitudes and outcomes. One is the strength of identification that the members of a culture have for their cultural group. Do the individuals in an encounter think of the person with whom they are interacting as a unique individual, or do they view that person primarily as a representative of a different cultural group? Similarly, do the interactants view themselves as unique individuals or as representatives of particular cultural groups? One study finds that the outcomes of intercultural encounters depend on the extent to which cultural identities are seen as an important component of people's interpersonal identities.[49] Identification with their culture increases if they have a relatively high status within the group, as well as if the bonds to their culture are strong and all their friends and social networks are associated with it.

Intercultural communication outcomes are also affected by the degree of perceived threat. If the members of a culture believe that certain fundamental aspects of their cultural identity—such as their language and special characteristics—are threatened, they are likely to increase their identification with their culture, and intercultural contacts are less likely to be favorable. Even groups that are in the majority sometimes see the presence of people from other cultures as threatening. For example, consider the perceived threat and consequent reactions of U.S. Americans to immigrants who are willing to work for a lower wage.

Another factor is the degree of typicality with which the other interactants are viewed. That is, participants in intercultural encounters make a judgment about the degree to which specific individuals are typical or atypical of their culture, which in turn influences the positive or negative character of their attitudes. More important, typicality affects the likelihood that experiences with one member of a culture are generalized to other members of that culture.[50] For example, if someone is viewed as unique and unrepresentative of the typical members of a culture, a positive experience with that individual will not necessarily result in positive attitudes toward other people from the same cultural group.

The nature of the interactants' cultural stereotypes is another factor in intercultural contacts. Miles Hewstone and Howard Giles propose that these stereotypes are used as filters to assess the behaviors of members of other groups.[51] They also suggest that if a person does not conform to the cultural stereotype in some important way, that person is dismissed as atypical. Consequently, negative stereotypes toward the culture can persist even when there are positive and favorable interactions with a member of the culture.

Outcomes of Intercultural Contact

Both fictional and nonfictional accounts of intercultural contacts are replete with references to individual and cultural changes. References are made to people who "go native" and who seem to adjust or adapt to life in the new culture. References are also made to those who retain their own cultural identity by using only their original language and by living in cultural ghettos. During the height of the British Empire in India, for example, many British officials and their families tried to recreate the British lifestyle in India, in a climate not conducive to tuxedos and fancy dresses, with layers and layers of slips and decorative fabrics.

CULTURE *connections*

I took a drink from every bottle held out to me. The man leaned over and slapped my knee—I was a good chap, I did not get drunk and fall on the floor. They laughed. I smiled to show I was cheerful and friendly, but I couldn't laugh because I didn't know what they were laughing at.

This, I thought, is what being a foreigner is really all about. It is not wandering through a strange country seeing unfamiliar people: it's when all the unfamiliar people stare at *you*, and find *you* strange; when you can't fit anonymously into a crowd; when your passing is an uncommon event. It's when you don't understand the joke, and the joke may very well be you.

—*Liza Cody*

It is generally accepted that intercultural communication creates stress for most individuals. In intercultural communication, the certainty of one's own cultural framework is gone, and there is a great deal of uncertainty about what other code systems mean. Individuals who engage in intercultural contacts for extended periods of time will respond to the stress in different ways. Most will find themselves incorporating at least some behaviors from the new culture into their own repertoire. Some take on the characteristics, the norms, and even the values and beliefs of another culture willingly and easily. Others resist the new culture and retain their old ways, sometimes choosing to spend time in enclaves populated only by others like themselves. Still others simply find the problems of adjusting to a new culture to be intolerable, and they leave if they can.

People's reactions also change over time. That is, the initial reactions of acceptance or rejection often shift as increased intercultural contacts produce different kinds of outcomes. Such changes in the way people react to intercultural contacts are called *adaptation*.

Adaptation   Words such as *assimilation, adjustment, acculturation,* and even *coping* are used to describe how individuals respond to their experiences in other cultures. Many of these terms refer to how people from one culture react to prolonged contact with those from another. Over the years, different emotional overtones have been attached to these terms. To some people, for instance, *assimilation* is a negative outcome; to others it is positive. Some consider *adjustment* to be "good," whereas for others it is "bad."

We offer an approach that allows you to make your own value judgment about what constitutes the right kind of outcome. We believe that competent adjustment to another culture will vary greatly from situation to situation and from person to person. We have used the broader term of *adaptation* to characterize these adjustments because it subsumes various forms of cultural or individual adaptation.

> *Adaptation is the process by which people establish and maintain relatively stable, helpful, and mutually shared relationships with others upon relocating to an unfamiliar cultural setting.*[52]

Note that this definition suggests that when individuals adapt to another culture they must learn how to "fit" themselves into it. Again remember that different individuals and different groups will make the fit in different ways.

Adaptation includes physical, biological, and social changes. Physical changes occur because people are confronted with new physical stimuli—they eat different food, drink different water, live in different climates, and reside in different kinds of housing. When people are exposed to a new culture, they may undergo actual physical or biological changes. People deal with new viruses and bacteria; new foods cause new reactions and perhaps even new allergies. Prolonged contact between groups results in intermarriage, and the children of these marriages are born with a mixture of the genetic features of the people involved. Social relationships change with the introduction of new people. Outgroups may become bonded with the ingroups, for example, in opposition to the new outgroup members. Such changes may also cause individuals to define themselves in new and different ways.[53]

Alternatively, the culture itself might change because of the influences of people from other cultures. The French, for example, have raised concerns about the effects of the English language on their own language and culture. Traditional societies have sometimes expressed this distress about the Westernization or urbanization of their cultures.

Culture Shock versus Adaptation   Sustained intercultural contact that requires total immersion in another culture may produce a phenomenon that has sometimes been called *culture shock*. The anthropologist Kalvero Oberg, who provided an early elaboration of the term, describes some of the reasons it occurs:

> Culture shock is precipitated by the anxiety that results from losing all our familiar signs and symbols of social intercourse. These signs or cues include the thousand and one ways in which we orient ourselves to the situations of daily life: when to shake hands and what to say when we meet people, when and how to give tips, how to give orders to servants, how to make purchases, when to accept and when to refuse invitations, when to take statements seriously and when not. Now these cues, which may be words, gestures, facial expressions, customs, or norms, are acquired by all of us in the course of growing up and are as much a part of our culture as the language we speak or the beliefs we accept. All of us depend for our peace of mind and our efficiency on hundreds of these cues, most of which we are not consciously aware.[54]

That is, culture shock is said to occur when people must deal with a barrage of new perceptual stimuli that are difficult to interpret because the cultural context has changed. Things taken for granted at home require virtually constant monitoring in the new culture to assure some degree of understanding. The loss of predictability, coupled with the fatigue that results from the need to stay consciously focused on what would normally be taken for granted, produces the negative responses associated with culture shock. These can include

> excessive washing of the hands; excessive concern over drinking water, food, dishes, and bedding; fear of physical contact with attendants or servants; the absent-minded, far-away stare (sometimes called the "tropical stare"); a feeling of helplessness and a desire for dependence on long-term residents of one's own nationality; fits of anger over delays and other minor frustrations; delay and outright refusal to learn the lan-

guage of the host country; excessive fear of being cheated, robbed, or injured; great concern over minor pains and eruptions of the skin; and finally, that terrible longing to be home, to be able to have a good cup of coffee and a piece of apple pie, to walk into that corner drugstore, to visit one's relatives, and in general, to talk to people who really make sense.[55]

Often associated with culture shock are the U-curve and W-curve hypotheses of cultural adaptation. In the U-curve hypothesis, the initial intercultural contacts are characterized by a positive, almost euphoric, emotional response. As fatigue mounts and culture shock sets in, however, the individual's responses are more and more negative, until finally a low point is reached. Then, gradually, the individual develops a more positive attitude and the new culture seems less foreign, until a positive emotional response once again occurs.

The U-curve hypothesis has been extended to the W-curve, which includes the person's responses to her or his own culture upon return. It posits that a second wave of culture shock, which is similar to the first and has been called *re-entry shock,* may occur when the individual returns home and must readapt to the once taken-for-granted practices that can no longer be followed without question.[56] Some returnees to the United States, for instance, have difficulties with the pace of life, the relative affluence around them, and the seemingly superficial values espoused by the mass media. Others are frustrated when their co-workers and friends seem uninterested in their intercultural experiences, which may have changed them profoundly, but instead want simply to fill them in on "what they missed." Such re-entry problems, of course, are not confined to U.S. Americans who have been to another culture.[57] Japanese school-age children who returned from living in English-speaking countries, for instance, have

CULTURE *connections*

Many people talk a lot about "cultural shock," but no one I've heard has come close to really describing the complete emotional disruption which accompanies cultural transition. In a very real sense, all the convenient cultural cushions we have become so accustomed to having around are in one moment totally dislodged. You're left flat on your back with only that *within* you for support. "Alone in the wilderness—inadequate description. For alone you certainly are not, though in unfamiliar terrain, you are. Not alone. For you are continually surrounded by people. Every action is under scrutiny for you are *indeed* a very strange intrusion. Yet, still very alone in the sense that you lack anyone to empathize with your discomfort and disorientation. There is nothing lonelier than the feeling that there is no one with whom you can communicate; that no one understands your problems and that even when you talk with someone, though he may understand you, he really doesn't understand *you.* Everything except that people still eat, sleep, talk, laugh, cry, and defecate is strange and different.

—*David Wallender*

Describe what your culture regards as the appropriate or correct way of doing these everyday activities:

1. Eating (how, when, with whom)
2. Bathing (how, where, how often, with whom)
3. Types of food (what is edible and not edible)
4. Personal hygiene (daily regime, use of deodorants or perfumes, teeth cleaning, etc.)
5. Sleeping (where, how, with whom)
6. Driving a car (who, which side of the road, how fast)
7. Greeting someone (how, whom, when, why)

Compare your responses to those of your classmates. Are there some ways that you do things that others regard as strange, or even offensive? Are there some responses of others that you would not deem as appropriate behavior? To what extent do we use our own cultural experiences and ways of behaving to evaluate the most basic of daily tasks?

identified readjustment problems because of their differences from their peers, the precise expectations for their behaviors in school, their reduced proficiency in the Japanese language, and their interpersonal styles.[58] One girl had to dye her hair black because it had lightened from the sun. Another had to remind herself continually, "I shouldn't be different from others; I should do the same as others in doing anything."[59]

Though initially regarded as plausible, the U-curve and the W-curve hypotheses do not provide sufficiently accurate descriptions of the adaptation process. They do not account, for instance, for those whose experiences remain favorable, for those who fail to adapt and return home prematurely, or for those whose level of discomfort changes little during the adaptation period. Rather, there seem to be a variety of possible adaptation patterns that individuals could experience, depending on their particular circumstances. The pattern of adaptation varies widely from one individual to the next, and therefore no single pattern can be said to characterize the typical adaptation process.[60]

The term *culture shock* can now be seen to describe a pattern in which the individual has severe negative reactions on contact with another culture. Such extreme responses, however, in which the person's knowledge, motivation, and skills are initially insufficient to cope with the strangeness of a new culture, are among many likely reactions. We therefore prefer the more general term *adaptation* to refer to the pattern of accommodation and acculturation that results from people's contact experiences with another culture. As many theorists have suggested, it is through adaptation that personal transformation from cultural contact takes place.[61]

The Adaptation Process   Recent efforts to describe the adaptation process suggest a more complex set of patterns than the U-curve and the W-curve hypotheses provide. Daniel J. Kealey found that the U-curve was an accurate description of the adaptation process for only about 10 percent of the individuals he studied; the majority experienced little change (30 percent remained highly satisfied, 10 percent stayed moderately satisfied, and 15 percent maintained a low level of satisfaction throughout); and another 35 percent had an extremely low level of satisfaction initially but improved continuously for the duration of their intercultural assignment.[62] Interestingly, many in this latter group, which experienced the most severe adjustment stress, eventually became the most competent in their ability to function in another culture.

Adapting to another culture often requires learning to eat unfamiliar foods in unfamiliar ways.

There is also ample evidence to suggest that the adaptation process has multiple dimensions or factors associated with it.[63] For example, Mitchell R. Hammer, William B. Gudykunst, and Richard L. Wiseman have suggested that intercultural effectiveness consists of three such dimensions: the ability to deal with psychological stress, skill in communicating with others both effectively and appropriately, and proficiency in establishing interpersonal relationships.[64] Colleen Ward and her colleagues have identified just two dimensions of adaptation: psychological and sociocultural. The former is similar to Hammer and his colleagues' first dimension, and the latter seems to combine the remaining two.[65] Similarly, Guo-Ming Chen found that communicator adaptability and interaction with others were major positive contributors to international students' ability to cope with adjustment difficulties in the United States.[66]

Despite such distinctions, however, the adaptation process has usually been viewed as a single "package" of related features that all follow the same trajectory of change for a given individual. However, distinct patterns of change likely characterize each dimension of adaptation. Thus, for instance, the time it takes to adjust to the pace of life in an unfamiliar culture may be very different from the rate of adaptation to the culture's expectations regarding the use of indirection in language.

Types of Adaptation   Answers to two important questions shape the response of individuals and groups to prolonged intercultural contact, thus producing different outcomes. The first concern is whether it is considered important to maintain one's cultural identity and to display its characteristics. The second concern involves whether people believe it is important to maintain relationships with their outgroups.[67]

Assimilation occurs when it is deemed relatively unimportant to maintain one's original cultural identity but it is important to establish and maintain relationships with other cultures. The metaphor of the United States as a melting pot, which envisions many cultures giving up their individual characteristics to build the new, homogenized cultural identity of the United States, illustrates the choice described in Figure 6.1 as assimilation. Assimilation means taking on the new culture's beliefs, values, and norms.

When an individual or group retains its original cultural identity while seeking to maintain harmonious relationships with other cultures, *integration* occurs. Countries such as Switzerland, Belgium, and Canada, with their multilingual and multicultural populations, are good examples. Integration produces distinguishable cultural groups that work cooperatively to ensure that the society and the individuals continue to function well. Both integration and assimilation promote harmony and result in an appropriate fit of individuals and groups to the larger culture.

When individuals or groups do not want to maintain positive relationships with members of other groups, the outcomes are starkly different. If a culture does not want positive relationships with another culture and if it also wishes to retain its cultural characteristics, *separation* may result. If the separation occurs because the more politically and economically powerful culture does not want the intercultural contact, the result of the forced separation is called *segregation*. The history of the United States provides numerous examples of segregation in its treatment of African Americans. If, however, a nondominant group chooses not to participate in the larger society in order to retain its own way of life, the separation is called *seclusion*. The Amish are a good example of this choice.

When individuals or groups neither retain their cultural heritage nor maintain positive contacts with the other groups, *marginalization* occurs. This form of adaptation is characterized by confusion and alienation. The choices of marginalization and separation are reactions against other cultures. The fit these outcomes achieve in the adaptation process is based on battling against, rather than working with, the other cultures in the social environment.[68]

For purposes of simplification, Figure 6.1 suggests that each of the questions must be answered as wholly "yes" or "no." In reality, however, people could choose a variety

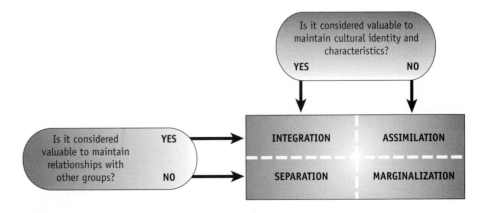

FIGURE 6.1

Forms of acculturation.

Source: John W. Berry, Uichol Kim, and Pawel Boski, "Psychological Acculturation of Immigrants," *Cross-Cultural Adaptation: Current Approaches,* ed. Young Yun Kim and William B. Gudykunst (Newbury Park, CA: Sage, 1988).

of points between these two extremes. The French, for example, while certainly not isolationists, have raised concerns about the effects of the English language on their own language and culture. Similarly, traditional societies have sometimes been distressed about the Westernization or urbanization of their cultures while simultaneously expressing a desire for increased contact and trade.

Becoming an Interculturally Competent Communicator

Obviously, not all individuals acculturate similarly. Some find the daily challenges of responding to another culture to be too stressful and overwhelming. If possible, such individuals will choose to return to their culture of origin; if they cannot do so, various kinds of maladaptive adjustments, or even mental illnesses, can occur.

At the opposite extreme, and of particular interest to us, are those individuals who move easily among many cultures. Such people generally have a profound respect for many varied points of view and are able to understand others and to communicate appropriately and effectively with people from a variety of cultures. Such individuals are able to project a sense of self that transcends any particular cultural group.

Young Yun Kim and Brent Ruben use the term *intercultural transformation* to describe the process by which individuals move beyond the thoughts, feelings, and behaviors of their initial cultural framework to incorporate other cultural realities. The process can be described as follows:

> The process of becoming intercultural—of personal transformation from cultural to intercultural—is a process of growth beyond one's original cultural conditioning. One consequence of extensive communication experiences and the subsequent internal transformation is the development of a cultural identity that is far from being "frozen." An intercultural person's cultural identity is characteristically open to further transformation and growth. This does not mean that a highly intercultural person's identity

CULTURE *connections*

Too often, to talk about identity in America is to hiss and boo. Blacks attack Jews, Hispanics attack blacks, Irish attack Italians, straights ridicule gays, feminists accuse men. And vice versa—a spiral, never-ending vice versa. To be secure in one's own group, it seems, requires denouncing everyone else. *Denuncio ergo sum.*

People are who they are by championing the superiority of their personal identity—superiority of heritage, of pigmentation and, most especially, of what Saul Bellow calls "the ideological fuse." Sometimes Americans seem to approach society as a boxing ring where everyone is free to defend himself from his own corner. The outcome is predictable—separatism and grand claims to a universal Truth.

—*Ilan Stavans*

is culture-free or cultureless. Rather, it is not rigidly bound by membership to any one particular culture. . . . A second consequence [of an intercultural transformation] . . . is a cognitive structure that enables a broadened and deepened understanding of human conditions and cultural differences and a view of things that are larger than any one cultural perspective. . . . The increased cognitive depth and breadth is, in turn, likely to facilitate corresponding emotional and behavioral capacities as well.[69]

Interculturally competent communicators integrate a wide array of culture-general knowledge into their behavioral repertoires, and they are able to apply that knowledge to the specific cultures with which they interact. They are also able to respond emotionally and behaviorally with a wide range of choices in order to act appropriately and effectively within the constraints of each situation. They have typically had extensive intercultural communication experiences, and they have learned to adjust to alternative patterns of thinking and behaving.

Identity, Biases, Contact, and Intercultural Competence

In Chapters 4 and 5 we suggested that learning about the preferences that describe your own culture's patterns, in order to understand better your own beliefs, values, and norms, was an important step toward improving intercultural competence. The discussion of cultural identity in this chapter should serve to reinforce this guideline. A good place to begin is by describing your own cultural identity. Is this relatively easy for you to do? Have you always been aware of your cultural background, or have you experienced events that have caused you to search for an understanding of your cultural identity? Do you place your cultural identity primarily in one cultural group or in several cultural groups? How does your cultural identity shape your social and personal identity? Does your cultural identity result in a strong sense of others as either in or out of your cultural group? If so, were you taught to evaluate negatively those who are not part of your cultural group? Conversely, do you sometimes feel excluded from and evaluated negatively by people from cultures that differ from your own? The answers to these questions will help you to understand the possible consequences, both positive and negative, of your cultural identity as you communicate interculturally.

In order to improve your intercultural competence by building positive motivations, or emotional reactions, to intercultural interactions, take an honest inventory of the various ways in which you categorize other people. Can you identify your obvious ethnocentric attitudes about appearance, food, and social practices? Make a list of the stereotypes, both positive and negative, that you hold about the various cultural groups with which you regularly interact. Now identify those stereotypes that others might hold about your culture. By engaging in this kind of self-reflective process, you are becoming more aware of the ways in which your social categorizations detract from an ability to understand communication from culturally different others.

Ethnocentrism, stereotyping, prejudice, discrimination, and racism are so familiar and comfortable that overcoming them requires a commitment both to learning about other cultures and to understanding one's own. A willingness to explore various cultural experiences without prejudgment is necessary. An ability to behave appropriately and effectively with culturally different others, without invoking prejudiced and stereotyped assumptions, is required. Although no one can completely overcome the obstacles to intercultural competence that naturally exist, the requisite knowledge, motivation, and skill can certainly help to minimize the negative effects of prejudice and discrimination.

The intercultural challenge for all of us now living in a world where interactions with people from different cultures are common features of daily life is to be willing to grapple with the consequences of prejudice, discrimination, and racism at the individual, social, and institutional levels. Because "prejudice" and "racism" are such emotionally charged concepts, it is sometimes very difficult to comment on their occurrence in our interactions with others. Individuals who believe that they have perceived discriminatory remarks and actions often feel that they cannot risk the resentment of their co-workers, fellow students, teachers, or service providers that would likely occur should they demand interactions that do not display prejudice against them. Conversely, those who do not regard themselves as having prejudiced or racist attitudes and who believe they never behave in discriminatory ways are horrified to learn that others might interpret their attitudes as prejudiced and their actions as discriminatory. While discussions about prejudice, discrimination, and racism can lead to a better understanding of the interpersonal dynamics that arise as individuals seek to establish mutually respectful relationships, they can just as easily lead to greater divisions and hostilities between people. The challenge for interculturally competent communicators is to contend with the pressing but potentially inflammatory issues of prejudice and discrimination in a manner that is both appropriate and effective.

We are also challenged to function competently in a world that, increasingly, is characterized by multiple cultures inhabiting adjacent and often-overlapping terrain. The ability to adapt to these intercultural settings—to maintain positive, healthy relationships with people from cultures other than your own—is the hallmark of the interculturally competent individual.

Summary

This chapter began with a discussion of cultural identity. The cultures with which you identify affect your views about where you belong and whom you consider to be "us" and "them." Next we discussed the biases that impede the development of intercultural competence. Ethnocentrism, stereotyping, prejudice, discrimination, and racism occur because of the human need to organize and streamline the processing of information. When people assume that these "thinking shortcuts" are accurate representations, intercultural competence is impaired.

Cultural biases are based on normal human tendencies to view ourselves as members of a particular group and to view others as not belonging to that group. Status, power, and economic differences heavily influence all intercultural contacts. Cultural biases are a reminder that all relationships take place within a political, economic, social, and cultural context. The intercultural challenge for all of us, as we live in a world where interactions with people from different cultures are common features of daily life, is to be willing to grapple with the consequences of prejudice, discrimination, and racism at the individual, social, and institutional levels.

When one cultural group lives near other cultural groups, various forms of adaptation occur. The desire to maintain both an identification with the culture of origin and positive relationships with other cultures influences the type of adaptation that is experienced. An intercultural transformation occurs when people are able to move beyond the limits of their own cultural experiences to incorporate the perspectives of other cultures into their own interpersonal interactions.

For Discussion

1. If people are born into one culture but raised in another, to which culture(s) do they belong?
2. What are the advantages and disadvantages for U.S. Americans who grow up with multiple cultural heritages?
3. What do people lose, and what do they gain, from having an ethnocentric perspective?
4. Are there historical examples in the United States of some groups dominating and subordinating other cultural groups? Are there contemporary examples?
5. Is it possible for European Americans to be the recipients of any form of racism in the United States?
6. Why might less obvious or less alarming forms of racism be just as dangerous as old-fashioned or symbolic racism?

For Further Reading

Gordon W. Allport, *The Nature of Prejudice* (Cambridge, MA: Addison-Wesley, 1954). A classic work establishing our understanding of the hows, whys, and nature of prejudice in human interaction.

Cathy N. Davidson, *36 Views of Mount Fuji: On Finding Myself in Japan* (New York: Plume, 1993). A well-written narrative that documents the adaptation of a European American woman to life in Japan, as well as describing her readjustments upon returning to her culture of origin.

Young Yun Kim, *Becoming Intercultural: An Integrative Theory of Communication and Cross-Cultural Adaptation* (Thousand Oaks, CA: Sage, 2001). The culmination of much previous work that has sought to understand the dynamics of adaptation and adjustment, Kim's book provides a framework for understanding the experience of individuals who move (either physically or psychologically) from one dominant cultural setting to another.

Stuart Oskamp (ed.), *Reducing Prejudice and Discrimination* (Mahwah, NJ: Erlbaum, 2000). Offers theories about and strategies to reduce both prejudice and discrimination.

Dolores V. Tanno and Alberto González, *Communication and Identity across Cultures* (Thousand Oaks, CA: Sage, 1998). Explores various aspects about who, how, when, where, and why individuals create and maintain their cultural and multicultural identities.

For additional information about intercultural films and about Web sites on specific cultures, turn to the Resources section at the back of this book.

Coding Intercultural Communication

chapter **7**   Nonverbal Intercultural Communication

chapter **8**   Verbal Intercultural Communication

chapter **9**   The Effects of Code Usage in Intercultural Communication

Nonverbal Intercultural Communication

Definition of Nonverbal Codes
Characteristics of Nonverbal Codes
Relationship of Nonverbal to Verbal
   Communication
**Cultural Universals in Nonverbal
   Communication**
**Cultural Variations in Nonverbal
   Communication**
**Nonverbal Messages in Intercultural
   Communication**
Body Movements

Space
Touch
Time
Voice
Other Nonverbal Code Systems
**Synchrony of Nonverbal
   Communication Codes**
**Nonverbal Communication
   and Intercultural Competence**
Summary

Learning to communicate as a native member of a culture involves knowing both the nonverbal and verbal code systems that are used. The verbal code system, which is considered in the next chapter, constitutes only a portion of the messages that people exchange when they communicate. In this chapter we explain the types of messages that are often regarded as more foundational or more elemental to human communication. Taken together, these messages constitute the nonverbal communication system.

Definition of Nonverbal Codes

The importance of nonverbal codes in communication has been well established. Nonverbal communication is a multichanneled process that is usually performed spontaneously; it typically involves a subtle set of nonlinguistic behaviors that are often enacted subconsciously.[1] Nonverbal behaviors can become part of the communication process when someone intentionally tries to convey a message or when someone attributes meaning to the nonverbal behavior of another, whether or not the person intended to communicate a particular meaning.

An important caution related to the distinction between nonverbal and verbal communication must be made as you learn about nonverbal code systems. Though we describe the communication of nonverbal and verbal messages in separate chapters for explanatory convenience, it would be a mistake to assume that they are actually separate and independent communication systems.[2] In fact, they are inseparably linked together to form the code systems through which the members of a culture convey their beliefs, values, thoughts, feelings, and intentions to one another. As Sheila Ramsey suggests:

> Verbal and nonverbal behaviors are inextricably intertwined; speaking of one without the other is, as Birdwhistell says, like trying to study "noncardiac physiology." Whether in opposition or complementary to each other, both modes work to create the meaning of an interpersonal event. According to culturally prescribed codes, we use eye movement and contact to manage conversations and to regulate interactions; we follow rigid rules governing intra- and interpersonal touch, our bodies synchronously join in the rhythm of others in a group, and gestures modulate our speech. We must internalize all of this in order to become and remain fully functioning and socially appropriate members of any culture.[3]

CULTURE *connections*

This was one of many elements of her culture that Katy just took for granted—like the Bulgarian penchant for teasing. "Bulgarians tease each other mercilessly," Doug says. "People kept making fun of me. Katy's nephew Chochi made fun of the way I walk, for example. Bulgarians have this very distinctive walk, very low down, bent knees, slouching, round shoulders." Doug gets up and hunches over to demonstrate. "But Americans tend to walk high and bouncy"—he takes another trip around the table in an upbeat manner—"and I am at the extreme. So Chochi kept making fun of me—walking on his toes and bouncing around. I was feeling very defensive." Finally, Katy explained that Bulgarians tease people they feel close to. "So it was a good sign. It was a way of making me welcome, like part of the family."

Differences in ideas about personal space and privacy also created discomfort for Doug. . . .

[S]haking his head even now as he remembers it, [Doug thinks] about the Bulgarian family's tendency to move together—in a group—from room to room. "As an American who needs his space," he tells us, "I'd get really tired. So I'd go into the bedroom to read a book in English, rest a little bit. Five or ten minutes later, somebody would wander in from the other room and then somebody else and somebody else until everybody was in the bedroom."

Sweet, we say.

"Yes," Doug agrees. "But it would drive me crazy! I just could not get away."

—*Jessie Carroll Grearson and Lauren B. Smith*

Thus our distinction between nonverbal and verbal messages is a convenient, but perhaps misleading, way to sensitize you to the communication exchanges within and between cultures.

Characteristics of Nonverbal Codes

Nonverbal communication messages function as a "silent language" and impart their meanings in subtle and covert ways.[4] People process nonverbal messages, both the sending and receiving of them, with less awareness than they process verbal messages. Contributing to the silent character of nonverbal messages is the fact that most of them are continuous and natural, and they tend to blur into one another. For example, raising your hand to wave goodbye is a gesture made up of multiple muscular movements, yet it is interpreted as one continuous movement.

Unlike verbal communication systems, however, there are no dictionaries or formal sets of rules to provide a systematic list of the meanings of a culture's nonverbal code systems. The meanings of nonverbal messages are usually less precise than are those of verbal codes. It is difficult, for example, to define precisely the meaning of a raised eyebrow in a particular culture.

Skill in the use of nonverbal message systems has only recently begun to receive formal attention in the educational process, a reflection of the out-of-awareness character of nonverbal codes.

Relationship of Nonverbal to Verbal Communication

The relationship of nonverbal communication systems to the verbal message system can take a variety of forms. Nonverbal messages can be used to accent, complement, contradict, regulate, or substitute for the verbal message.

Nonverbal messages are often used to *accent* the verbal message by emphasizing a particular word or phrase, in much the same way as *italics* add emphasis to written messages. For instance, the sentence "He did it" takes on somewhat different meanings, depending on whether the subject (*He* did it), the verb (He *did* it), or the object of the verb (He did *it*) is emphasized.

Nonverbal messages that function to clarify, elaborate, explain, reinforce, and repeat the meaning of verbal messages *complement* the verbal message. Many U.S. Americans shake their heads up and down while saying yes to reinforce the verbal affirmation. Similarly, smiling while talking to someone helps to convey a generally pleasant tone and encourages a positive interpretation of the verbal message. Pointing forcefully at someone while saying "*He* did it!" helps to elaborate and underscore the verbal message.

Nonverbal messages can also *contradict* the verbal message. These contradictions could occur purposefully, as when you say yes while indicating no with a wink or a gesture; or they may be out of your conscious awareness, as when you say, "I'm not upset," while your facial expression and tone of voice indicate just the opposite. Contradictions between the verbal and nonverbal channels often indicate that something is amiss. Though the contradictory cues might indicate an attempt at deception, a less evaluative interpretation might simply be that the verbal message is not all that the person could convey. In intercultural communication, these apparent incongruities, when they occur, might serve as a cue that something is wrong.

When nonverbal messages help to maintain the back-and-forth sequencing of conversations, they function to *regulate* the interaction. Conversations are highly structured, with people typically taking turns at talking in a smooth and highly organized sequence. Speakers use nonverbal means to convey that they want the other person to talk or that they do not wish to be interrupted, just as listeners indicate when they wish to talk and when they prefer to continue listening. Looking behaviors, vocal inflections, gestures, and general cues of readiness or relaxation all help to signal a person's conversational intentions.

Finally, nonverbal messages that are used in place of the verbal ones function as a *substitute* for the verbal channel. They are used when the verbal channel is blocked or when people choose not to use it. Head nods, hand gestures, facial displays, body movements, and various forms of physical contact are often used as a substitute for the verbal message.

The specific nonverbal messages used to accent, complement, contradict, regulate, or substitute for the verbal messages will vary from culture to culture. In intercultural communication, difficulties in achieving competence in another verbal code are compounded by variations in the nonverbal codes that accompany the spoken word.

Cultural Universals in Nonverbal Communication

Charles Darwin believed that certain nonverbal displays were universal.[5] The shoulder shrug, for example, is used to convey such messages as "I can't do it," "I can't stop it from happening," "It wasn't my fault," "Be patient," and "I do not intend to resist." Michael Argyle has listed a number of characteristics of nonverbal communication that are universal across all cultures: (1) the same body parts are used for nonverbal expressions; (2) nonverbal channels are used to convey similar information, emotions, values, norms, and self-disclosing messages; (3) nonverbal messages accompany verbal communication and are used in art and ritual; (4) the motives for using the nonverbal channel, such as when speech is impossible, are similar across cultures; and (5) nonverbal messages are used to coordinate and control a range of contexts and relationships that are similar across cultures.[6]

Paul Ekman's research on facial expressions demonstrates the universality of many nonverbal emotional displays.[7] Ekman discovered three separate sets of facial muscles that operate independently and can be manipulated to form a variety of emotional expressions. These muscle sets include the forehead and brow; the eyes, eyelids, and base of the nose; and the cheeks, mouth, chin, and rest of the nose. The muscles in each of these facial regions are combined in a variety of unique patterns to display emotional states. For example, fear is indicated by a furrowed brow, raised eyebrows, wide-open eyes, creased or pinched base of the nose, taut cheeks, partially open mouth, and upturned upper lip. Because the ability to produce such emotional displays is consistent across cultures, there is probably a biological or genetic basis that allows these behaviors to be produced in all humans in a particular way.

Another universal aspect of nonverbal communication is the need to be territorial. Robert Ardrey, an ethologist, has concluded that territoriality is an innate, evolutionary characteristic that occurs in both animals and humans.[8] Humans from all cultures mark and claim certain spaces as their own.

Although some aspects of nonverbal code systems are universal, it is also clear that cultures choose to express emotions and territoriality in differing ways. These variations are of particular interest in intercultural communication.

Cultural Variations in Nonverbal Communication

Most forms of nonverbal communication can be interpreted only within the framework of the culture in which they occur. Cultures vary in their nonverbal behaviors in three ways. First, cultures differ in the specific *repertoire* of behaviors that are enacted. Movements, body positions, postures, vocal intonations, gestures, spatial requirements, and even dances and ritualized actions are specific to a particular culture.

Second, all cultures have *display rules* that govern when and under what circumstances various nonverbal expressions are required, preferred, permitted, or prohibited. Thus, children learn both how to communicate nonverbally and the appropriate display rules that govern their nonverbal expressions. Display rules indicate such things as how far apart people should stand while talking, whom to touch and where, the speed and timing of movements and gestures, when to look directly at others in a conversation and when to look away, whether loud talking and expansive gestures or quietness and controlled movements should be used, when to smile and when to frown, and the overall pacing of communication.

The norms for display rules vary greatly across cultures. For instance, Judith N. Martin, Mitchell R. Hammer, and Lisa Bradford found that Latinos and European

Behaviors that are insignificant in one culture may be very meaningful in another. This African American surgeon relaxes and shows the soles of her shoes to visitors. In many cultures, this behavior would be regarded as an insult.

Americans differ in their judgments about the importance of displaying behaviors that signal approachability (smiling, laughing, and pleasant facial expressions) and poise (nice appearance, appropriate conversational distance, and appropriate posture) in con-

Consider your own nonverbal communication. Identify at least two nonverbal behaviors that have shared meaning with others, two that have idiosyncratic meaning, and two that have random meaning.

versations. The differences are related to whether the interaction is viewed as primarily task-oriented or socially oriented, and whether the conversational partners are from their own or from different cultural groups. Specifically, approachability and poise behaviors are most important for Latinos when working with other Latinos and when socializing with people from other cultures. In contrast, European Americans think it most important to display these behaviors only when socializing with another European American.[9]

Such differences in display rules can cause discomfort and misinterpretations. For instance, a Mexican American female visited her relatives in Mexico. Upon her arrival, she reports:

> All of the relatives came to greet me and everyone shook my hand, hugged me, and kissed me on the cheek. I didn't find this very odd at first, because even though I had never seen some of these relatives, we were family and being affectionate doesn't bother me. The difference occurred when I would go out with my cousins and their friends. When Maria would drop off Monica and me, they would kiss each other on the cheek. When a friend would come to the house, the greeting would always be a kiss on the cheek. It didn't matter if it was in public or private. It was as natural to them as shaking hands or hugging.

Display rules also indicate the intensity of the behavioral display that is acceptable. In showing grief or intense sadness, for instance, people from southern Mediterranean cultures may tend to exaggerate or amplify their displays, European Americans may try to remain calm and somewhat neutral, the British may understate their emotional displays by showing only a little of their inner feelings, and the Japanese and Thai may attempt to mask their sorrow completely by covering it with smiling and laughter.[10]

Third, cultures vary in the *interpretations* or meanings that are attributed to particular nonverbal behaviors. Three possible interpretations could be imposed on a given instance of nonverbal behavior: it is random, it is idiosyncratic, or it is shared.[11] An interpretation that the behavior is random means that it has no particular meaning to anyone. An idiosyncratic interpretation suggests that the behaviors are unique to special individuals or relationships, and they therefore have particular meanings only to these people. For example, family members often recognize that certain unique behaviors of a person signify a specific emotional state. Thus, a family member who tugs on her ear may indicate, to other family members, that she is about to explode in anger. The third interpretation is that the behaviors have shared meaning and significance, as when a group of people jointly attribute the same meaning to a particular nonverbal act.

However, cultures differ in what they regard as random, idiosyncratic, and shared. Thus, behaviors that are regarded as random in one culture may have shared significance in another. For example, John Condon and Fathi Yousef describe an incident in which a British professor in Cairo inadvertently showed the soles of his shoes to his class while leaning back in his chair; the Egyptian students were very insulted.[12] The professor's random behavior of leaning back and allowing the soles of his shoes to be seen was a nonverbal behavior with the shared meaning of insult in Egyptian culture. Such differences in how cultures define *random* can lead to problems in intercultural communication; if one culture defines a particular behavior as random, that behavior will probably be ignored when someone from a different culture uses it to communicate something.

Even nonverbal behaviors that have shared significance in each of two cultures may mean something very different to their members. As Ray Birdwhistell suggests, "A smile in one society portrays friendliness, in another embarrassment, and in still another may contain a warning that unless tension is reduced, hostility and attack will follow."[13] Aaron Wolfgang noted similar differences in interpretations when he compared Jamaican and Canadian reactions to such commonplace behaviors as clapping the hands for attention:

> In Barbados, a waiter in the dining room attempting to get the attention of some Canadian diners to show them to their table by clapping, shrugged his shoulders when they would not respond. In the English-Canadian culture clapping the hands would be considered inappropriate, or for that matter almost any expressive or gestural movement for attention would be frowned upon.[14]

Nonverbal repertoires, their corresponding display rules, and their preferred interpretations are not taught verbally. Rather, they are learned directly through observation and personal experience in a culture. Because they are frequently acquired outside of conscious awareness, they are rarely questioned or challenged by their users and are often noticed only when they are violated. In intercultural communication, therefore, misunderstandings often occur in the interpretations of nonverbal behaviors because different display rules create very different meanings about the appropriateness and effectiveness of particular interaction sequences. Consider, for instance, the following example:

> An American college student, while having a dinner party with a group of foreigners, learns that her favorite cousin has just died. She bites her lip, pulls herself up, and politely excuses herself from the group. The interpretation given to this behavior will vary with the culture of the observer. The Italian student thinks, "How insincere; she doesn't even cry." The Russian student thinks, "How unfriendly; she didn't care enough to share her grief with her friends." The fellow American student thinks, "How brave; she wanted to bear her burden by herself."[15]

As you can see, cultural variations in nonverbal communication alter the behaviors that are displayed, the meanings that are imposed on those behaviors, and the interpretations of the messages.

Nonverbal Messages in Intercultural Communication

Messages are transmitted between people over some sort of channel. Unlike written or spoken words, however, nonverbal communication is *multichanneled*. Thus, several types of nonverbal messages can be generated by a single speaker at a given instant.

CULTURE *connections*

A loud voice from the doorway interrupted him.

"Chee!" The speaker was a beefy young man with reddish-blond hair and a complexion that suffered from too many hours of dry air and high-altitude sun. . . .

He was pointing at Chee, a violation of the Dine rules of courtesy. Now he beckoned to Chee with his finger—rude in a multitude of other cultures.

Chee rose, his face darkened a shade.

—*Tony Hillerman*

When we "read" or observe the nonverbal behaviors of others, we might notice where they look, how they move, how they orient themselves in space and time, what they wear, and the characteristics of their voice. All of these nonverbal codes use particular channels or means of communicating messages, which are interpreted in a similar fashion by members of a given culture. We will discuss six types of nonverbal codes to demonstrate their importance in understanding how members of a culture attempt to understand, organize, and interpret the behaviors of others. We will consider body movements, space, touch, time, voice, and other nonverbal code systems.

Body Movements

The study of body movements, or body language, is known as *kinesics*. Kinesic behaviors include gestures, head movements, facial expressions, eye behaviors, and other physical displays that can be used to communicate. Of course, like all other forms of communication, no single type of behavior exists in isolation. Specific body movements can be understood only by taking the person's total behavior into account.

Paul Ekman and Wallace Friesen have suggested that there are five categories of kinesic behaviors: emblems, illustrators, affect displays, regulators, and adaptors.[16] We will consider each type of kinesic behavior in turn.

Emblems   Emblems are nonverbal behaviors that have a direct verbal counterpart. Emblems that are familiar to most U.S. Americans include such gestures as the two-fingered peace symbol and arm waving to indicate hello or goodbye. Emblems are typically used as a substitute for the verbal channel, either by choice or when the verbal channel is blocked for some reason. Underwater divers, for example, have a rich vocabulary of kinesic behaviors that are used to communicate with their fellow divers. Similarly, a baseball coach uses kinesic signals to indicate a particular pitch or type of play, which is usually conveyed by an elaborate pattern of hand motions that involve touching the cap, chest, wrist, and other areas in a pattern known to the players.

Emblems, like all verbal languages, are symbols that have been arbitrarily selected by the members of a culture to convey their intended meanings. For example, there is nothing peacelike in the peace symbol, which is a nonverbal emblem that can be

This Latino man stands in a doorway and gestures to others. Do you know what the gesture means?

displayed by extending the index and middle fingers upward from a clenched fist. Indeed, in other cultures the peace symbol has other meanings; Winston Churchill used the same symbol to indicate victory, and to many people in South American countries it is regarded as an obscene gesture. The meanings of emblems are learned within a culture and, like verbal codes, are used consciously by the culture's members when they wish to convey specific ideas to others. Because emblems have to be learned to be understood, they are culture-specific.

Emblems can be a great source of misunderstanding in intercultural communication because the shared meanings for an emblem in one culture may be different in another. In Turkey, for instance, to say "no" nonverbally:

> Nod your head up and back, raising your eyebrows at the same time. Or just raise your eyebrows; that's "no." . . .
>
> By contrast, wagging your head from side to side doesn't mean "no" in Turkish; it means "I don't understand." So if a Turk asks you, "Are you looking for the bus to Ankara?" and you shake your head, he'll assume you don't understand English, and will probably ask you the same question again, this time in German.[17]

Illustrators   Illustrators are nonverbal behaviors that are directly tied to, or accompany, the verbal message. They are used to emphasize, explain, and support a word or phrase. They literally illustrate and provide a visual representation of the verbal message. In saying "the huge mountain," for example, you may simultaneously lift your arms and move them in a large half-circle. Similarly, you may point your index finger to emphasize an important idea or use hand motions to convey directions to a particular address. Unlike emblems, however, none of these gestures has meaning in itself. Rather, the meaning depends on the verbal message it underscores.

Illustrators are less arbitrary than emblems, which makes them more likely to be universally understood. But differences in both the rules for displaying illustrators and in the interpretations of them can be sources of intercultural misunderstanding. In Asian cultures, for example, calling for a person or a taxi while waving an index finger is very inappropriate, akin to calling a dog. Instead, the whole right hand is used, palm down, with the fingers together in a scooping motion toward the body. Similarly, punching the fist into the open palm as a display of strength may be misinterpreted as an obscene gesture whose meaning is similar to a Westerner's use of the middle finger extended from a closed fist.

Affect Displays   Affect displays are facial and body movements that show feelings and emotions. Expressions of happiness or surprise, for instance, are displayed by the face and convey a person's inner feelings. Though affect displays are shown primarily through the face, postures and other body displays can also convey an emotional state.

The namaste gesture is an emblem that is used in India both as a greeting and to say goodbye.

Many affect displays may be universally recognized. The research of Paul Ekman and his colleagues indicates that regardless of culture, the primary emotional states include happiness, sadness, anger, fear, surprise, disgust, contempt, and interest.[18] In addition to these *primary affect displays,* there are about thirty *affect blends,* combinations of the primary emotions. While recent evidence supports Ekman's view,[19] James A. Russell argues that more information is needed to prove that there are indeed universal interpretations of emotional displays. He suggests that the categories for interpreting affect displays may actually vary somewhat across cultures.[20]

While talking to your friends, try not to display any emotion nonverbally. What does this do to your ability to communicate your views and experiences?

Affect displays may be unconscious and unintentional, such as a startled look of surprise, a blush of embarrassment, or dilated pupils due to pleasure or interest. Or affect displays may be conscious and intentional, as when we purposely smile and look at another person to convey warmth and affection. Cultural norms often govern both the kind and amount of affect displays shown. The Chinese, for instance, typically have lower frequency, intensity, and duration of affect displays than their European counterparts.[21]

Regulators   Regulators are nonverbal behaviors that help to synchronize the back-and-forth nature of conversations. This class of kinesic behaviors helps to control the flow and sequencing of communication and may include head nods, eye contact, postural shifts, back-channel signals (such as "Uh huhm" or "Mmm-mmm"), and other turn-taking cues.

Regulators are used by speakers to indicate whether others should take a turn and by listeners to indicate whether they wish to speak or would prefer to continue listening. They also convey information about the preferred speed or pacing of conversations and the degree to which the other person is understood and believed.

Regardless of culture, taking turns is required in all conversations. Thus, for interpersonal communication to occur, talk sequences must be highly coordinated. Regulators are those subtle cues that allow people to maintain this high degree of coordination.

Regulators are culture-specific. For instance, people from high-context cultures such as Korea and Japan are especially concerned with meanings conveyed by the eyes. In an interesting study comparing the looking behaviors of African Americans and European Americans in a conversation, Marianne LaFrance and Clara Mayo found that there were many differences in the interpretations of turn-taking cues. European Americans tend to look directly into the eyes of the other person when they are the listeners, whereas African Americans prefer to look away. Unfortunately, to African Americans such behaviors by European Americans may be regarded as invasive or confrontational when interest and involvement are intended. Conversely, the behaviors of African Americans could be regarded by European Americans as a sign of indifference or inattention when respect is intended. LaFrance and Mayo also found that when African American speakers pause while simultaneously looking directly at their European American listeners, the listeners often interpret this as a signal to speak, only to find that the African American person is also speaking.[22]

Adaptors   Adaptors are personal body movements that occur as a reaction to an individual's physical or psychological state. Scratching an itch, fidgeting, tapping a pencil, and smoothing one's hair are all behaviors that fulfill some individualized need.

Adaptors are usually performed unintentionally, without conscious awareness. They seem to be more frequent under conditions of stress, impatience, enthusiasm, or nervousness, and they are often interpreted by others as a sign of discomfort, uneasiness, irritation, or other negative feelings.

Space

The use of space functions as an important communication system in all cultures. Cultures are organized in some spatial pattern, and that pattern can reveal the character of the people in that culture. Two important features of the way cultures use the space around them are the different needs for personal space and the messages that are used to indicate territoriality.

Cultural Differences in the Use of Personal Space

Wherever you go, whatever you do, you are surrounded at all moments by a personal space "bubble." Edward Hall, who coined the term *proxemics* to refer to the study of how people differ in their use of personal space, has suggested that people interact within four spatial zones or distance ranges: intimate, personal, social, and public.[23] These proxemic zones are characterized by differences in the ways that people relate to one another and in the behaviors that

TABLE 7.1   Zones of Spatial Difference

Spatial Distance Zone	Spatial Distance (in feet)	Usage	Other Characteristics
Intimate	0–1½	Loving; comforting; protecting; fighting	Minimal conversation; smell and feel of other; eye contact unlikely
Personal	1½–4	Conversations with intimates, friends, and acquaintances	Touch possible; much visual detail
Social	4–12	Impersonal and social gatherings	More formal tone; some visual detail lost; eye contact likely
Public	12–up	Lectures; concerts; plays; speeches; ceremonies; protection	Subtle details lost; only obvious attributes noticed

typify the communication that will probably occur in them. Table 7.1, which is based on Hall's observations of U.S. Americans, displays the differences from zone to zone in the types and intensity of sensory information that is received by those who are involved in a communication experience.

Personal space distances are culture specific. People from colder climates, for instance, typically use large physical distances when they communicate, whereas those from warm-weather climates prefer close distances. The personal space bubbles for northern Europeans are therefore large, and people expect others to keep their distance. The personal space bubbles for Europeans get smaller and smaller, however, as one travels south toward the Mediterranean. Indeed, the distance that is regarded as intimate in Germany, Scandinavia, and England overlaps with what is regarded as a normal conversational distance in France and the Mediterranean countries of Italy, Greece, and Spain. Consequently, northern Europeans think their southern counterparts get "too close for comfort," whereas the southern Europeans regard their northern neighbors as "too distant and aloof."

CULTURE *connections*

Umeeta has herself changed since she came to the United States, absorbed some elements of American-style interaction. "When I was in India recently," she says, "people would walk close to me, and I found myself moving away." Time is less elastic for her, too, than it once was. "Being in the United States has affected how I experience time. I wish I could spend more of it talking, sitting together with friends without a goal, never thinking about the hour. But I myself am on a schedule; work takes up to much of my life."

—*Jessie Carroll Grearson and Lauren B. Smith*

The habitual use of the culturally proper spacing distance is accompanied by a predictable level and kind of sensory information. For example, if the standard cultural spacing distance in a personal conversation with an acquaintance is about three feet, people will become accustomed to the sights, sounds, and smells of others that are usually acquired at that distance. For someone who is accustomed to a larger spacing distance, at three feet the voices will sound too loud, it might be possible to smell the other person's breath, the other person will seem too close and perhaps out of the "normal" focal range, and the habitual ways of holding the body may no longer work. Then, the culturally learned cues that are so helpful within one's culture can become a hindrance. One European American student, for instance, in commenting on a party that was attended by many Italians and Spaniards, exclaimed, "They would stand close enough that I could almost feel the air coming from their mouths." Similar reactions to intercultural encounters are very common. As Edward and Mildred Hall have suggested:

For one day, intentionally stand about three to six inches closer to people than you normally would. Keep track of their reactions and your own comfort levels. Do they change over time?

> Since most people don't think about personal distance as something that is culturally patterned, foreign spatial cues are almost inevitably misinterpreted. This can lead to bad feelings which are then projected onto the people from the other culture in a most personal way. When a foreigner appears aggressive and pushy, or remote and cold, it may mean only that her or his personal distance is different from yours.[24]

Cultural Differences in Territoriality

Do you have a favorite chair or classroom seat that you think "belongs" to you? Or do you have a room, or perhaps just a portion of a room, that you consider to be off limits to others? The need to protect and defend a particular spatial area is known as *territoriality,* a set of behaviors that people display to show that they "own" or have the right to control the use of a particular geographic area.

People mark their territories in a variety of ways. It can be done formally using actual barriers such as fences and signs that say "No Trespassing" or "Keep Off the Grass." Territories can also be marked informally by nonverbal markers such as clothing, books, and other personal items that indicate a person's intent to control or occupy a given area.

Cultural differences in territoriality can be exhibited in three ways. First, cultures can differ in the general degree of territoriality that its members tend to exhibit. Some cultures are far more territorial than others. For instance, as Hall and Hall point out in their comparison of Germans and French:

> People like the Germans are highly territorial; they barricade themselves behind heavy doors and soundproof walls to try to seal themselves from others in order to concentrate on their work. The French have a close personal distance and are not as territorial. They are tied to people and thrive on constant interaction and high-information flow to provide them the context they need.[25]

Second, cultures can differ in the range of possible places or spaces about which they are territorial. A comparison of European Americans with Germans, for example, reveals that both groups are highly territorial. Both have a strong tendency to establish areas that they consider to be their own. In Germany, however, this feeling of territoriality extends to "all possessions, including the automobile. If a German's car is touched, it is as though the individual himself has been touched."[26]

Finally, cultures can differ in the typical reactions exhibited in response to invasions or contaminations of their territory. Members of some cultures prefer to react by withdrawing or avoiding confrontations whenever possible. Others respond by insulating themselves from the possibility of territorial invasion, using barriers or other boundary markers. Still others react forcefully and vigorously in an attempt to defend their "turf" and their honor.

Touch

Touch is probably the most basic component of human communication. It is experienced long before we are able to see and speak, and it is a fundamental part of the human experience.

The Meanings of Touch   Stanley E. Jones and A. Elaine Yarbrough have identified five meanings of touch that are important in understanding the nature of intercultural communication.[27] Touch is often used to indicate *affect,* the expression of positive and negative feelings and emotions. Protection, reassurance, support, hatred, dislike, and disapproval are all conveyed through touch; hugging, stroking, kissing, slapping, hitting, and kicking are all ways in which these messages can be conveyed. Touch is also used as a sign of *playfulness.* Whether affectionately or aggressively, touch can be used

Cultures differ in the use of touching and space. These soldiers hold hands, which in many cultures is a commonly-accepted behavior among male friends.

to signal that the other's behavior should not be taken seriously. Touch is frequently used as a means of *control*. "Stay here," "move over," and similar messages are communicated through touch. Touching for control may also indicate social dominance. High-status individuals in most Western countries, for instance, are more likely to touch than to be touched, whereas low-status individuals are likely to receive touching behaviors from their superiors.[28] Touching for ritual purposes occurs mainly on occasions involving introductions or departures. Shaking hands, clasping shoulders, hugging, and kissing the cheeks or lips are all forms of greeting rituals. Touching is also used in *task-related* activities. These touches may be as casual as a brief contact of hands when passing an object, or they may be as formal and prolonged as a physician taking a pulse at the wrist or neck.

Cultural Differences in Touch   Cultures differ in the overall amount of touching they prefer. People from high-contact cultures such as those in the Middle East, Latin America, and southern Europe touch each other in social conversations much more than do people from noncontact cultures such as Asia and northern Europe. These cultural differences can lead to difficulties in intercultural communication. Germans, Scandinavians, and Japanese, for example, may be perceived as cold and aloof by Brazilians and Italians, who in turn may be regarded as aggressive, pushy, and overly familiar by northern Europeans. As Edward and Mildred Hall have noted, "In northern Europe one does not touch others. Even the brushing of the overcoat sleeve used to elicit an apology."[29] A comparable difference was observed by Dean Barnlund, who found that U.S. American students reported being touched twice as much as did Japanese students.[30]

Cultures also differ in where people can be touched. In Thailand and Malaysia, for instance, the head should not be touched because it is considered to be sacred and the locus of a person's spiritual and intellectual powers. In the United States, the head is far more likely to be touched.[31]

Cultures vary in their expectations about who touches whom. In Japan, for instance, there are deeply held feelings against the touch of a stranger. These expectations are culture-specific, and even cultures that exist near one another can have very different norms. Among the Chinese, for instance, shaking hands among people of the opposite sex is perfectly acceptable; among many Malay, it is not. Indeed, for those who practice the Muslim religion, casual touching between members of the opposite sex is strictly forbidden. Both men and women have to cleanse themselves ritually before praying if they happen to make physical contact with someone of the opposite sex. Holding hands, for example, or walking with an arm across someone's shoulder or around the waist, or even grabbing an elbow to help another cross the street, are all considered socially inappropriate behaviors between men and women. In some places there are legal restrictions against public displays of hugging and kissing, even among married couples. However, this social taboo refers only to opposite-sex touching; it is perfectly acceptable for two women to hold hands or for men to walk arm in arm. Many European Americans, of course, have the opposite reaction; they react negatively to same-sex touching (particularly among men) but usually do not mind opposite-sex touching.

Finally, cultures differ in the settings or occasions in which touch is acceptable. Business meetings, street conversations, and household settings all evoke different norms for what is considered appropriate. Cultures make distinctions between those settings that they regard as public and those considered private. Although some cultures regard touching between men and women as perfectly acceptable in public conversations, others think that such activities should occur only in the privacy of the home; to them, touch is a highly personal and sensitive activity that should not occur where others might see it.

Time

The study of time—how people use it, structure it, interpret it, and understand its passage—is called *chronemics.* We consider chronemics from two perspectives: time orientations and time systems.

Time Orientations   Time orientation refers to the value or importance the members of a culture place on the passage of time. In Chapter 2 we indicated that communication is a process, which means that people's behaviors must be understood as part of an ongoing stream of events that changes over a period of time. Chapters 5 and 6 suggested that members of a culture share a similar worldview about the nature of time. We also indicated that different cultures can have very different conceptions about the appropriate ways to comprehend events and experiences. Specifically, some cultures are predominantly past-oriented, others are present-oriented, and still others prefer a future-oriented worldview. As we briefly review these cultural orientations about time, take note of the amazing degree of interrelationship—in this case the link between a culture's nonverbal code system and its cultural patterns—that characterizes the various aspects of a culture.

Past-oriented cultures regard previous experiences and events as most important. These cultures place a primary emphasis on tradition and the wisdom passed down from older generations. Consequently, they show a great deal of deference and respect for parents and other elders, who are the links to these past sources of knowledge. Events are circular, as important patterns perpetually recur in the present; therefore, tried-and-true methods for overcoming obstacles and dealing with problems can be applied to current difficulties. Many aspects of the British, Chinese, and Native American experiences,

CULTURE *connections*

The meeting was set for 8 o'clock on a Wednesday evening. Mary told me, "The door will be open, just walk in."

I arrived at Mary's basement apartment at 8:10. Not only was the door not open, there was no response when I knocked on it. . . . Mary explained that she had lain down when she got home from work and had fallen asleep. Like so many other Irish women, she seemed to have no awareness of the passage of time and no embarrassment at having forsaken her own plans. Oddly, in this situation, it was I who was always embarrassed by my too literal interpretation of time.

—*Rosemary Mahony*

for instance, can be understood only by reference to their reverence for traditions, past family experiences, or tribal customs. Consider this example of a past-oriented culture the Samburu, a nomadic tribe from northern Kenya that reveres its elders:

> The elders are an invaluable source of essential knowledge, and in an environment that by its very nature allows only a narrow margin for error, the oldest survivors must possess the most valuable knowledge of all. The elders know their environment intimately—every lie and twist of it. The land, the water, the vegetation; trees, shrubs, herbs—nutritious, medicinal, poisonous. They know each cow, and have a host of specific names for the distinctive shape and skin patterns of each animal in just the same way that Europeans distinguish within the general term flower, or tree.[32]

Present-oriented cultures regard current experiences as most important. These cultures place a major emphasis on spontaneity and immediacy and on experiencing each moment as fully as possible. Consequently, people do not participate in particular events or experiences because of some potential future gain; rather, they participate because of the immediate pleasure the activity provides. Present-oriented cultures typically believe that unseen and even unknown outside forces, such as fate or luck, control their lives. Cultures such as those in the Philippines and many Central and South American countries are usually present-oriented, and they have found ways to encourage a rich appreciation for the simple pleasures that arise in daily activities.

European American culture is considered to be monochronic. Name as many consumer items as you can that reflect this orientation toward time.

Future-oriented cultures believe that tomorrow—or some other moment in the future—is most important. Current activities are not accomplished and appreciated for their own sake but for the potential future benefits that might be obtained. For example, you go to school, study for your examinations, work hard, and delay or deny present rewards for the potential future gain that a rewarding career might provide. People from future-oriented cultures, which include many European Americans, believe that their fate is at least partially in their own hands and that they can control the consequences of their actions.

Time Systems   Time systems are the implicit cultural rules that are used to arrange sets of experiences in some meaningful way. There are three types of time systems: technical, formal, and informal.

Technical time systems are the precise, scientific measurements of time that are calculated in such units as nanoseconds. Typically, members of a culture do not use technical time systems because they are most applicable to specialized settings such as the research laboratory. Consequently, technical time systems are of little relevance to the common experiences that members of a culture share.

Formal time systems refer to the ways in which the members of a culture describe and comprehend units of time. Time units can vary greatly from culture to culture. Among many Native American cultures, for instance, time is segmented by the phases of the moon, the changing seasons, the rise and fall of the tides, or the movements of the sun. Similarly, when a Peruvian woman was asked for the distance to certain Inca ruins, she indicated their location by referring nonverbally to a position in the sky that represented the distance the sun would travel toward the horizon before the journey would be complete.[33] Among European Americans, the passage of time is segmented into seconds, minutes, hours, days, weeks, months, and years.

Time's passage may likewise be indicated by reference to significant events such as the birth of a royal son or an important victory in battle. Time intervals for particular events or activities may also be based on significant external events such as the length of a day or the phases of the moon. Alternatively, time intervals may be more arbitrary, as in the length of a soccer game or the number of days in a week. These ways of representing the passage of time, however arbitrary, are the culture's formal time system. Sequences such as the months in the year are formally named and are explicitly taught to children and newcomers as an important part of the acculturation process.

The formal time system includes agreements among the members of a culture on such important issues as the extent to which time is regarded as valuable and tangible. European Americans, of course, typically regard time as a valuable, tangible commodity that is used or consumed to a greater or lesser degree.

Informal time systems refer to the assumptions cultures make about how time should be used or experienced. How long should you wait for someone who will be ready soon, in a minute, in a while, or shortly? When is the proper time to arrive for a 9:00 A.M. appointment or an 8:00 P.M. party? As a dinner guest, how long after your arrival would you expect the meal to be served? How long should you stay after the meal has been concluded? Cultures have unstated expectations about the timing and duration of such events. Although these expectations differ, depending on such factors as the occasion and the relative importance of those being met or visited, they are widely held and consistently imposed as the proper or appropriate way to conduct oneself as a competent member of the culture. In this regard, Edward Hall has reported:

> The time that it takes to reach an agreement or for someone to make up his mind operates within culturally defined limits. In the U.S. one has about four minutes in the business world to sell an idea. In Japan the well-known process of "nemawashi"—consensus building, without which nothing can happen—can take weeks or months. None of this four-minute sell.[34]

Perhaps the most important aspect of the culture's informal time system is the degree to which it is monochronic or polychronic.[35] A *monochronic* time system means that things should be done one at a time, and time is segmented into precise, small units. In a monochronic time system, time is viewed as a commodity; it is scheduled, managed, and arranged. European Americans, like members of other monochronic cultures, are very time-driven. The ubiquitous calendar or scheduler that many European Americans carry, which tells them when, where, and with whom to engage in activities, is an apt symbol of a monochronic culture. An event is regarded as separate and distinct from all others and should receive the exclusive focus of attention it deserves. These events also have limits or boundaries, so that there are expected beginning and ending points that have been scheduled in advance. Thus European Americans

> find it disconcerting to enter an office overseas with an appointment only to discover that other matters require the attention of the man we are to meet. Our ideal is to center the attention first on one thing and then move on to something else.[36]

A *polychronic* time system means that several things are being done at the same time. In Spain and among many Spanish-speaking cultures in Central and South America, for instance, relationships are far more important than schedules. Appointments will be quickly broken, schedules readily set aside, and deadlines unmet without guilt or apology when friends or family members require attention. Those who use polychronic time systems often schedule multiple appointments simultaneously, so keeping "on schedule" is an impossibility that was never really a goal. European Americans, of course, are upset when they are kept waiting for a scheduled appointment, particularly when they discover that they are the third of three appointments that have been scheduled at exactly the same hour.

Cultural Differences in Perceptions and Use of Time   Cultures differ in their time orientations and in the time systems they use to give order to experiences. Misunderstandings can occur between people who have different time orientations. For instance, someone from a present-oriented culture might view people from past-oriented cultures as too tied to tradition and people from future-oriented cultures as passionless slaves to efficiency and materialism. Alternatively, someone from a future-oriented culture might view those from present-oriented cultures as self-centered, hedonistic, inefficient, and foolish.[37] This natural tendency to view one's own practices as superior to all others is a common source of problems in intercultural communication.

Cultures also differ in the formal and informal time systems they use to determine how long an event should take, and even how long "long" is. Misinterpretations often occur when individuals from monochronic and polychronic cultures attempt to interact. Each usually views the other's responses to time "commitments" as disrespectful and unfriendly.

Voice

Earlier in this chapter we stated that nonverbal messages are often used to accent or underscore the verbal message by adding emphasis to particular words or phrases. Indeed, the many qualities of the voice itself, in addition to the actual meaning of the words, form the *vocalic* nonverbal communication system. Vocalics also include many nonspeech sounds such as belching, laughing, and crying and vocal "filler" sounds such as *uh, er, um,* and *uh-huh.*

Vocal versus Verbal Communication   Vocalic qualities include pitch (high to low), rate of talking (fast to slow), conversational rhythm (smooth to staccato), and volume (loud to soft). Because spoken (i.e., verbal) language always has some vocal elements, it is difficult to separate the meaning conveyed by the language from that conveyed by the vocalic components. However, if you can imagine that these words you are now reading are a transcript of a lecture we have given, you will be able to understand clearly the distinctions we are describing. Although our words—the language spoken—are here on the printed page, the vocalics are not. Are we speaking rapidly or slowly? How does our inflection change to emphasize a point or to signal a question? Are we yelling, whispering, drawling, or speaking with an accent? Do our voices indicate that we are tense, relaxed, strained, calm, bored, or excited? The answers to these types of questions are conveyed by the speaker's voice.

Cultural Differences in Vocal Communication   There are vast cultural differences in vocalic behaviors. For example, unlike English, many Asian languages are tonal. The same Chinese words when said with a different vocalic tone or pitch can have vastly different meanings. Mà, for example, could mean "mother," "a pileup," "horse," or "scold," depending on the tone used in its expression.

In addition to differences in tone or pitch, there are large cultural differences in the loudness and frequency of speaking. Latinos, for instance, perceive themselves as talking more loudly and more frequently than European Americans.[38]

The emotional meanings conveyed by the voice are usually taken for granted by native language users, but they can be the cause of considerable problems when they fail to conform to preconceived expectations. For instance, when a Saudi Arabian man is speaking in English, he will usually transfer his native intonation patterns without necessarily being aware that he has done so. In Arabic, the intonation pattern is such that many of the individual words in the sentence are stressed. Although a flat intonation pattern is used in declarative sentences, the intonation pattern for exclamatory sentences is much stronger and more emotional than that in English. The higher pitch of Arabic speakers also conveys a more emotional tone than that of English speakers. Consequently, differences in vocal characteristics may result in unwarranted negative impressions. The U.S. American may incorrectly perceive that the Saudi Arabian is excited or angry when in fact he is not. Questions by the Saudi that merely seek information may sound accusing. The monotonous tone of declarative sentences may be

CULTURE *connections*

When she and Muzzafer came to Boston, Bibi found it almost unbearable. It was more than missing her parents' airy, flower-filled house, her socialite friends, or her father's smoky study. It wasn't the long hours spent utterly alone, speaking to no one except the cashier at the supermarket. She'd been saved from desolate evenings waiting for Muzzafer to return by a friend, another young Indian woman called Meera, who had recently come abroad with her husband, an American painter.

The worst was not the dark, dirty apartment, not the walls stained black with mildew or the long climb up the concrete stairs. It was the smell. All around her was that smell, stronger than car exhaust or garbage or urine. The smell of white skin. Pink and damp like a newborn kitten or a hairless baby bird. The smell of their sweat seemed artificial and sick, even through all their perfumes and deodorants. She wondered why she'd never noticed in India or during her art classes in Europe. Sometimes, on a crowded bus in the winter, the steam escaping from the folds of damp wool and nylon, the smell was suffocating and Bibi thought she wouldn't live until the next stop. Now, fourteen years later, with most of her family settled in America, she suddenly realized that she'd stopped noticing it.

—Ameena Meer

perceived as demonstrating apathy or a lack of interest. Vocal stress and intonation differences may be perceived as aggressive or abrasive when only polite conversation is intended. Conversely, the Saudi Arabian may incorrectly interpret certain behaviors of the U.S. American speaker as an expression of calmness and pleasantness when anger or annoyance is being conveyed. Similarly, a statement that seems to be a firm assertion to the U.S. American speaker may sound weak and doubtful to the Saudi Arabian.[39]

Other Nonverbal Code Systems

Many other nonverbal code systems are relevant to an understanding of intercultural communication because virtually everything we say, do, create, and wear can communicate messages about our culture and ourselves. These other codes include the chemical, dermal, physical, and artifactual systems that create a multichanneled set of nonverbal messages.

Chemical Code System   The interpretations made from chemically based body functions form the chemical code system. Chemical codes include natural body odor, tears, sweat, gas, household smells, and similar phenomena. People have distinct chemical code systems that are affected by their way of living, food preferences, habits, and environment. These differences are often used to make judgments or interpretations about members of a culture. For instance, most meat-eating Westerners have a distinct body odor that may be unpleasant to cultures that do not consume red meat. Similarly, many hotels in Malaysia have posted signs that say "No Durians" to discourage their guests from bringing in the pungent, sweet-tasting fruit that many consider to be a delicacy. Among many Arabic-speaking cultures, attempts to mask body odors with perfumes is considered an insult; this chemical information is so favorably regarded that close spatial distances in conversations are used to obtain it.

Dermal Code System   The short-term changes in skin texture or sensitivity that result from physical or psychological reactions to the environment form the dermal code system. Dermal codes include blushing, blanching, goose flesh, and related experiences. Particularly in high-context cultures, subtle changes in skin tonalities may be carefully observed to obtain the information needed to act appropriately.

Physical Code System   The relatively unchanging aspects of the body form the physical code system: weight, body shape, facial features, skin color, eye color, hair, characteristics that denote age and gender, and similar features. Indeed, the cultural standards for beauty vary greatly, as can expectations about how people should look.

Artifactual Code System   The creations that people make, use, or wear are the artifactual code system. These aspects of material culture include the tools, clothing, buildings, furnishings, jewelry, lighting, and color schemes that are common to the members of a culture. Clothing styles, cosmetics, and body ornamentations, for instance, are used to fulfill the culture's needs for modesty, self-expression, or privacy. Differences in privacy needs, in particular, are often indicated by such features as closed doors in the United States, sound-proofed doors in Germany, tree-lined barriers at property lines in England, or paper-thin walls in Japan.

Synchrony of Nonverbal Communication Codes

Cultures train their members to synchronize the various nonverbal behaviors to form a response pattern that typifies the expected behaviors in that culture. Subtle variations in the response patterns are clearly noticed, even when they differ by only a few thousandths of a second. William Condon, who describes himself as "a white, middle-class male," suggests that interactional synchrony is learned from birth and occurs within a fraction of a second. Condon compares the differences in the speech and gestures of African Americans and European Americans:

> If I say the word "because" both my hands may extend exactly together. In Black behavior, however, the right hand may begin to extend with the "be" portion slightly ahead of the left hand and the left hand will extend rapidly across the "cause" portion. This creates the syncopation, mentioned before, which can appear anywhere in the body. A person moves in the rhythm and timing of his or her culture, and this rhythm is in the whole body. . . . It may be that those having different cultural rhythms are unable to really "synch-in" fully with each other. . . . I think that infants from the first moments of life and even in the womb are getting the rhythm and structure and style of sound, the rhythms of their culture, so that they imprint to them and the rhythms become part of their very being.[40]

Behavioral synchrony in the use of nonverbal codes can be found in virtually all cultures. Not only must an individual's many behaviors be coordinated appropriately, they must also mesh properly with the words and movements of the other interactants. Coordination in Japanese bowing behaviors, for example, requires an adaptation to the status relationships of the participants; the inferior must begin the bow, and the superior decides when the bow is complete. If the participants are of equal status, they must begin and end their bows simultaneously. This is not as easy as it seems. As one Japanese man relates:

> Perfect synchrony is absolutely essential to bowing. Whenever an American tries to bow to me, I often feel extremely awkward and uncomfortable because I simply cannot synchronize bowing with him or her. . . . bowing occurs in a flash of a second, before you have time to think. And both parties must know precisely when to start bowing, how deep, how long to stay in the bowed position, and when to bring their heads up.[41]

CULTURE *connections*

Nepalis do not knock before they enter closed doors as it is assumed one will always be decently covered. I suppress a wave of indignation when someone bursts in unannounced. This whole experience is a challenge to the right of privacy we assume at home. In Nepal the need to be alone would be culturally aberrant and usually physically impossible. I think with some amusement now of the festering family argument that occasionally resurfaced because each of my sons felt entitled to a room of his own.

—Barbara J. Scott

Similar degrees of coordination and synchrony can be found in most everyday activities. Sensitivity to these different nonverbal codes can help you to become more interculturally competent.

Nonverbal Communication and Intercultural Competence

The rules and norms that govern most nonverbal communication behaviors are both culture-specific and outside of conscious awareness. That is, although members of a culture know and follow their culture's expectations, they probably learned the norms for proper nonverbal expressiveness very early in childhood, and these norms may never have been articulated verbally.[42] Sometimes, therefore, the only way you will know that a cultural norm exists is when you break it!

An important consequence of this out-of-awareness aspect is that members of a culture use their norms to determine appropriate nonverbal behaviors and then make negative judgments about others' feelings, motives, intentions, and even their attractiveness if these norms are violated.[43] Often the violations will be inaccurately attributed to aspects of personality, attitudes, or intelligence rather than to a mismatch between learned nonverbal codes. U.S. Americans, for instance, highly value positive nonverbal displays and typically regard someone who smiles as more intelligent than someone who does not; the Japanese, however, whose cultural norms value constraint in nonverbal expressiveness, do not equate expressiveness with intelligence.[44] The very nature of nonverbal behaviors makes inaccurate judgments difficult to recognize and correct.

These two women illustrate several kinds of nonverbal messages. Notice the meanings that you attribute to their gestures, facial expressions, body postures, clothing, and the distance they stand from one other.

CULTURE *connections*

By then, I was used to the averted gaze of devout Muslim men, and it seemed normal to me to be conversing with someone whose eyes were focused on a floor tile an inch in front of my shoe. He was considering whether to let me meet his wife.

—*Geraldine Brooles*

The following suggestions will help you use your knowledge of nonverbal communication to improve your intercultural competence. These suggestions are designed to help you notice, interpret, and use nonverbal communication behaviors to function more appropriately and more effectively in intercultural encounters.

Researchers have been known to take weeks or even months to analyze the delicate interaction rhythms involved in a single conversation. Of course, most people do not have the luxury of a month to analyze someone's comments before responding. However, the knowledge that the patterns of behavior will probably be very complex will help sensitize you to them and may encourage you to notice more details.

No set of behaviors is universally correct, so the "right" behaviors can never be described in a catalog or list. Rather, the proper behaviors are those that are appropriate and effective in the context of the culture, setting, and occasion. What is right in one set of circumstances may be totally wrong in another. Although it is useful to gather culture-specific information about appropriate nonverbal behaviors, even this knowledge should be approached as relative because prescriptions of "right" behavior rarely identify all of the situational characteristics that cultural natives "know."

By monitoring your emotional reactions to differences in nonverbal behaviors, you can be alert to the interpretations you are making and, therefore, to the possibility of alternative meanings. Strong visceral responses to differences in smell, body movement, and personal spacing are quite common in intercultural communication. Knowledge that these might occur, followed by care in the interpretation of meanings, is critical.

Skillful interpretation includes observation of general tendencies. Focus on what members of the other culture prefer and the ways in which they typically behave. How, when, and with whom do they gesture, move, look, and touch? How are time and space used to define and maintain social relationships? It is much harder to pay attention to these general tendencies than you might think because in all likelihood you have not had much practice in consciously looking for patterns in the commonplace, taken-for-granted activities through which cultural effects are displayed. Nevertheless, it is possible, with practice, to improve your observation skills.

Even after making observations, be tentative in your interpretations and generalizations. You could be wrong. You will be far more successful in making sense of others' behaviors if you avoid the premature closure that comes with assuming you know for certain what something means. Think of your explanations as tentative working hypotheses rather than as unchanging facts.

Next, look for exceptions to your generalizations. These exceptions are very important because they help you to recognize that no one individual, regardless of the thoroughness and accuracy with which you have come to understand a culture, will exactly fit the useful generalizations you have formed. The exceptions that you note can help you to limit the scope of your generalizations and to recognize the boundaries beyond which your judgments may simply not apply. Maybe your interpretations apply only to men, or students, or government officials, or strangers, or the elderly, or potential customers. Maybe your evaluations of the way time and space are structured apply only to business settings, or among those whose status is equal, or with particular people like yourself. Though it is necessary to make useful generalizations to get along in another culture, it is equally necessary to recognize the limits of these generalizations.

Finally, practice to improve your ability in observing, evaluating, and behaving in appropriate and effective ways. Practice increases your skills in recognizing specific patterns to people's behaviors, in correctly interpreting the meanings and likely consequences of those behaviors, and in selecting responses that are both appropriate and effective. Like all skills, your level of intercultural competence will improve with practice. Of course, the best form of practice is one that closely approximates the situations in which you will have to use the skills you are trying to acquire. Therefore, we encourage you to seek out and willingly engage in intercultural communication experiences.

Summary

Although there is some evidence that certain nonverbal communication tendencies are common to all humans, cultures vary greatly in the repertoire of behaviors and circumstances in which nonverbal exchanges occur. A smile, a head nod, and eye contact may all have different meanings in different cultures.

This chapter considered the important nonverbal code systems used to supplement, reinforce, or substitute for the verbal code systems. Nonverbal code systems are the silent language of communication. They are less precise and less consciously used and interpreted than verbal code systems, but they can have powerful effects on perceptions of and interpretations about others. The nonverbal code systems relating to body movements, space, touch, time, voice, and other nonverbal code systems were each described. Finally, the interrelationship of these nonverbal code systems with one another and with the verbal code system was explored.

For Discussion

1. What are some examples of cultural universals? Can you think of examples from your personal experiences that either confirm or contradict the idea of cultural universals?

2. It is widely believed by many that "a smile is universally understood." Do you agree with this statement? Why or why not.

3. Touch is one of the most fundamental parts of the human experience. But cross-cultural differences in the norms for touching can cause problems in intercultural interactions. Provide examples of your touching norms that you believe differ for people from cultures other than your own.

4. What are some of the ways that U.S. Americans have been taught (or have unconsciously learned) to synchronize their nonverbal behaviors?

For Further Reading

Peter A. Andersen, Michael L. Hecht, Gregory D. Hoobler, and Marya Smallwood, "Nonverbal Communication Across Cultures," *Handbook of International and Intercultural Communication,* 2nd ed., ed. William B. Gudykunst and Bella Mody (Thousand Oaks, CA: Sage, 2002) 89–106. The authors identify six dimensions of cultural differences in which nonverbal variations are described. These include immediacy, individualism–collectivism, gender, power distance, uncertainty avoidance, and high versus low context. This is a useful summary because it is up-to-date and links well to other key concepts presented in *Intercultural Competence.*

Edward T. Hall, *The Hidden Dimension* (Garden City, NY: Doubleday, 1966). An exploration of the variations in the use of space across cultures and how that use reflects cultural values and establishes rules for interactions.

Edward T. Hall, *The Silent Language* (New York: Anchor Books, 1981). The classic work that launched explorations into the impact of culture on the ways that people from different cultures interpret various cultural symbols, including time and distance.

David Matsumoto, Brenda Franklin, Jung-Wook Choi, David Rogers, and Haruyo Tatani, "Cultural Influences on the Expression and Perception of Emotion," *Handbook of International and Intercultural Communication,* 2nd ed., ed. William B. Gudykunst and Bella Mody (Thousand Oaks, CA: Sage, 2002) 107–125. A scholarly summary that explores the culturally universal and culturally specific displays and expressions of emotions.

For additional information about intercultural films and about Web sites on specific cultures, turn to the Resources section at the back of this book.

Verbal Intercultural Communication

**The Power of Language in
   Intercultural Communication**
Definition of Verbal Codes
The Features of Language
Rule Systems in Verbal Codes
Interpretation and Intercultural
   Communication
**Language, Thought, Culture, and
   Intercultural Communication**

The Sapir–Whorf Hypothesis
   of Linguistic Relativity
Language and Intercultural
   Communication
**Verbal Codes and Intercultural
   Competence**
Summary

In this chapter we consider the effects of language systems on people's ability to communicate interculturally. In so doing we explore the accuracy of a statement by the world-famous linguistic philosopher Ludwig Wittgenstein, who asserted that "the limits of my language are the limits of my world."

The Power of Language in Intercultural Communication

Consider the following examples, each of which illustrates the pivotal role of language in human interaction:

A U.S. business executive is selected by her company for an important assignment in Belgium, not only because she has been very successful but also because she speaks French. She prepares her materials and presentation and sets off for Belgium with high expectations for landing a new contract for her firm. Once in Belgium, she learns that although the individuals in the Belgian company certainly speak French, and there are even individuals who speak German or English, their first language and the preferred language for conducting their business is Flemish. Both the U.S. business executive and her company failed to consider that Belgium is a multicultural and multilingual country populated by Walloons who speak French and Flemings who speak Flemish.

Vijay is a student from India who has just arrived in the United States to attend graduate school at a major university. Vijay began to learn English in primary school, and since his field of study is engineering, even his classes in the program leading to his bachelor's degree were conducted in English. Vijay considers himself to be proficient in the English language. Nevertheless, during his first week on campus the language of those around him is bewildering. People seem to talk so fast that Vijay has difficulty differentiating one word from another. Even when he recognizes the words, he cannot quite understand what people mean by them. His dormitory roommate seemed to say, "I'll catch you later" when he left the room. The secretary in the departmental office tried to explain to him about his teaching assistantship and the students assigned to the classes he was helping to instruct. Her references to students who would attempt to "crash" the course were very puzzling to him. His new faculty advisor, sensing Vijay's anxiety about all of these new situations, told him to "hang loose" and "go with the flow." When Vijay inquired of another teaching assistant about the meaning of these words, the teaching assistant's only reaction was to shake his head and say, "Your advisor's from another time zone!" Needless to say, Vijay's bewilderment continued.

Language—whether it is English, French, Swahili, Flemish, Hindi, or one of the world's other numerous languages—is a taken-for-granted aspect of people's lives. Language is learned without conscious awareness. Children are capable of using their language competently before the age of formal schooling. Even during their school years, they learn the rules and words of the language and do not attend to how the lan-

CULTURE *connections*

My first "word" was "milk." I said it in sign language, reaching my little hands out from the crib. The sign for "milk" in my family was two closed fists rubbing knuckles together up and down in a loose imitation of milking a cow. I was 6 months old, according to my parents. That I signed before I spoke proves what scientists now have discovered: children of the deaf babble with their fingers, just as children of the hearing babble with their tongues.

Sign was my native language. It is a language inextricably tied to my inner feelings, more so than speech. To a native signer who can also hear, there is a strong and nostalgic feeling about sign language that is intimately connected to earliest childhood. To this day if I sign "milk," I feel more milky than if I say the word. When I make the sign and facial gestures for "hate"—a face contorted with anger as both hands hurl the hate with flinging fingers—I feel the kind of hate a child feels, emotion unmediated by polite adult expectations. Likewise "love," indicated by crossing arms against chest and giving oneself a hug, feels far more encompassing and visceral than the word "love" stated with the lips.

—*Lennard J. Davis*

guage influences the way they think and perceive the world. It is usually only when people speak their language to those who do not understand it or when they struggle to become competent in another language that they recognize language's central role in the ability to function, to accomplish tasks, and, most important, to interact with others. It is only when the use of language no longer connects people to others or when individuals are denied the use of their language that they recognize its importance.

There is a set of circumstances involving communication with people from other cultural backgrounds in which awareness of language becomes paramount. Intercultural communication usually means interaction between people who speak different languages. Even when the individuals seem to be speaking the same language—a person from Spain interacting with someone from Venezuela, a French Canadian conversing with a French-speaking citizen of Belgium, or an Australian person visiting the United States—the differences in the specific dialects of the language and the different cultural practices that govern language use can mystify those involved and they can realistically be portrayed as two people who speak different languages.

In this chapter we explore the nature of language and how verbal codes affect communication between people of different cultural backgrounds. Because this book is written in English and initially intended for publication and distribution in the United States, many of the examples and comparisons refer to characteristics of the English language as it is used in the United States. We begin with a discussion of the characteristics and rule systems that create verbal codes and the process of interpretation from one verbal code to another. We then turn to a discussion of the all-important topic of the relationship among language, culture, thought, and intercultural communication. As we consider this issue, we explore the Sapir–Whorf hypothesis of linguistic relativity and assess the scholarly evidence that has been amassed both in support of the hypothesis and in opposition to it. We also consider the importance of language in the identity of ethnic and cultural groups. The chapter concludes with a consideration of verbal codes and intercultural competence.

Definition of Verbal Codes

Discussions about the uniqueness of human beings usually center on our capability to manipulate and understand symbols that allow interaction with others. In a discussion of the importance of language, Charles F. Hockett noted that language allows people to understand messages about many different topics from literally thousands of people. Language allows us to talk with others, to understand or disagree with them, to make plans, to remember the past, to imagine future events, and to describe and evaluate objects and experiences that exist in some other location. Hockett also pointed out that language is taught to individuals by others and thus is transmitted from generation to generation in much the same way as culture. In other words, language is learned.[1]

Popular references to language often include not only spoken and written language but also "body language." However, we have already discussed the latter topic in the previous chapter on nonverbal codes. Here we will concentrate on understanding the relationship of spoken and written language, or verbal codes, to intercultural communication competence.

The Features of Language

Verbal means "consisting of words." Therefore, a *verbal code* is a set of rules about the use of words in the creation of messages. Words can obviously be either spoken or written. Verbal codes, then, include both oral (spoken) language and nonoral (written) language.

Children first learn the oral form of a language. Parents do not expect two-year-olds to read the words on the pages of books. Instead, as parents speak aloud to a child, they identify or name objects in order to teach the child the relationship between the language and the objects or ideas the language represents. In contrast, learning a second language as an adolescent or adult often proceeds more formally, with a combination of oral and nonoral approaches. Students in a foreign language class are usually required to buy a textbook that contains written forms of the language, which then guide students in understanding both the oral and the written use of the words and phrases.

Although English is spoken in many parts of the world, its use varies greatly. This sign on a sidewalk in Europe for a WC (water closet) differs from what you would find in the U.S.

The concept of a written language is familiar to all students enrolled in U.S. college and university classes, as they all require at least reasonable proficiency in the nonoral form of the English language. Fewer and fewer languages exist only in oral form. When anthropologists and linguists discover a culture that has a unique oral language, they usually attempt to develop a written form of it in order to preserve it. Indeed, many Hmong who immigrated to the United States from their hill tribes in Southeast Asia have had to learn not only the new language of English but also, in many instances, the basic fact that verbal codes can be expressed in written form. Imagine the enormous task it must be not only to learn a second language but also first to understand that language can be written.

Our concern in this chapter is principally with the spoken verbal codes that are used in face-to-face intercultural communication. Nevertheless, because the written language also influences the way the language is used orally, written verbal codes play a supporting role in our discussion, and some of our examples and illustrations draw on written expressions of verbal codes in intercultural communication.

An essential ingredient of both verbal and nonverbal codes is symbols. As you recall from Chapter 1, symbols are words, actions, or objects that stand for or represent a unit of meaning. The relationship between symbols and what they stand for is often highly arbitrary, particularly for verbal symbols.

CULTURE *connections*

It was my first year of school, my first days away from the private realm of our house and tongue. I thought English would be simply a version of our Korean. Like another kind of coat you could wear. I didn't know what a difference in language meant then. Or how my tongue would tie in the initial attempts, stiffen so, struggle like an animal booby-trapped and dying inside my head. Native speakers may not fully know this, but English is a scabrous mouthful. In Korean, there are no separate sounds for L and R, the sound is singular and without a baroque Spanish trill or roll. There is no B and V for us, no P and F. I always thought someone must have invented certain words to torture us. *Frivolous. Barbarian. . . .*

I will always make bad errors of speech. I remind myself of my mother and father, fumbling in front of strangers. Lelia says there are certain mental pathways of speaking that can never be unlearned. Sometimes I'll say *riddle* for *little,* or *bent* for *vent,* though without any accent and so whoever's present just thinks I've momentarily lost my train of thought. But I always hear myself displacing the two languages, conflating them—maybe conflagrating them—for there's so much rubbing and friction, a fire always threatens to blow up between the tongues. Friction, affliction. In kindergarten, kids would call me "Marble Mouth" because I spoke in a garbled voice, my bound tongue wrenching myself to move in the right ways.

—*Chang-rae Lee*

Another critical ingredient of verbal codes is the system of rules that governs the composition and ordering of the symbols. Everyone has had to learn the rules of a language—how to spell, use correct grammar, and make appropriate vocabulary choices—and thereby gain enough mastery of the language to tell jokes, to poke fun, and to be sarcastic. Even more than differences in the symbols themselves, the variations in rules for ordering and using symbols produce the different languages people use.

Rule Systems in Verbal Codes

Five different but interrelated sets of rules combine to create a verbal code, or language. These parts or components of language are called phonology, morphology, semantics, syntactics, and pragmatics.

Phonology   When you listen to someone who speaks a language other than your own, you will often hear different (some might even say "strange") sounds. The basic sound units of a language are called *phonemes,* and the rules for combining phonemes constitute the *phonology* of a language. Examples of phonemes in English include the sounds you make when speaking, such as [k], [t], or [a].

The phonological rules of a language tell speakers which sounds to use and how to order them. For instance, the word *cat* has three phonemes: a hard [k] sound, the short [a] vowel, and the [t] sound. These same three sounds, or phonemes, can be rearranged to form other combinations: *act, tack,* or even *tka.* Of course, as someone who speaks and writes English, your knowledge of the rules for creating appropriate combinations of phonemes undoubtedly suggests to you that *tka* is improper. Interestingly, you know that *tka* is incorrect even though you probably cannot describe the rules that make it so.[2]

Languages have different numbers of phonemes. English, for example, depends on about forty-five phonemes. The number of phonemes in other languages ranges from as few as fifteen to as many as eighty-five.[3]

Mastery of another language requires practice in reproducing its sounds accurately. Sometimes it is difficult to hear the distinctions in the sounds made by those proficient in the language. Native U.S. English speakers often have difficulty in hearing phonemic distinctions in tonal languages, such as Chinese, that use different pitches for many sounds, which then represent different meanings. Even when the differences can be heard, the mouths and tongues of those learning another language are sometimes unable to produce these sounds. In intercultural communication, imperfect rendering of the phonology of a language—in other words, not speaking the sounds as native speakers do—can make it difficult to be understood accurately. Accents of second-language speakers, which we discuss in more detail later in this chapter, can sometimes provoke negative reactions in native speakers.

In your living spaces (house, room, apartment, etc.), arbitrarily choose a different word to refer to such common items as tables, chairs, couches, and televisions. Consistently use those words for a day or two and note people's reactions. Do others begin using the same labels as you? Do they try to get you to "behave" properly and return to the "correct" terminology?

Morphology   Phonemes combine to form *morphemes,* which are the smallest units of meaning in a language. The 45 English phonemes can be used to generate more than 50 million morphemes! For instance, the word *comfort,* whose meaning refers to a state of ease and contentment, contains one morpheme. But the word *comforted* contains two morphemes: *comfort* and *-ed.* The latter is a suffix that means that the comforting action or activity happened in the past. Indeed, though all words contain at least one morpheme, some words (such as *uncomfortable,* which has three morphemes) can contain two or more. Note that morphemes refer only to meaning units. Though the word *comfort* contains smaller words such as *or* and *fort,* these other words are coincidental to the basic meaning of *comfort.* Morphemes, or meaning units in language, can also differ depending on the way they are pronounced. In Chinese, for instance, the word pronounced as "Ma" can have four different meanings—mother, toad, horse, or scold—depending on the tone with which it is uttered.[4] Pronunciation errors can have very unintended meanings!

Semantics   As noted earlier, morphemes—either singly or in combination—are used to form words. The study of the meaning of words is called *semantics.* The most convenient and thorough source of information about the semantics of a language is the dictionary, which defines what a word means in a particular language. A more formal way of describing the study of semantics is to say that it is the study of the relationship between words and what they stand for or represent. You can see the semantics of a language in action when a baby is being taught to name the parts of the body. Someone skilled in the language points to and touches the baby's nose and simultaneously vocalizes the word *nose.* Essentially, the baby is being taught the vocabulary of a language. Competent communication in any language requires knowledge of the words needed to express ideas. You have probably experienced the frustration of trying to describe an event but not being able to think of words that accurately convey the intended meaning. Part of what we are trying to accomplish with this book is to give you a vocabulary that can be used to understand and explain the nature of intercultural communication competence.

Communicating interculturally necessitates learning a new set of semantic rules. The baby that grows up where people speak Swahili does not learn to say *nose* when the protruding portion of the face is touched; instead, she or he is taught to say *pua.* For an English speaker to talk with a Swahili speaker about his or her nose, at least one of them must learn the word for nose in the other's language. When learning a second language, much time is devoted to learning the appropriate associations between the words and the specific objects, events, or feelings that the language system assigns to them. Even those whose intercultural communication occurs with people who speak the "same" language must learn at least some new vocabulary. The U.S. American visiting Great Britain will confront new meanings for words. For example, *boot* refers to the storage place in a car, or what the U.S.-English-speaking person would call the *trunk. Chips* to the British are *French fries* to the U.S. American. A Band-Aid in the United States is called a *plug* in Great Britain. As Winston Churchill so wryly suggested, the two countries are indeed "divided by a common language."

The discussion of semantics is incomplete without noting one other important distinction: the difference between the denotative and connotative meanings of words. *Denotative meanings* are the public, objective, and legal meanings of a word. Denotative meanings are those found in the dictionary or law books. In contrast, *connotative meanings* are personal, emotionally charged, private, and specific to a particular person.

Can you order from this menu in Budapest, Hungary?

As an illustration, consider a common classroom event known as a *test*. When used by a college professor who is speaking to a group of undergraduate students, *test* is a relatively easy word to define denotatively. It is a formal examination that is used to assess a person's degree of knowledge or skill. But the connotative meanings of *test* probably vary greatly from student to student; some react to the idea with panic, and others are blasé and casual. Whereas denotative meanings tell us, in an abstract sense, what the words mean objectively, our interest in intercultural communication suggests that an understanding of the connotative meanings—the feelings and thoughts evoked in others as a result of the words used in the conversation—is critical to achieving intercultural competence.

As an example of the importance of connotative meanings, consider the experience reported by a Nigerian student who was attending a university in the United States. When working with a fellow male student who was African American, the Nigerian called to him by saying, "Hey, boy, come over here." To the Nigerian student, the term *boy* connotes a friendly and familiar relationship, is a common form of address in Nigeria, and is often used to convey a perception of a strong interpersonal bond. To the African American student, however, the term *boy* evokes images of racism, oppression, and an attempt to place him in an inferior social status. Fortunately, the two students were friends and were able to talk to each other to clarify how they each interpreted the Nigerian student's semantic choices; further misunderstandings were avoided. Often, however, such opportunities for clarification do not occur.

Another example is seen in the casual conversation of a U.S. American student and an Arab student. The former had heard a radio news story about the intelligence of pigs and was recounting the story as "fact" when the Arab student forcefully declared, "Pigs are dirty animals, and they are very dumb." The U.S. American student describes her reaction: "In my ignorance, I argued with him by telling him that it was true and had been scientifically proven." It was only later that she learned that as part of the religious beliefs of devout Muslims, pigs are believed to be unclean. Learning the connotative meanings of language is essential in achieving competence in another culture's verbal code.

Syntactics   The fourth component of language is *syntactics,* the relationship of words to one another. When children are first learning how to combine words into phrases, they are being introduced to the syntactics of their language. Each language stipulates the correct way to arrange words. In English it is not acceptable to create a sentence such as the following: "On by the book desk door is the the." It is incorrect to place the preposition *by* immediately following the preposition *on.* Instead, each preposition must have an object, which results in phrases such as "on the desk" and "by the door." Similarly, articles such as *the* in a sentence are not to be presented one right after the other. Instead, the article is placed near the noun, which produces a sentence that includes "the book," "the door," and "the desk." The syntactics of English grammar suggest that the words in the preceding nonsense sentence might be rearranged to form the grammatically correct sentence "The book is on the desk by the door." The order of the words helps establish the meaning of the utterance.

Each language has a set of rules that govern the sequence of the words. To learn another language you must learn those rules. The sentence "John has, to the store to buy

CULTURE *connections*

"Spanglish"—a Spanish-English hybrid dialect—was once the street slang of tough, colorful Mexican-American *cholos.* Today Spanglish is the region's third language, spoken by young and old, Latino and Anglo. Here's how:

▶ With hybrid words:
Ahí nos watchamos (See you later, *hasta luego*—literally, we'll watch each other there)
Shawerear (to shower, *bañarse*)
Wifa (wife, *esposa*)

▶ Using Spanish colloquialisms unique to the region:
Biroles (*frijoles,* beans)
¿Cómo la juegas¿ (*¿Cuál es tu trabajo?,* what's your line of work?)
¿Qué cura¿ (*¿Qué hay de nuevo?,* What's up?)
¡A la brava ése! (Let's cut the bull!)

▶ Blending Spanish and English phrases in the same sentence:
Cómo se llama that place? (inversion: What's the name *de ese lugar?*)
Quieres ir a dancing? (inversion: Want to go *a bailar?*)
What are you doing este fin de semana? (inversion: *Qué haces* this weekend?)

some eggs, gone" is an incorrect example of English syntax but an accurate representation of German syntax.

Pragmatics   The final component of all verbal codes is *pragmatics,* the effect of language on human perceptions and behaviors. The study of pragmatics focuses on how language is actually used. A pragmatic analysis of language goes beyond phonology, morphology, semantics, and syntactics. Instead, it considers how users of a particular language are able to understand the meanings of specific utterances in particular contexts. By learning the pragmatics of language use, you understand how to participate in a conversation and you know how to sequence the sentences you speak as part of a conversation. For example, when you are eating a meal with a group of people and somebody says, "Is there any salt?" you know that you should give the person the salt shaker rather than simply answering "yes."

To illustrate how the pragmatics of language use can affect intercultural communication, imagine yourself as a dinner guest in a Pakistani household. You have just eaten a delicious meal. You are relatively full but not so full that it would be impossible for you to eat more if it was considered socially appropriate to do so. Consider the following dialogue:

> *Hostess:* I see that your plate is empty. Would you like some more curry?
>   *You:* No, thank you. It was delicious, but I'm quite full.
> *Hostess:* Please, you must have some more to eat.
>   *You:* No, no thank you. I've really had enough. It was just great, but I can't eat another bite.
> *Hostess:* Are you sure that you won't have any more? You really seemed to enjoy the brinjals. Let me put just a little bit more on your plate.

What is your next response? What is the socially appropriate answer? Is it considered socially inappropriate for a dinner guest not to accept a second helping of food? Or is the hostess pressing you to have another helping because in her culture your reply is not interpreted as a true negative response? Even if you knew Urdu, the language spoken in Pakistan, you would have to understand the pragmatics of language use to respond appropriately—in this instance, to say "no" at least three times.

The rules governing the pragmatics of a language are firmly embedded in the larger rules of the culture and are intimately associated with the cultural patterns discussed in Chapters 4 and 5. For example, cultures vary in the degree to which they encourage people to ask direct questions and to make direct statements. Imagine a student from the United States who speaks some Japanese and who subsequently goes to Japan as an exchange student. The U.S. American's culturally learned tendency is to deal with problems directly, and she may therefore confront her Japanese roommate about the latter's habits in order to "clear the air" and establish an "open" relationship. Given the Japanese cultural preference for indirectness and face-saving behaviors, the U.S. American student's skill in Japanese does not extend to the pragmatics of language use. As Wen Shu Lee suggests, these differences in the pragmatic rule systems of languages also make it very difficult to tell a joke—or even to understand a joke—in a second language.[5] Humor requires a subtle knowledge of both the expected meanings of the words (semantics) and their intended effects (pragmatics).

CULTURE *connections*

Walking in the city, the financial heartland of London, I overheard a bit of conversation between two British businesspersons that went something like this:

"Yes, it is a pity that Ian's in queer street."
"Too much hire purchase was the problem, wasn't it?"
"Yes, and too many purchases of bespoken clothes and other things."
"And now his personal and business current accounts are badly overdrawn?"
"Precisely. He's been forced to retain a solicitor, and his position as commercial traveler is in jeopardy."

Hearing that conversation made one thing very apparent to me, a native speaker of American English: significant differences sometimes exist in the vocabulary that American and British businesspersons use to convey messages, and a sound grasp of one of the two globally dominant forms of English isn't always sufficient to ensure accurate message comprehension across cultures.

The conversation between two British businesspersons converted to its equivalent English form:

"Yes, it is unfortunate that Ian's seriously in debt."
"Was too much installment buying the problem?"
"Yes, and too many purchases of custom-made clothes and other things."
"And now his personal and business checking accounts are badly overdrawn?
"Precisely. He's been forced to hire a lawyer, and his job as a traveling salesman is in jeopardy.

—*James Calvert Scott*

Interpretation and Intercultural Communication

Translation can be defined as the use of verbal signs to understand the verbal signs of another language.[6] Translation usually refers to the transfer of written verbal codes between languages. *Interpretation* refers to the oral process of moving from one code to another. When heads of state meet, an interpreter accompanies them. The translator, in contrast to the interpreter, usually has more time to consider how she or he wants to phrase a particular passage in a text. Interpreters must make virtually immediate decisions about which words or phrases would best represent the meanings of the speaker.

The Role of Interpretation in Today's World   Issues surrounding the interpretation of verbal codes from one language to another are becoming more and more important for all of us. Such issues include whether the words or the ideas of the original should be conveyed, whether the translation should reflect the style of the original or that of the translator, and whether an interpreter should correct cultural mistakes.

Using a dictionary that shows the origin of words, find five English words that originated in different languages. In class, compare your words to those of others. Are there certain languages that seem to predominate? Can you make generalizations about the types of words that come to the English language from other languages?

In today's global marketplace, health care workers, teachers, government workers, and businesspeople of all types find that they are increasingly required to use professional interpreters to communicate verbally with their clients and thus fulfill their professional obligations.[7] Similarly, instructions for assembling consumer products that are sold in the United States but manufactured in another country often demonstrate the difficulty in moving from one language to another. Even though the words on the printed instruction sheet are in English, the instructions may not be correct or accurately interpreted.

Issues in interpretation, then, are very important. People involved in intercultural transactions must often depend on the services of multilingual individuals who can help to bridge the intercultural communication gap.

Types of Equivalence   If the goal in interpreting from one language to another is to represent the source language as closely as possible, a simpler way of describing the goal is with the term *equivalence*. Those concerned about developing a science of translation have described a number of different types of equivalence. *Dynamic equivalence* has been offered as one goal of good translation and interpretation.[8] Five kinds of equiva-

These signs in Navajo, English, and Spanish reflect the many languages used by the people of New Mexico.

lence must be considered in moving from one language to another: vocabulary, idiomatic, grammatical–syntactical, experiential, and conceptual equivalence.[9]

Vocabulary Equivalence   To establish vocabulary equivalence, the interpreter seeks a word in the target language that has the same meaning in the source language. This is sometimes very difficult to do. Perhaps the words spoken in the source language have no direct equivalents in the target language. For instance, in Igbo, a language spoken in Nigeria, there is no word for *window*. The word in Igbo that is used to represent a window, *mpio,* actually means "opening." Likewise, there is no word for *efficiency* in the Russian language, and the English phrase "A house is not a home" has no genuine vocabulary equivalent in some languages. Alternatively, there may be several words in the target language that have similar meanings to the word in the source language, so the interpreter must select the word that best fits the intended ideas. An interpreter will sometimes use a combination of words in the target language to approximate the original word, or the interpreter may offer several different words to help the listener understand the meaning of the original message.

Idiomatic Equivalence   An idiom is an expression that has a meaning contrary to the usual meaning of the words. Phrases such as "Eat your heart out," "It's raining cats and dogs," and "Eat humble pie" are all examples of idioms. Idioms are so much a part of language that people are rarely aware of using them. Think of the literal meaning of the following idiom: "I was so upset I could have died." Or consider the plight of a Malaysian student who described his befuddlement when his fellow students in the United States initiated conversations by asking, "What's up?" His instinctive reaction was to look up, but after doing so several times he realized that the question was an opening to conversation rather than a literal reference to something happening above him. Another example is the request a supervisor in a university media center made to a student assistant from India, who tended to take conversations and instructions literally. The supervisor instructed the assistant to "put this videotape on the television." The supervisor was later surprised to learn that the videotape was literally placed on top of the television, instead of being played for the class. The challenge for interpreters is to understand the intended meanings of idiomatic expressions and to translate them into the other language.

Grammatical–Syntactical Equivalence   The discussion later in this chapter about some of the variations among grammars highlights the problems in establishing equivalence

CULTURE *connections*

The in-law situation was overwhelming for me, an only child. There is no Kikuyu word for uncle or aunt so Joseph had six fathers and the mamas were even more numerous— small, wiry women who smelled like butter when they hugged me.

—*Kathleen Coskran*

in grammatical or syntactical rule systems. Quite simply, some languages make grammatical distinctions that others do not. For instance, when translating from the Hopi language into English, the interpreter has to make adjustments for the lack of verb tenses in Hopi because tense is a necessary characteristic of every English utterance.

Experiential Equivalence   Differing life experiences are another hurdle the interpreter must overcome. The words presented must have some meaning within the experiential framework of the person to whom the message is directed. If people have never seen a television, for instance, a translation of the phrase "I am going to stay home tonight and watch television" would have virtually no meaning to them. Similarly, although clocks are a common device for telling time and they govern the behaviors of most U.S. Americans, many people live in cultures in which there are no clocks and no words for this concept. Some Hmong people, upon moving to the United States, initially had difficulty with the everyday experience of telling time with a clock.

CULTURE *connections*

What Language Do You Speak?

U.S. English	British English
Bomb (failure)	Bomb (success)
Closet	Cupboard
Cookie	Biscuit
Dessert	Pudding
Drug store	Chemist's shop
Flashlight	Torch
Hamburger bun	Bap
Hamburger meat	Mince
Hardware store	Ironmonger
Hotdog bun	Bridge roll
Mailbox	Pillar box
Notions	Haberdashery
Pacifier	Dummy
Potato chips	Crisps
Rubber cement	Cow gum
Round-trip ticket	Return ticket
Scab	Blackleg
Second floor	First floor
Stove	Cooker
Sweater	Jumper
Two weeks	Fortnight
Undershirt	Vest
Washcloth	Face flannel

Conceptual Equivalence   Conceptual equivalence takes us back to the discussions in Chapters 4 and 5 about cultural patterns being part of a person's definition of reality. Conversation with people with radically different cultural patterns requires making sense of the variety of concepts that each culture defines as real and good.

Language, Thought, Culture, and Intercultural Communication

Every language has its unique features and ways of allowing those who speak it to identify specific objects and experiences. These linguistic features, which distinguish each language from all others, affect how the speakers of the language perceive and experience the world. To understand the effects of language on intercultural communication, questions such as the following must be explored:

- How do initial experiences with language shape or influence the way in which a person thinks?
- Do the categories of a language—its words, grammar, and usage—influence how people think and behave?

More specifically, consider the following question:

- Does a person growing up in Saudi Arabia, who learns to speak and write Arabic, "see" and "experience" the world differently than does a person who grows up speaking and writing Tagalog in the Philippines?

Although many scholars have advanced ideas and theories about the relationships among language, thought, culture, and intercultural communication, the names most often associated with these issues are Benjamin Lee Whorf and Edward Sapir. Their theory is called *linguistic relativity*.

The Sapir–Whorf Hypothesis of Linguistic Relativity

Until the early part of the twentieth century, in Western Europe and the United States language was generally assumed to be a neutral medium that did not influence the way people experienced the world.[10] During that time, the answer to the preceding question would have been that, regardless of whether people grew up learning and speaking Arabic or Tagalog, they would experience the world similarly. The varying qualities of language would not have been expected to affect the people who spoke those languages. Language, from this point of view, was merely a vehicle by which ideas were presented, rather than a shaper of the very substance of those ideas.

In 1921 anthropologist Edward Sapir began to articulate an alternative view of language, asserting that language influenced or even determined the ways in which people thought.[11] Sapir's student, Benjamin Whorf, continued to develop Sapir's ideas through the 1940s. Together, their ideas became subsumed under several labels, including the theory of linguistic determinism, the theory of linguistic relativity, the Sapir–Whorf hypothesis, and the Whorfian hypothesis. The following quotation from Sapir is typical of their statements:

> Human beings do not live in the objective world alone, nor alone in the world of social activity as ordinarily understood, but are very much at the mercy of the particular language which has become the medium of expression for their society. It is quite an

illusion to imagine that one adjusts to reality essentially without the use of language and that language is merely an incidental means of solving specific problems of communication or reflection. The fact of the matter is that the "real world" is to a large extent unconsciously built up on the language habits of the group. . . . The worlds in which different societies [cultures] live are distinct worlds, not merely the same world with different labels attached. . . . We see and hear and otherwise experience very largely as we do because the language habits of our community predispose certain choices of interpretation.[12]

This young man in Mauritania is practices writing. The Sapir-Whorf hypothesis underscores the relationship between his language and his experiences in the world.

Our discussion of the Sapir–Whorf hypothesis is not intended to provide a precise rendering as articulated by Sapir and Whorf, which is virtually impossible to do. During the twenty years in which they formally presented their ideas to the scholarly community, their views shifted somewhat and their writings include both "firmer" or more deterministic views of the relationship between language and thought and "softer" views that describe language as merely influencing or shaping thought.

In the "firm" or deterministic version of the hypothesis, language functions like a prison—once people learn a language, they are irrevocably affected by its particulars. Furthermore, it is never possible to translate effectively and successfully between languages, which makes competent intercultural communication an elusive goal.

The "softer" position is a less causal view of the nature of the language–thought relationship. In this version, language shapes how people think and experience their world, but this influence is not unceasing. Instead, it is possible for people from different initial language systems to learn words and categories sufficiently similar to their own so that communication can be accurate.

If substantial evidence had been found to support the firmer version of the Sapir–Whorf hypothesis, it would represent a dismal prognosis for competent intercultural communication. Because so few people grow up bilingually, it would be impossible to transcend the boundaries of our linguistic experiences. Fortunately, the weight of the scholarly evidence, which we summarize in the following section, debunks the notion that people's first language traps them inescapably in a particular pattern of thinking. Instead, evidence suggests that language plays a powerful role in *shaping* how people think and experience the world. Although the shaping properties of language are significant, linguistic equivalence can be established between people from different language systems.[13]

Sapir and Whorf's major contribution to the study of intercultural communication is that they called attention to the integral relationship among thought, culture, and language. In the following section, we discuss some of the differences in the vocabulary and grammar of languages and consider the extent to which these differences can be used as evidence to support the two positions of the Sapir–Whorf hypothesis. As you consider the following ideas, examine the properties of the languages you know. Are there specialized vocabularies or grammatical characteristics that shape how you think and experience the world as you use these languages?

CULTURE *connections*

When I was learning to read and speak the Tamil language I slowly came to realize that it had no word for "hope." When I questioned my Hindu teacher about this, he asked me in turn what I meant by hope. Does hope mean anything? Things will be what they will be. . . . This conversation helped me to realize that in English also the word "hope" often stands for nothing more than a desire for what may or may not be.

—*Diana L. Eck*

Variations in Vocabulary   The best-known example of vocabulary differences associated with the Sapir–Whorf hypothesis is the large number of words for snow in the Eskimo language. (The language is variously called Inuktitut in Canada, Inupit in Alaska, and Kalaallisut in Greenland.) Depending on whom you ask, there are from seven to fifty different words for snow in the Inuktitut language.[14] For example, there are words that differentiate falling snow (*gana*) and fully fallen snow (*akilukak*). The English language has fewer words for snow and no terms for many of the distinctions made by Eskimos. The issue raised by the Sapir–Whorf hypothesis is whether the person who grows up speaking Inuktitut actually perceives snow differently than does someone who grew up in Southern California and may only know snow by second-hand descriptions. More important, could the Southern Californian who lives with the Inupit in Alaska learn to differentiate all of the variations of snow and to use the specific Eskimo words appropriately? The firmer version of the Sapir–Whorf hypothesis suggests that linguistic differences are accompanied by perceptual differences, so that the English speaker looks at snow differently than does the Eskimo speaker.

There are numerous other examples of languages that have highly specialized vocabularies for particular features of the environment. For instance, in the South Sea islands, there are numerous words for coconut, which not only refer to the object of a coconut but also indicate how the coconut is being used or to a specific part of the coconut.[15] Similarly, in classical Arabic thousands of words are used to refer to a camel.[16]

Another variation in vocabulary concerns the terms a language uses to identify and divide colors in the spectrum. For example, the Kamayura Indians of Brazil have a single word that refers to the colors that English speakers would call blue and green. The best translation of the word the Kamayuras use is "parakeet colored."[17] The Dani of West New Guinea divide all colors into only two words, which are roughly equivalent in English to "dark" and "light."[18] The important issue, however, is whether speakers of these languages are able to distinguish among the different colors when they see them or can experience only the colors suggested by the words available for them to use. Do the Kamayura Indians actually see blue and green as the same color because they use the same word to identify both? Or does their language simply identify colors differently than does English?

Do you think that you could learn to distinguish all of the variations of the object "snow" that are important to the Eskimos? Could you be taught to see all of the important characteristics of a camel or a coconut? Such questions are very important in

---

Interview people who speak a language other than English. What words do they use to refer to the following relatives?

▶ *Grandparent:* father's mother, mother's mother, father's father, mother's father
▶ *Sibling:* oldest brother, older brother, younger brother, youngest brother, oldest sister, older sister, younger sister, youngest sister
▶ *Aunt:* father's older sister, father's younger sister, mother's older sister, mother's younger sister
▶ *Uncle:* father's older brother, father's younger brother, mother's older brother, mother's younger brother
▶ *Cousin:* father's brother's son, father's brother's daughter, mother's brother's son, mother's brother's daughter
▶ *Child:* first-born male child, first-born female child, youngest child

accepting or rejecting the ideas presented in the firm and soft versions of the Sapir–Whorf hypothesis.

Researchers looking at the vocabulary variations in the color spectrum have generally found that although a language may restrict how a color can be labeled verbally, people can still see and differentiate among particular colors. In other words, the Kamayura Indians can, in fact, see both blue and green, even though they use the same linguistic referent for both colors.[19] The evidence on color perception and vocabulary, then, does not support the deterministic version of the Sapir–Whorf hypothesis.

What about all those variations for snow, camels, and coconuts? Are they evidence to support the firm version of the Sapir–Whorf hypothesis? A starting point for addressing this issue is to consider how English speakers use other words along with essentially the one word English has for "particles of water vapor that when frozen in the upper air fall to earth as soft, white, crystalline flakes." English speakers are able to describe verbally many variations of snow by adding modifiers to the root word. People who live in areas with a lot of snow are quite familiar with *dry snow, heavy snow, slush,* or *dirty snow.* Skiers have a rich vocabulary to describe variations in snow on the slopes. It is possible, therefore, for a person who has facility in one language to approximate the categories of another language. The deterministic position of Sapir–Whorf, then, is difficult to support. Even Sapir and Whorf's own work can be used to argue against the deterministic interpretation of their position because in presenting all of the Eskimo words for snow, Whorf provided their approximate English equivalents.

A better explanation for linguistic differences is that variations in the complexity and richness of a language's vocabulary reflect what is important to the people who speak that language. To an Eskimo, differentiating among varieties of snow is much more critical to survival and adaptation than it is to the Southern Californian, who may never see snow. Conversely, Southern Californians have numerous words to refer to four-wheeled motorized vehicles, which are very important objects in their environment. However, we are certain that differences in the words and concepts of a language do affect the ease with which a person can change from one language to another because there is a dynamic interrelationship among language, thought, and culture.

Variations in Linguistic Grammars   A rich illustration of the reciprocal relationship among language, thought, and culture can be found in the grammatical rules of different languages. In the following discussion, you will once again see how the patterns of a culture's beliefs, values, and norms, as discussed in Chapters 4 and 5, permeate all aspects of the culture. Because language shapes how its users organize the world, the patterns of a culture will be reflected in its language and vice versa.

Cultural Conceptions of Time   Whorf himself provided detailed descriptions of the Hopi language that illustrate how the grammar of a language is related to the perceptions of its users. Hopi do not linguistically refer to time as a fixed point or place but rather as a movement in the stream of life. The English language, in contrast, refers to time as a specific point that exists on a linear plane divided into past, present, and future. Hopi time is more like an ongoing process; the here and now (the present) will never actually arrive, but it will always be approaching. The Hopi language also has no tenses, so the people do not place events into the neat categories of past, present, and future that native speakers of English have come to expect. As Stephen Littlejohn has suggested, the consequences of these linguistic differences is that

> Hopi and SAE [Standard Average European] cultures will think about, perceive, and behave toward time differently. For example, the Hopi tend to engage in lengthy preparing activities. Experiences (getting prepared) tend to accumulate as time gets later. The emphasis is on the accumulated experience during the course of time, not on time as a point or location. In SAE cultures, with their spatial treatment of time, experiences are not accumulated in the same sense. Elaborate and lengthy preparations are not often found. The custom in SAE cultures is to record events (space-time analogy) such that what happened in the past is objectified in space (recorded).[20]

Because a culture's linguistic grammar shapes its experiences, the speakers of Hopi and English will experience time differently and each may find it difficult to understand the view of time held by the other. Judgments about what is "natural," "right," or "common sense" will obviously vary and will be reinforced by the linguistic habits of each group.

Showing Respect and Social Hierarchy   Languages allow, and to a certain extent force, speakers to display respect for others. For instance, it is much easier to show respect in Spanish than it is in English. Consider the following sentences:

¿Sabe Usted dónde está la profesora?

Know you where is the professor? [Do you know where the professor is?]

¿Sabes dónde está la profesora?

Know you where is the professor? [Do you know where the professor is?]

These distinctly different Spanish sentences are identical when translated into English. The sentences in Spanish reflect the differences in the level of respect that must be shown between the person speaking and the person being addressed. The pronoun *Usted* is used in the first example to mark the speaker's question as particularly formal or polite. The *s* in *Sabes* in the second example marks the relationship between the speaker and the person being addressed as familiar or informal. In the actual practice of Spanish, a younger person would not use the informal grammatical construction to address an older person, just as an older person would not use the formal *Usted* with a person who was much younger.

This example illustrates once again that the grammar of a language can at least encourage its users to construct their interactions with others in particular ways. When a language directs a speaker to make distinctions among the people with whom the speaker interacts, in this instance by showing linguistically a greater respect for some and not others, the language helps to remind its users of social distinctions and the behaviors that are appropriate to them. Thus, language professors who teach Spanish to English-speaking students often note that the English speaker is not behaving respectfully.

The degree to which a language demands specific words and grammatical structures to show the nature of the relationship between the communicators suggests how much a culture values differences between people. In the frameworks of the ideas presented in Chapters 4 and 5, Spanish-speaking cultures would be more likely to value a hierarchical social organization and a large power distance. Chinese, Japanese, and Korean languages also reflect the relative social status between the addresser and addressee. In

CULTURE *connections*

Language is useful in contrasting both worldviews. Spanish, labyrinthine in nature, has at least four conjugations to address the past; the lone future tense is hardly used. One can portray a past event in multiple ways, but when it comes to one of tomorrow, a speaker in Buenos Aires, Lima, Mexico City, and Caracas has little choice. The fact is symptomatic: Hispanics, unable to recover from history, are obsessed with memory. English, on the other hand, is exact, matter-of-fact—in Jorge Luis Borges's words, "mathematical," a tongue with plenty of room for conditionals, ready to seize destiny.

Spanish makes objects female and male, while in English the same things lack gender. As if one were not enough, Spanish has two verbs for *to be:* one used to describe permanence, another to refer to location and temporality. Thus, a single sentence, say Hamlet's famous dilemma, *To be, or not to be,* is inhabited in Spanish by a double, never self-negating, clear-cut meaning: to be or not to be alive; to be or not to be here. English simplifier: to be, period—here and now. Again, Spanish has two verbs for *to know:* one used to characterize knowledge through experience, the other to designate memorized information. To know Prague is not the same as to know the content of the Declaration of Independence. Much less baroque, English refuses complication.

—Ilan Stavans

Hindi, Korean, and other languages, there are specific words for older brother, older sister, younger brother, and younger sister, which remind all siblings of their relative order in the family and the norms or expectations appropriate to specific familial roles. Languages with grammatical and semantic features that make the speakers decide whether to show respect and social status to others are constant reminders of those characteristics of social interaction. In contrast, a language with few terms to show status and respect tends to minimize those status distinctions in the minds of the language's users.

Pronouns and Cultural Characteristics   English is the only language that capitalizes the pronoun *I* in writing. English does not, however, capitalize the written form of the pronoun *you*. Is there a relationship between the individualism that characterizes most of the English-speaking countries and this feature of the English language? In contrast, consider that there are more than 12 words for *I* in Vietnamese, in Chinese more than 10, and over 100 in Japanese.[21] Does a language that demands a speaker to differentiate the self (the "I") from other features of the context (for example, other people or the type of event) shape the way speakers of that language think about themselves? If "I" exist, but "I" am able to identify myself linguistically only through reference to someone else, will "I" not have a different sense of myself than the English-speaking people who see themselves as entities existing apart from all others?[22]

As an example of the extreme contrasts that exist in the use and meanings of pronouns, consider the experiences of Michael Dorris, who lived in Tyonek, Alaska, an Athabaskan-speaking Native American community:

Much of my time was spent in the study of the local language, linguistically related to Navajo and Apache but distinctly adapted to the subarctic environment. One of its most difficult features for an outsider to grasp was the practice of almost always speaking and thinking in a collective plural voice. The word for people, "dene," was used as a kind of "we"—the subject for virtually every predicate requiring a personal pronoun—and therefore any act became, at least in conception, a group experience.[23]

Imagine having been trained in the language that Dorris describes. Would speaking such a language result in people who think of themselves as part of a group rather than as individuals?[24] Alternatively, if you are from a culture that values individualism, would you have difficulty communicating in a language that requires you always to say *we* instead of *I*? If your cultural background is more group-oriented, would it be relatively easy for you to speak in a language that places you as part of a group?

Linguistic Relativity and Intercultural Communication   The semantic and syntactic features of language are powerful shapers of the way people experience the physical and social world. Sapir and Whorf's assertions that language *determines* our reality have proved to be false. Language does not determine our ability to sense the physical world, nor does the language first learned create modes of thinking from which there is no escape. However, language shapes and influences our thoughts and behaviors. The vocabulary of a language reflects what you need to know to cope with the environment and the patterns of your culture. The semantics and syntactics of language gently nudge you to notice particular kinds of things in your world and to label them in particular ways. All of these components of language create habitual response patterns to the people, events, and messages that surround you. Your language intermingles with other aspects of your culture to reinforce the cultural patterns you are taught.

The influence of a particular language is something you can escape; it is possible to translate to or interact in a second language. But as the categories for coding or sorting the world are provided primarily by your language, you are predisposed to perceive the world in a particular way, and the reality you create is different from the reality created by those who use other languages with other categories.

When the categories of languages are vastly different, people will have trouble communicating with one another. Differences in language affect what is relatively easy to say and what seems virtually impossible to say. As Wilma M. Roger has suggested, "Language and the cultural values, reactions, and expectations of speakers of that language are subtly melded."[25]

We offer one final caution. For purposes of discussion we have artificially separated vocabulary and grammar, as if language is simply an adding together of these two elements. In use, language is a dynamic and interrelated system that has a powerful effect on people's thoughts and actions. The living, breathing qualities of language as spoken and used, with all the attendant feelings, emotions, and experiences, are difficult to convey adequately in an introductory discussion such as this one.

Language and Intercultural Communication

The earlier sections of this chapter may have given the impression that language is stable and used consistently by all who speak it. However, even in a country that has predominantly only one language, there are great variations in the way the language is spoken (accents) and there are wide deviations in how words are used and what they mean. Among U.S. Americans who speak English, it is quite common to hear many different accents. It is also quite common to hear words, phrases, and colloquial expressions that are common to only one region of the country. Think of the many voices associated with the speaking of English in the United States. Do you have an auditory image of the way someone sounds who grew up in New York City? How about someone who grew up in Georgia? Wisconsin? Oregon? The regional variations in the ways English is spoken reflect differences in accents and dialects.

Increasingly, U.S. Americans speak many first languages other than English. As noted in Chapter 1, multiple language systems are represented in U.S. schools. Employers in businesses must now be conscious of the different languages of their workers. In addition, specialized linguistic structures develop for other functions within the context of a larger language. Because language differences are powerful factors that influence the relationships between ethnic and cultural groups who live next to and with each other in communities and countries, we will examine the variations among languages of groups of people who essentially share a common political union.[26] We begin by considering the role of language in maintaining the identity of a cultural group and in the relationship between cultural groups who share a common social system. We then talk about nonstandard versions of a language, including accents, dialects, and argot, and we explore their effects on communication with others.

Language, Ethnic Group Identity, and Dominance   Each person commonly identifies with many different social groups. For example, you probably think of yourself as part of a certain age grouping, as male or female, as married or unmarried, and as a college student or someone who is simply interested in learning about intercultural communication. You may also think of yourself as African American, German American, Vietnamese American, Latino, Navajo, or one of the many other cultural groups composing the population of the United States. You may also identify with a culture from outside of the United States.

Henri Tajfel argues that humans categorize themselves and others into different groups to simplify their understanding of people. When you think of someone as part of a particular social group, you associate that person with the values of that group.[27] In this section we are particularly concerned with the ways in which language is used to identify people in a group, either by the group members themselves or by outsiders from other groups. Some of the questions we are concerned with include the following: How important is language to the members of a culture? What is the role of language in the maintenance of a culture? Why do some languages survive over time while others do not? What role does language play in the relationship of one culture to another?

The importance that cultures attribute to language has been well established.[28] In fact, some would argue that the very heart of a culture is its language and that a culture dies if its language dies.[29] However, it is difficult to determine the exact degree of importance that language has for someone who identifies with a particular group because there are so many factors that affect the strength of that identification. For example, people are more likely to have a strong sense of ethnic and linguistic identity if members of other important cultural groups acknowledge their language in some way. In several states within the United States, for example, there have been heated legal battles to allow

Can you guess what the yellow vehicle identified in Malay as "Bas Sekolah" is used for?

election ballots to be printed in languages other than English. Those advocating this option are actually fighting to gain official status and support for their languages.

A language will remain vital and strong if groups of people who live near one another use the language regularly. The sheer number of people who identify with a particular language and their distribution within a particular country or region have a definite effect on the vigor of the language. For people who are rarely able to speak the language of their culture, the centrality of the language and the cultural or ethnic identity that goes with it are certainly diminished. Their inability to use the language results in lost opportunities to express their identification with the culture that it symbolizes.

The extent to which a culture maintains a powerful sense of identification with a particular language is called *perceived ethnolinguistic vitality,* which refers to "the individual's subjective perception of the status, demographic characteristics, and institutional support of the language community."[30] Very high levels of perceived ethnolinguistic vitality mean that members of a culture will be unwilling to assimilate their linguistic behavior with other cultures that surround them.[31] Howard Giles, one of the foremost researchers in how languages are used in multilingual societies, concludes that there are likely to be intense pressures on cultural members to adopt the language of the larger social group and to discontinue the use of their own language when

Within a culture, slang is often used differently across generations. For a typical day, keep track of the slang words that you use. Are there differences between those words and the slang words that people who are a generation older or a generation younger than you use?

1. the members of a culture lack a strong political, social, and economic status;
2. there are few members of the culture compared to the number of people in other groups in the community; and
3. institutional support to maintain their unique cultural heritage is weak.[32]

When multiple languages are spoken within one political boundary, there are inevitably political and social consequences. In the United States, for example, English has maintained itself as the primary language over a long period of time. Immigrants to the United States have historically been required to learn English in order to participate in the wider political and commercial aspects of the society. Schools offered classes only in English, television and radio programs were almost exclusively in English, and the work of government and business also required English. The English-only requirement has not been imposed without social consequences, however. In Micronesia, for example, where there are nine major languages and many dialects, people are demonstrably apprehensive about communicating with others when they must use English instead of their primary language.[33]

In recent years in the United States, there has been a change in the English-only pattern. Now in many areas of the country there are large numbers of people for whom English is not the primary language. As a consequence, teaching staffs are multilingual; government offices provide services to non-English speakers; and cable television has an extensive array of entertainment and news programming in Spanish, Chinese, Japanese, Arabic, and so on.

In some countries formal political agreements acknowledge the role of multiple languages in the government and educational systems. Canada has two official languages: English and French. Belgium uses three: French, German, and Flemish. In Singapore, English, Mandarin, Malay, and Tamil are all official languages, and India has over a dozen.

When India was established in 1948, one of the major problems concerned a national language. Although Hindi was the language spoken by the largest number of people, the overwhelming majority of the people did not speak it. India's solution to this problem was to identify sixteen national languages, thus formalizing in the constitution the right for government, schools, and commerce to operate in any of them. Even that solution has not quelled the fears of non-Hindi speakers that Hindi will predominate. In the mid-1950s there was political agitation to redraw the internal state boundaries based on the languages spoken in particular regions. Even now, major political upheavals periodically occur in India over language issues.

Because language is such an integral part of most people's identities, a great deal of emotion is attached to political choices about language preferences. However, what is most central to intercultural competence is the way in which linguistic identification influences the interaction that occurs between members of different cultural groups. In interpersonal communication, language is used to discern ingroup and outgroup members. That is, language provides an obvious and highly accurate cue about whether people share each other's cultural background. If others speak as you do, you are likely to assume that they are similar to you in other important ways.

Howard Giles has developed *communication accommodation theory* to explain why people in intercultural conversations may choose to *converge* or *diverge* their communication behaviors to that of others.[34] At times, interactants will converge their language use to that of their conversational partners by adapting their speech patterns to the behaviors of others. They do so when they desire to identify with others, appear similar to them, gain their approval, and facilitate the development of smooth and harmonious relationships. At other times, interactants' language use will diverge from their conversational partners and will thus accentuate their own cultural memberships, maintain their individuality, and underscore the differences between themselves and others. Giles suggests that the likelihood that people will adapt and accommodate to others depends on such factors as their knowledge of others' communication patterns, their motivations to converge or diverge, and their skills in altering their preferred repertoire of communication behaviors.

People also make a positive or negative evaluation about the language that others use. Generally speaking, there is a pecking order among languages that is usually buttressed and supported by the prevailing political order. Thus,

> In every society the differential power of particular social groups is reflected in language variation and in attitudes toward those variations. Typically, the dominant group promotes its patterns of language use as dialect or accents by minority group members reduce their opportunities for success in the society as a whole. Minority group members are often faced with difficult decisions regarding whether to gain social mobility by adopting the language patterns of the dominant group or to maintain their group identity by retaining their native speech style.[35]

In the United States, there has been a clear preference for English over the multiple other languages that people speak, and those who speak English are evaluated ac-

As these signs in New York City illustrate, a beneficial consequence of intercultural contacts is the opportunity to share and learn new languages and cultural patterns.

cording to their various accents and dialects. African Americans, for instance, have often been judged negatively for their use of Black Standard English, which has grammatical forms that differ from those used in Standard American English.[36] In the next section, we discuss the consequences of these evaluations and the effects of alternative forms of language use on intercultural communication competence.

Alternative Versions of a Language   No language is spoken precisely the same way by all who use it. The sounds made when speaking English by someone from England, Australia, or Jamaica differ from the speech of English-speaking U.S. Americans. Even among those who share a similar language and reside in the same country, there are important variations in the way the language is spoken. These differences in language use include the way the words are pronounced, the meanings of particular words or phrases, and the patterns for arranging the words (grammar). Terms often associated with these alternative forms of a language include *dialect, accent, argot* (pronounced "are go"), and *jargon*.

Dialects   Dialects are versions of a language with distinctive vocabulary, grammar, and pronunciation that are spoken by particular groups of people or within particular regions. Dialects can play an important role in intercultural communication because they often trigger a judgment and evaluation of the speaker. Dialects are measured against a "standard" spoken version of the language. The term *standard* does not describe inherent or naturally occurring characteristics but, rather, historical circumstances. For example, among many U.S. Americans, Standard American English is often the preferred dialect and conveys power and dominance. But as John R. Edwards has suggested, "As a dialect, there is nothing intrinsic, either linguistically or esthetically, which gives Standard English special status."[37]

Occasionally, use of a nonstandard dialect may lead to more favorable evaluations of the speaker. Thus, a U.S. American may regard someone speaking English with a British accent as more "cultured" or "refined." However, most nonstandard dialects of English are frequently accorded less status and are often considered inappropriate or unacceptable in education, business, and government. For example, speakers of Spanish- or Appalachian-accented English, as well as those who speak Black Standard English, are sometimes unfairly assumed to be less reliable, less intelligent, and of lower status than those who speak Standard American English.[38]

One dialect frequently used in the United States has been variously called Black Standard English, Black English, African American Vernacular English, and Ebonics. Linguists have estimated that about 90 percent of the African American community uses Ebonics at least some of the time. Geneva Smitherman explains some of the linguistic forces that underlie Ebonics by providing an example of some African American women at a beauty shop, one of whom exclaims, "The Brotha be looking good; that's what got the Sista nose open!" According to Smitherman:

> In this statement, *Brotha* refers to an African American man, *looking good* refers to his style (not necessarily the same thing as physical beauty in Ebonics), *Sista* is an African American woman, and her passionate love for the Brotha is conveyed by the phrase *nose open* (the kind of passionate love that makes you vulnerable to exploitation). *Sista nose* is standard Ebonics grammar for denoting possession, indicated by adjacency/

context (rather than the /'s, s'/). The use of *be* means that the quality of *looking good* is not limited to the present moment but reflects the Brotha's past, present, and future essence. As in the case of Efik and other West African languages, aspect is important in the verb system of US Ebonics, conveyed by the use of the English verb *be* to denote a recurring, habitual state of affairs. (Contrast *He be looking good* with *He looking good,* which refers to the present moment only—certainly not the kind of *looking good* that opens the nose!). Note further that many Black writers and today's Hip Hop artists employ the spellings "Brotha" and "Sista" to convey a pronunciation pattern showing West African language influence, i.e., a vowel sound instead of an /r/ sound. The absence of the /r/ at the end of words like "Sista" parallels /r/ absence in many West African languages, many of which do not have the typical English /r/ sound. Also in these communities, kinship terms may be used when one is referring to other African people, whether they are biologically related or not.[39]

Like all dialects, Ebonics is not slang, sloppy speech, incorrect grammar, or broken English. Rather, it reflects an intersection of West African languages and European American English, which initially developed during the European slave trade and the enslavement of African peoples throughout the Americas and elsewhere.

Accents   Distinguishable marks of pronunciation are called *accents.* Accents are closely related to dialects. Research studies repeatedly demonstrate that speakers' accents are used as a cue to form impressions of them.[40] Those of you who speak English with an accent or in a nonstandard version may have experienced the negative reactions of others, and you know the harmful effects such judgments can have on intercultural communication. Studies repeatedly find that accented speech and dialects provoke stereotyped reactions in listeners, so that the speakers are usually perceived as having less status, prestige, and overall competence. Interestingly, these negative perceptions and stereotyped responses sometimes occur even when the listeners themselves use a nonstandard dialect.[41]

If you are a speaker of Standard American English, you speak English with an "acceptable" accent. Can you recall conversations with others whose dialect and accent did not match yours? In those conversations, did you make negative assessments of their character, intelligence, or goodwill? Such a response is fairly common. Negative judgments that are made about others simply on the basis of how they speak are obviously a formidable barrier to competence in intercultural communication. For example, an Iranian American woman describes the frustration and anger experienced by her father, a physician, and her mother, a nurse, when they attempted to communicate with others by telephone. Though both of her parents had immigrated to the United States many years before, they spoke English with a heavy accent. These educated people were consistently responded to as if they lacked intelligence simply because of their accent. Out of sheer frustration they usually had their daughter, who spoke English with a U.S. accent, conduct whatever business needed to be accomplished on the telephone.

Move through your radio dial, stopping at the first five stations you find. Listen to the accents of the radio announcers. Are they all the same? Different? What about the accents makes them seem similar or different?

CULTURE *connections*

"I love your grandmother's accent," my high school friend told me after a visit to my house. I looked at her in confusion. "What accent?"

She assured me my grandmother spoke with an accent, although she wasn't sure what kind. I knew Grandma's parents had come from Norway, but it had never occurred to me that she had an accent. She just spoke like Grandma. The next time she came to our house, I tried to listen to her words more objectively. Sure enough, all those round, musical vowels of hers weren't just her unique way of talking; she had a Norwegian accent.

It made me wonder what else I hadn't realized about my relatives, just because I knew them too well to see them clearly. A few years later, my friend Sue gave me a clear reminder of how easy it can be to take things for granted.

Sue's husband, Daniel, had come to the United States from Kenya. They had met and married in Minnesota. When their son, Jeff, was born, they decided that Sue would speak to him in English and Daniel in Kikuyu, so that he would be bilingual right from the start. The plan worked well, and Jeff spoke both English and Kikuyu with ease from an early age.

When Jeff was seven years old, several members of Daniel's family came from Kenya for a visit. Sue and Daniel were thrilled. Wouldn't they be proud when Jeff conversed freely with his relatives in Kikuyu! They explained to Jeff that Daddy's family would be coming to stay with them, and Jeff eagerly helped them plan activities for the visitors. He seemed excited to have them come.

At the airport on the big day, Daniel greeted his family and introduced them to his wife. Then he proudly introduced his son in Kikuyu and waited for the conversation to begin. But as soon as the relatives started speaking to Jeff, he stared at them in surprise and clammed up. He wouldn't say a word to anyone in any language. Daniel's family tried to be polite, and Daniel assured them Jeff really did know how to talk, but the conversation on the way back to the house was a little strained, with Jeff remaining absolutely silent.

It wasn't until Daniel got everyone home and settled that he had a chance to talk with his son and find out what had upset him. Jeff had never met anyone else who spoke Kikuyu, only his dad. All his life Jeff had assumed that this was a special secret language between him and his father that no one else knew. And then all these strangers had shown up, speaking their private language! It had been a shock.

—*Sharon Huntington*

Jargon and Argot   Both jargon and argot are specialized forms of vocabulary. *Jargon* refers to a set of words or terms that are shared by those with a common profession or experience. For example, students at a particular university share a jargon related to general education requirements, registration techniques, add or drop procedures, activity fees, and so on. Members of a particular profession depend on a unique set of meanings for words that are understood only by other members of that profession. The shorthand code used by law-enforcement officers, lawyers, those in the medical profession, and even professors at colleges and universities are all instances of jargon.

CULTURE *connections*

An increasing number of my students who come from homes in which a language other than English is spoken, and in which at least two cultures coexist, may not, in fact, experience a disruption in their sense of themselves. Code-switching (the alternate use of two or more languages in the same utterance) is, for many of them, a normal state of discourse. That is the case not only for my international students, but also for many of my students who are members of various ethnic groups. Hispanic-American students, in particular, now proudly assert their once-precarious position on the borderlands, refusing to choose among identities or languages. Indeed, despite the politics that swirl around the issue, we are increasingly coming to realize that code-switching is a sophisticated communicative strategy.

—*Isabelle de Courtivron*

Argot refers to a specialized language that is used by a large group within a culture to define the boundaries of their group from others who are in a more powerful position in society. As you might expect, argot is an important feature in the study of intercultural communication. Unlike jargon, argot is typically used to keep those who are not part of the group from understanding what members say to one another. The specialized language is used to keep those from the outside, usually seen as hostile, at bay.

Code Switching   Because of the many languages spoken in the United States, you will likely have many opportunities to hear and perhaps to participate in a form of language use called *code switching*. Code switching refers to the selection of the language to be used in a particular interaction by individuals who can speak multiple languages. The decision to use one language over another is often related to the setting in which the interaction occurs— a social, public, and formal setting versus a personal, private, and informal one. In his poignant exploration about speaking Spanish in an English-speaking world, Richard Rodriguez describes his attachment to the language associated with this latter setting.

When I was a boy, things were different. The accent of *los gringos* was never pleasing nor was it hard to hear. Crowds at Safeway or at bus stops would be noisy with sound. And I would be forced to edge away from the chirping chatter above me. . . .

But then there was Spanish. *Español:* my family's language. *Español:* the language that seemed to me to be a private language. I'd hear strangers on the radio and in the Mexican Catholic church across town speaking in Spanish, but I couldn't really believe that Spanish was a public language, like English. Spanish speakers, rather, seemed related to me, for I sensed that we shared—through our language—the experience of feeling apart from *los gringos.* . . . Spanish seemed to me the language of home. . . .

A family member would say something to me and I would feel myself specially recognized. My parents would say something to me and I would feel embraced by the sounds of their words. Those sounds said: *I am speaking with ease in Spanish. I am addressing you in words I never use with* los gringos. *I recognize you as someone special, close, like no one outside. You belong with us. In the family.*[42]

A person's conversational partner is another important factor in code-switching decisions. Many African Americans, for instance, switch their linguistic codes based on the culture and gender of their conversational partners.[43]

The topic of conversation is another important influence on the choice of a linguistic code. One study found that Moroccans, for instance, would typically use French when discussing scientific or technological topics and Arabic when discussing cultural or religious ones. Interestingly, people's attitudes toward a particular topic were found to be consistent with the underlying beliefs, values, and norms of the culture whose language they choose to speak.[44]

Verbal Codes and Intercultural Competence

The link between knowledge of other verbal codes and intercultural competence is obvious. To speak another language proficiently requires an enormous amount of effort, energy, and time. The opportunity to study another language in your college curriculum is a choice we highly recommend to prepare you for a multicultural and multilingual world. Those world citizens with facility in a second or third language will be needed in every facet of society.

Many English speakers have a false sense of security because English is studied and spoken by so many people around the world. There is arrogance in this position that should be obvious because it places all of the responsibility for learning another language on the non-English speaker. Furthermore, even if two people from different cultures are using the verbal code system of one of the interactants, significant influences on their communication arise from their initial languages.

The multicultural nature of the United States and the interdependence of world cultures means that multiple cultures and multiple languages will be a standard feature of people's lives. Despite our strong recommendation that you learn and be tolerant of other languages, it is virtually impossible for anyone to be proficient in all of the verbal codes that might be encountered in intercultural communication. However, there are important ways to improve competence in adjusting to differences in verbal codes when communicating interculturally.

First, the study of at least one other language is extraordinarily useful in understanding the role of differences in verbal codes in intercultural communication. Genuine fluency in a second language demonstrates experientially all of the ways in which language embodies another culture. It also reveals the ways in which languages vary and how the nuances of language use influence the meanings of symbols. Even if you never become genuinely proficient in it, the study of another language teaches much about the culture of those who use it and the categories of experience the language can create. Furthermore, such study demonstrates, better than words written on a page or spoken in a lecture, the difficulty in gaining proficiency in another language and may lead to an appreciation of those who are struggling to communicate in second or third languages.

Short of becoming proficient in another language, learning about its grammatical features can help you understand the messages of the other person. Study the connections between the features of a verbal code and the cultural patterns of those who use it. Even if you are going to communicate with people from another culture in your own first language, there is much that you can learn about the other person's language

CULTURE *connections*

It is one of the remarkable aspects of language that we can appear to take on different personalities simply by making different sounds than the ones to which we are accustomed. For those who are truly bilingual this seems so obvious as to hardly bear mentioning: they flit easily between tongues—an English set of vowels and mannerisms flows into Urdu patterns and intonations with scarcely a ripple—though they will talk casually about "my Pakistani self" and "my English persona." But for those of us who came late to another language, it is always something of an odd experience to see and feel it happen, the moment when you notice another personality overtaking your familiar one, the moment when you become "Italian" or "Japanese." It's the moment when you stop worrying about grammar and accent, and allow the other language to possess you, to pass through you, to transform you.

When I speak Spanish, the language that I know best besides English, I find my facial muscles set in a different pattern, and new, yet familiar gestures taking over my hands. I find myself shrugging and tossing my head back, pulling down the corners of my mouth and lifting my eyebrows. I touch people all the time and don't mind that they stand so close to me and blow cigarette smoke into my face. I speak more rapidly and fluidly and I use expressions that have no counterpart in English, expressions that for all my experience as a translator, I simply can't turn into exact equivalents. To speak another language is to lead a parallel life; the better you speak any language, the more fully you live in another culture.

—*Barbara Wilson*

and the corresponding cultural patterns that can help you to behave appropriately and effectively.

Knowledge of another language is one component of the link between competence and verbal codes. Motivation, in the form of your emotional reactions and your intentions toward the culturally different others with whom you are communicating, is another critical component. Trying to get along in another language can be an exhilarating and very positive experience, but it can also be fatiguing and frustrating. The attempt to speak and understand a new verbal code requires energy and perseverance. Most second-language learners, when immersed in its cultural setting, report a substantial toll on their energy.

Functioning in a culture that speaks a language different from your own can be equally tiring and exasperating. Making yourself understood, getting around, obtaining food, and making purchases all require a great deal of effort. Recognizing the possibility of irritability and fatigue when functioning in an unfamiliar linguistic environment is an important prerequisite to intercultural competence. Without such knowledge, the communicator may well blame his or her personal feelings of discomfort on the cultures that are being experienced.

The motivation dimension also concerns your reactions to those who are attempting to speak your language. In the United States, for example, those who speak English often lack sympathy for and patience with those who do not. If English is your first lan-

Learning other languages is an important feature of intercultural competence.

guage, notice those learning it and provide whatever help you can. Respond patiently. If you do not understand, ask questions and clarify. Try making your verbal point in alternative ways by using different sets of words with approximately equivalent meanings. Speak slowly, but do not yell. Lack of skill in a new language is not caused by a hearing impairment. Be aware of the jargon in your speech and provide a definition of it. Above all, to the best of your ability, withhold judgments and negative evaluations; instead, show respect for the enormous difficulties associated with learning a new language.

An additional emotional factor to monitor in promoting intercultural competence is your reaction to nonstandard versions of a language. The negative evaluations that nonstandard speech often triggers are a serious impediment to competence.

Competence in intercultural communication can be assisted by behaviors that indicate interest in the other person's verbal code. Even if you have never studied the language of those with whom you regularly interact, do attempt to learn and use appropriate words and phrases. Get a phrase book and a dictionary to learn standard comments or queries. Learn how to greet people and to acknowledge thanks. At the same time, recognize your own limitations and depend on a skilled interpreter when needed.

Intercultural competence requires knowledge, motivation, and actions that recognize the critical role of verbal codes in human interaction. Though learning another language is a very important goal, it is inevitable that you will need to communicate with others with whom you do not share a common verbal code.

Summary

In this chapter we have explored the vital role of verbal codes in intercultural communication. The features of language and the five rule systems were discussed. Phonology, the rules for creating the sounds of language, and morphology, the rules for creating the meaning units in a language, were described briefly. The study of the meaning of words (semantics), the rules for ordering the words (syntactics), and the effects of language on human perceptions and behaviors (pragmatics) were also described. We then described the difficulties in establishing equivalence in the process of interpretation from one language to another.

The important relationships among language, thought, culture, and behavior were explored. The Sapir–Whorf hypothesis of linguistic relativity, which concerns the effects of language on people's thoughts and perceptions, was discussed. We noted that the firmer version of the hypothesis portrays language as the determiner of thought and the softer version portrays language as a shaper of thought; variations in words and grammatical structures from one language to another provide important evidence in the debate on the Sapir–Whorf hypothesis; and that each language, with its own unique features, serves as a shaper rather than determiner of human thought, culture, and behavior.

Finally, variations in language use within a nation were considered. Language plays a central role in establishing and maintaining the identity of a particular culture. Language variations also foster a political hierarchy among cultures within a nation; nonstandard versions of a language, including accents, dialects, jargon, and argot, are often regarded less favorably than the standard version. The concept of code switching, and some factors that affect the selection of one language over another, were also discussed. The chapter concluded with a discussion of intercultural competence and verbal communication.

For Discussion

1. Based on the examples at the beginning of this chapter, what do you think Ludwig Wittgenstein meant when he said that "the limits of my language are the limits of my world"?
2. Is accurate translation and interpretation from one language to another possible? Explain.
3. Do you identify yourself as a member of one or more social groups? If so, which one(s)?
4. What is the difference between a dialect and an accent? Between jargon and argot? Give an example of each of these terms.
5. If you speak more than one language (or language dialect), when is each of them used? That is, in what places, relationships, or settings do you use each of them?
6. If you could construct an ideal society, would it be one in which everyone spoke the same language? Or does a society in which people speak different languages offer greater advantages? Explain.

For Further Reading

John J. Gumperz and Stephen C. Levinson (eds.), *Rethinking Linguistic Relativity* (Cambridge: Cambridge University Press, 1996). A good source for additional information on the Sapir-Whorf hypothesis.

Fern L. Johnson, *Speaking Culturally: Language Diversity in the United States* (Thousand Oaks, CA: Sage, 2000). An excellent exploration and description of various cultural discourse patterns within the United States. Provides solid evidence that the United States is not a monolingual, monocultural society.

Steven Pinker, *Words and Rules: The Ingredients of Language* (New York: Basic Books, 1999). A very readable explanation of how phonemes, morphemes, and syntax combine to create language.

Richard Rodriguez, *Hunger of Memory: The Education of Richard Rodriguez* (Toronto: Bantam Books, 1982). Rodriquez's work has often been a point of controversy because of its opposition to bilingual education. We suggest this book to students because of Rodriquez's poignant, vivid descriptions of the experiences in living with one language at home and another in the rest of his world.

Geneva Smitherman, *Talkin That Talk: Language, Culture, and Education in African America* (New York: Routledge, 2000). Offers insights into Ebonics as a language that shapes the culture and experiences of African Americans.

Stella Ting-Toomey and Felipe Korzenny (eds.), *Language, Communication, and Culture: Current Directions* (Newbury Park, CA: Sage, 1989). A good overview of various issues about communication and culture. Explains how the structure of a language, as well as its use, shapes and influences the deeply embedded understandings that people bring to their conversations with others.

For additional information about intercultural films and about Web sites on specific cultures, turn to the Resources section at the back of this book.

chapter 9

The Effects of Code Usage in Intercultural Communication

Preferences in the Organization of Verbal Codes
Organizational Preferences in the Use of U.S. English
Organizational Preferences in Other Languages and Cultures
Cultural Variations in Persuasion
Persuasion in Intercultural Encounters
Cultural Differences in What Is Acceptable as Evidence

Cultural Differences in What Is Considered Reasonable
Cultural Differences in Styles of Persuasion
Cultural Variations in the Structure of Conversations
Value of Talk and Silence
Rules for Conversations
Effects of Code Usage on Intercultural Competence
Summary

Practical, everyday communication experiences—greeting a friend, buying something from a shopkeeper, asking directions, or describing a common experience—require messages to be organized in a meaningful way. Cultures differ, however, in the patterns that are preferred for organizing ideas and communicating them to others. These differences affect what people regard as logical, rational, and a basis for sound reasoning and conclusions.

This chapter focuses on the consequences for intercultural communication of differences in the way cultures use verbal and nonverbal communication. Do people in particular cultures have distinctive preferences for what, where, when, and with whom to speak? Are there differences in what are regarded as the ideal ways to organize ideas and present them to others? What constitutes appropriate forms of reasoning, evidence, and proof in a discussion or argument? Is proof accomplished with a statistic, an experience, an expert's testimony, or a link between some aspect of the problem and the emotions of the listener? What is considered "rational" and "logical"? In short, how do conversations differ because of the differences in culture, language, and nonverbal codes?

CULTURE *connections*

"The American style of learning is to ask questions, discuss the theory and then go do it and ask more questions," he said. "The Japanese style is to observe the master, not ask questions and then get your hands dirty at the very beginning. If you ask questions, it can suggest that the master didn't do his job properly. The different styles can cause problems."

Intercultural communication competence requires more than just an accurate translation of the verbal and nonverbal codes that others use. The "logic" of how those codes are organized and used must also be understood.

The chapter begins by considering alternative preferences for the organization of messages. Next we discuss cultural variations in persuasive communication. Finally, differences in the structure of conversations are presented as another way in which code systems influence intercultural competence.

Preferences in the Organization of Verbal Codes

Cultures have distinct preferences for organizing ideas and presenting them in writing and in public speeches. Consider what you have been taught in English composition courses as the "correct" way to structure an essay, or recall the organizational patterns you have used to structure the content of a speech. The premise underlying our discussion is that cultures provide preferred ways for people to organize and convey thoughts and feelings. These preferences influence the ways people communicate and the choices they make to arrange ideas in a specific pattern.

The effects of code usage on the organization of ideas are visible to teachers of English as a second language (ESL). Even after nonnative English speakers have mastered the vocabulary and grammar of the English language, they are unlikely to write an essay in what is considered "correct" English form. In fact, because of the particular style for the organization and presentation of ideas, ESL teachers can often identify the native language of a writer even when the essay is written in English. Robert Kaplan, one of the most influential investigators of cultural and linguistic differences in organizational patterns, refers to speaking and writing correctly as learning the "logic" of the language.[1]

In this section, we first describe the organizational features of the English language as it is used in the United States. We then explore the organizational features associated with other languages used in particular cultures.

Organizational Preferences in the Use of U.S. English

For most cultures, the correct use of language is most easily observed when the language is formally taught in the school system. English is a standard feature of the U.S. high school curriculum, and English composition is a requirement for virtually all U.S.

college students. The development of oral communication skills, which usually includes training in public speaking, is also a common requirement for many college students. In both written and oral communication courses, users of U.S. English explicitly learn rules that govern how ideas are to be presented. Indeed, the features that characterize a well-organized essay in U.S. English are very similar to the features of a well-organized public speech.

The structure of a good essay or speech in U.S. English requires the development of a specific theme. A thesis statement, which is the central organizing idea of the speech or essay, is the foundation on which speakers or writers develop their speech or essay. Ideally, thesis statements are clear and specific; speakers and writers must present their ideas in a straightforward and unambiguous manner. In many instances, the stu-

This African American student practices his persuasive skills. Cultures differ in the types of arguments considered to be persuasive.

dent of U.S. English is taught to provide the thesis statement in the opening paragraph of the essay or in the beginning of the speech.

The paragraph is the fundamental organizational unit of written English. As a standard textbook for college writing courses indicates,

> A paragraph is a unit of thought composed of sentences, [which are themselves] smaller units of thoughts, relating to a single topic. . . . The main idea of the paragraph often appears in a topic sentence, usually located at or near the beginning of the paragraph.[2]

There are other rules that guide how paragraphs are combined into an essay or main points into a speech. Generally, correct organization in U.S. English means that writers or speakers clearly state their thesis at the beginning and provide the audience

CULTURE *connections*

What's confusing to English speakers about Athabaskans

They do not speak
They keep silent
They avoid situations of talking

They only want to talk to close acquaintances
They play down their own abilities
They act as if they expect things to be given to them
They deny planning

They avoid direct questions
They never start a conversation
They talk off the topic

They never say anything about themselves
They are slow to take a turn in talking

They ask questions in unusual places

They talk with a flat tone of voice
They are too indirect, inexplicit
They don't make sense
They just leave without saying anything

What's confusing to Athabaskans about English speakers

They talk too much
They always talk first
They talk to strangers or people they don't know
They think they can predict the future

They brag about themselves
They don't help people even when they can
They always talk about what is going to happen later
They ask too many questions
They always interrupt
They only talk about what they are interested in
They don't give others a chance to talk

They are always getting excited when they talk
They aren't careful when they talk about things or people

—*Ronald Scollon and Suzanne Wong-Scollon*

with an overview of their main points. As the key to good organization, students are taught to outline the main points of the essay or speech by subordinating supporting ideas to the main ideas. In fact, most teachers give students explicit instructions to help them learn to organize properly.

In U.S. English there is also a preferred way to develop the main points. If a speaker is talking about scuba diving, with main points on equipment and safety tips, he or she is expected to develop the point on equipment by talking only about equipment. Safety tips should not be mentioned in the midst of the discussion about equipment. If the speaker gave examples related to safety tips in the middle of the discussion on equipment, listeners (or readers) trained in the preferences embedded in U.S. English would become confused and would think the speaker was disorganized. A teacher would probably comment on the organizational deficiencies and might lower the student's grade because the speech does not match the expected form of a well-organized speech.

The organizational pattern preferred in the formal use of U.S. English can best be described as linear. This pattern can be visualized as a series of steps or progressions that move in a straight line toward a particular goal or idea. Thus, the preferred organizational pattern forms a series of "bridges," where each idea is linked to the next.

Organizational Preferences in Other Languages and Cultures

Some years ago Robert Kaplan systematically began to study the preferred organizational patterns of nonnative speakers of English. In an article that is usually credited with launching a specialization called contrastive rhetoric, Kaplan characterized the preferences for the organization of paragraphs among people from different language and cultural groups.[3]

Satoshi Ishii elaborates on Kaplan's depiction of organizational preferences when he describes the preferred structure of a paragraph in Japanese as a "gyre."[4] Ishii characterizes a gyre as an approach to an idea by "indirection" and explains the Japanese paragraph as a series of "stepping stones" that depend on indirection and implication, rather than on explicit links, to connect ideas and provide a main point. The rules for language use in Japan demand that speakers not tell the listener the specific point being conveyed; to do so is considered rude and inappropriate. Rather, the Japanese delicately circle a topic in order to imply its domain. The U.S. English concepts of thesis statements and paragraph topic sentences have no real equivalent in many languages. Studies of Korean, Thai, Chinese, and Japanese language use indicate that in these languages the thesis statement is often buried in the passage.[5]

Imagine the consequences of an intercultural interaction between a Japanese person and a U.S. American. What might happen if one of them is able to speak in the other's language and is sufficiently skilled to convey meaning linguistically but is not adept at the logic of the language? The Japanese person is likely to think that the U.S. American is rude and aggressive. Conversely, the U.S. American is likely to think that the Japanese person is confusing and imprecise. Both people in this intercultural interaction are likely to feel dissatisfied, confused, and uncomfortable.

The circularity in the structure of the Japanese paragraph also characterizes the writing of those whose first language is Hindi, one of India's national languages. Yamuna Kachru indicates that a Hindi paragraph does not develop just one unified thought or idea.[6] Rather, the preferred style allows the writer to digress and to include material related to many ideas. When using English, speakers of Hindi exhibit characteristics of the Hindi organizational style in their English paragraphs.

How do you think U.S. teachers of English would grade an assignment that was written in English by a native Hindi speaker? We can easily imagine the comments about the lack of organization and the poor development of the ideas. Kachru, in fact, concludes that Indian writing and speaking conventions show a marked preference for nonlinearity and are therefore perceived, from a Western perspective, as illogical.

Speakers of Indian English like to provide many minor contextual points of a story before advancing the thesis, whereas speakers of British English tend first to provide the thesis of the story and then give the relevant information.[7] Chinese discourse styles are similar to those of Indian English. Rather than relying on a preview statement to orient the listener to the discourse's overall direction, the Chinese rely heavily on contextual cues. Chinese speech also tends to use single words such as *because, as,* and *so* to replace whole clause connectives, such as "in view of the fact that" "to begin with," or "in conclusion," that are commonly used in English.[8] In Arabic, writing is structured using repetition, parallelism, and coordination between sentences.[9]

Another difference in organizational structure concerns languages that are speaker-responsible and those that are listener-responsible. In English, which is a speaker-responsible language, the speaker provides the structure and therefore much of the specific meaning of the statement.[10] Because the speaker tells the listener exactly what is going to be talked about and what the speaker wants the listener to know, prior knowledge of the speaker's intent is not necessary. In Japanese, which is a listener-responsible language, speakers need to indicate only indirectly what they are discussing and what they want the listener to know when the conversation is over. The listener is forced to construct the meaning, and usually does so, based on shared knowledge between the speaker and the listener.

In sum, cultural patterns interact with code systems to create expectations about what is considered the proper or logical way to organize the presentation of ideas. What is considered the right way to organize ideas within one culture may be regarded as illogical, disorganized, unclear, and perhaps even rude, discourteous, and ineffective in another. In intercultural communication, people make judgments about the clarity and logic of others' thoughts, and their assumptions about what is rational or logical may vary greatly and may lead to misunderstandings.

Cultural Variations in Persuasion

Persuasion, or the use of symbols to influence others, is most often identified with formal, public settings, such as when a candidate for political office tries to win votes through speeches and advertisements. Increasingly, persuasive messages are mediated through photographs, television, film, and even music. Persuasion, however, also occurs in everyday interactions between people.

Persuasion in Intercultural Encounters

Attempts to influence others to accept an idea or to engage in some behavior are a common feature of everyday conversation. For example, you might have tried to convince your employer to give you a day off from work. Or perhaps you negotiated with

CULTURE *connections*

Growing up in Africa I did not have the sense of history that seems so important in other parts of the world. Our language, Somali, did not have a written script until 1973, so we did not learn to read or write. Knowledge was passed down by word of mouth—poetry or folktales—or, more important, by our parents teaching us the skills we needed to survive. . . .

In Somalia, we lived the way our ancestors had for thousands of years; nothing had changed dramatically for us. As nomads we did not live with electricity, telephones, or automobiles, much less computers, television, or space travel. These facts, combined with our emphasis on living in the present, gave us a much different perspective on time than the one that dominates the Western world.

—*Waris Dirie and Cathleen Miller*

a salesperson on the price of a new television. Or maybe you tried to convince your teacher that the due date for your term paper should be delayed a week. All of these events involve persuasion.

In today's multicultural world, any of the preceding examples could involve culturally heterogeneous representatives. An Asian student may need to ask a European American teacher for an extension on an assignment. An African American who supervises employees from a variety of cultural groups may need to convince them to implement a change in office procedures. The Latino businessperson may want to sell his company's new information system to a Brazilian manager of a company in Argentina. The tourist in Nigeria may want hotel room service in the middle of the night. All of these communicative situations require knowledge and skill in using the appropriate means of persuasion; whereas members of some cultures genuinely enjoy the persuasive or argumentative encounter, many others shun such confrontations.[11]

The effective use of verbal and nonverbal codes in persuasion varies greatly from culture to culture. For instance, there are differences in what cultures consider to be acceptable evidence, who is regarded as an authority, how evidence is used to create persuasive arguments, and what ideas are reasonable. These preferred ways to convince others are called the culture's *persuasive style*. When people from diverse cultures communicate, the differences in their persuasive styles are often very evident.

The word *logical* is often used to describe the preferred persuasive style of a culture. Logic and rationality seem to be invoked as though there were some firm "truth" somewhere that simply has to be discovered and used in order to be convincing. We are suggesting, however, that "because logic has cultural aspects, an understanding of social life requires an understanding of how people think in their own cultural context."[12] In fact, Stephen Toulmin, a leading philosopher who studies human reasoning, claims that what people call rationality varies from culture to culture and from time to time:

CULTURE *connections*

Many more "Vivas!" greeted his call to the youth to "rededicate themselves for the final offensive" (i.e., the elections). Then Allan Boesak spoke—in English, but using African oratorical devices. Listening to him, I remembered the comment of a white friend who lectures in UWC's English department. In her view, black students writing in English are at a peculiar disadvantage. Often their tutors criticize them for being repetitive and beating about the bush, not realizing that, in African languages, such "flaws" are cultivated as component parts of an art much admired throughout Africa.

—*Dervla Murphy*

> Within different cultures and epochs, reasoning may operate according to different methods and principles, so that different milieus represent (so to say) the parallel "jurisdictions" of rationality.[13]

In other words, what is regarded as logical and rational varies from culture to culture. A phrase that sums up these variations is *ethno-logics* or *alternative logics.*

Persuasion involves an interaction between a speaker and his or her audience, in which the speaker intends to have the audience accept a point of view or a conclusion. Persuasion usually involves evidence, establishing "logical" connections between the pieces of evidence, and ordering of the evidence into a meaningful arrangement—all of which is used to convince the audience to accept the speaker's point of view or conclusion. In each of these elements of persuasion, there are substantial variations from culture to culture. In the following sections we describe some of these variations.

Cultural Differences in What Is Acceptable as Evidence

Evidence is what a persuader offers to those she or he is trying to persuade. In any given persuasive situation, we have available to us a myriad of sensory information or ideas. For example, suppose that students are trying to persuade a teacher to give an extension on a paper's due date. There have probably been numerous events that students could select as evidence. Maybe many students had been ill for a day, or perhaps the teacher had been sick. Or perhaps during one critical lecture, the noise of construction workers just outside the classroom made it difficult to pay attention to the discussion. Any of these events might be used as evidence to support the conclusion that the paper's due date ought to be postponed. An idea or experience does not become evidence, however, until it is selected for use in the persuasive interaction. What we choose from among all of the available cues is highly influenced by our culture.

There are no universally accepted standards about what constitutes evidence. Among many devout Muslims and Christians, for instance, parables or stories—particularly from the Koran or Bible—are a powerful form of evidence. The story is offered, and the lesson from the story is assumed to be conclusive. In other cultures, the story itself must be scrutinized to determine how illustrative it is compared to other possible cases. Persuasive messages in cultures influenced by Confucianism, for instance, often depend on metaphors and analogies as evidence.[14]

The European American culture prefers physical evidence and eyewitness testimony, and members of that culture see "facts" as the supreme kind of evidence. Popular mysteries on television or in best-selling books weave their tales by giving clues through the appearance of physical evidence or facts—a button that is torn off a sleeve, a record of calls made from one person's telephone to another, or a bankbook that shows regular deposits or withdrawals. From all of these pieces of evidence, human behavior and motivation are regarded as apparent. In certain portions of Chinese culture, however, physical evidence is discounted because no connection is seen between those pieces of the physical world and human actions. People from cultures that view the physical world as indicative of human motivation have difficulty understanding this Buddhist point of view.

The use of expert testimony in the persuasive process also varies greatly from one culture to another. In certain African cultures, the words of a witness would be discounted or even totally disregarded because people believe that if you speak up about seeing something, you must have a particular agenda in mind; in other words, no one is regarded as objective. The U.S. legal system, however, depends on the testimony of others; witnesses to traffic accidents, for example, are called to give testimony concerning the behavior of the drivers involved in the accident. Teachers of adults who are learning English indicate that these students may not understand the relative weight or authority to give to a scholarly presentation in a journal or academic work versus opinions found in an editorial column of a newspaper or magazine.[15]

Cultural Differences in What Is Considered Reasonable

Perhaps the best way to think about what a culture might deem to be logical or reasonable is to refer to the discussion of cultural patterns in Chapters 4 and 5. Cultural patterns supply the underlying assumptions that people within a culture use to determine what is "correct" and reasonable, and they therefore provide the persuader's justification for linking the evidence to the conclusions desired from the audience.

Michael Cole and Sylvia Scribner offer the following illustration of cultural differences in what might be considered reasonable in a persuasive situation:

> In central Liberia, as well as many other parts of Africa, it is believed that certain men (variously called *zos, shamen,* and *witchdoctors*) can control lightning and direct it to hit anyone or anything they choose. As evidence of such powers, a college student from this region offered the following story: In his town, there was an occasion upon which someone stole meat from the cooking pot of the lightning *zo*. Angered, the *zo* announced that if the meat was not returned immediately, he would direct lightning to hit the guilty person on the following Saturday. On the appointed day, the meat had not been returned and the people all took to their houses in fear; a storm blew up, and when it was over the people found a dead dog, apparently killed by lightning. The student, and all the townspeople, took the dog's death as *prima facie* evidence of the power of the *zo*.[16]

In Liberia, the cultural assumption that underlies the logical sequence described above is that the material (human) world interacts with the natural or spiritual world. Within other cultural frameworks it would not be considered reasonable to accept the

Read the following scenarios and describe the cultural reasoning that underlies each of the responses. Do some of the responses seem more "logical" to you than others?

1. A murder has been committed and one man has been accused of the crime. You want to know whether he is guilty or innocent. You should
   a. observe the accused man. Guilty people usually give themselves away in how they talk or act.
   b. look for physical evidence. You must find some footprint, fingerprint, or property that connects the accused man with the crime.
   c. find witnesses. You should talk with all who know the accused man, were at the scene of the crime, and so forth.
   d. put the accused person to a test and see how he behaves. This might be a psychological test or some physical test that will give you proof.

2. You are a very fortunate person. You are happy, healthy, and intelligent. You have a strong and loving family. Almost everything you have set out to do turns out well. You think:
   a. I am just lucky. Some people are lucky, some people are not. I happen to be lucky.
   b. I must be careful; good and bad tend to balance, and one of these days things will begin to go badly for me.
   c. Life is what you make it. To be happy you have to "think happy," as happiness is all up to the individual's attitude and frame of mind.
   d. Somebody or some force is watching over me. Call it "God" or a guardian angel or some other supernatural power—I have such faith.

3. You are a farmer. There has been a long dry spell throughout the growing season, and there is little hope for rain soon. Without rain, you and your family may starve during the next year. What is the best thing for you to do?
   a. Pray for rain. Only God (or the gods) can deliver you from this dry spell.
   b. Ask scientists or technical people for methods to create rain, perhaps by seeding the clouds with chemicals.
   c. Ask the elders and wise men of the community; they have lived the longest, and they know best what to do.
   d. You are probably being punished; the dry spell is a curse. Discover the source of this curse, remove it, and the rains will come.*

*Adapted from John Condon and Fathi Yousef, *An Introduction to Intercultural Communication* (Indianapolis: Bobbs-Merrill, 1975) 225–227.

dog's death as evidence, because a fundamental belief is that the human world does not interact with the spiritual world.

Another example of the relationship of evidence, "reasonableness," and persuasive impact occurred in mid-1997 in the United States. At that time, meteorologists noted evidence that included an unusually large haul of squid off the coast of California, increased rainfall in Chile, and dramatic increases in water temperatures along the equator in the central Pacific.[17] Such developments, they argued, were signs that a weather pattern commonly known as "El Niño" would occur the following winter and would result in a series of intense storms in 1998 that would cause severe flooding along the west coast of the United States. Heeding these dire predictions, the Office of Disaster Preparedness used

CULTURE *connections*

Out of the corner of my eye I saw the dogs, pointing their noses. Their heads were very high. They weren't moving, just standing there. Then, they started to go around and around in a circle. I wanted to go get my father. He was in the village. Did he know a storm was coming? I told the missionary, finally, that we were in danger, and we'd better go get my mother, who was with my aunt, and my father. The missionary looked up at the sky. It was clear. He said that there was no storm coming. I said there was, I knew there was. He wanted to know how I knew. I told him: the dogs. He asked me to explain. I did. He laughed. He told me I was superstitious. It was the first time I heard the word, and I didn't know what he was talking about. How often I would hear that word over the years. The Eskimos were always hearing, then, that they were superstitious. But I knew what I knew! I told the missionary that I had to leave, right away. He said I wasn't being a good Eskimo; I was leaving *him!* I asked him to come along with me. He did. We reached my mother, and she joined us, and we found my father, and we went home. I remember seeing some clouds in the sky, as we came home. The dogs were beginning to howl. They were hungry, but not howling hungry. They were upset with us. Why weren't we doing something faster to protect ourselves from the storm? A dog keeps a close eye on his neighbors—people.

Before we could do anything, the missionary had to leave; otherwise, to be polite, we would have to stand there talking with him. My father called me away to the back of our house, and said I should pretend to get sick. He told me to hold my stomach and come to him and say it hurts. I waited for him to go back to the minister, and then I came over and did what my father wanted me to do. The minister excused himself and left—after my father excused himself because he wanted to take me in the house and look after me. My mother could tell that my father and I had figured out a way to send the minister off. We watched him leaving, and suddenly the storm came upon us—like lightning in the summer. The wind pushed at us; it wanted to sweep us away. My father realized that the minister might not make it back to his church. I went with my father on the sled, to get the minister. We caught up with him, but he wanted to keep moving. . . . We stayed inside for a long, long time—over a week, my grandchildren would say. It was a bad storm, but we had a good time. I helped my mother sew. We had enough food. The baby cried, but the wind was noisier than the baby. It was very hard to clear a path from the house to the shed. Later, we heard that the minister had died on his way back to the church. The storm had taken his spirit. My mother believed that the storm lasted such a long time because the minister was trying to break away from the storm; the longer his spirit fought with the wind, the worse the wind became. When the wind left us, it went to the mountains, far inland. That is where the minister's spirit is. Our ancestors are there, and I'm sure they are looking after the minister.

—Robert Coles

public funds to increase their stock of sandbag supplies. The evidence of the squid, the increased rainfall, and the increases in water temperature were considered reasonable and, therefore, persuasive within the European American cultural framework.

Concurrently, in Israel, a cow inseminated with sperm from a Swiss bull produced the first red heifer born in the Holy Land in two millennia. In ancient times, the Bible relates, the ashes of a red heifer were used to purify the priests before they entered the Temple. The red heifer's birth in 1997 was therefore viewed by some as a sign (evidence) that it was the time to rebuild the Temple on its original site, where the Dome of the Rock and the al-Aqsa Mosque—two of Islam's holiest shrines—are currently housed. Mainstream Jewish groups and secular Israelis regarded the meaning of the red heifer with skepticism, and they suggested that it was an unreasonable threat to prospects for a comprehensive peace in the region.[18] In sum, different expectations about what constitutes evidence and reasoning can yield very different justifications for subsequent actions.

Cultural Differences in Styles of Persuasion

We have suggested that every culture has preferred choices for the types of evidence that people will accept. The underlying cultural patterns function as assumptions in the persuasive process, and these also vary among cultures. Thus, cultures differ in the ways people prefer to arrange their evidence, assumptions, and claims; this constitutes the culture's "persuasive style."[19]

Anne Bliss describes variations in persuasive style displayed by students whose first language is not English. Lakota speakers, for example, offer stories that are related to their persuasive point, but the speaker/persuader may not even make explicit the link to the conclusion. Bliss also suggests that native speakers of Spanish often have difficulties when using English because they do not aggressively or deliberately offer a conclusion; instead, they assume that passive sentence constructions and descriptions will lead the listeners to a conclusion.[20]

John Condon says that many U.S. Americans may also have difficulty with the persuasive style of someone from Mexico because Mexicans are more emotional and dramatic and have less concern about the accuracy of details. When a U.S. American visiting Mexico asks a shopkeeper a question, the shopkeeper's goal is to keep the visitor happy; thus an answer is provided even if it is not accurate.[21]

Much of the tradition of persuasion and rhetoric among U.S. Americans is influenced by the rhetoric of Aristotle, who emphasized the separation of logic and reason from emotion. This separation is antithetical to good rhetorical practices in Chinese discourse, for example, as well as in Hindu rhetoric and philosophy. These Asian rhetorical traditions emphasize the importance of emotion in learning the truthfulness of a situation.[22] Similarly, Stanley Lubman describes a fundamental difference between U.S. Americans and Chinese in a persuasive encounter. U.S. Americans use alternative ways of saying the same thing, and they display changes in their positions during the course of a discussion. The Chinese, on the other hand, simply restate their position repeatedly; they would never publicly change their position without private consultation among themselves.[23]

We would like to elaborate on the idea of persuasive style because, like many of the other characteristics of a culture, it is an important cultural attribute that is taken for granted within a culture but affects communication between cultures. As we have cautioned elsewhere, not every person in a culture will select the culture's preferred style. Rather, we are describing a cultural tendency, a choice or preference that most people in the culture will select most of the time.

Barbara Johnstone describes three general strategies of persuasion that can form a culture's preferred style: the quasilogical, presentational, and analogical.[24] Each of these styles depends on different kinds of evidence, organizational patterns, and conclusions. As you read the descriptions of these styles, try to imagine what a persuasive encounter would be like and what might happen if others preferred a different persuasive style.

Quasilogical Style   The preferred style for members of many Western cultures is one that Johnstone calls quasilogical. In this style, the preference is to use statistics and testimony from expert, objective witnesses as evidence. The evidence is then connected to the conclusion in a way that resembles formal logic. In formal logic, once the listener accepts or believes the individual pieces of evidence, the conclusions follow "logically" and must also be accepted. In the quasilogical style, the speaker or persuader will connect the evidence to the persuasive conclusion by using such words as *thus, hence,* and *therefore.* The form or arrangement of the ideas is very important.

The dominance of the quasilogical style for English speakers is underscored by advice given to students of English as a second language: "English-speaking readers are convinced by facts, statistics, and illustrations in arguments; they move from generalizations to specific examples and expect explicit links between main topics and subtopics; and they value originality."[25] The underlying assumption of this style is that if the idea is "true," it simply needs to be presented in a logical way so that its truthfulness becomes apparent to all. Those who prefer the quasilogical style assume that it is possible to discover what is true or false and right or wrong about a particular experience. In other words, they believe that events can be objectively established and verified.

Presentational Style   The presentational style emphasizes and appeals to the emotional aspects of persuasion. In this style, it is understood that people, rather than the idea itself, are what make an idea persuasive. That is, ideas themselves are not inherently persuasive; what makes them compelling is how they are presented to others. Thus, an immutable truth does not exist, and there are no clear rights or wrongs to be discovered.

In the presentational style, the persuader uses language to create an emotional response. The rhythmic qualities of words and the ability of words to move the hearer visually and auditorily are fundamental to this style of persuasion. You have probably read poetry or literature that stimulated a strong emotional reaction. Those who use a presentational style persuade in the same way. By the use of words, the ideas of the speaker become so vivid and real that the persuasive idea almost becomes embedded in the consciousness of the listener. The language of this style of persuasion is filled with sensory words that induce the listener to *look, see, hear, feel,* and ultimately *believe.*

Analogical Style   The analogical style seeks to establish an idea (a conclusion) and to persuade the listener by providing an analogy, a story, or a parable in which there is either an implicit or explicit lesson to be learned. The storybook pattern that begins "Once upon a time" is one example of this style, as are the sermons of many ministers and preachers. An assumption underlying the analogical style is that the collective ex-

CULTURE *connections*

Native American people hesitate to tell anyone directly what they *should* do. With many Native American people, it is not customary to say, "You must not do that." A story indirectly says to children, "You may act this way, but look at the consequences." . . .

There are cultural storytelling conventions in Native American tradition that vary sharply from European American tradition and which may account, in part, for the observed powerful effects of the telling of *lesson* stories: (1) while European heroes are praised for succeeding, Native American heroes are honored for their attempt, even if they fail; (2) when animals talk in European stories, they usually imitate human characteristics and failures, but when they talk in Native American stories, it is because they are respected as equals in the natural world, with wisdom to share; (3) many characters are not given names, underlining the universality of human experience over situation-specific events; (4) nonverbal communication through gesture and voice is given an equal rather than a supplementary role in oral tales, which may appear verbally lean; and (5) the spirit world and the physical world exist side by side and are so close that it is possible to move back and forth between the two without effort. . . .

Consistent with an appreciation for indirect teaching, a Native American lesson story is told without further explication of meaning and contains no surprise endings, shocks, or ironic twists. To an analytical mind a lesson story may seem to have no deductive conclusion, ending only with the teller saying something like, "That's how it was." Tellers do not lift out the "moral" of the story for the listener or offer the accepted point of view, which might be consistent with the linear and discursive nature of traditional American education.

—Sunwolf

perience of groups of people—the culture—is persuasive, rather than the ideas themselves or the characteristics of a dynamic individual. Historical precedent takes on great importance because what convinces is a persuader's ability to choose the right historical story to demonstrate the point. In the analogical style, skill in persuasion is associated with the discovery and narration of the appropriate story—a story that captures the essence of what the persuader wants the listeners to know.

Persuasive encounters involving people with different stylistic preferences may result in neither person being persuaded by the other. To a person with a cultural preference for a quasilogical style, the presentational style will appear emotional and intuitive, and the analogical style will appear irrelevant. To those using the presentational style, the quasilogical style will appear dull, insignificant, and unrelated to the real issues. To those using the analogical style, the quasilogical style will seem blunt and unappealing.

Even seemingly "objective" reporting of news may convey a subtle persuasive message. Japanese newspapers and television news shows, for example, routinely refer to Japanese adults by their family name plus *san,* the latter word being an address term denoting respect or honor. As Daniel Dolan suggests, however, "this respect is *conditional,* because in most instances of reporting about a person associated with criminal

A Guatemalan man uses his sales pitch to influence a shopper. People the world over depend on persuasion to transform interested customers into purchasing customers.

activity, mass media reporters will publicly divest an individual of the personal address term *san* and in its place use *yogisha* [suspect], *hikoku* [accused], or family name alone. The effect is to banish the person, at least temporarily, from functioning citizenry."[26]

An interesting example of the clash in preferences for persuasive styles is found in Jesse Jackson's speech given to the 1988 Democratic Presidential Nominating Convention, when Jackson was running for that nomination. Jackson's speaking style was mis-

CULTURE *connections*

The black [American] culture is characterized by an oral tradition. Knowledge, attitudes, ideas, notions are traditionally transmitted orally, not through the written word. It is not unusual, then, that the natural leader among black people would be one with exceptional oratorical skills. He must be able to talk, to speak—to preach. In the black religious tradition, the successful black preacher is an expert orator. His role involves more, however. His relationship with his parishioners is reciprocal; he talks to them, and they talk back to him. That is expected. In many church circles this talk-back during a sermon is a firm measure of the preacher's effectiveness.

—*Charles V. Hamilton*

interpreted by many in the media, who were primarily European Americans, because they did not understand that his presentational speaking style followed the oral tradition of African American speakers. Jackson was accused of factual exaggeration, lying, and being overly dramatic and emotional. Yet his speaking style was grounded in a rich rhetorical tradition in which "argument" and "reasoning" are presented as part of a performance, with dramatic emphases to make the ideas clear and vivid.[27]

Cultural Variations in the Structure of Conversations

All conversations differ on a number of important dimensions: how long one talks; the nature of the relationship between the conversants; the kinds of topics discussed; the way information is presented; how signals are given to indicate interest and involvement; and even whether conversation is regarded as a useful, important, and necessary means of communicating. In this section, we explore some of the differences in the way cultures shape the use of codes to create conversations. Our usual caution applies: when cultural tendencies are described, remember that not all members of the culture will necessarily reflect these characteristics.

Value of Talk and Silence

The importance given to words varies greatly from one culture to the next. Among African Americans and European Americans, for example, words are considered very important. In informal conversations between friends, individuals often "give my word" to assure the truth of their statement. In the legal setting, people swear that their words constitute "the truth, the whole truth, and nothing but the truth." Legal obligations are contracted with formal documents to which people affix their signatures—another set of words. The spoken word is seen as a reflection of a person's inner thoughts. Even the theories of communication that are presented in most books about communication—including this one—are highly influenced by underlying assumptions that give words the ability to represent thoughts. In this characteristically Western approach to communication, people need words to communicate accurately and completely with one another. Conversely, silence is often taken by many Western Europeans and European Americans to convey a range of negative experiences—awkwardness, embarrassment, hostility, disinterest, disapproval, shyness, an unwillingness to communicate, a lack of verbal skills, or an expression of interpersonal incompatibility.[28]

Other cultures can be far more hesitant about the value of words. Asian cultures such as those of Japan, Korea, and China, and southern African cultures, such as those of Swaziland, Zambia, and Lesotho, have quite a different evaluation of words and talking. D. Lawrence Kincaid says that "the Eastern perspective places more emphasis than the Western on the meaning of silence and on saying nothing or as little as is necessary."[29] Because of a combination of historical and cultural forces, spoken words in Japan, Korea, and China are viewed with some suspicion and disregard. Taoist sayings such as "One who speaks does not know" and "To be always talking is against nature" convey this distrust of talking and wordiness.[30]

Have two people enact a typical beginning to a telephone conversation. Try to identify the underlying rules that govern such typical telephone conversation openings.

In Japan, the term *haragei* (wordless communication) describes the cultural preference to communicate without using language. Donald Klopf elaborates on this Japanese penchant:

> The desire not to speak is the most significant aspect or feature of Japanese language life. The Japanese hate to hear someone make excuses for his or her mistakes or failures. They do not like long and complicated explanations. Consequently, the less talkative person is preferred and is more popular than the talkative one, other conditions being equal. If one has to say something normally, it is said in as few words as possible.[31]

In Korea, the strong religious and cultural influence of Confucian values has devalued oral communication and made written communication highly regarded. June Ock Yum, in an interesting exploration of the relationship between Korean philosophy and communication, says, "Where the written communication was dominant, spoken words were underrated as being apt to run on and on, to be mean and low. To read was the profession of scholars, to speak the act of menials."[32] Buddhism, also a major influence on Korean thought, teaches, "True communication is believed to occur only when one speaks without the mouth and when one hears without the ears."[33]

In Swaziland people are similarly suspicious of those who talk excessively. As Peter Nwosu has observed:

> The Swazis are quick to attribute motives when a person during negotiations is very pushy, engages in too much self-praise, or acts like he or she knows everything. "People who talk a lot are not welcome; be calm, but not too calm that they suspect you are up to some mischief," remarks an official of the Swazi Embassy in Washington, D.C. Indeed, there is such a thin line between talkativeness and calmness that it is difficult for a foreigner to understand when one is being "too talkative" or "too calm."[34]

People from Finland are also less willing than European Americans to talk, even among close friends.[35]

The consequences of these differences in preferences for talking are illustrated by a Japanese American student and an African American student who became roommates. Over a period of a few weeks, the African American student sought social interaction and conversation with his Japanese American roommate, who seemed to become less

CULTURE *connections*

He had yet to say anything. She knew the trick; keep silent long enough, the other person felt compelled to fill that silence. Pastor Seabolt did not know with whom he was in competition, however. Alaska Native children learn by watching and listening. Direct questions are not often asked, and when words finally are used, they are honored and remembered and so not wasted in trivia. The lack of verbal communication could frustrate and bewilder an Anglo dealing with a Native for the first time, as witness the three classes Kate had dropped her first year in college because the teachers kept asking her questions.

—*Dana Stabenow*

and less willing to converse. The African American student interpreted this reticence as an indication of dislike and disinterest rather than as an indication of cultural differences in conversational preferences. Finally, he decided to move to a different room, because he felt too uncomfortable with the silence to remain.

There are also different cultural preferences for silence and the place of silence in conversations. Keith Basso describes a number of interpersonal communication experiences in which members of the Apache tribe prefer silence, whereas non–Native Americans might prefer to talk a lot: meetings between strangers, the initial stages of a courtship, an individual returning home to relatives and friends after a long absence, a person verbally expressing anger, someone being sad, and during a curing ceremony.[36] Basso gives this assessment of the value placed on introductions:

> The Western Apache do not feel compelled to "introduce" persons who are unknown to each other. Eventually, it is assumed, strangers will begin to speak. However, this is a decision that is properly left to the individuals involved, and no attempt is made to hasten it. Outside help in the form of introductions or other verbal routines is viewed as presumptuous and unnecessary.
>
> Strangers who are quick to launch into conversations are frequently eyed with undisguised suspicion. A typical reaction to such individuals is that they "want something," that is, their willingness to violate convention is attributed to some urgent need which is likely to result in requests for money, labor, or transportation.[37]

In sum, the fundamental value and role of talk as a tool for conversation vary from culture to culture.

Rules for Conversations

Cultures provide an implicit set of rules to govern interaction. Verbal and nonverbal codes come with a set of cultural prescriptions that determine how they should be used. In this section we explore some of the ways in which conversational structures can vary from one culture to another. Communication scholars using an ethnographic perspective have been at the forefront of these investigations, and we draw heavily on their efforts.[38] In Chapter 11 we also consider some aspects of conversational structures that are particularly relevant to the development of intercultural relationships.

Some of the ways in which conversational rules can vary are illustrated in the following questions:

- How do you know when it is your turn to talk in a conversation?
- When you talk to a person you have never met before, how do you know what topics are acceptable for you to discuss?
- In a conversation, must your comments be directly related to those that come before?
- When you are upset about a grade, how do you determine the approach to take in a conversation with the teacher, or even *if* you should have a conversation with the teacher?
- When you approach your employer to ask for a raise, how do you decide what to say?
- If you want someone to do something for you, do you ask for it directly or do you mention it to others and hope that they will tell the first person what it is that you want?

▶ If you decide to ask for something directly, do you go straight to the point and say, "This is what I need from you," or do you hint at what you want and expect the other person to understand?

▶ When you speak, do you use grand language filled with images, metaphors, and stories or do you simply and succinctly present the relevant information?

Cultural preferences would produce many different answers to these questions. For example, European Americans signal a desire to speak in a conversation by leaning forward a small degree, slightly opening their mouth, and establishing eye contact. In another culture, those same sets of symbols could be totally disregarded because they have no meaning, or they could mean something totally different (for example, respectful listening). Acceptable topics of conversations for two U.S. American students meeting in a class might include their majors, current interests, and where they work. Those same topics in some other cultures might be regarded as too personal for casual conversations, but discussions about religious beliefs and family history might seem perfectly acceptable. Though European Americans expect comments in a conversation to be related to previous ones, Japanese express their views without necessarily responding to what the other has said.[39]

William Gudykunst and Stella Ting-Toomey describe cultural variations in conversational style along four dimensions: direct–indirect, elaborate–succinct, personal–contextual, and instrumental–affective.[40] Cultures that prefer a direct style, such as European Americans, use verbal messages that are explicit in revealing the speaker's true intentions and desires. In contrast, those that prefer indirection will veil the speaker's true wants and needs with ambiguous statements. African American, Japanese, and Korean cultures, for example, prefer the indirect style.

Like all exchanges, this conversation is governed by a complex set of rules about who talks to whom, for how long, and on what topics. Yet the participants are unlikely to be consciously aware of these rules until someone breaks them.

Cultural conversational styles also differ on a dimension of elaborate to succinct. The elaborate style, which is found in most Arab and Latino cultures, results in the frequent use of metaphors, proverbs, and other figurative language. The expressiveness of this style contrasts with the succinct style, in which people give precisely the amount of information necessary. In the succinct style, there is a preference for understatement and long pauses, as in Japanese American and Chinese American cultures.

In cultures that prefer a personal style, in contrast to those that prefer a contextual style, there is an emphasis on conversations in which the individual, as a unique human being, is the center of action. This style is also characterized by more informality and less status-oriented talk. In the contextual style, the emphasis is on the social roles that people have in relationships with others. Japanese, Chinese, and Indian cultures all emphasize the social role or the interpersonal community in which a particular person is embedded. The style is very formal and heightens awareness of status differences by accentuating them.

In the instrumental style, communication is goal-oriented and depends on explicit verbal messages. Affective styles are more emotional and require sensitivity to the underlying meanings in both the verbal and nonverbal code systems. Min-Sun Kim suggests that this goal-oriented style, which is characterized by a heightened concern for "getting the job done," is preferred by people from individualistic cultures, whereas the affective style, which is concerned with the feelings and emotions of others, typifies people from collectivistic cultures.[41] Thomas Kochman has articulated some of the differences in conversational styles between European Americans and African Americans:

At the dinner table with your family or friends, try to determine the rules for passing food, getting more food, giving others more food, and saying "no" to more food.

> The differing potencies of black and white public presentations are a regular cause of communicative conflict. Black presentations are emotionally intense, dynamic, and demonstrative; white presentations are more modest and emotionally restrained.[42]

Melanie Booth-Butterfield and Felecia Jordan similarly found that African American females were more expressive, more involved with one another, more animated, and more at ease than were their European American counterparts, who appeared more formal and restrained.[43] Because of these differences in conversational style, an African American and a European American may judge each other negatively.

Ronald Scollon and Suzanne Wong-Scollon, who have studied the Athabaskan, a cultural group of native peoples in Alaska and northern Canada, describe similar problems in intercultural communication:

> When an Athabaskan and a speaker of English talk to each other, it is very likely that the English speaker will speak first. . . . The Athabaskan will feel it is important to know the relationship between the two speakers before speaking. The English speaker will feel talking is the best way to establish a relationship. While the Athabaskan is waiting to see what will happen between them, the English speaker will begin speaking, usually asking questions in fact, to find out what will happen. Only where there is a longstanding relationship and a deep understanding between the two speakers is it likely that the Athabaskan will initiate the conversation.[44]

Regulating conversations is also problematic for the English speaker and an Athabaskan because the latter uses a longer pause—about a half second longer—between

CULTURE *connections*

To an English speaker, a sudden intake of breath implies a gasp of shock or fear. But in Scandinavian conversation, a sucking in of breath that sounds like "ya" is a way of assuring a conversation partner you are listening, just as English speakers will mutter "mm-hmm" from time to time, especially on the telephone. Linguists call it "back-channeling."

Another common use of interjections is as "placeholders," hesitation sounds that give the speaker a moment to think. English speakers use "uh" or "um," meaning: Don't give up, don't interrupt, I'm going to get to my point eventually. Russians similarly use the particle "vot"; Arabic speakers pause with the word "yahni."

Unlike ordinary words, such sounds are "semantically empty," says David Murray, a Washington anthropologist. "It's hard to say what they mean outside the context of a conversation." But pronounced in midsentence, they can be rich with significance. "Uh . . . I don't think so," can be much more emphatic than, "I don't think so."

"We are all performance artists when we speak," he says.

—*Scott Shane*

turns. The effects of this slightly longer pause would be comical if the consequences for intercultural communication were not so serious.

> When an English speaker pauses, he waits for the regular length of time (around one second or less), that is, *his* regular length of time, and if the Athabaskan does not say anything, the English speaker feels he is free to go on and say anything else he likes. At the same time the Athabaskan has been waiting his regular length of time before coming in. He does not want to interrupt the English speaker. This length of time we think is around one and one-half seconds. It is just enough longer that by the time the Athabaskan is ready to speak the English speaker is already speaking again. So the Athabaskan waits again for the next pause. Again, the English speaker begins just enough before the Athabaskan was going to speak. The net result is that the Athabaskan can never get a word in edgewise (an apt metaphor in this case), while the English speaker goes on and on.[45]

These very real differences in the nature of conversations play a critical role in intercultural communication. The ultimate result is often a negative judgment of other people rather than a recognition that the variability in cultural preferences is creating the difficulties.

Effects of Code Usage on Intercultural Competence

Developing competence in the practical, everyday use of verbal and nonverbal codes is undoubtedly a major challenge for the intercultural communicator. But simply knowing the syntactic rules of other code systems is not sufficient to be able to use those code systems well.

The most important knowledge you can take away from this chapter is the realization that people from other cultures may organize their ideas, persuade others, and

CULTURE *connections*

I looked at her and didn't know what to say. Could she really think that this was appropriate wording for an application to an international lending group? I finally asked her as much. She did not look up from her work. "Mm. Is there something wrong with the grammar?" I said no, the grammar seemed fine, but the content seemed a bit weak, perhaps. Her expression did not change at all. "But this is a translation of the text written by the officials of our college. This is the Chinese way of writing this sort of thing. I am only an English teacher, I cannot presume to change it." I told her that perhaps from a Chinese point of view this kind of language was acceptable, but that from a Western point of view it seemed repetitive, and since they were applying to an institution run according to Western principles, they might want to draft a more Western-sounding text. She sighed, still without looking at me, and said nothing. I got the impression that she was quietly hoping I wouldn't press the issue, so I didn't, and pointed out a misspelling.

—*Mark Salzman*

structure their conversations in a manner that differs from yours. You should attempt, to the greatest extent possible, to understand your own preferences for using verbal and nonverbal codes to accomplish practical goals. If you can, mentally set aside your beliefs and the accompanying evaluative labels. Instead, recognize that your belief system and the verbal and nonverbal symbols that are used to represent it were taught to you by your culture and constitute only one among many ways of understanding the world and accomplishing one's personal objectives.

Look for the differences in the ways that people from other cultures choose to accomplish their interpersonal objectives. Look for alternative logics. Approach the unfamiliar as a puzzle to be solved rather than as something to be feared or dismissed as illogical, irrational, or wrong. Much can be learned about the effects of code usage by observing others. If your approach is not successful, notice how members of the culture accomplish their objectives.

Summary

The chapter described the effects on intercultural communication of cultural differences in the way verbal and nonverbal codes are used. These differences affect how people attempt to understand messages, organize ideas, persuade others, and engage in discussions and conversations.

We began with a discussion of differences in cultural preferences for organizing and arranging messages, and we contrasted the organizational preferences of U.S. English, which are typically linear, with those of other languages and cultures.

Cultural variations in persuasion and argumentation were considered next. We emphasized that appropriate forms of evidence, reasoning, and rationality are all culturally based and can affect intercultural communication. Indeed, there are major differences in persuasive styles that are taken for granted within a culture but that affect the communication between cultures.

Cultural variations also exist in the structure of conversations. The importance given to talk and silence, the social rules and interaction styles that are used in conversations, and even the cues used to regulate the back-and-forth sequencing of conversations can all create problems for intercultural communicators.

Finally, we noted that differences in the way people prefer to communicate can affect the ability to behave appropriately and effectively in intercultural encounters. These cultural preferences typically operate outside of awareness and may lead to judgments that others are "wrong" or "incorrect" when they are merely different.

For Discussion

1. What does it mean to learn the "logic" of a language?
2. In what ways does the U.S. legal system reflect the European American view of argumentation and persuasion?
3. Does your culture value a particular style of persuasion? Do your own preferred ways of persuading others reflect your culture's style of persuasion?
4. What does silence communicate to you? How is your culture's use of silence connected to Hall's cultural patterns of low and high context?
5. Members of some cultures will invariably say "yes" even though, given the situation and their true feelings, the answer is most likely "no." How do you explain this phenomenon?

For Further Reading

Ulla Connor, *Contrastive Rhetoric: Cross-Cultural Aspects of Second-Language Writing* (New York: Cambridge University Press, 1996). Provides detailed explanations and examples of the influence of culture on oral and written use of language, particularly as seen from the perspective of second-language learners.

Alberto González and Dolores V. Tanno (eds.), *Rhetoric in Intercultural Contexts* (Thousand Oaks, CA: Sage, 2000). This collection explores how different cultural traditions influence what are considered to be good rhetorical practices.

Clayann G. Panetta (ed.), *Contrastive Rhetoric Revisited and Redefined* (Mahwah, NJ: Erlbaum 2001). This volume probes the impact of culturally grounded rhetoric on how people write and persuade others.

Ron Scollon and Suzanne Wong-Scollon, *Intercultural Communication: A Discourse Approach*, 2nd ed. (Malden, MA: Blackwell, 2001). Offers numerous examples of the relationships between a person's language, thinking, and logical actions. Explores how language and culture provide a preferred structure to conversations.

For additional information about intercultural films and about Web sites on specific cultures, turn to the Resources section at the back of this book.

part four

Communication in Intercultural Relationships

chapter **10** Intercultural Competence in Interpersonal Relationships

chapter **11** Episodes, Contexts, and Intercultural Interactions

chapter **12** The Potential for Intercultural Competence

Intercultural Competence in Interpersonal Relationships

Cultural Variations in Interpersonal Relationships
Types of Interpersonal Relationships
Dimensions of Interpersonal Relationships
Dynamics of Interpersonal Relationships
The Maintenance of Face in Interpersonal Relationships
Types of Face Needs
Facework and Interpersonal Communication
Facework and Intercultural Communication

Improving Intercultural Relationships
Learning about People from Other Cultures
Sharing Oneself with People from Other Cultures
Handling Differences in Intercultural Relationships
Interpersonal Relationships and Intercultural Competence
Summary

All relationships imply connections. When you are in an interpersonal relationship you are connected—in a very important sense, you are bound together—with another person in some substantial way. Of course, the nature of these ties is rarely physical. Rather, in interpersonal relationships you are connected to others by virtue of your shared experiences, interpretations, perceptions, and goals.

Cultural Variations in Interpersonal Relationships

In Chapter 2 we indicated that communication is interpersonal as long as it involves a small number of participants who can interact directly with one another and who therefore have the ability to adapt their messages specifically for one another. Of course, different patterns of interpersonal communication are likely to occur with different types of interpersonal relationships. We believe it is useful to characterize the various types of interpersonal relationships by the kinds of social connections the participants share.

Types of Interpersonal Relationships

Some interpersonal connections occur because of blood or marriage. Others exist because of overlapping or interdependent objectives and goals. Still others bind people together because of common experiences that help to create a perception of "we-ness."

However, all interpersonal relationships have as their common characteristic a strong connection among the individuals.

The number of interpersonal relationships that you have throughout your life is probably very large. Some of these relationships are complex and involved, whereas others are simple and casual; some are brief and spontaneous, while others may last a lifetime. Some of these relationships, we hope, have involved people from different cultures.

Interpersonal relationships between people from different cultures can be difficult to understand and describe because of the contrasts in culturally based expectations about the nature of interpersonal communication. However, regardless of the cultures involved or the circumstances surrounding the relationship's formation, there is always some sort of bond or social connection that links or ties the people to one another. The participants may be strangers, acquaintances, friends, romantic partners, or family or kinship members. Each relationship carries with it certain expectations for appropriate behaviors that are anchored within specific cultures. People in an intercultural relationship, then, may define their experiences very differently and may have dissimilar expectations; for example, a stranger to someone from one culture may be called a friend by someone from another culture.

Strangers   You will undoubtedly talk to many thousands of people in your lifetime, and most of them will be strangers to you. But what exactly is a stranger? Certainly, a stranger is someone whom you do not know and who is therefore unfamiliar to you. But is someone always a stranger the first time you meet? How about the second time, or the third? What about the people you talked with several times, although the conversation was restricted to the task of seating you in a restaurant or pricing your groceries, so names were never actually exchanged? Are these people strangers to you? Your answers to these questions, like so many of the ideas described in this book, depend on what you have been taught by your culture.

In the United States, for instance, the social walls that are erected between strangers may not be as thick and impenetrable as they are in some collectivistic cultures. European Americans, who are often fiercely individualistic as a cultural group, may not have developed the strong ingroup bonds that would promote separation from outsiders. Among the Greeks, however, who hold collectivistic values, the word for "non-Greek" translates as "stranger."

Even in the United States, the distinction between stranger and nonstranger is an important one; young children are often taught to be afraid of people they do not know. Compare, however, a U.S. American's reaction toward a stranger to that of a Korean in a similar situation. In Korea, which is a family-dominated collectivist culture, a stranger is anyone to whom you have not been formally introduced. Strangers in Korea are "nonpersons" to whom the rules of politeness and social etiquette simply do not apply. Thus, Koreans may jostle you on the street without apologizing or, perhaps, even noticing. However, once you have been introduced to a Korean, or the Korean anticipates in other ways that he or she may have an ongoing interpersonal relationship with you, elaborate politeness rituals are required.

Acquaintances   An acquaintance is someone you know, but only casually. Therefore, interactions tend to be on a superficial level. The social bonds that link acquaintances

CULTURE *connections*

In China, once you began to "see" a person, you were locked in, to the exclusion of all others of the opposite sex. There were no degrees of involvement. Everyone knew that you were a couple, and that was a clear signal to all others. As a woman tied to a man in Shanghai, I was safe from the advances of others. Most women married the first person they dated, just as my mother had done, and as all my siblings eventually would. A female considered paired would be viewed as a loose woman if she developed friendships with other men. Even those who broke up with their boyfriends were looked down upon by friends and family if they dated again right away. It was a holdover from feudal society, when a woman whose husband died was expected to remain single all her life, regardless of her age.

—*Ting-Xing Ye*

are very slight. Acquaintances will typically engage in social politeness rituals, such as greeting one another when first meeting or exchanging small talk on topics generally viewed as more impersonal such as the weather, hobbies, fashions, and sports. But acquaintances do not typically confide in one another about personal problems or discuss private concerns. Of course, the topics appropriate for small talk, which do not include personal and private issues, will differ from one culture to another. Among European Americans, it is perfectly appropriate to ask a male acquaintance about his wife; in the United Arab Emirates, it would be a major breach of social etiquette to do so. In New Zealand, it is appropriate to talk about national and international politics; in Pakistan, these and similar topics should be avoided. In Austria, discussions about money and religion are typically sidestepped; elsewhere, acquaintances may well be asked "personal" questions about their income and family background.

Friends   As with many of the other terms that describe interpersonal relationships, *friend* is a common expression that refers to many different types of relationships. "Good friends," "close friends," and "just friends" are all commonly used expressions among U.S. Americans. Generally speaking, a friend is someone you know well, someone you like, and someone with whom you feel a close personal bond. A friendship usually includes higher levels of intimacy, self-disclosure, involvement, and intensity than does acquaintanceship. In many ways, friends can be thought of as close acquaintances.

> Make a list of the people you would regard as acquaintances, friends, romantic partners, and family members. Compare the number and types of people in these categories with others in your class. What does this comparison reveal?

Unlike kinships, friendships are voluntary, even though many friendships start because the participants have been thrust together in some way. Because they are voluntary, friendships usually occur between people who see themselves as similar in some important ways and who belong to the same social class.

European American friendships tend to be very compartmentalized because they are based on a shared activity, event, or experience. The European American can study with one friend, play racquetball with another, and go to the movies with a third. As suggested in Chapter 4, this pattern occurs because European Americans typically classify people according to what they do or have achieved rather than who they are. Relations among European Americans are therefore fragmented, and they view themselves and others as a composite of distinct interests. Conversely, the Thai are likely to react more to the other person as a whole and will avoid forming friendships with those whose values and behaviors are in some way deemed undesirable.[1] Unlike friendships in the United States, in Thailand a friend is accepted completely or not at all; a person cannot disapprove of some aspect of another's political beliefs or personal life and still consider her or him to be a friend.

These Moroccan women hold hands to convey their friendship. In every culture, expectations about the social behaviors are influenced by a set of rules.

CULTURE *connections*

A friendly American is not necessarily an American friend. Though an American may be willing to have long, intimate conversations with a stranger, that doesn't mean a dinner invitation is forthcoming.

—*Sophia Dembling*

John Condon has noted that the language people use to describe their interpersonal relationships often reflects the underlying cultural values about their meaning and importance. Thus, Condon says, friendships among European Americans are expressed by terms such as *friends, allies,* and *neighbors,* all of which reflect an individualistic cultural value. However, among African Americans and some Southern whites, closeness between friends is expressed by such terms as *brother, sister,* or *cousin,* suggesting a collectivist cultural value. Mexican terms for relationships, like the cultural values they represent, are similar to those of African Americans. Thus when European Americans and Mexicans speak of close friendships, the former will probably use a word such as *partner,* which suggests a voluntary association, whereas Mexicans may use a word such as *brother* or *sister,* which suggests a lasting bond that is beyond the control of any one person.[2]

From your own cultural perspective, identify the expectations and responsibilities that you have for the role of friend. Find another person in your class and compare the responsibilities that each of you has identified. Are there obvious differences?

As interpersonal relationships move from initial acquaintance to close friendship, five types of changes in perceptions and behaviors will probably occur. First, friends interact more frequently; they talk to each other more often, for longer periods of time, and in more varied settings than acquaintances do. Second, the increased frequency of interactions means that friends will have more knowledge about and shared experiences with each other than will acquaintances, and this unique common ground will probably develop into a private communication code to refer to ideas, objects, and experiences that are exclusive to the relationship. Third, the increased knowledge of the other person's motives and typical behaviors means that there is an increased ability to predict a friend's reactions to common situations. The powerful need to reduce uncertainty in the initial stages of relationships, which we discuss in greater detail later in this chapter, suggests that acquaintanceships are unlikely to progress to friendships without the ability to predict the others' intentions and expectations. Fourth, the sense of "we-ness" increases among friends. Friends often feel that their increased investment of time and emotional commitment to the relationship creates a sense of interdependence, so that individual goals and interests are affected by and linked to each person's satisfaction with the relationship. Finally, close friendships are characterized by a heightened sense of caring, commitment, trust, and emotional attachment to the other person, so that the people in a friendship view it as something special and unique.[3]

These students, who are both friends and co-workers, are finishing the latest edition of their school's newspaper. In intercultural communication, differences in cultural patterns may cause difficulties in managing personal relationships.

Intercultural friendships can vary in a variety of ways: whom a person selects as a friend, how long a friendship lasts, the prerogatives and responsibilities of being a friend, the number of friends that a person prefers to have, and even how long a relationship must develop before it becomes a friendship. African American friends, for instance, expect to be able to confront and criticize one another, sometimes in a loud and argumentative manner.[4] Latinos, Asian Americans, and African Americans feel that it takes them, on the average, about a year for an acquaintanceship to develop into a close friendship, whereas European Americans feel that it takes only a few months.[5] For intercultural friendships to be successful, therefore, they may require an informal agreement between the friends about each of these aspects for the people involved to have shared expectations about appropriate behaviors.

Romantic Partners   The diversity of cultural norms that govern romantic relationships is an excellent example of the wide range of cultural expectations. Consider, for instance, the enormous differences in cultural beliefs, values, and norms about love, romance, dating, and marriage.

Among European Americans, dating usually occurs for romance and companionship. A dating relationship is not viewed as a serious commitment that will necessarily, or even probably, lead to an engagement. If they choose to do so, couples will marry because of love and affection for each other. Although family members may be consulted before a final decision is made, the choice to marry is made almost exclusively by the couples themselves.

In Argentina and Spain, dating is taken more seriously. Indeed, dating the same person more than twice may mean that the relationship will lead to an engagement and, ultimately, marriage. Yet engagements in these Spanish-speaking cultures typically last a long time and may extend over a period of years, as couples work, save money, and prepare themselves financially for marriage.

In Indonesia, the opportunities for men and women to be together, particularly in unchaperoned settings, are much more restricted. In India, casual dating relationships and similar opportunities for romantic expression among unmarried individuals are still quite rare; marriages are likely to be arranged by parents, usually with the consent of the couple. This pattern of familial involvement can also be found in Arabic-speaking cultures, where marriage imposes great obligations and responsibilities on the families of the couple. In Algeria, for instance, a marriage is seen as an important link between families, not individuals. Consequently, the selection of a spouse may require the approval of the entire extended family. Moreover, in both India and Algeria, romantic love is believed to be something that develops after marriage, not before. Even in Colombia, where because of changes in customs and cultural practices arranged marriages are no longer fashionable, the decision to get married requires family approval. Yet research by Stanley Gaines on the nature of intercultural romantic relationships found a great deal of similarity in the communication across cultures.[6]

Family   Family or kinship relationships are also characterized by large cultural variations. Particularly important to the development of intercultural relationships are these factors: how the family is defined, or who is considered to be a member of the family; the formality of roles and behavioral expectations for particular family members; and the importance of the family in social relationships and personal decisions.

Among European Americans, and even among members of most European cultures, family life is primarily confined to interactions among the mother, father, and children. Households usually include just these family members, though the extended family unit also includes grandparents, aunts, uncles, and cousins. Though the amount and quality of interaction among extended family members will vary greatly from family to family, members of the extended family rarely live together in the same household or take an active part in the day-to-day lives of the nuclear family members.

Family relationships in other cultures can be quite different. Among Latinos, for instance, the extended family is very important.[7] Similarly, in India the extended family dominates; grandparents, aunts, uncles, and many other relatives may live together in one household. Families in India include people who would be called second or third cousins in the European American family, and the unmarried siblings of those who have become family members through marriage may also be included in the household. These "family members" would rarely be defined as such in the typical European American family. Among Native Americans family refers to all members of the clan.[8] No particular pattern of family relationships can be said to typify the world's cultures. Many Arab families, for instance, include multiple generations of the male line. Often three

Because culture influences expectations about appropriate and effective behaviors, intercultural families may need to pay more attention to the negotiation of their relationship rules.

generations—grandparents, married sons and their wives, and unmarried children—will live together under one roof. Among certain cultural groups in Ghana, however, just the opposite pattern can be found; families have a matrilineal organization, and the family inheritance is passed down through the wife's family rather than the husband's.

Expected role behaviors and responsibilities also vary among cultures. In Argentina, family roles are very clearly defined by social custom; the wife is expected to raise the children, manage the household, and show deference to the husband. In India, the oldest male son has specific family and religious obligations that are not requirements for other sons in the same family. Languages sometimes reflect these specialized roles. In China, for example,

> [a] sister-in-law is called by various names, depending on whether she is the older brother's wife, the younger brother's wife, or the wife's sister. Aunts, uncles, and cousins are named in the same way. Thus, a father's sister is "ku," a mother's sister is "yi," an uncle's wife is "shen," and so on.[9]

Families also differ in their influence over a person's social networks and decision making. In some cultures, the family is the primary means through which a person's social life is maintained. In others, such as among European Americans, families are almost peripheral to the social networks that are established. In the more collectivist cultures such as Japan, Korea, and China, families play a pivotal role in making decisions for children, including the choice of university, profession, and even marital partner. In

CULTURE *connections*

I remember asking a twenty-year-old student in economics at Delhi University . . . if she loved the childhood friend her parents had decided she should marry. "That's a very difficult question," she answered. "I don't know. This whole concept of love is very alien to us. We're more practical. I don't see stars, I don't hear little bells. But he's a very nice guy, and I think I'm going to enjoy spending my life with him. Is that love?" She shrugged.

—Elisabeth Bumiller

contrast, in individualistic cultures, where children are taught from their earliest years to make their own decisions, a characteristic of "good parenting" is to allow children to "learn for themselves" the consequences of their own actions.

The increasing number of people creating intercultural families, in which husband and wife represent different cultural backgrounds, poses new challenges for family communication. Often, the children in these families are raised in an intercultural household that is characterized by some blending of the original cultures. Differences in the expectations of appropriate social roles—of wife and husband, son and daughter, older and younger child, or husband's parents and wife's parents—require a knowledge of and sensitivity to the varying influences of culture on family communication.

Dimensions of Interpersonal Relationships

People throughout the world use at least three primary dimensions to interpret interpersonal communication messages: control, affiliation, and activation.[10]

Control   Control involves status or social dominance. We have control to the extent that we have the power and prestige to influence the events around us. Depending on the culture, control can be communicated by a variety of behaviors including touching, looking, talking, and the use of space. Supervisors, for instance, are more likely to touch their subordinates than vice versa. In many cultures, excessive looking behaviors are viewed as attempts to "stare down" the other person and are usually seen as an effort to exert interactional control. Similarly, high-power individuals seek and are usually given more personal space and a larger territory to control than their low-power counterparts. Of course, many of these same behaviors, when used in a different context, could also indicate other aspects of the interpersonal relationship. Excessive eye contact, for example, might not be an indication of power; it may merely mean that the two individuals are deeply in love. Usually, however, there are other situational cues that can be used to help interpret the behaviors correctly.

Control is often conveyed by the specific names or titles used to address another person. Do you address physicians, teachers, and friends by their first names, or do you say *Doctor, Professor,* or *Mr.* or *Ms.*? In Malaysia and many other places, personal names are rarely used among adults because such use might imply that the other person has little social status. Instead,

CULTURE *connections*

But then there is another word, or phrase, worth learning: *Mai pen rai*. In conversation, *mai pen rai* is a richer "no problem" or "never mind," a kind of verbal shrug. Beyond conversation, the phrase speaks volumes. It means that clashes are dealt with in something other than the Western, head-on way. In a year spent in a Thai newsroom, I never heard an angry voice, or a slamming door. "We recognize problems when they arrive, not before"—that line, with a smile, from a chief advisor to the prime minister.

a shortened form or a pet name is often used if a kin term is not appropriate. This is to avoid showing disrespect, since it is understood that the more familiar the form of address to a person, the more socially junior or unimportant he must be regarded.[11]

In cultures that are very attuned to status differences among people, such as Japan, Korea, and Indonesia, the language system requires distinctions based on people's degree of social dominance. In Indonesia, for instance,

[t]he Balinese speak a language which reflects their caste, a tiered system where (like the Javanese) at each level their choice of words is governed by the social relationship between the two people having a conversation.[12]

Intercultural communication is often characterized by an increased tendency to *mis*interpret nonverbal control and status cues. In both the United States and Germany, for instance, private offices on the top floors and at the corners of most major businesses are reserved for the highest-ranking officials and executives; in France, executives typically prefer an office that is centrally located, in the middle of their subordinates if possible, in order to stay informed and to control the flow of activities. Thus, the French may infer that the Germans are too isolated and the Germans that the French are too easily interrupted to manage their respective organizations well.

Affiliation Members of a culture use affiliation to interpret the degree of friendliness, liking, social warmth, or immediacy that is being communicated. Affiliation is an evaluative component that indicates a person's willingness to approach or avoid others. Albert Mehrabian suggests that we approach those people and things we like and we avoid or move away from those we do not like.[13] Consequently, affiliative behaviors are those that convey a sense of closeness, communicate interpersonal warmth and accessibility, and encourage others to approach.

Affiliation can be expressed through eye contact, open body stances, leaning forward, close physical proximity, touching, smiling, a friendly tone of voice, and other communication behaviors. Edward Hall has called those cultures that display a high degree of affiliation "high-contact" cultures; those that display a low level are called "low-contact" cultures.[14]

Compared to low-contact cultures, members of high-contact cultures tend to stand closer, touch more, and have fewer barriers such as desks and doors to separate themselves from others. High-contact cultures, which are generally located in warmer climates, include many of the cultures in South America, Latin America, southern Europe, and the Mediterranean region; most Arab cultures; and Indonesia. Low-contact cultures, which tend to be located in colder climates, include the Japanese, Chinese, U.S. Americans, Canadians, and northern Europeans. One explanation for these climate-related differences is that the harshness of cold-weather climates forces people to live and work closely with one another in order to survive, and some cultures have compensated for this forced togetherness by developing norms that encourage greater distance and privacy.[15]

> Compare your relationship with two friends or two family members. How do the relationships differ on the dimensions of control, affiliation, and activation?

Activation   Activation refers to the ways people react to the world around them. Some people seem very quick, excitable, energetic, and lively; others value calmness, peacefulness, and a sense of inner control. Your perception of the degree of activity that another person exhibits is used to evaluate that person as fast or slow, active or inactive, swift or sluggish, relaxed or tense, and spirited or deliberate.

Cultures differ in what they consider acceptable and appropriate levels of activation in a conversation. For instance, among many of the black tribes of southern Africa, loud talking is considered inappropriate. Similarly, among Malaysians,

> [t]oo much talk and forcefulness on the part of an adult speaker is disapproved. . . . A terse, harmonious delivery is admired. . . . The same values—of evenness and restraint—hold for Malay interpersonal relations generally. Thus Malay village conversation makes little use of paralinguistic devices such as facial expression, body movement, and speech tone. . . . Malays are not highly emotive people.[16]

Thais, like Malays, often dampen or moderate their level of responsiveness. As John Feig suggests,

> Thais have a tendency to neutralize all emotions; even in a very happy moment, there is always the underlying feeling: I don't want to be too happy now or I might be correspondingly sad later; too much laughter today may lead to too many tears tomorrow.[17]

Iranians tend to have the opposite reaction, as they are often very emotionally expressive in their conversations. Particularly when angry, a man's conversation may consist of behaviors such as "turning red, invoking religious oaths, proclaiming his injustices for all to hear, and allowing himself to be held back."[18]

European Americans are probably near the midpoint of this dimension. Compared to the Japanese, for instance, European Americans tend to be fairly active and expressive in their conversations. As Harvey Taylor suggested:

> An American's forehead and eyebrows are constantly in motion as he speaks, and these motions express the inner feelings behind the words. The "blank," nearly motionless Japanese forehead reveals very little of the Japanese person's inner feelings to the American (but not necessarily to the Japanese). Therefore the American feels that the Japanese is not really interested in the conversation or (worse yet) that the Japanese is hiding the truth.[19]

Compared to Jordanians, Iranians, African Americans, and Latinos, however, European Americans are passive and reserved in conversational expressiveness.

It is useful once again to remind you that all beliefs, values, and cultural norms lie on a continuum. How a particular characteristic is displayed or perceived in a specific culture is interpreted against the culture with which it is being compared. Thus it is possible for an African American to seem very active and emotionally expressive to the Japanese but quite calm and emotionally inexpressive to the Kuwaitis.

Dynamics of Interpersonal Relationships

Interpersonal relationships are dynamic. That is, they are continually changing, as they are pushed and pulled by the ongoing tugs of past experiences, present circumstances, and future expectations.

One useful way to think about relational dynamics is to view people in interpersonal relationships as continually attempting to maintain their balance amidst changing circumstances. To illustrate, imagine that you and your partner are attempting to do a common dance routine such as a country line dance, a tango, or a waltz. Now imagine that you are dancing aboard a ship at sea: the floor rises and falls to the pulsing of the waves; uneven electrical power makes the music speed up and slow down; and your partner wants to add graceful variations to the typical sequence of steps. Your efforts to stay "in rhythm" and coordinate your movements with the music and with your partner are analogous to the adaptations that people must continually make to the ongoing dynamics of interpersonal relationships.

Leslie Baxter suggests that the changing dynamics in interpersonal relationships are due to people's attempts to maintain a sense of "balance" among opposing and seemingly contradictory needs. These basic contradictions in relationships, called "dialectics," create ongoing tensions that affect the way people connect to one another.[20] Three dialectics have been identified as important in interpersonal relationships: autonomy–connection, novelty–predictability, and openness–closedness. Each of the dialectics has corresponding cultural-level components.

The autonomy–connection dialectic is perhaps the most central source of tensions in interpersonal relationships. Individuals inevitably vary, at different moments of their interpersonal relationships, in the extent to which they want a sense of separation from others (autonomy) and a feeling of attachment to others (connection). Note the word *and* in the previous sentence; both types of interpersonal needs, though they may seem contradictory, occur simultaneously. As we implied in our discussions of individualism–collectivism in Chapter 5, a culture teaches its members both the "correct" range of autonomy and connection and how these should be expressed when communicating with others. Thus, while the general level of autonomy desired by someone from an individualistic culture may be relatively high, one's specific needs for autonomy and connection will vary across time and relationships.

The novelty–predictability dialectic relates to people's desire for change and stability in their interpersonal relationships. All relationships require moments of novelty and excitement, or they will be emotionally dead. They also require a sense of predictability, or they will be chaotic. The novelty–predictability dialectic refers to the dynamic tensions between these opposing needs. The cultural dimension of uncertainty avoidance provides a way of understanding the general range of novelty and predictability that people desire. At specific moments within each relationship, however, individuals can vary in their preferences for novelty and predictability.

The openness–closedness dialectic relates to people's desire to share or withhold personal information. To some extent, openness and self-disclosure are necessary to establish and maintain relational closeness and intimacy. However, privacy is an equally important need; the desire to establish and maintain boundaries is basic to the human condition. For instance, a person may be open to interpersonal contact at certain moments, or with specific individuals, or about certain topics. There will also be times when that person may want to shut the office door or find another way to lessen the degree of interpersonal contact. The openness–closedness dialectic operates not only within a relationship but also in decisions about the public presentation of the relationship to others. Individuals in interpersonal relationships must continually negotiate what kinds of information about their relationship they want to reveal or withhold from others. Several cultural dimensions may affect openness–closedness. Collectivist cultures, for instance, with their tightly knit ingroups and relatively large social distances from outgroups, typically encourage openness within the ingroup and closedness to outgroup members. Alternatively, cultures that value large power distances may expect openness within interpersonal relationships to be asymmetric, such that those relatively lower in social status are expected to share personal information with their superiors.

Each of these relational dialectics, and others as well, contributes to a dynamically changing set of circumstances that affect what people expect, want, and communicate in interpersonal relationships. As the following section explains, how people in interpersonal relationships maintain an appropriate balance among these dialectics relates to their maintenance of face.

The Maintenance of Face in Interpersonal Relationships

A very important concept for understanding interpersonal communication among people from different cultures is that of face, or the public expression of the inner self. Erving Goffman defined *face* as the favorable social impression that a person wants others to have of him or her.[21] Face therefore involves a claim for respect and dignity from others.

The definition of *face* suggests that it has three important characteristics. First, face is *social*. This means that face is not what an individual thinks of himself or herself but rather how that person wants others to regard his or her worth. Face therefore refers to the public or social image of an individual that is held by others. Face, then, always occurs in a relational setting. Since it is social, one can only gain or lose face through actions that are known to others. The most heroic deeds, or the most bestial ones, do not affect a person's face if they are done in complete anonymity. Nor can face be claimed independent of the social perceptions of others. For instance, the statement "No matter what my teachers think of me, I know I am a good student" is not a statement about face. Since face has a social component, a claim for face would occur only when the student conveys to others the idea that teachers should acknowledge her or his status as a good student. In this sense, the concept of *face* is only meaningful when considered in relation to others in the social network.[22] Consequently, it differs from such psychological concepts as self-esteem or pride, which can be claimed for oneself independently of others and can be increased or decreased either individually or socially.

CULTURE *connections*

Korean interpersonal relationships operate on the principle of harmony. Maintaining a peaceful, comfortable atmosphere is more important than attaining immediate goals or telling the absolute truth. Koreans believe that to accomplish something while causing unhappiness or discomfort to individuals, is to accomplish nothing at all. If relationships are not kept harmonious, it is difficult, if not impossible, to work toward any goal. All cultures value how its members feel emotionally, but few cultures value it as much as Koreans do. To Koreans, to put greater emphasis on efficiency, honesty, or some other form of moral integrity is to be cold and unfeeling.

—*Sonja Vegdahl Hur and Ben Seunghwa Hur*

Second, face is an *impression,* which may or may not be shared by all, that may differ from a person's self-image. People's claims for face, therefore, are not requests to know what others actually think about them; instead, they are solicitations from others of favorable expressions about them. To maintain face, people want others to act toward them with respect, regardless of their "real" thoughts and impressions. Thus, face maintenance involves an expectation that people will act as though the others are appreciated and admired.

Third, face refers only to the *favorable* social attributes that people want others to acknowledge. Unfavorable attributes, of course, are not what others are expected to admire. However, cultures may differ in the behaviors that are highly valued, and they may have very different expectations, or norms, for what are considered to be desirable face behaviors.

Types of Face Needs

Penelope Brown and Stephen Levinson extended Goffman's ideas by proposing a universal model of social politeness.[23] They pointed out that, regardless of their culture, all people have face and a desire to maintain and even gain more of it. Face is maintained through the use of various politeness rituals in social interactions, as people try to balance the competing goals of task efficiency and relationship harmony.[24] Tae-Seop Lim suggests that there are three kinds of face needs: the need for control, the need for approval, and the need for admiration.[25] We now describe these three universal face needs.

The Need for Control   Control face is concerned with individual requirements for freedom and personal authority. It is related to people's need for others to acknowledge their individual autonomy and self-sufficiency. As Lim suggests, it involves people's

> image that they are in control of their own fate, that is, they have the virtues of a full-fledged, mature, and responsible adult. This type of face includes such values as "independent," "in control of self," "initiative," "mature," "composed," "reliable," and "self-sufficient." When persons claim these values for themselves, they want to be self-governed and free from others' interference, control, or imposition.[26]

CULTURE *connections*

As Chinese New Year of 1956 drew near, one of us came up with the idea of selling fire-crackers. I'd procure the fireworks; he'd do most of the selling.

No problem. We scraped together whatever money we had, and I got the explosives. Fireworks weren't easy to find, but they were legal. Each morning, I'd haul a sack of the red packages, ranging from tiny firecrackers bundled together by their fuses, to the regular, two-inch numbers, to a few specialty items like cherry bombs. If I knew of kids who were interested in buying, I'd take a supply. Otherwise, Leo took the parcel and went about business.

Chinese New Year was shaping up nicely when the bubble burst.

I was at Lincoln Park when Mr. Pichotto, my teacher, asked me to accompany him to the principal's office.

I shook the entire way. I knew we—or at least I—had been busted.

The principal came right to the point.

"Do you want to tell me about the firecrackers?" he asked.

"What firecrackers?"

"The ones you and Leo have been selling?"

Ah, yes . . . *those* firecrackers. Apparently, two things had happened. A fellow student had told a teacher that we were peddling fireworks. Coincidentally, Leo was giving a prospective client a sample of a rare specialty item, the slightly more expensive and profoundly more explosive cherry bomb. It was noticed.

For my parents, and particularly for my mother, my bust was a personal humiliation. To them, our citizenship grades were just as important as our scholastic marks. Getting caught and reprimanded was *seet-meen* (losing face) of the worst sort.

—*Ben Fong Torres*

The claim for control face, in other words, is embodied in the desire to have freedom of action.

The Need for Approval   Approval face is concerned with individual requirements for affiliation and social contact. It is related to people's need for others to acknowledge their friendliness and honesty. This type of face is similar to what the Chinese call *lien*,[27] or the integrity of moral character, the loss of which makes it impossible for a person to function appropriately within a social group. As Hsien Chin Hu relates,

A simple case of *lien*-losing is afforded by the experience of an American traveler in the interior of China. In a little village she had made a deal with a peasant to use his donkey for transportation. On the day agreed upon the owner appeared only to declare that his donkey was not available, the lady would have to wait one day. Yet he would not allow her to hire another animal, because she had consented to use his ass. They argued back and forth first in the inn, then in the courtyard; a crowd gathered around them, as each stated his point of view over and over again. No comment was made, but some of the older people shook their heads and muttered something, the peasant getting more and more excited all the time trying to prove his right. Finally he turned and left the place without any more arguments, and the American was free to hire another beast. The man had felt the disapproval of the group. The condemnation of his community of his attempt to take advantage of the plight of the traveler made him feel he had "lost *lien*."[28]

Lien is maintained by acting with good *jen,* the Chinese term for "man." As Francis Hsu explains:

> When the Chinese say of so-and-so "*ta pu shih jen*" (he is not *jen*), they do not mean that this person is not a human animal; instead they mean that his behavior in relation to other human beings is not acceptable."[29]

Hsu regards the term *jen* as similar in meaning to the Yiddish term *mensh,* which refers to a good human being who is kind, generous, decent, and upright. Such an individual should therefore be admired for his or her noble character. As Leo Rosten says of this term,

> It is hard to convey the special sense of respect, dignity, approbation, that can be conveyed by calling someone "a real *mensh*." . . . The most withering comment one might make on someone's character or conduct is: "He is not (did not act like) a *mensh*." . . . The key to being "a real *mensh*" is nothing less than—character: rectitude, dignity, a sense of what is right, responsible, decorous. Many a poor man, many an ignorant man, is a *mensh*.[30]

Thus approval face reflects the desire to be treated with respect and dignity.

The Need for Admiration   Admiration face is concerned with individual needs for displays of respect from others. It is related to people's need for others to acknowledge their talents and accomplishments. This type of face is similar to what the Chinese call *mien-tzu,* or prestige acquired through success and social standing. One's *mien-tzu*

> is built up through high position, wealth, power, ability, through cleverly establishing social ties to a number of prominent people, as well as through avoidance of acts that would cause unfavorable comment. . . . All persons growing up in any community have the same claim to *lien,* an honest, decent "face"; but their *mien-tzu* will differ with the status of the family, personal ties, ego's ability to impress people, etc.[31]

Thus admiration face involves the need for others to acknowledge a person's success, capabilities, reputation, and accomplishments.

Facework and Interpersonal Communication

The term *facework* refers to the actions people take to deal with their own and others' face needs. Everyday actions that impose on another, such as requests, warnings, compliments, criticisms, apologies, and even praise, may jeopardize the face of one or more participants in a communicative act. Ordinarily, say Brown and Levinson,

> people cooperate (and assume each other's cooperation) in maintaining face in interaction, such cooperation being based on the mutual vulnerability of face. That is, normally everyone's face depends on everyone else's being maintained, and since people can be expected to defend their faces if threatened, and in defending their own to

threaten others' faces, it is in general in every participant's best interest to maintain each others' face.[32]

The degree to which a given set of actions may pose a potential threat to one or more aspects of people's face depends on three characteristics of the relationship.[33] First, the potential for face threats is associated with the control dimension of interpersonal communication. Relationships in which there are large power or status differences among the participants have a great potential for people's actions to be interpreted as face-threatening. Within a large organization, for instance, a verbal disagreement between a manager and her employees will have a greater potential to be perceived as face-threatening than will an identical disagreement among employees who are equal in seniority and status.

Second, face-threat potential is associated with the affiliation dimension of interpersonal communication. That is, relationships in which participants have a large social distance, and therefore less social familiarity, have a great potential for actions to be perceived as face-threatening. Thus, very close family members may say things to one another that they would not tolerate from more distant acquaintances. Relationships where strangers have no formal connection to one another but are, for example, simply waiting in line at the train station, the taxi stand, or the bank, may sometimes be seen as an exception to this general principle.[34] As Ron Scollon and Suzie Wong-Scollon suggest, "Westerners often are struck with the contrast they see between the highly polite and deferential Asians they meet in their business, educational, and governmental contacts and the rude, pushy, and aggressive Asians they meet on the subways of Asia's major cities."[35] At many train stations in the People's Republic of China, for example,

> people are not in the midst of members of their own community, so the drive to preserve face and act with proper behavior is much lower. Passengers usually wait in waiting rooms until the attendant moves a barrier and they can cross the area between them and the train. The competition is quite fierce as passengers rush toward the train with their luggage, and they have little regard for the safety of other passengers. Often, fellow travelers are injured by luggage, knocked to the ground, or even pushed between the platform and the train, where they fall to the tracks.[36]

Third, face-threat potential is related to culture-specific evaluations that people make. That is, cultures may make unique assessments about the degree to which particular actions are inherently threatening to a person's face. Thus, certain actions within one culture may be regarded as face-threatening, whereas those same actions in another culture may be regarded as perfectly acceptable. In certain cultures, for instance, passing someone a bowl of soup with only one hand, or with one particular hand, may be regarded as an insult and therefore a threat to face; in other cultures, however, those same actions are perfectly acceptable.

Stella Ting-Toomey[37] and Min-Sun Kim[38] both suggest that cultural differences in individualism–collectivism affect the facework behaviors that people are likely to use. In individualist cultures, concerns about message clarity and preserving one's own face are more important than maintaining the face of others, because tasks are more important than relationships and individual autonomy must be preserved. Consequently, direct, dominating, and controlling face-negotiation strategies are common, and there is a low

CULTURE *connections*

An amusing but revealing example of how [face] is achieved occurs in one popular Chinese television program aired in Taiwan. The program, roughly similar to the American program, "The Love Connection," allows a contestant to choose among five potential dating partners. However, in the Chinese version, the four contestants who are not chosen are matched with dating partners from the audience at the conclusion of the program! Since each of the pairs of contestants is given a chance to express appreciation for their "date," everyone's *mien-tzu* [face] is protected.

—*Hui-Ching Chang and G. Richard Holt*

degree of sensitivity to the face-threatening capabilities of particular messages. Conversely, in collectivist cultures, the mutual preservation of face is extremely important, because it is vital that people be approved and admired by others. Therefore, indirect, obliging, and smoothing face-negotiation strategies are common, direct confrontations between people are avoided, concern for the feelings of others is heightened, and ordinary communication messages are seen as having a great face-threatening potential.

Facework and Intercultural Communication

Competent facework, which lessens the potential for specific actions to be regarded as face-threatening, encompasses a wide variety of communication behaviors. These behaviors may include apologies, excessive politeness, the narration of justifications or excuses, displays of deference and submission, the use of intermediaries or other avoidance strategies, claims of common ground or the intention to act cooperatively, or the use of implication or indirect speech. The specific facework strategies a person uses, however, are shaped and modified by his or her culture. For instance, the Japanese and U.S. Americans have very different reactions when they realize that they have committed a face-threatening act and would like to restore the other's face. The Japanese prefer to adapt their messages to the social status of their interaction partners and provide an appropriate apology. They want to repair the damage if possible, but without providing reasons that explain or justify their original error. Conversely, U.S. Americans would prefer to adapt their messages to the nature of the provocation and provide verbal justifications for their initial actions. They may use humor or aggression to divert attention from their actions but do not apologize for their original error.[39]

As another example of culture-specific differences in facework behaviors, consider the comments that are commonly appended to the report cards of high school students in the United States and in China. In the United States, evaluations of high school students include specific statements about students' strengths and weaknesses. In China, however, the high school report cards that are issued at the end of each semester never criticize the students directly; rather, teachers use indirect language and say "I wish that you would make more progress in such areas as . . ." in order to save face while conveying his or her evaluations.[40]

Facework is a central and enduring feature of all interpersonal relationships. Facework is concerned with the communication activities that help to create, maintain, and sustain the connections between people. As Robyn Penman says:

> Facework is not something we do some of the time, it is something that we unavoidably do all the time—it is the core of our social selves. That it is called face and facework is curious but not critical here. What is critical is that the mechanism the label stands [for] seems to be as enduring as human social existence. In the very act of communicating with others we are inevitably commenting on the other and our relationship with them. And in that commenting we are maintaining or changing the identity of the other in relationship to us.[41]

Improving Intercultural Relationships

Competent interpersonal relationships among people from different cultures do not happen by accident. They occur as a result of the knowledge and perceptions people have about one another, their motivations to engage in meaningful interactions, and their ability to communicate in ways that are regarded as appropriate and effective. To improve these interpersonal relationships, then, it is necessary to learn about and thereby reduce anxiety and uncertainty about people from other cultures, to share oneself with those people, and to handle the inevitable differences in perceptions and expectations that will occur.

Learning about People from Other Cultures

The need to know, to understand, and to make sense of the world is a fundamental necessity of life. Without a world that is somewhat predictable and that can be interpreted in a sensible and meaningful way, humankind itself would not survive.

We have already suggested in Chapter 5 that both individuals and cultures can differ in their need to reduce uncertainty and in the extent to which they can tolerate ambiguity and, therefore, in the means they select to adapt to the world. The human need to learn about others, to make sense of their actions, and to understand their beliefs, values, and behaviors has typically been studied under the general label of *uncertainty reduction theory*.[42] This theory explains the likelihood that people will seek out additional information about one another, but it deals primarily with the knowledge component of communication competence. William B. Gudykunst has recently revised uncertainty reduction theory and renamed it *anxiety/uncertainty management theory*.[43] It now focuses more clearly on intercultural communication, incorporates the emotional or motivational component of intercultural competence, and emphasizes ways to cope with or manage the inherent tensions and anxieties that inevitably occur in many intercultural encounters. In the sections that follow, we describe the components, causes, and consequences of uncertainty management behaviors and some strategies for reducing uncertainty in interpersonal relationships among people from different cultures.

Components of Uncertainty and Anxiety Management   While some degree of unpredictability exists in all interpersonal relationships, it is typically much higher in intercultural interactions. There are two broad components involved in the management of uncertainty behaviors: uncertainty and anxiety. *Uncertainty* refers to the extent to

Competent intercultural communication often leads to a reduction in uncertainty and anxiety in intercultural interactions.

which a person lacks the knowledge, information, and ability to understand and predict the intentions and behaviors of another. *Anxiety* refers to an individual's degree of emotional tension and her or his inability to cope with change, to live with stress, and to contend with vague and imprecise information.

Uncertainty and anxiety are influenced by culture. In Chapter 5, when we discussed Hofstede's value dimensions, we suggested that cultures differ in the extent to which they prefer or can cope with uncertainty. It should now be obvious that Hofstede's uncertainty avoidance dimension is related to what is here being referred to as anxiety/uncertainty management.

Causes of Uncertainty and Anxiety   Three conditions are related to uncertainty and anxiety management behaviors. These are your expectations about future interactions with other people, the incentive value or potential rewards that relationships with other people may have for you, and the degree to which other people exhibit behaviors that deviate from or do not match your expectations.

The first condition is your *expectations about future interactions* with another person. If you believe that you are very likely to interact with some person on future occasions, the degree to which you can live with ambiguity and insufficient information about that person will be low, and your need for more knowledge about that person will

CULTURE *connections*

When one American passes another on the street, in the middle of the day and in a neighborhood not known to be dangerous, there is a good chance, if one exchanges glances with the other, that he or she will smile or nod, or even say hello to the stranger, without it going any further. This often surprises French visitors in the United States. As a respectable, gray-haired man said to me, "If I were younger, I would think all these pretty girls were giving me the eye. . . . They seem like such flirts when they smile at you like that. . . . If this were France . . ." This same sudden and fleeting rapport among strangers can be established just as well through conversation in the United States, here again without consequence. It can even last a long time, as at American dinners and parties, at which one meets "very nice" people, with whom one has long conversations, and whom one will never see again (which French people find deeply disturbing).

—*Raymonde Carroll*

be high. Conversely, if you do not expect to see and talk with someone again, you will be more willing to remain uncertain about her or his motives and intentions, your anxiety level will be relatively low, and you will therefore not attempt to seek out any additional information. This person will continue to be a stranger. Anxiety/uncertainty management theory suggests that sojourners and immigrants who know they will be interacting in a new culture for a long period of time will be more likely to try to reduce their uncertainty about how and why people behave than will a tourist or temporary visitor.

The second condition, *incentive value,* refers to the perceived likelihood that the other person can fulfill various needs that you have, give you some of the resources that you want, or provide you with certain rewards that you desire. If a person's incentive value is high—that is, if the other person has the potential to be very rewarding to you—your need to find out more about that person will be correspondingly high. As you might expect, a high incentive value also increases the degree to which a person will be preferred or viewed as interpersonally attractive. Of course, the needs or rewards that people might want vary widely; the incentive value of a given person is related to his or her ability to provide such benefits as status, affection, information, services, goods, money, or some combination of these resources.[44]

One form of incentive value that has been widely investigated is the perceived similarity of the other person. The *similarity–attraction hypothesis* suggests that we like and are attracted to those whom we regard as comparable to ourselves in ways that we regard as important. Conversely, we are unlikely to be attracted to those who are very different from us. This hypothesis implies that, at least in the initial stages of intercultural encounters, the dissimilarities created by cultural differences may inhibit the development of new interpersonal relationships.

The third condition is the *degree of deviance* that the other person exhibits. Deviant behaviors are those that are not typically expected because they are inconsistent with the common norms that govern particular social situations. When a person acts deviantly, both your level of anxiety and your degree of uncertainty about that person increase, because he or she is far less predictable to you. Conversely, when a person conforms to your expectations by behaving in a predictable way, your level of anxiety and your degree of uncertainty about that person decrease. A person who behaves in deviant and unexpected ways is often disliked and is regarded as interpersonally unattractive, whereas one who conforms to others' expectations and is therefore predictable is often most liked and preferred. In intercultural communication, it is extremely likely that the other person will behave "deviantly" or differently from what you might expect. Thus, uncertainty about people from other cultures will typically be high, as will the level of anxiety and tension that you experience.

Consequences of Uncertainty and Anxiety Management   Because intercultural communication involves people from dissimilar cultures, each person's behaviors are likely to violate the others' expectations and create uncertainty and anxiety. Consequently, there is always the possibility that fear, distrust, and similar negative emotions may prevail. Often, but not always, the negative emotions can be overcome, and positive outcomes can result.

Judee Burgoon has developed *expectancy violations theory* to explain when deviations from expectations will be regarded as positive or as negative.[45] All behaviors that differ from expectations will increase the degree of uncertainty in an interaction. Burgoon suggests that how a person interprets and reacts to the deviations of another depends on how favorably that person is perceived. If the other person is perceived positively, violations of your expectation that increase interaction involvement will be seen as favorable, whereas violations of expectations that decrease interaction involvement will be viewed as unfavorable. To illustrate, imagine that you are having a conversation with someone who is standing closer to you than you would expect. This is clearly a violation of your expectations, but how would you likely react to this situation? Burgoon suggests that, if the person is positively valenced—because, for example, you regard the person as physically attractive—then you may view the violation and the other person favorably, whereas if the other person is negatively valenced, then you will regard the violation and the other person unfavorably and may attempt to back away or escape. Conversely, imagine that your conversation is with someone who is standing farther away than your typical or expected interaction distance. If the person is positively valenced, you may attempt to compensate for the violation by moving closer, whereas if the person is negatively valenced you will likely attribute negative connotations—he or she is aloof, cold—to the person.

The positive consequences of anxiety and uncertainty management behaviors that are applicable to intercultural communication can be grouped under two general labels: informational consequences and emotional consequences. Informational consequences result from the additional knowledge that has been gained about other people, including facts or inferences about their culture; increased accuracy in the judgments made about their beliefs, values, and norms; and an increased degree of confidence that they are being perceived accurately.

Emotional consequences may include increased levels of self-disclosure, heightened interpersonal attraction, increases in intimacy behaviors, more frequent nonverbal displays of positive emotions, and an increased likelihood that future intercultural contacts will be regarded as favorable. Of course, these positive outcomes all presume that the reduction in anxiety and uncertainty about another person will result in an increase in positive communicator valence, which is not necessarily so. Unfortunately, as Gudykunst suggests, negative perceptions in intercultural encounters frequently occur because people are not *mindful*—focused, aware, open to new information, and tolerant of differences. This allows our cultural assumptions to remain unchallenged. As we have seen, the perception that a person is acting in a deviant way (as defined by one's own cultural expectations) will often lead to decreased satisfaction with the encounter.

Strategies for Reducing Uncertainty and Anxiety   To behave both appropriately and effectively in an intercultural encounter, you must make an accurate assessment about many kinds of information: the individual characteristics of the person with whom you interact, the social episodes that are typical of the particular setting and occasion, the specific roles that are being played within the episode, the rules of interaction that govern what people can say and do, the setting or context within which the interaction occurs, and the cultural patterns that influence what is regarded as appropriate and effective. Thus, uncertainty is not reduced for its own sake, but occurs every day for strategic purposes. As Charles R. Berger suggested:

> To interact in a relatively smooth, coordinated, and understandable manner, one must be able both to predict how one's interaction partner is likely to behave, and, based on these predictions, to select from one's own repertoire those responses that will optimize outcomes in the encounter.[46]

There are three general types of strategies—passive, active, and interactive—that can be used to gain information about other people and thus reduce one's level of uncertainty and degree of anxiety. Passive strategies involve quiet and surreptitious observation of another person to learn how he or she behaves. Active strategies include efforts to obtain information about another person by asking others or structuring the environment to place the person in a situation that provides the needed information. Interactive strategies involve actually conversing with the other person in an attempt to gather the needed information. As you might expect, there are large cultural differences in the preferred strategies that are used to reduce uncertainty and manage anxiety in intercultural encounters. For example, European Americans are more likely than their Japanese counterparts to use active strategies such as asking questions and self-disclosing as a way to obtain information about another person, whereas the Japanese are more likely to use passive strategies.[47]

Sharing Oneself with People from Other Cultures

The human tendency to reveal personal information about oneself and to explain one's inner experiences and private thoughts is called *self-disclosure*. Self-disclosure occurs among people of all cultures, but there are tremendous cultural differences in the breadth, depth, valence, timing, and targets of self-disclosing events.

The *breadth* of self-disclosing information refers to the range of topics that are revealed, and European Americans tend to self-disclose about more topics than do members of most other cultures. For example, Tsukasa Nishida found that European Americans discussed a much wider range of topics that were related to the self (such as health and personality) with strangers than did Japanese; also, Japanese had far more self-related topics than did European Americans that they would never discuss with others.[48] Ghanaians tend to self-disclose about family and background matters, whereas U.S. Americans self-disclose about career concerns.[49] In contrast,

> Chinese culture takes a conservative stand on self-disclosure. For a Chinese, self-centered speech would be considered boastful and pretentious. Chinese tend to scorn those who often talk about themselves and doubt their motives when they do so. Chinese seem to prefer talking about external matters, such as world events. For Americans, self-disclosure is a strategy to make various types of relationships work; for Chinese, it is a gift shared only with the most intimate relatives and friends.[50]

The *depth* of the self-disclosing information refers to the degree of "personalness" about oneself that is revealed. Self-disclosure can reveal superficial aspects ("I like broccoli") or very private thoughts and feelings ("I'm afraid of my father"). Of the many cultures that have been studied, European Americans are among the most revealing self-disclosers. European Americans disclose more than African Americans, who in turn disclose more than Mexican Americans.[51] European Americans also disclose more than the British,[52] French,[53] Germans, Japanese,[54] and Puerto Ricans.[55]

Valence refers to whether the self-disclosure is positive or negative, and thus favorable or unfavorable. Not only do European Americans disclose more about themselves than do members of many other cultures, but they are also more likely to provide negatively valenced information. Compared to many Asian cultures, for example, European Americans are far less concerned with issues of "face" and are therefore more inclined to share information that may not portray them in the most favorable way.

Timing refers to when the self-disclosure occurs in the course of the relationship. For European Americans, self-disclosure in new relationships is generally high because the participants share information about themselves that the others do not know. A person's name, hometown, employment or educational affiliations, and personal interests are all likely to be shared in initial interactions. As the relationship progresses, the amount of self-disclosure diminishes because the participants have already learned what they need to know to interact appropriately and effectively. Only if the relationship becomes more personal and intimate will the amount of self-disclosure again begin to increase. But the timing of the self-disclosure process can be very different in other cultures. For example, Native Americans typically reveal very little about themselves initially because they believe that too much self-disclosure at that stage is inappropriate. A similar pattern may be found among members of Asian cultures.

Target refers to the person to whom self-disclosing information is given. Among European Americans, spouses are usually the targets of a great deal of self-disclosure, and mutual self-disclosure is widely regarded as contributing to an ideal and satisfactory marriage.[56] The breadth and depth of self-disclosure among other European American family members are of much lesser degree. Other cultures have different patterns. Among the Igbos of Nigeria, for instance, age is used to determine the appropriate degree of self-disclosure among interactants, younger interactants being expected to self-disclose far more than their older counterparts. As a cultural norm, when elder Igbos are in an initial encounter with someone who is younger, they have the right to

Which of the following topics are public? Private?

Private: I would discuss only with self, family, and/or intimate friends.
Public: I would discuss with casual friends, acquaintances, and/or strangers.

Attitudes and Opinions
1. What I think and feel about my religion; my personal religious views
2. My views on religion
3. My views on racial integration
4. My views on sexual morality
5. The things I regard as desirable for a person to be

Tastes and Interests
1. My favorite foods; my food dislikes
2. My likes and dislikes in music
3. My favorite reading matter
4. The kinds of movies and TV programs I like best
5. The kind of party or social gathering I like best; the kind that bores me

Work or Studies
1. What I feel are my shortcomings that prevent me from getting ahead
2. What I feel are my special strong points for work
3. My goals and ambitions in my work
4. How I feel about my career; whether I am satisfied with it
5. How I really feel about the people I work for or with

Money
1. How much money I make at work
2. Whether or not I owe money; if so how much?
3. My total financial worth
4. My most pressing need for money right now
5. How I budget my money

Personality
1. Aspects of my personality I dislike
2. What feelings I have trouble expressing or controlling
3. Facts of my present sex life
4. Things I feel ashamed or guilty about
5. Things that make me feel proud

Body
1. My feelings about my face
2. How I wished I looked
3. My feelings about parts of my body
4. My past illnesses and treatment
5. Feelings about my sexual adequacy

Family
1. Inquiries about the health of family members
2. Descriptions of family disagreements
3. Problems of siblings, parents, or children
4. The family's financial situation
5. Social activities of the family*

*Adapted from Dean Barnlund, *Public and Private Self in Japan and the United States: Communication Styles of Two Cultures* (Yarmouth, ME: Intercultural Press, 1975).

CULTURE *connections*

As two American women who have married men from other nations, we wanted to better understand the dynamics of intercultural families, those formed by partners from different countries. How do intercultural parents raise their children? What kinds of cultural identities do they encourage in their offspring? How important are adults' cultural identities in the contexts of their multinational families? How do intercultural couples organize their homes and their lives to reflect these different identities? What potential losses and misunderstandings are involved in these choices?

—*Jessie Carroll Grearson and Lauren B. Smith*

inquire about the young person's background, parents, hometown, and similar information that may ultimately lead to contact with distant relatives or old friends.

Handling Differences in Intercultural Relationships

Conflict in interpersonal relationships is a major nemesis for most people. Add the complications of different cultural backgrounds, and problems in managing conflict can become even more severe. Stella Ting-Toomey and John Oetzel's work provides some direction for managing intercultural conflict.[57]

Ting-Toomey and Oetzel use the distinction between collectivism and individualism, which is discussed more fully in Chapter 5. Briefly, in collectivist cultures, interpersonal bonds are relatively enduring, and there are distinct ingroups and outgroups. Collectivist cultures are often very traditional. In individualistic cultures, the bonds between people are more fragile, and because people belong to many different groups that often change, membership in ingroups and outgroups is very flexible. Individualistic cultures are therefore often characterized by rapid innovation and change.

Conflict may involve either task or instrumental issues. Task issues are concerned with how to do something or how to achieve a specific goal, whereas instrumental issues are concerned with personal or relationship problems such as hostility toward another person. The distinction therefore focuses on conflict about ideas versus conflict about people.

Ting-Toomey and Oetzel believe that people in collectivistic and individualistic cultures typically define and respond to conflict differently. In collectivistic cultures, people are more likely to merge task and instrumental concerns, and conflict is therefore likely to be seen as personal. To shout and scream publicly, thus displaying the conflict to others, threatens everyone's face to such an extreme degree that such behavior is usually avoided at all costs. In contrast, people from individualistic cultures are more likely to separate the task and the instrumental dimensions. Thus, they are able to express their agitation and anger (perhaps including shouting and strong nonverbal actions) about an issue and then joke and socialize with the other person once the disagreement is over. It is almost as if once the conflict is resolved, it is completely forgotten.

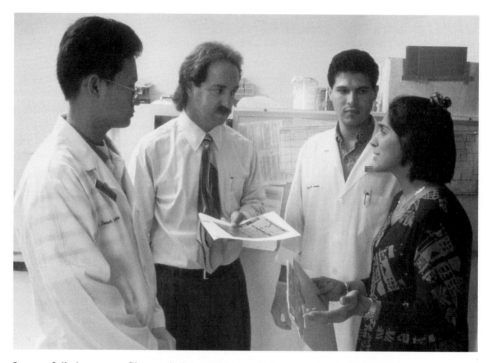

Issues of disclosure, conflict resolution, and face maintenance affect all interpersonal relationships. These technicians in a DNA Testing Lab confer about their work.

Because there is a great deal of volatility and variability in people's behaviors in individualistic cultures, there is often considerable potential for conflict. Because people are encouraged to be unique, their behaviors are not as predictable as they would be in collectivistic cultures. Also, because expectations are individually based rather than group-centered, there is always the possibility that the behavior of any one person will violate the expectations of another, possibly producing conflict.

Cultures also shape attitudes toward conflict. In collectivistic cultures, which value indirectness and ambiguity, conflicts and confrontations are typically avoided. Thus, rather than trying to resolve the problem directly, people in collectivistic cultures will attempt to maintain the external smoothness of the relationship. In individualistic cultures, which are also more likely to be "doing" or activity-oriented cultures, people's approach to conflict will be action-oriented. That is, the conflict precipitates actions, and the conflict is explicitly revealed and named.[58]

A very important concept for understanding how people from different cultures handle conflict is that of face, which we discussed earlier in this chapter. In conflicts, in particular, face is very likely to be threatened, and all participants are vulnerable to the face-threatening acts that can occur.

The actions of people in conflict can include attempts to save face for themselves, others, or all participants. Members of collectivistic cultures are likely to deal with face

CULTURE *connections*

Presented by the couples as an often unresolvable problem was the loss of place, culture and family that resulted from one partner's leaving his or her home of origin. The immigrant partner in the couple almost invariably expressed a longing for his or her own landscape and climate, and a deep sadness about the distance from extended family members. Other topics that frequently arose were loss of religion and language. While many couples were originally optimistic about importing religion and language from their native lands, they found that the United States exerted a pressure to assimilate that was very difficult to resist. As a result, these essential elements of culture were preserved only through great effort, if at all. For example, while Hueping Chin has managed to teach her son to speak Chinese fluently, as he grows older, their dialogue in Chinese sometimes falters in the face of new topics: "How does the space shuttle work? I find it hard to explain that to him in Chinese." The words of Jat Aluwalia capture the sense of regret that some felt: "I admit defeat; I guess the sense of being Indian ends with me."

—*Jessie Carroll Grearson and Lauren B. Smith*

threats such as conflicts by selecting strategies that smooth over their disagreements and allow them to maintain the face of both parties, that is, mutual face-saving. As Ringo Ma suggests, however, such strategies do not simply ignore the conflicting issues; after all, conflicts do get resolved in high-context cultures. Rather, nonconfrontational alternatives are used to resolve differences. Often, for instance, a friend of those involved in the conflict, or an elderly person respected by all, will function as an unofficial intermediary who attempts to preserve the face of each person and the relationship by preventing rejection and embarrassment.[59] Members of individualistic cultures, conversely, are likely to deal with face threats in a direct, controlling way. It is important to their sense of self to maintain their own face, to take charge, to direct the course of action, and in so doing to protect their own dignity and self-respect even at the expense of others.[60]

Imagine a scene involving two employees assigned to an important and high-tension project. Perhaps they are operating under serious time constraints, or perhaps the lives of many people depend on their success. Inevitably, disagreements about how to approach the assignment, as well as the specifics of the assignment itself, are likely to occur. Now assume that one employee is from a collectivistic culture such as Korea and the other is from an individualistic culture such as England. The difficulties inherent in completing their assignment will probably be increased by the great differences in their approaches to the problems that will arise. Each person's attempt to maintain face may induce the other to make negative judgments and evaluations. Each person's attempt to cope with the conflict and accomplish the task may produce even more conflict.[61] As Ting-Toomey and Oetzel suggest, these differences will need to be addressed before the work can be accomplished successfully.

Interpersonal Relationships and Intercultural Competence

Intercultural competence in interpersonal relationships requires knowledge, motivation, and skill in using verbal and nonverbal codes, as described in previous chapters. In addition, it requires behaviors that are appropriate and effective for the different types and dimensions of interpersonal relationships described in this chapter.

Recall a recent disagreement you had with a close friend or family member. How was the disagreement expressed, and how did you "manage" the disagreement? What are the cultural beliefs, values, and norms that underlie how you chose to deal with the disagreement?

Competence in intercultural relationships requires that you understand the meanings attributed to particular types of interpersonal relationships. Whom should you consider to be a stranger, an acquaintance, a friend, or a family member? What expectations should you have for people in these categories? What clues do people from other cultures offer about their expectations for you? Your expectations about the nature of interpersonal relationships affect how you assign meaning to other people's behaviors.

Your willingness to understand the face needs of people from other cultures and to behave appropriately in order to preserve and enhance their sense of face is critical to your intercultural competence. Always consider a person's need to maintain a favorable face in her or his interactions with others. Perceptions of autonomy, approval, and respect by others are important, but you must meet these face needs with facework that is appropriate to the other's cultural beliefs.

Your expectations about self-disclosure, obtaining information about others, and handling disagreements will not, in all likelihood, be the same as those of people from other cultures. Competence in developing and maintaining intercultural relationships requires knowledge of differences, a willingness to consider and try alternatives, and the skill to enact alternative relational dynamics.

Summary

People in an intercultural relationship may have very different expectations about the preferred nature of their social interactions. The types of interpersonal relationships, including those among strangers, acquaintances, friends, romantic partners, and family members, may also vary greatly across cultures.

Interpersonal relationships can be interpreted along the three dimensions of control, affiliation, and activation. The control dimension provides interpretations about status or social dominance. The affiliation dimension indicates the degree of friendliness, liking, and social warmth that is being communicated. The activation dimension is concerned with interpersonal responsiveness.

The concept of face refers to the positive social impressions that people want to have and would like others to acknowledge. Face includes the need for autonomy or individual freedom of action, approval or inclusion in social groups, and admiration or respect from others because of one's accomplishments. The need for facework depends on the control and affiliation dimensions of interpersonal communication and on culture-specific judgments about the extent to which certain actions inherently threaten one's face.

To improve intercultural relationships, you must learn about people from other cultures and thereby reduce the degree of uncertainty. Sharing yourself in appropriate ways with people from other cultures and learning to use culturally sensitive ways to handle the differences and disagreements that may arise are additional ways to improve intercultural relationships.

For Discussion

1. What is a friend to you? What do you expect of your friends?
2. What is meant by the concept of "face"?
3. Describe the relationship among the following terms: face, face maintenance, facework, embarrassment, truthfulness, dishonesty, fear, and withdrawal.
4. Why do anxiety and uncertainty management play a particularly powerful role in intercultural communication?
5. Do differences in what we categorize as "public" and "private" information hold any consequences for the development of a relationship?

For Further Reading

Rosemary Breger and Rosanna Hill (eds.), *Cross-Cultural Marriage: Identity and Choice* (New York: Berg, 1998). Contributions in this volume explore the personal experiences of those in intercultural marriages, as well as placing the positive and negative issues that emerge in such marriages in social, legal, and psychological contexts.

William B. Gudykunst, Stella Ting-Toomey, and Tsukasa Nishida (eds.), *Communication in Personal Relationships across Cultures* (Thousand Oaks, CA: Sage, 1996). An in-depth look at interpersonal relationships in Chinese, Japanese, Korean, Mexican, Brazilian, Iranian, African, and former Soviet bloc countries, as well as the presentation of a theoretical framework for understanding cross-cultural variations in interpersonal relationships.

Stella Ting-Toomey (ed.), *The Challenge of Facework: Cross-Cultural and Interpersonal Issues* (Albany: State University of New York Press, 1994). Essays that provide a thorough description of the concept of "face" as a general cultural construct, as well as a cross-cultural analysis of how face influences interpersonal relationships.

Stella Ting-Toomey and John G. Oetzel, *Managing Intercultural Conflict Effectively* (Thousand Oaks, CA: Sage, 2001). Directly addresses the effects that differing cultural backgrounds have on how conflict occurs, develops, and is resolved.

For additional information about intercultural films and about Web sites on specific cultures, turn to the Resources section at the back of this book.

chapter 11

Episodes, Contexts, and Intercultural Interactions

Social Episodes in Intercultural Relationships
The Nature of Social Episodes
Components of Social Episodes
Contexts for Intercultural Communication

The Health Care Context
The Educational Context
The Business Context
Episodes, Contexts, and Intercultural Competence
Summary

There is a repetitiveness to everyday communication experiences that helps to make them understandable and predictable. The recurring features of these common events, which we call social episodes, allow you to anticipate what people may do, what will likely happen, and what variations from the expected sequence of events could mean.

Social Episodes in Intercultural Relationships

People undertake intercultural relationships in predictable ways. In this section we describe how communication experiences are grouped into common events. Our point is that people's interactions are structured by their participation in events that are quite predictable and routine.

The Nature of Social Episodes

Think about how your daily life is structured. If you are like most people, there is a great deal of predictability in what you do each day and even with whom you do it. If you are attending a college or university, much of your life is taken up with such activities as attending class, studying, talking with a classmate in the cafeteria, working at a job, going shopping, meeting a friend after work, attending a party, and eating dinner. These are the kinds of structures in your life that we refer to as *social episodes,* that is, interaction sequences that are repeated over and over again. Not only do these social episodes recur, but their structure is also very predictable. The individuals who participate in these episodes generally know what to expect from others and what others expect from them. It is almost as if there were an unwritten script that tells you roughly what to say, whom to say it to, and how to say it.

Take the example of going to class. You probably attend class in a room filled with chairs, or tables with chairs, that face the front of the room. When you take a seat, you put your notebooks and other texts on the floor or under the desk. You keep your chair oriented in the way all the other chairs are oriented. The room is arranged so that you can look at the teacher, and there is a clearly marked space in the front of the room for

CULTURE *connections*

Washington finally sent Adm. William Fallon, the Navy's No. 2 officer, to the town of Uwajima to meet with the families of nine Japanese presumed dead in the Feb. 9 accident off Hawaii. And in Honolulu, Cmdr. Scott Waddle finally apologized, after merely expressing regret earlier. But the U.S. did several things backward, the experts say, and often only after significant political pressure—underscoring the very different roles apologies play and the varied meanings they have in the two societies.

At one level, Japanese apologize dozens of times a day—when entering a room, initiating a phone call, visiting a neighbor, giving a gift. Although in literal terms these are expressions of regret, in reality they are largely formulaic and don't carry much weight.

"It's a bit like Americans saying, 'Nice to meet you,' " said Tatsumi Tanaka, president of Risk Hedge, a crisis management company. "It's not as though they necessarily mean it."

A very different set of rules and expectations applies, however, when a dispute or accident is more serious or contentious. In these cases, apologies play a key role in a nation that eschews confrontation and highly values group harmony.

In the Japanese context, Waddle, as the person most directly responsible for the accident, should have apologized first and quickly—well before President Bush. And ideally, he should have done so in person, by traveling to Uwajima, the tightknit community that is home to the families of the missing.

"What apologies represent is very different for Japanese than for Americans," said Tamami Kondo, head of the Seishikai finishing school in Tokyo. "The first consideration isn't how guilty you are but rather a desire to show your concern for hurting the other person's heart."

Those cultural differences are reflected in the respective legal systems as well. In the U.S. apologies carry a stronger connotation of guilt, so most people facing a legal challenge tend to sidestep responsibility or clam up early on. Waddle's decision not to apologize or speak publicly about the accident was largely tied to his fears of legal liability, U.S. Ambassador Thomas S. Foley has repeatedly told the Japanese media in recent weeks.

In Japan, on the other hand, it's important to apologize right away in court or even before a trial because it's culturally expected and evidence of contrition can result in a greatly reduced sentence. "An apology comes first," said Takao Tanase, law professor at Kyoto University. "In the U.S., you deny everything."

—*Mark Magnier*

the teacher to stand or sit. When you enter the classroom, you never consider taking that spot. You expect the teacher, when she or he walks into the room, to do so. You do not expect the teacher to walk into the room and take the chair next to you.

If you get to class early enough, you might engage in small talk with another student. There are fairly predictable topics you might discuss, depending on how well you know each other. You probably talk about the class, whether you have done the reading, how your work is going, and the assignments. You might talk about the teacher and analyze his or her strengths and weaknesses. You might talk about the weather, the latest sports scores, or other common topics.

You expect the teacher to give a lecture or in some other way provide a sense of structure for the class. You take notes if the teacher gives a lecture, trying to summarize the key points. If you talk to a classmate while the teacher is lecturing, you whisper rather than talk in a loud voice. If the teacher did not enact the behaviors you expect for the person playing the part of "teacher," you might complain about it to others. Similarly, if one of your fellow classmates did not follow the expected behaviors for "being a student," you might think there was something wrong.

The purpose of this extended example is to underscore our point that much of what people do is made up of social episodes, which are repetitive, predictable, and routine behaviors that form the structure of their interactions with others. These social episodes provide information about how to interpret the verbal and nonverbal symbols of the interactants. The meanings of the symbols are understood because of the context in which they are given. Because those who participate in a social episode usually have the same understanding about what is to take place, they usually know how to behave, what to say, and how to interpret the actions and intentions of others.

In social episodes that include intercultural interactions, however, those involved may—and in all likelihood will—have very different expectations and interpretations about people's behaviors and intentions. As the interaction becomes more and more ambiguous, the expected behaviors that pattern the social episode also become more unpredictable and problematic. Though your culture teaches you to interpret the meanings and behaviors in social episodes in particular ways, other cultures may provide their members with very different interpretations of these same experiences.

Components of Social Episodes

There are five components of social episodes, each of which influences intercultural communication: cultural patterns, social roles, rules of interaction, interaction scenes, and interaction contexts.

Cultural Patterns   Cultural patterns are shared judgments about what the world is and what it should be, and widely held expectations about how people should behave. The patterns of a culture's beliefs and values, described in Chapters 4 and 5, permeate the ways in which members of a culture think about their world.

Cultural patterns are like tinted glasses that color everything people see and to which they respond. The episodes that are used to structure people's lives—attending class, eating dinner, playing with a friend, going to work, talking with a salesperson—are certainly common to many cultures. But the interpretations that are imposed on these behaviors vary greatly, depending on the cultural patterns that serve as the lens through which the social episodes are viewed. Tamar Katriel, for example, describes a common episode in middle-class Israeli life called *mesibot kiturim,* or "griping party." She argues that, while these griping parties might occur in other cultures, they are particularly important in Israel and reflect a communally oriented cultural pattern.[1]

Joseph Forgas and Michael Bond found that Hong Kong Chinese and Australian students, although leading superficially very similar lives—going to classes, studying, and so on—perceived various social episodes very differently. The perceptions of the Chinese students reflected values and cultural patterns associated with that culture's emphasis on community, the collective good, and acceptance of authority. The Australian students saw the same episodes in terms of self-confidence, competition, and the pleasure they might receive from the interactions in which they participated.[2]

Social Roles   A social role is a set of expected behaviors associated with people in a particular position. Common roles that exist in most cultures include student, mother, father, brother, sister, boss, friend, service person, employee, sales clerk, teacher, manager, soldier, woman, man, and mail carrier. The role that you take in a particular social episode strongly suggests to you the way in which you should act. If you are participating in an episode of a boss giving an employee a performance review, you would expect to behave very differently if you were the employee rather than the boss. If another person is upset about the comments of a co-worker, your response would be influenced by the particular role you play in relationship to the upset person. Are you in the role of friend, relative, or employer? Your answer to the question will definitely affect how you respond to the person's concerns. In many episodes you play clearly defined roles that give you guidance about what you should say to the other person and even how you should say it. Furthermore, the role you are playing is matched by the roles of others in the episode. You have expectations for yourself based on your roles, and you also have expectations for others based on their roles.

The expectations for appropriate behavior for the roles of student and teacher are quite apparent in the example at the beginning of this section. However, appropriate behaviors for these roles will vary greatly among cultures. In many Asian cultures it is not acceptable to ask a teacher questions or to whisper to another student. Students are expected to stand up when the teacher enters the room and again when the teacher leaves the room. The students would never call a teacher by his or her first name but only by a formal title.

The role of friends also varies greatly from culture to culture. As discussed in Chapter 10, European Americans have a tendency to call a lot of people "friends," and they often separate their friends into different categories based on where the friendship is established. They might have friends at work, friends from their neighborhoods, and friends from clubs or organizations to which they belong. Many of these friendships are fairly transitory and might last only as long as people work for the same organization or live in the same neighborhood. When the place in which the friendship is conducted is no longer shared in common, the friendship no longer exists in any active sense. In many other cultures, people may have fewer friends, but these friendships are often maintained for longer periods of time.

The importance of this discussion to your participation in intercultural communication should be obvious. Even though you may think you are fulfilling a particular role

Weddings, such as this Laotian one, illustrate the components of social episodes: cultural patterns, social roles, rules of interaction, interaction scenes, and interaction contexts.

(such as that of student, friend, house guest, or customer), the expectations of the role may vary widely between your culture and the culture in which you are interacting. There are also sets of rules that generally govern the interactions among people in an episode. Some of these rules are related to specific roles, but others are simply norms or guides to govern behavior.

CULTURE *connections*

At the end of dinner, my mother and Dolores fought over the check. Fighting over the check is the only appropriate way to end a Chinese meal unless one man is dining with a group of women. In that instance, the man is expected to pay. In all other cases, not to fight over the check indicates a lack of breeding. In spite of Dolores's isolation and her poverty, she had not relinquished all her ties to the past.

"*Gai wo*," she demanded when the waiter appeared with the check. "Give it to me."

"*Bu dwei*," my mother said. "That's not right. *Gai wo*."

The waiter stood between them, a look of boredom on his face. He had probably seen many meals end the exact same way. The older couple across the way from us were not so blasé. The wife, who had a head of dignified-looking gray hair, kept craning her neck around to stare at us. The exchange dragged on through a few more rounds of "*Gai wo*" and "*Bu dwei, gai wo*" when my mother suddenly changed tack.

"Ah," she said and pointed to me. "*Gai ta*."

She managed to startle the waiter out of his indifference.

"*Gai ta?!*" he demanded. He shook his head indignantly, no.

"*Dwei*," I said, and reached for the check.

"*Bu gai ta*," he said firmly. "No."

He spoke to my mother. In his eyes, I was still too young to be addressed directly in the presence of elders, much less to be responsible for paying the bill. While he was admonishing my mother, Dolores took advantage of the distraction and grabbed the check out of his hand. My mother, thinking equally fast, stole Dolores's pocketbook off her lap and threw it across the table at me. When Dolores reached for the bag, waving her hands frantically in the air, my mother expertly plucked the check out of her fingers. She handed it to me.

"Go pay," she said.

I nodded back, unable to speak. I was in the presence of a master. Dolores, indignant but laughing, gave in. For a moment, the two women giggled, heads together.

—Leslie Chang

Rules of Interaction   Rules of interaction provide a predictable pattern or structure to social episodes and give relationships a sense of coherence.[3] Rules of interaction are not written down somewhere, nor are they typically shared verbally. Instead, they operate at the level of unwritten, unspoken expectations. Most of the time, people are not even consciously aware of the rules that govern a social episode until they are broken. Think about the various kinds of rules, for example, that govern the interactions at a wedding. In addition to the various roles (bride, groom, parents, bridesmaids, groomsmen, and guests), there are a host of rules embedded in the different types of weddings that occur. A wedding invitation from a U.S. American couple that is engraved on heavy linen paper and announces a candlelight ceremony at dusk suggests something about the rules governing what a guest should wear and how a guest should act. In contrast, a photocopied invitation on colored paper announcing that pizza and beer will be served following the ceremony suggests a very different set of rules. As B. Aubrey Fisher indicates:

> Virtually every social relationship has rules to determine what is appropriate and what is inappropriate for that relationship. For some relationships, the most important rules can be found in a larger social context. Meet someone at a church social, and you will probably conform to rules appropriate to interpersonal communication in a church. For other relationships, the important rules are created during the process of interaction. After you get to know someone, you are more likely to be innovative and to do something "different."[4]

Rules of interaction include such diverse aspects as what to wear, what is acceptable to talk about, the sequence of events, and the artifacts that are part of the event. In France, for instance, you would never talk about your work at a dinner party, even if all of the people there were in some way connected to the same place of work. Among most U.S. American businesspeople, however, it is commonplace to expect talk about business at a dinner table. An invitation to a dinner party can mean that immediately upon arrival, you will be given the meal and only after you have eaten will you sit and talk leisurely with your hosts;

What are the rules for initial conversations between strangers?

or the invitation may mean that you must spend a substantial period of time before a meal is served in having drinks and talking with your hosts. Do you bring gifts such as flowers, wine, or candy? If so, are there particular artifacts that are taboo, such as wine or other forms of alcohol in Saudi Arabia or chrysanthemums in Italy (which are only given at a funeral)? The rules of interaction provide culture-specific instructions about what should and should not occur in particular social episodes.

Interaction Scenes   Interaction scenes are made up of the recurring, repetitive topics that people talk about in social conversations. Most conversations are organized around these ritualized and routinized scenes, which are the chunks of conversational behavior adapted to the particular circumstances.

Kathy Kellermann describes a standard set of interaction scenes that are commonly used by college students in U.S. universities when engaged in informal conversations. As Figure 11.1 indicates, Kellermann's research suggests that interaction scenes are organized into subsets, so that the scenes in subset 1 come before those in subset 2, and so on; however, within a particular subset, no specific order of scenes exists. Consequently, an informal conversation among acquaintances might include such topics as a ritualized greeting ("Hello!"), a reference to the other person's health ("How are you?"), a reference to the present situation, a discussion of the weather, a comment on people known in common, other common interests, a positive evaluation of the other person ("Nice to see you again!"), a reason for terminating the conversation ("I'm late for a meeting"), and finally a good-bye sequence.[5] Notice that certain scenes are part of more than one subset; these scenes function as a bridge to link the subsets together and thus help the conversation to flow from idea to idea.

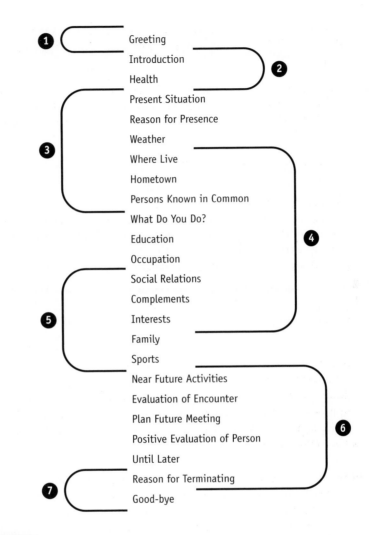

FIGURE 11.1

Typical interaction scenes.

Source: Kathy Kellermann, "The Conversation MOP: II. Progression through Scenes in Discourse," *Human Communication Research 17* (1991): 388.

Conversations among people from other cultures have a similar structure. That is, a standard set of scenes or topics is used to initiate and maintain conversations, and the conversations flow from beginning to end in a more-or-less predictable pattern, which is typically understood and followed by the interactants. However, there are important differences in the ways the conversations of people from other cultures are organized and sequenced, including the types of topics discussed and the amount of time given to each one.

CULTURE *connections*

The Danish mother who left her 14-month-old daughter unattended for about an hour outside a Manhattan restaurant Saturday night will not be allowed to be alone with the infant until charges against her are cleared up, according to a ruling by a family court judge here.

Wednesday evening, after a family court hearing, the mother was reunited with her daughter in a private home in New York City. They will live there with others until criminal and family court hearings next week, according to a spokesman for the city's Administration for Children's Services.

Danish actress Annette Sorensen, 30, said in court here this week that leaving a baby outside while adults chat inside a restaurant is accepted parenting behavior in Denmark. Her view is being loudly echoed in the Danish press, which has portrayed the behavior of the mother as normal and the behavior of New York City police as bizarre.

The actual topics in an interaction scene can vary widely from one culture to another. In Hong Kong, for instance, conversations among males often include inquiries about the other person's health and business affairs. In Denmark or the French portion of Belgium, questions about people's incomes are to be avoided. In Algeria, topics such as the weather, health, or the latest news are acceptable, but one would almost never inquire about female family members. In Ecuador and Chile, it is appropriate, almost obligatory, to inquire politely about the other person's family. Among Africans, a person is expected to inquire first about a person's well-being before making a request.

The amount of time given to each topic may also vary from one culture to another. It is well known, for instance, that European Americans like to get down to business in their conversations and will typically avoid elaborate sequences of small talk. Social and business conversations among the Saudis and Kuwaitis, on the other hand, will include far more elaborate greeting rituals, some phrases actually being repeated several times before the conversation moves on to subsequent sequences. Similarly, when Africans meet they typically inquire extensively about the health and welfare of each other's parents, relatives, and family members. Although the Japanese do not typically repeat words or phrases, they also prefer to spend considerably more time in the "getting to know you" phase of social conversations.

Difficulties can arise in intercultural interactions when the participants differ in their expectations. At a predominantly African American university in Washington, D.C., for example, an encounter took place between an African American student; African students from Tanzania, Nigeria, and Kenya; and Caribbean students from Jamaica, Trinidad, and Tobago. The African American student, who did not share the others' expectations about the need for elaborate greeting rituals before making a simple request, walked into the graduate assistant's office to inquire about the time.

In your culture, what makes a wedding a wedding? That is, what are the rules for (and the variations on the rules for) getting married?

CULTURE *connections*

We were married in a traditional Navajo ceremony. My family entered the hogan first, bearing gifts for my wife's family and a saddle: a sign that I was ready to make a new home. Then my wife's family entered the hogan carrying corn mush prepared by her grandmother. White cornmeal, representing the woman's family, was mixed with the male's yellow cornmeal and set in a wedding basket. My wife and I grabbed fingerfuls of mush and ate them, and we were married. Two lives combined into one. Navajos say it is a new life.

"Hi! Does anyone know what time it is?" he asked, without any formal greetings. No one responded. After a few moments, he repeated his question, apparently frustrated. The African and Caribbean students looked up but continued with their work without responding. At this point the Nigerian student, who realized that the problems were due to incompatible expectations, responded to the first student's question. The student thanked him and left the room. When the African American had gone, the other students wondered aloud why the Nigerian had answered the question. "He has no respect," one of them remarked. "How could he walk into the room and ask about the time without greeting anyone?" another argued. Interestingly, both the African American and the other students were simply attempting to conform to their own expectations about the appropriate behaviors in an interaction scene involving strangers who are making requests.

Interaction Contexts   Interaction contexts are the settings or situations within which social episodes occur. Contexts impose a "frame" or reference point around communication experiences by helping people to determine what specific actions should mean, what behaviors are to be expected, and how to act appropriately and effectively in a particular interaction.

Contexts for Intercultural Communication

U.S. Americans are increasingly being asked to participate in social episodes within three specific contexts that we would like to highlight: health care, education, and business. Each provides an important and recurring meeting ground where people from many cultures converge and interact. We now describe in greater detail the particular importance and challenge of these three contexts.

The Health Care Context

In Chapter 1 we indicated that the need for intercultural competence arises, in part, because of the increased cultural mixing that has occurred across national boundaries and within the United States itself. The consequences to human life and suffering from a

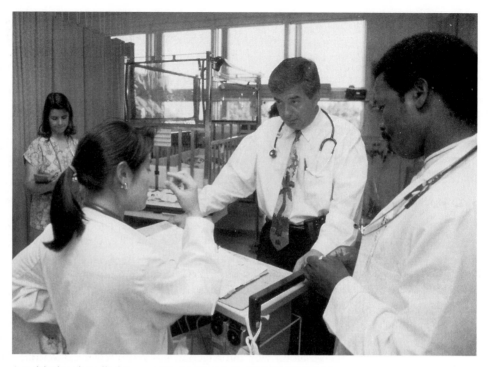

A multicultural medical team meets to discuss their patients' needs.

lack of intercultural competence in the health care context should be obvious. The health care context affects doctors, nurses, counselors, and health care workers, as well as patients, families, communities, and cultural groups.

Communication scholars have begun to study the specific characteristics of the intercultural health care context in an effort to improve communication competence.[6] Similarly, health care professionals have responded to the intercultural imperative by including courses that are designed to increase intercultural communication skills within their professional training and development programs. The nursing profession, for instance, has developed both a specialization in "transcultural nursing" and a new professional organization, the Transcultural Nursing Society.[7] Textbooks and training materials are now readily available to assist nursing students in their academic preparations for intercultural communication challenges, as courses in transcultural nursing are standard offerings in many nursing degree programs.[8] Resource materials are now available to assist all health care providers as they interact with people representing a range of cultural backgrounds.[9] Indeed, as a prerequisite to their certification, many health care providers are asked to demonstrate their competence in interacting with diverse cultural groups.[10]

Culture's Influence on the Health Care Context   Cultural patterns provide the lenses through which people come to understand their world. All participants in the health care context—the providers, the patients, their families, and the larger social world—draw upon their own cultural patterns and expectations about what constitutes appropriate and effective medical care. These cultural patterns often lead to very clear expectations about the right and wrong ways to treat illnesses and help people—expectations that are not necessarily shared by those from other cultures. While scholars have offered several ways to conceptualize the systematic relationship of cultural patterns to health care, there is a remarkable similarity among their presentations. Three general approaches characterize beliefs about health that cultures might adopt to explain issues of illness and wellness: magico-religious or personalistic, holistic or naturalistic, and biomedical or Western.[11] These three approaches bear a strong resemblance to elements in the cultural patterns we described in Chapters 4 and 5.

In the *magico-religious* or *personalistic approach,* health and illness are closely linked to supernatural forces. Mystical powers, typically outside of human control, cause health and illness. A person's health is therefore at the mercy of these powerful forces for good or evil. Sometimes illnesses occur because of transgressions or improper actions; the restoration of health is thus a gift, or even a reward, for proper conduct. Within this approach, health and illness are usually seen as anchored in or related to the whole community rather than to a specific individual. The actions of one person, then, can dramatically affect others. Treatments for illnesses within this framework are directed toward soothing or removing problematic supernatural forces rather than toward changing something organic within the individual. Healers, who are best equipped to deal with both the spiritual and the physical worlds, perform such treatments. Some African cultures, for example, believe that demons and evil spirits cause illness.[12] Many Asian cultures also believe in the supernatural as an important source of illness.[13] Within the United States, cultural groups with many members who share such beliefs include various Latino and African American cultures.

In the *holistic* or *naturalistic* approach, humans desire to maintain a sense of harmony with the forces of nature. Illness is explained in systemic terms and occurs when organs in the body (such as the heart, spleen, lungs, liver, and kidneys) are out of balance with some aspect of nature. There is thus a great emphasis on the prevention of illness by maintaining a sense of balance and good health. Good health, however, means more than just an individual's biological functioning. Rather, it includes her or his relationship to the larger social, political, and environmental circumstances. Some diseases, for instance, are thought to be caused by external climatic elements such as wind,

CULTURE *connections*

After hanging his coat Somdali turned to greet the others. When we had come in they had just glanced at us and resumed their conversation. The African way of entering the company of others is for the newcomer to announce himself by greeting first. It is the "umthakathi" (wizard) who arrives unseen.

—*Norman Hodge*

cold, heat, dampness, and dryness. Native Americans, for example, often define health in terms of a person's relationship to nature; health occurs if a person is in harmony with nature, whereas sickness occurs because a principle of nature has been violated. As Richard Dana suggests, "healing the cultural self for American Indians and Alaska Natives must be holistic to encompass mind, body, and spirit."[14] A common distinction within this approach is contrasting of both foods and diseases as either hot or cold. The classification of a disease as hot or as cold links it both to a diagnosis and to a treatment.[15] The ancient Chinese principle of yin and yang captures the essence of this distinction; everything in the universe is either positive or negative, cold or hot, light or dark, male or female, plus or minus, and so on, and people should have a harmonious balance between these opposing forces in their approach to all of life's issues.

In the *biomedical* or *Western* approach, people are thought to be controlled by biochemical forces. Consequently, objective, physical data are sought. Good health is achieved by knowing which biochemical reactions to set in motion. Disease occurs when a part of the body breaks down, resulting in illness or injury. Doctors and nurses, who fix the biochemical problem affecting the "broken part," thus making the body healthy again, provide treatments. This approach is closely linked to European American cultural patterns and has had a major influence on the development of the health care system in the United States. Indeed, the biomedical approach is so dominant within the United States that it is sometimes very difficult for individuals—providers and patients alike—to act competently in and adapt themselves to alternative cultural patterns.[16]

Family and Gender Roles in the Health Care Context   The role of the individual patient, in contrast to the role of the family, is an important difference in the functioning of health care systems. The health care system in the United States typically focuses solely on the individual patient as the source of the medical problems in need of a cure. Yet many cultures in the United States are more collectivist and group-oriented, and this difference can be the basis for serious problems and misunderstandings. Cultures that value the community or the extended family, for instance, may influence people's willingness to keep important health care appointments. Navajo women, for example, who often give priority to family members' needs, have been known to forego clinic appointments when someone from the extended family stops in to visit and ask for help.[17] Likewise, competent treatment for Latino patients may require the involvement and agreement of other family members, not just the patient.[18]

The responsibilities of family members in the health care context differ widely across cultures. Among the Amish communities in the United States, for example, the family includes a large, extended group, with adult members of the extended family having obligations and responsibilities to children other than their own biological ones. Hospital rules that give rights and responsibilities only to members of the immediate family pose challenges when an Amish child is hospitalized. The large number of people who expect to make lengthy visits to the child may prove difficult for the medical staff.[19] Similarly, when suggesting health care intervention strategies for Pacific Islanders and Hawaiians, experts recommend focusing on the entire family, rather than on just the identified patient, in order to be effective.[20]

In many cultures, health care providers are expected to talk about the nature of the illness and its prognosis with family members but not with the patient. It is the family members, not the patient, who are expected to make decisions about the nature of treatment.[21] Of course, intercultural difficulties may occur when the family's ideas about the appropriate course of treatment differ from those of the medical staff. A Latino teenager, for example, was hospitalized on an oncology unit. Problems occurred when his family took him home for a day but did not follow the medical rules for such visits. He ate forbidden foods, did not return to the hospital at the specified time, and generally did not follow other aspects of his treatment. The medical team was upset with the family because their patient suffered a setback. The parents, however, knew that their son had only a limited time to live and wanted him to be with his family and enjoy what little time he had.[22]

Many cultures have strong expectations about modesty, and expectations about bodily displays for women can make the medical examination itself a source of intercultural difficulties. In some cultures, for instance, role requirements governing appropriate behaviors for women do not permit undressing for an examination by male physicians or nurses. Among many Latina women, for example, there are strong social taboos against showing the body to others; disrobing for a medical examination may be embarrassing and difficult.[23] Similarly, Latina women are uncomfortable revealing personal information in the presence of sons and daughters who may accompany them to the medical appointment.

Conversational Structures and Language   Because of different interaction rules, the medical interview between caregiver and patient can be another source of intercultural communication problems. Latinos and Arabs, for example, may engage in extensive small talk before indicating their reasons for the medical interview. Interviews with Native Americans may be punctuated with extensive periods of silence. Medical interviewers may consider such small talk or silence a "waste of time" rather than a vital component of the person's cultural pattern that affects his or her comfort level and willingness to proceed with the interview.[24] Similarly, direct and explicit discussions with many Asians and Asian Americans may pose serious threats to their face, and the use of indirection or other face-saving strategies may be preferred.[25]

In many cultures, doctors are perceived as authority figures with whom one must agree in the face-to-face medical interview. A patient may know that he or she will not be able to follow a proposed treatment plan but may be reluctant to respond to the doctor in a way that might appear to be a challenge to the doctor's authority.[26] Similarly, individuals from cultures that see health care workers as authority figures will be reluctant to initiate interaction and ask questions.[27] Patients from individualistic and low-context cultures, for instance, often feel that it is very important to communicate verbally with their physicians, and they are therefore very motivated to do so. Conversely, patients from collectivistic and high-context cultures may be much more apprehensive about participation as a patient in their medical care, and they may therefore avoid conversing with their physicians during medical interviews.[28]

Ambiguities in the use of language can present additional difficulties in diagnosing and treating illnesses. Consider the case of a nurse or pharmacist who instructs a patient to "take three pills a day at mealtime" and expects that the patient will take one pill at each of three meals. Patients who come from cultures that do not separate their day into three major mealtimes may instead take all three pills simultaneously at the one

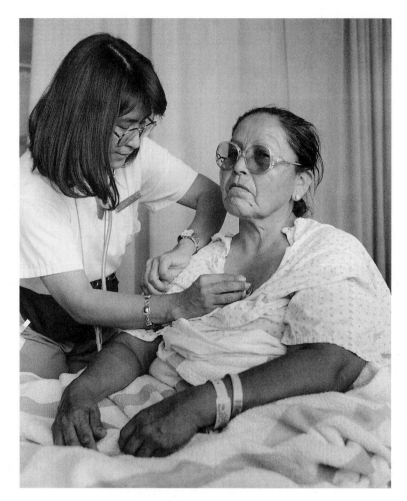

Because health care may require the display of and access to one's body in ways that are private and personal, cultural expectations about what behaviors are permitted or prohibited are particularly important in such settings.

large meal that is eaten every day.[29] A misunderstanding with very serious ramifications happened to a non-native speaker of English who had signed a consent form for a tubal ligation, or "having her tubes tied." The woman thought that "tied" meant that the procedure could be reversed should she later decide to have more children. Only the skilled intervention of an interculturally competent health care worker, who understood the ambiguity in the language and clearly explained to the woman the consequences of her decision, prevented a medical procedure that was not wanted.[30]

It is not just ambiguities in understanding and in translating the English language that challenges health care

Recall your last visit to a doctor. Identify the features of that episode that are typical of social episodes in the medical context. Are there cultural characteristics that are unique to the culture(s) represented in this medical appointment?

CULTURE *connections*

The Mien people believe the hospital is haunted. At night, the spirits of the dead rove the corridors like a poisonous wind. In their minds, the hospital is a forbidding forest of restless souls and muffled cries.

In their language, there is no word for cancer. Or antibiotics. They don't believe in surgery. Or "bad news." They believe in herbal remedies, in bodily humors, in animal sacrifice and tribal shamans—in appeasement. They believe illness is caused by evil spirits, by ancestral transgressions, by ineluctable destiny. With no philosophic immune system, so to speak, they are resigned to their mortality, however premature. . . .

Since sickness is perceived as a communal affliction, often the entire Mien clan will attempt to crowd into the hospital room to witness the proceedings. In grave cases, even the shaman might appear to perform a rite.

—*Bob Sylva*

workers. The Spanish language, for example, which is used by several U.S. cultures, has many words and grammatical constructions that vary from one cultural group to another.[31] Such cases highlight problems of intercultural misunderstandings and the implications for "informed consent" in the intercultural health care context.

The effective treatment of a patient's pain by the health care professional requires an ability to interpret the patient's nonverbal and verbal symbols so that a culturally appropriate medical intervention can occur. In many cultures, for instance, individuals are taught to be more stoic and circumspect in verbally identifying the severity of their pain. In other cultures, there is an expectation that one will use very emotional and dramatic terms to describe one's experience of pain.[32]

Intercultural Competence in the Health Care Context Health care professionals assume a special responsibility in assuring that they understand their patients in order to treat them effectively. This responsibility requires a willingness to attempt to understand the cultural patterns—the beliefs, values, and interaction norms—of their patients. There are excellent reference books now available to health care professionals in which the general characteristics of various cultures are presented. However, in the health care context, as in all others, you must remember that each individual may or may not share the preferences of her or his cultural group.

The Educational Context

The U.S. educational system increasingly requires competent intercultural communication skills from its participants. Because of the culturally diverse student populations throughout the U.S. educational system, people must give increased attention to the factors that students, parents, teachers, administrators, other educational professionals, and ordinary citizens face when challenged to communicate in the educational context.

CULTURE *connections*

I gave birth in a Manila hospital to the son we had planned to call Martin, who died a few hours later. For me, the death of my baby was something that should not have happened, unthinkable, unbearable. But for the gentle Filipina nurses, the loss was sad but part of life, bound to happen from time to time. Their sympathy was firmly mixed with a cheerful certainty that I would be back next year with another one—as so many women are in the Philippines, whether the infant lives or dies.

It was our good fortune that my time in the village had allowed me to observe and compare responses to death. On the afternoon of Martin's birth, I described to Barkev the way Filipinos would express their sympathy. Don't expect to be left alone, I said, and don't expect people tactfully to avoid the subject. I expect friends to seek us out and to show their concern by asking specific factual questions. Rather than a euphemistic handling of the event and a denial of the ordinary course of life, we should be ready for the opposite. An American colleague of my husband might shake hands, nod his head sadly, perhaps murmuring, "We were so sorry to hear," and beat a swift retreat; a Filipino friend would say, "It was so sad that your baby died. Did you see him? Who did he look like? Was he baptized? How much did he weigh? How long were you in labor?"

Stereotypes often conceal their opposites. In other contexts Filipinos describe Americans as "brutally frank," while Americans find Filipinos frustratingly indirect and invasive. Yet in the handling of death, Filipinos behave in a manner which Americans might characterize as "brutally frank" and seem to go out of their way to evoke the expression of emotion, while Americans can only be called euphemistic and indirect, going to great lengths to avoid emotional outbreaks.

—*Mary Catherine Bateson*

Culture's Influence on the Educational Context   All participants in the educational context—teachers, students, parents, school administrators, and other staff—bring their cultures' beliefs, values, and norms with them. Differences in cultural backgrounds may produce developmental variations in children's cognitive, physical, and motor abilities, as well as in their language, social, and emotional maturity.[33]

Communication within a classroom, in the playground of an elementary school, or within a college dormitory is typically governed by a set of rules based within one cultural group. In the United States, the patterns associated with the European American culture have tended to dominate educational systems, often making it difficult for students and parents from other cultures to participate effectively in the schools.[34] Yet for most teachers in the U.S. schools, it is an everyday occurrence to have students who come from cultural backgrounds other than their own. As a student in high school or college, you may have already experienced classrooms of people from diverse cultural backgrounds. Alternatively, you may be a parent interacting within your children's school system. Students in intercultural communication classes may be preparing to teach in elementary or high schools. As the statistics presented in Chapter 1 demonstrate, many current teachers, and certainly most future teachers, will work in a setting that demands the knowledge, motivations, and skills of a competent intercultural communicator.

For many students, attending school can itself be an intercultural experience. Elvira, for example, is a junior Filipina American student who daily crosses the cultural boundary from her Filipino home to her U.S. American high school. While she attends regularly and receives very high grades, she is concerned that the school experiences cut her off from her sister and friends. Sonia, similarly, is a Mexican American high school student who is very popular with her Latina friends but consistently feels like an outsider at school. This makes it very difficult for her to be academically and socially successful in the educational context.[35]

Scholars in communication and education have begun to document the many ways that cultural differences can lead to dissimilarities in interpretations and expectations about competent behaviors for students and teachers. Problematic issues include differences in expectations concerning such classroom behaviors as the rules for participation and turn taking, discipline and control, and even pedagogical approaches such as lectures, group learning, and self-paced work. Intercultural problems also arise when parents and other family members attempt to communicate with various officials representing the school.

Classroom Interaction   Recall from Chapter 4 that cultures differ in the ways they choose to define activities, social relations, the self, the world, and the passage of time.

The intercultural nature of classrooms, from elementary school through college, require educators to adapt their approaches to teaching and learning.

All of these choices can influence preferences for how students and teachers relate to each other in the classroom.[36]

Those who prefer a more hierarchical relationship between individuals will structure the relationship between student and teacher with greater status differences. German instructors, for example, tend to be more formal, aloof, and socially distant than their U.S. counterparts.[37] Similarly, within many Asian and Asian American cultures teachers are highly revered and respected. Students and parents would not openly and directly question the authority and statements of a teacher. Consider, for example, the types of communication messages and the proper role behaviors of students and teachers in Chinese classrooms. If you are familiar with U.S. classrooms, compare your experiences to the following:

> Students who are late for class should get the teacher's permission to enter the classroom. Even in college, students have to sit quietly in rows that face the teacher, listen attentively, and take careful notes. Students must also raise their hands and stand at attention when they answer or want to ask questions. Not raising a hand is a violation of classroom rules, and not standing up is a violation of the reverence rule.[38]

As this description conveys, the Chinese classroom is characterized by a high degree of formality. Many people from cultures with similar preferences for formality are shocked to find European American teachers with their penchant for informality. Many U.S. professors, for instance, encourage students to call them by their first names; while many students prefer such informality, some feel uncomfortable because it suggests disrespect.

Students from collectivistic cultures are generally more accepting of messages about appropriate classroom behaviors and will comply with teachers' requests about classroom management.[39] Even the nature of teachers' persuasive messages differs across cultures. Chinese college teachers, for instance, appeal to the group in gaining student compliance, whereas European American teachers, with a cultural preference for individualism, stress the benefit to the specific student.[40] Within the classroom, the treatment of personal property is also influenced by the culture of the students, with "personal" items such as toys, books, and clothing perceived very differently in individualistic and in collectivistic cultures.[41]

Classroom discussion and participation also vary greatly across cultures. Because of the basic rules for interaction that are taught within their culture, some Native American children have a difficult time asking straightforward questions and looking directly at their teacher.[42] Similarly, many Native American and Asian American students are unwilling to volunteer, speak out, or raise problems or concerns unless the teacher specifically calls on them by name. Korean students, for instance, are often unwilling to talk with their teachers even when the teachers have incorrectly calculated the students' scores on an exam.[43] Questions for clarification are rarely asked of the teacher directly; to do so might be regarded as a challenge to the teacher's authority and could threaten her or his face should the answer not be known.

Students from many cultures who go to school in the United States sometimes find it difficult to adapt to the verbal style expected of them. Conversely, when U.S. students study overseas, they often experience similar difficulties in understanding the cultural

This typical elementary school classroom depicts the intercultural character of many schools across the United States.

expectations related to the educational context.[44] Yet a willingness to speak in class is a communication characteristic highly valued by European American teachers and students, whose cultural framework celebrates individual achievement and responsibility. To students from cultures that emphasize the collective good and the maintenance of face, however, such behaviors in the classroom are too competitive, as they disrupt the group's harmony and separate people from one another. Native American fifth- and sixth-graders, for example, perceived their high-verbal teachers to have less competence in their oral delivery of messages.[45] Similarly, African American children, whose culture emphasizes the development of verbal skills and expressiveness, are often affected in their classroom interactions with their European American teachers:

> In both verbal and nonverbal language, they [African American children] are more the-atrical, show greater emotion, and demonstrate faster responses and higher energy. . . . African-American speakers are more animated, more persuasive, and more active in the communication process. They often are perceived as confrontational because of this style. On the other hand, the school, and most Anglo-American teachers, are more oriented toward a passive style, which gives the impression that the communicator is somewhat detached, literal, and legalistic in use of the language. Most African-American students find this style distancing and dissuasive.[46]

Turn taking within the classroom is also governed by cultural expectations. Watch how teachers in your various classes regulate the flow of conversations and contributions. A teacher has a particular set of expectations about who speaks in the classroom as well as when and how to speak. Is it acceptable for students to talk among themselves? How loudly can they talk to each other? How long can private conversations continue before the teacher asks for them to stop? How do students get permission to speak in class? All of these classroom behaviors, which are crucial to how teachers evaluate their students and how students evaluate teachers and classroom environments, are grounded in cultural expectations.

Cultural patterns directly affect preferred ways to learn in the classroom. Think for a moment about the classroom experiences you have had. Did they encourage students to work cooperatively in groups? Or were classroom activities designed to encourage students to work alone, succeeding or failing on their individual merits? Latino children, whose culture teaches the importance of family and group identities, are more likely to value cooperativeness than competitiveness.[47] Because Native American cultural patterns emphasize the group, harmony with nature, and circularity, children from that culture often respond better to learning approaches that are noncompetitive, holistic, and cooperative.[48] European American children, in contrast, often prefer learning approaches that emphasize competition, discrete categories for information, and individual achievement.

Families and the Educational System   Another key set of relationships in which competent intercultural communication is essential is in the interaction of parents, and sometimes other family members, with school personnel, including teachers, administrators, and others. Because the value of education itself differs from one culture to another, the importance of a student's success in school will also vary. For Thais and Filipinos, for instance, education affects the entire family's status and social standing.

CULTURE *connections*

In high school, I tried to emulate the five-paragraph essay. I was in honors and AP classes and always got A's, but I was never totally proficient like the other students in their writing. Grammar and usage was natural for them, but not for me. Remember, my first language was Spanish. I spoke Spanish at home to my parents and siblings, so I intermixed my sentence structures and rhetorical patterns. Oftentimes they'd see this as a deficiency. I wanted to go on tangents and use imagery, like my father did when he told his cuentos y historias. I wanted to incorporate my oral skills from my culture into the written text, but was not allowed to do so. I emulated this plastic voice until I went to college. And even then, only a select few teachers encouraged this form of writing.

This writing was the personal narrative. I learned to use personal narrative in my essays and short stories and incorporated personal narrative characteristics in my poetry. I had never been given this freedom. I had never been validated in this way. I wish I had been allowed to use personal narrative from day one of my second shot at first grade. I know I would be a more effective writer today.

—*Maria J. Estrada*

By excelling in school, therefore, children bring honor to their families while preparing for future successes that will further enhance the family stature. Education is thus a family concern, rather than an individual achievement.[49]

Even the need for the customary parent–teacher conferences may not make much sense to parents from cultures in which there is no expectation that parents will play an active role in decisions about their children's education.[50] Many Middle Eastern parents, for instance, expect their children will do well in school. Thus, when the children actually do well, there is generally less overt praise or material reward than is common in the United States; children are doing what is expected of them. However, when children do not do well, parents may present a variety of attitudes including denial, blaming the school, blaming the child, and feeling ashamed.[51]

Similar expectations exist among many Asian and Asian American parents. A teacher's request for a routine conference, therefore, may be met with a sense of skepticism or a deep concern that a disobedient child may have dishonored the family. Because of face-saving needs, the parents may even assume that the exact nature of this problem will not be stated explicitly but must be discerned through a clever analysis and interpretation of the teacher's subtle clues. The teacher's bland statements that their child behaves well are therefore regarded as merely a social politeness. Not wanting to heap unlimited praise on the child for fear of setting false expectations, the teacher may unwittingly provide the parents with just the sort of high-context hints and generalities about the child's faults and weaknesses that they will interpret as an indication of a deeper and more difficult problem in need of correction.

A poignant example of the consequences of differing cultural expectations, complicated by linguistic difficulties, is the story of Magdalena, a Mexican immigrant mother, and her son Fabian. Because Fabian was not behaving appropriately in the school, the school officials asked Magdalena to have Fabian evaluated by a professional. Concerned about Fabian and wanting to be responsive to the school's request, Magdalena took Fabian to see their family doctor. As the situation at the school became more negative, the teachers and administrators believed that Magdalena was ignoring the seriousness of the problem and was not responding to their request. Ultimately, Fabian was expelled from school.[52] As Jerry McClelland and Chen Chen conclude:

> The combination of the school's instructions, the interpreter's translation, and her comprehension of the message resulted in Magdalena not understanding that a counselor's report, rather than a physician's report, was being requested. Given the Mexican culture in which she grew up, Magdalena was puzzled by the message to have Fabian checked. Magdalena said that in Mexico, if there is a problem with a child, the teacher and parent talk to each other and do not bring in a third person to give an opinion.[53]

Intercultural Competence in the Educational Context   The challenge to develop one's intercultural competence and fulfill the promise that cultural diversity brings to the educational context is aptly summarized by Josina Macau. She suggests that creating a constructive learning environment in an age of cultural diversity requires that people be sensitive to different and sometimes competing experiences.[54]

The starting point for developing intercultural competence in the educational context is to understand one's own cultural background. It is particularly important that teachers and administrators recognize their culture's influence on expectations about how classrooms should operate and how students should behave. The stakes for developing intercultural competence in education are very high. While the following example focuses on Native Americans, it is equally true of students from a variety of cultural backgrounds. It illustrates the importance of the educational context and the potential for both permanent and harmful consequences as a result of interactions within that context.

> When many young Native American children enter the classroom, they frequently find themselves in foreign environments where familiar words, values, and lifestyles are absent. As the classroom activities and language become increasingly different from the familiar home environment, the students suffer a loss of self-confidence and self-esteem, a loss that is sometimes irreparable.[55]

The Business Context

The business context is increasingly intercultural. Just as those working and receiving services in the health care and educational contexts must look to the development of competent intercultural communication, intercultural competence in our work lives is a critical asset.[56] Commerce and trade are global and affect us daily. Indeed, bookstores now regularly stock reference materials that provide insights into specific cultures and suggest some of the do's and don'ts of conducting business with individuals from those cultures.[57] Just look at your possessions and you will see ample evidence of the products that have crossed national and cultural boundaries. People, however, are the key ingredients in the intercultural business world.

Throughout most people's working lives, they will be within an intercultural business context; customers, co-workers, supervisors, and subordinates may all come from cultures that differ from their own. Unfortunately, many U.S. employees have been poorly prepared for these intercultural assignments. U.S. managers, for instance, who have been on temporary overseas assignments for U.S. multinational corporations, are far more likely to fail in their missions and to return home prematurely than are their Japanese or European counterparts. Whereas over one-half of the Western European and three-fourths of the Japanese firms have failure rates that are under 5 percent, a majority of U.S. multinational corporations have failure rates in the 10 to 20 percent range.[58] The underlying problem, experts agree, is top management's ethnocentricity and its corresponding failure to provide adequate preparation and rewards for these intercultural assignments.[59] Even within corporations and small businesses that are wholly owned and operated in the United States, there is an enormous degree of commerce and connection with people from a variety of cultural backgrounds, again creating the need to communicate competently in the intercultural business context.

Conduct an interview with a professional who works in a multicultural health, business, or educational context. What issues and concerns do they identify because of the presence of cultural differences? How do they deal with the cultural differences?

Culture's Influence on the Business Context   The discussion of cultural patterns in Chapter 5 described Geert Hofstede's work on cultural patterns. Using middle-level man-

Work settings are increasingly culturally diverse, providing opportunities to improve intercultural competence.

agers from a large multinational corporation with over fifty subsidiaries throughout the world, Hofstede delineated four dimensions of cultural differences: individualism–collectivism, power distance, uncertainty avoidance, and masculinity–femininity. While each of these dimensions is useful for understanding issues in the intercultural business context, our discussion will highlight the individualism–collectivism dimension.

Cultural variations in people's relationships to their organizations are important in understanding the intercultural business context. Is the critical unit of analysis and of human action the individual or the group? Specific areas of intercultural business that are associated with variations in individualism–collectivism include the following:

▶ *Who speaks for the organization?* In organizations within individualistic cultures, a single person may represent a company in its negotiations. In collectivistic cultures, a group of representatives would likely be involved in negotiations.

▶ *Who decides for the organization?* Organizations within individualistic cultures likely empower their negotiators to make decisions that are binding on the company. Such decisions are often made rapidly and without consultation from the home office once the negotiations have begun. Organizations within collectivistic cultures often require extensive consultations among the delegation members and with the home office at each step in the negotiation process, as no single individual has the exclusive power for decision making.

▶ *What motivates people to work?* Do people work because they are motivated by the possibility of individual rewards, as is common in individualistic cultures, or is group support and solidarity with one's colleagues a primary motivator?

Reward systems to encourage employees' best efforts vary widely. In Mexico, for instance, though the individual is valued, rewards for independent actions and individual achievements that are successful with U.S. Americans may not be strong motivators. Thus production contests and "employee of the month" designations to encourage Mexican employees are often unsuccessful.[60]

▶ *What is the basis for business relationships?* In collectivistic cultures, it is vital that businesspeople establish cordial interpersonal relationships and maintain them over time. The assumption that it is possible to have a brief social exchange that will produce the degree of understanding necessary to establish a business agreement is simply incorrect. In many African cultures, for example, friendship takes precedence over business. Similarly, most Middle Easterners extend their preference for sociability to business meetings, where schedules are looser and the first encounter is only for getting acquainted and not for business.[61] A similar regard for establishing social relationships as a prelude to doing business is also common in China, Japan, and Korea.[62] Indeed, the very notion of trustworthiness differs across intercultural business relationships, with individualistic cultures often emphasizing personal integrity in judging another's trustworthiness while collectivistic cultures emphasize one's commitment to the group or the organization.[63]

Another scholar-practitioner who has studied the impact of cultural patterns on communication competence in the intercultural workforce is Fons Trompenaars.[64] After many years of studying companies around the globe, Trompenaars identified the cultural dimension of *universalism–particularism* as especially useful in understanding how business practices vary because of culture. Universalistic cultures prefer to make business decisions based on a consistent application of rules, whereas particularistic cultures choose instead to adapt the rules to specific circumstances and relationships. William B. Gudykunst and Yuko Matsumoto indicate that universalism–particularism is related to the individualism–collectivism dimension. They suggest that businesspeople from individualistic cultures tend to be universalistic and apply the same value standards to all, whereas those from collectivistic cultures tend to be particularistic and apply different value standards to ingroups and outgroups.[65] Some features of the impact of this variation on the conduct of international business include the following:

▶ *What is the meaning of a contract?* Someone from a universalistic culture may view the signed contract as binding on all, whereas someone from a particularistic culture may view the contract as valid only if the circumstances remain unchanged, which may include whether the person who signed the contract is still

CULTURE *connections*

In New Delhi, India, where cows are sacred, the flagship burger at McDonald's is called the Maharaja Mac and is made of lamb.

part of his or her company. For example, the Chinese concept of legal or contractual agreements differs from the U.S. concept. In the United States, of course, a business contract is binding and should be implemented precisely as agreed. In China, however, contracts are regarded more as statements of intent rather than as promises of performance. Therefore, they are binding only if the circumstances and conditions that were in effect when the contract was signed are still present when the contract should be implemented.[66]

▶ *Are job evaluations conducted uniformly or adapted to specific individuals?* Within universalistic cultures, all individuals in similar jobs are evaluated using standardized criteria. Within particularistic cultures, the performance criteria depend upon people's relationships with others and their standing within the organization.

▶ *Are corporate office directives typically heeded or circumvented?* In universalistic cultures, directives from corporate headquarters are valued and are heeded throughout the organization. In particularistic cultures, such directives are often ignored or circumvented because they don't apply to the particular circumstances of a specific subsidiary or branch office.

Doing Business Interculturally   There are many illustrations of the influence of cultural patterns on the conduct of business across cultures. Business practices display cultural differences in interaction preferences, the importance and strategic use of

Conducting business among intercultural teams can be both challenging and rewarding.

interpersonal relationships, the desired social hierarchies for decision making, the expectations regarding work and gender roles, the nature of performance appraisals and specific achievements, and indeed the entire gamut of issues that businesspeople must confront.

Cultures differ in the preferred flow or pacing of business negotiations. In the initial stages of a negotiation, for example, German business managers may ask numerous questions about technical details. In Scandinavia, there is a great deal of initial frankness and a desire to get right down to business. Among the French, however, the early emphasis is on laying out all aspects of the potential deal. In contrast, many Italian and Asian managers may use these same initial stages to get to know the other person by

CULTURE *connections*

A neatly folded pocket square peeking out from under the lapel of his blue blazer, Takeo Sekine beams as he shows off the workbooks that are the tools of his trade.

Carefully combed and politely spoken, Mr. Sekine instructs people in the rituals and etiquette of corporate culture: how to address clients and superiors in polite forms of speech, when to offer one's business card, and even what color socks to wear. . . .

The essence of Sekine's teaching and that of a small industry of "business manner" promulgators, is how to communicate and behave within the hierarchies of Japan's big corporations.

In late 1994, for instance, a major bank contacted Sekine and asked if he would adapt some pages from one of his textbooks for inclusion in the bank's pocket date-book. Tokai Bank, based in the central city of Nagoya, gives its date-books to selected clients and its employees.

Sekine provided two pages, including one with diagrams detailing where people should sit or stand according to hierarchies in various business settings. Among the rules:

- ▶ If businesspeople are traveling together on a train, the most senior executive gets the window seat facing the direction in which the train is moving. The next most senior person sits opposite the boss, and the third most senior settles in next to him (women are rarely top managers in Japanese companies).
- ▶ In a taxi, the "top" seat is behind the driver. If three people ride in the rear, the most junior sits in the middle. The seat next to the driver is the "lowest" seat.
- ▶ In an elevator, the senior passenger stands at the rear, in the center, facing the door. The most junior stands near the buttons.
- ▶ Guests in an office should be seated in order to appreciate a painting, display case, or a mantlepiece if possible.
- ▶ When entering rooms, if the door pulls open, allow the guests to enter first. If it pushes open, you should enter first and hold the door. Do not fail to knock before entering any room, even if you know it is empty.

—*Cameron W. Barr*

talking about subjects other than the business deal. Likewise, preliminaries in Spain may take several days.[67] Similarly, problems often characterize Mexican and U.S. American negotiations, which arise from a greater emphasis on relational concerns by Mexican negotiators and on task behaviors by U.S. negotiators.[68]

In the United States and in other Western countries where individual achievement is valued, advancements occur because of one's accomplishments, there is a shorter-term and results-oriented approach to negotiating, and a high priority is placed on getting the job done and accomplishing task-related objectives. Interpersonal communication is typically direct, confrontational, face-to-face, and informal. Negotiating teams are willing to make decisions and concessions in the public negotiation setting, where individuals within the team may disagree publicly with one another. One individual is usually given the authority to make decisions that are binding on all.[69] Among the Japanese, however, who value group loyalty and age, advancement is based on seniority, there is a longer-term approach to negotiating, and the formation and nurturance of longer-lasting business relationships are extremely important. Interpersonal communication is likely to be indirect, conciliatory in tone, and formal. Often an intermediary is used, the real decision making occurs privately and away from the actual negotiations, the negotiating teams make group decisions, and all team members are expected to present a united front. In Table 11.1, Farid Elashmawi and Philip Harris highlight some of the key differences in expectations for business negotiations among U.S. American, Japanese, and Arab cultures.

Cultural differences in business practices are also evident in the use of interpersonal relationships for strategic purposes. In Columbia and other Latin American countries, for example, achieving objectives by using interpersonal connections to obtain jobs, contracts, supplies, and other contacts—that is, giving and receiving personal favors to create an interdependent network of relationships—is regarded very positively.[70] Similar customs exist in India and elsewhere. While not as widespread throughout the multicultural U.S. workplace, such practices as providing emotional support to fellow workers, and thereby building informal social networks that can be used strategically to circumvent the bureaucracy, is a common practice.[71]

The importance and value of social hierarchy is illustrated by many Chinese businesses. Chinese businesspeople will likely have to check with their superiors before making any real decisions. In Chinese organizations, superiors are expected to participate in many decisions that U.S. managers might routinely delegate to subordinates. The Chinese process of consulting the next higher level in the hierarchy often continues up the bureaucratic ladder to the very top of the organization. Thus, autonomy that is expected and rewarded in the United States may be regarded as insubordination in China.[72] Similarly, Mexicans often emphasize status differences in business and prefer formality in their business relationships, whereas European Americans prefer informality and minimal status differences in their business relationships.[73]

Work roles also differ across cultures. Among the Japanese, work roles are an extension of the family hierarchy. That is,

> presidents are "family heads," executives "wise uncles," managers "hard-working big brothers," workers "obedient and loyal children." American workers employed in Japanese-managed companies do not see themselves as "loyal and obedient children" and instead hold traditional American values of individualism, competitiveness, and social mobility.[74]

TABLE 11.1   Intercultural Negotiations with U.S., Japanese, and Arab Businesspeople

	U.S. American	Japanese	Arab
Group Composition	Marketing oriented	Function oriented	Committee of specialists
Number Involved	2–3	4–7	4–6
Space Orientation	Confrontational; competitive	Display harmonious relationship	Status
Establishing Rapport	Short period; Direct to task	Longer period; Until harmony established	Long period; Until trusted
Exchange of Information	Documented; Step-by-step; Multimedia	Extensive; Concentrate on receiving side	Less emphasis on technology, more on relationship
Persuasion Tools	Time pressure; Loss of opportunity; Saving/making money	Maintain relationship references; Intergroup connections	Go-between; Hospitality
Use of Language	Open/direct; Sense of urgency	Indirect; Appreciative; Cooperative	Flattery; Emotional; Religious
First Offer	Fair +/– 5 to 10%	+/– 10 to 20%	+/– 20–50%
Second Offer	Add to package; Sweeten the deal	–5%	–10%
Final Offer	Total package	Makes no further concessions	–25%
Decision-making Process	Top management team	Middle line with team consensus	Senior manager
Risk-Taking	Calculated; Personal responsibility	Low group responsibility	Religion-based
Time Orientation	Short-time/task orientation	Considerable time spent in negotiation	Longer negotiation period than U.S. and Japanese
Relationship Orientation	Personal relationships not as important	Group consensus and harmony	Establish trust through references and personal relationships

Source: Farid Elashmawi and Philip R. Harris, *Multicultural Management 2000: Essential Cultural Insights for Global Business Success* (Houston: Gulf, 1998) 196, 198.

Another area in which cultural differences affect the business context is in gender expectations. Cultures differ in their prescriptive roles for men and women, and in many cultures women are unlikely to have managerial or supervisory positions in business. Women from the United States may have to make careful adjustments in order to be interculturally competent in the business setting.[75]

Something seemingly as simple as the exchange of business cards can set the tone for subsequent business relationships. Many U.S. businesspeople simply take the business cards offered to them and, after a perfunctory glance, tuck them away; in most Asian cultures, however, the exchange of business cards requires a more involved ritual in which the cards are examined carefully upon their receipt.

The ease of international telecommunications brings businesspeople from around the globe into interactions using the common communication episode of "making an introductory telephone call." Yet something as straightforward as the protocol for a common telephone call is shaped by a multitude of differences that one's culture creates. Variations in the purposes of telephone calls, their degree of formality, the expectations about appropriate opening and closing remarks, and the anticipated length of the conversation all present intricate choices for achieving intercultural communication competence.[76]

Expectations about the "proper" way to conduct employee performance appraisals and provide a rationale for judgments and actions are another source of cultural differences. For example, Chinese managers do not provide their subordinates with the detailed performance appraisals that are customary in many U.S. firms. Feedback on failures and mistakes, for instance, is often withheld, which allows subordinates to save face and maintain their sense of esteem for future tasks within the organization. Similarly, while decisions to approve or reject specific requests or proposals may be communicated clearly by Chinese managers, justifications for such decisions are often vague or omitted in an effort to protect the face of the employees. In a business negotiation involving Chinese and U.S. Americans, therefore, attempts by the U.S. team to insist on explanations for Chinese decisions may communicate a lack of respect and a failure to acknowledge the Chinese attempts at face maintenance.

Even the seating arrangements and protocol during many business negotiations are highly prescribed. Among the Japanese, tables are never round in such business settings, and the expression "head of the table" is meaningless. Rather, as Figure 11.2 indicates, the two sides sit opposite one another, with the power position in the middle of each side. The power seat is flanked by advisors and, if necessary, an interpreter. Next come information suppliers and note takers, followed by other interested parties and junior people, who are closest to the door. Contrary to the usual practice in the United States, the power seat is not necessarily occupied by the most senior person present. Rather, whoever is most knowledgeable about the specific discussion topic takes the power seat and is designated as the company's official spokesperson for this aspect of the negotiations. At the conclusion of the business meeting, ritualistic thank-you's are uttered while all are still seated, both sides arise simultaneously and begin bowing, and the power person from the host company is expected to stay with the "guests" until they are outside the premises and are able to depart.[77]

Such differences in role expectations and in the rules for interactions between Japanese and U.S. American businesspeople are not confined to meetings that take place in Japan, nor are they limited to negotiations among teams from different organizations. Young Yun Kim and Sheryl Paulk found that communication problems and misunderstandings occurred within a Japanese-owned company in the United States because of the Japanese preference for indirectness and the U.S. American preference for directness.[78]

In Korea, the most important concept when doing business, and indeed the most important concern for all Korean interpersonal relationships, is that of *kibun. Kibun*

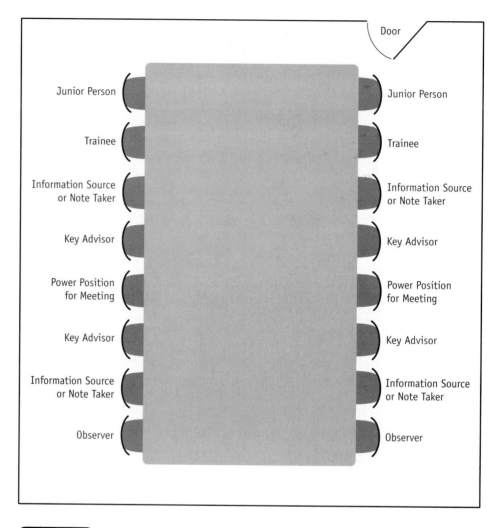

FIGURE 11.2

Conference table seating arrangements for Japanese business negotiations.

Source: Adapted from Richard H. Reeves-Ellington, "Using Cultural Skills for Cooperative Advantage in Japan," *Human Organization 52* (1993): 209.

refers to an individual's personal harmony, pleasurable inner feelings, positive state of mind, sense of pride, and dignity. In Korean relationships, keeping *kibun* in good order takes precedence over virtually all other considerations. In the business context, people must maintain a harmonious atmosphere that enhances the *kibun* of all, for to damage people's *kibun* may irreparably damage interpersonal relationships and create lifelong enemies.[79] Koreans believe that maintaining *kibun* is more important than attaining immediate goals, accomplishing task-related objectives, or telling the absolute truth. That is,

Kibun enters into every aspect of Korean life. Knowing how to judge the state of other people's *kibun,* how to avoid hurting it, and keeping your own *kibun* in a satisfactory state are important skills. . . . For example, a Korean's *kibun* is damaged when his subordinate does not show proper respect, that is, by not bowing soon enough, not using honorific words, not contacting the superior within an appropriate period of time, or worse, handing something to him with the left hand. Most of these rules of etiquette are well known to Koreans, and while they are often difficult or cumbersome to remember, they must be heeded to avoid hurting *kibun.*[80]

Intercultural Competence in the Business Context   What kinds of knowledge, motivations, and skills constitute "competence" in the business context? The very nature of competence itself may differ across cultures. That is, cultures often can hold fundamentally different expectations about how competence ought to be displayed. Compare, for example, the organizations with which you are familiar to the typical Thai organization. In Thai companies, people are perceived as communicatively competent only if they know how to avoid conflict with others, can control their emotional displays (both positive and negative), can use polite forms of address when talking to others, and can demonstrate respect, tactfulness, and modesty in their behaviors.[81]

As the workforce has become more culturally diverse, scholars and practitioners have tried to provide managers and their employees with the tools to work together successfully. Many managers now receive ongoing training about diversity issues, and company employees are often given similar opportunities to improve their knowledge, motivation, and skills. Most people recognize that the cultural heterogeneity of the workforce brings with it special challenges and opportunities, both for companies and for the individuals who work in them.[82] Work teams that are culturally diverse, for example, are often more innovative and creative than are culturally homogeneous work groups,[83] but only if the team can use its differences to its advantage.[84] Percy W. Thomas bluntly summarizes the challenge to us all:

> Twenty years of studying, teaching, and seeking to understand human reactions to differences of all sorts has led me to three conclusions: (1) People lack the communication skills, sensitivity, understanding, flexibility, and trust necessary to establish effective relationships; (2) many reactions to people who are culturally, racially, ethnically, and sexually different are based on irrational fears and nonsensical stereotypes; and (3) people do not know how to deal with their irrational fears, attitudes, beliefs, and behaviors as they relate to inappropriate and counterproductive responses to diversity.[85]

The stakes for businesses are very high. Companies can lose the valuable talent of good employees when cultural differences affect their work negatively. Employees themselves experience their work environments in such way as to affect their own mental well-being. As Thomas says:

> Companies lose millions of dollars "chasing the wind" by settling employee grievances, EEO complaints, and expensive class-action suits, and furthermore, they lose their competitive edge in the marketplace. The costs that stem from maintaining a culturally insensitive environment can be staggering. Many studies show that employee dissatisfaction costs the company large sums of money. Increased use of sick leave, high absenteeism, and simple anomie among workers are often indicators of a culturally insensitive environment.[86]

CULTURE *connections*

It is interesting to compare what happens in France and in the United States in the supermarket when the store is crowded, with a long line in front of the cash register and a long wait. In France, in most cases, one quickly shows signs of impatience, by raising one's eyes to the ceiling with an exasperated expression, by taking on an exhausted look, by stiffening or clamming up, or by exchanging with others glances of complicity. But one does not speak to others—all is expressed through body movements. At most, one might protest, "grumble" out loud while looking at one's neighbor, but without speaking to him directly. One simply makes him an accomplice against the cashier, the store, the system, those who "are going too far." In the United States, the situation is completely different. One turns to one's neighbors; people strike up rather general conversations, help each other pass the time, and joke about the situation—even sympathize with the cashier—and, when they finally get to the register, encourage the person there with a few kind words. I've seen strangers show each other family photos, exchange advice, recipes, or useful addresses, compare pregnancies and births, all just as calmly as if they were talking about the quality of a product or the use of an unusual vegetable in one's shopping cart. Most of all I've seen them joke around lot. A French woman who heard me speaking French to a friend I had met in the supermarket introduced herself to us, gave us her address and telephone number, and invited us to come see her if we were passing by the city in which she lived. Then, just before leaving us, she apologized for her behavior by saying, "Excuse me for having come up to you like that, but I heard you speaking French. I've become very American, you know. . . ."

—*Raymonde Carroll*

Charles R. Bantz describes the lessons he learned from working in a multicultural research team engaged in a long-term project spanning several years and several continents. Bantz recommends that increased attention and effort in four key areas would be most useful: gathering information about the multiple perspectives that will inevitably be present; maintaining flexibility and a willingness to adapt to differing situations, issues, and needs; building social relationships as well as task cohesion; and clearly identifying and emphasizing mutual long-term goals.[87]

Episodes, Contexts, and Intercultural Competence

Recall from Chapter 3 that interaction contexts are a component of intercultural competence related to the associations between two people interacting in specific settings. The discussion in this chapter on social episodes and interaction contexts elaborates on these important ideas. Just as a picture hung on the wall has a frame around it, each intercultural encounter is surrounded or defined by a cultural frame. Competence in intercultural communication requires understanding the nature of this cultural frame.

People frame their intercultural encounters by the definitions or labels they give to particular social episodes. The activities in which you interact are chunked or grouped into social episodes that are influenced by your cultural patterns, roles, rules, interaction scenes, and interaction contexts. Someone else may take a social episode that to you is "small talk with a classmate" as "an offer of friendship." What is to you a businesslike episode of "letting off steam with a co-worker about one of her mildly irritating habits" may be viewed as a "public humiliation." Do not assume that what you regard as appropriate social roles and sensible rules of interaction will necessarily be comfortable or even acceptable to another.

Summary

Social episodes are the repetitive, predictable, and routine behaviors that form the structure of one's interactions with others. Social episodes are made up of cultural patterns, social roles, rules of interaction, interaction scenes, and interaction contexts. People frame intercultural interactions by the expectations they have for particular social episodes.

Three specific social contexts—health care, education, and business—have become prominent meeting grounds where people from many cultures converge and interact. Each context was described in some detail to illustrate the importance of intercultural competence in everyday experiences.

For Discussion

1. What are social episodes? When, if ever, are people affected by them?
2. What are interaction contexts? How does culture affect interaction contexts?
3. Describe an intercultural encounter you have had in the health care, education, or business context. What issues or concerns surfaced as a result of this intercultural encounter? How did you deal with these concerns?
4. What actions can people take to be more interculturally competent in everyday contexts?

For Further Reading

Charles Braithwaite, "Sa'Ah Naagháí Bik'Eh Hózhóón: An Ethnography of Navajo Educational Communication Practices," *Communication Education 46* (1997): 219–233. A description of educational practices within a Navajo community that provides an understanding of how Navajo cultural characteristics define what is good and appropriate within the educational context.

Kenneth Cushner, Averil McClelland, and Philip Safford, *Human Diversity in Education: An Integrative Approach,* 3rd ed. (Boston: McGraw-Hill, 2000). Geared to those who will be teaching in a multicultural classroom, this book provides a philosophy of learning and an inclusive learning environment that can be applied to all students.

Elashmawi Farid and Philip R. Harris, *Multicultural Management 2000: Essential Cultural Insights for Global Business Success* (Houston: Gulf, 1998). A compendium of insights into how various business functions, ranging from human resources to business negotiations, are influenced by differences in the cultures of those in the organization.

Anne Fadiman, *The Spirit Catches You and You Fall Down: A Hmong Child, Her American Doctors, and the Collision of Two Cultures* (New York: Farrar, Straus, and Giroux, 1997). A case study of one Hmong family's experiences within the U.S. health care system. Illustrates the dramatic differences in expectations of competent health care within the two cultural frameworks.

Larry D. Purnell and Betty J. Paulanka (eds.), *Transcultural Health Care: A Culturally Competent Approach* (Philadelphia: F. A. Davis, 1998). An excellent guide to the effects of the beliefs, values, and norms of cultures within the United States on expectations of appropriate and effective communication within the health care setting.

Elise Trumbull, Carrie Rothstein-Fisch, Patricia M. Greenfield, and Blanca Quiroz with Marie Altchech, Catherine Daley, Kathryn Eyler, Elvia Hernandez, Giancario Mercado, Amada Irma Pérez, and Pearl Saiyzyk, *Bridging Cultures between Home and School: A Guide for Teachers, with a Special Focus on Immigrant Latino Families* (Mahwah, NJ: Erlbaum, 2001). While subtitled as a guide for teachers, this book provides insights for all who participate in the educational process. Describes how to navigate cultural differences among students, parents, teachers, and the expectations of the educational system.

For additional information about intercultural films and about Web sites on specific cultures, turn to the Resources section at the back of this book.

chapter 12

The Potential for Intercultural Competence

The Ethics of Intercultural Competence
When in Rome . . .
Are Cultural Values Relative or Universal?
Do the Ends Justify the Means?
Ethics—Your Choices
The Perils and Prospects for
 Intercultural Competence

Impact of National and International
 Events on Intercultural
 Communication
Forces That Pull Us Together
 and Apart
Summary
Concluding Remarks

It should be clear by now that we are personally committed to understanding the dynamics of culture and its effects on interpersonal communication. William Shakespeare suggested that the world is a stage filled with actors and actresses, but they come from different cultures and they need to coordinate their scripts and actions in order to accomplish their collective purposes. The image of a multicultural society is one that we firmly believe will characterize most people's lives in the twenty-first century. Intercultural communication will become far more commonplace in people's day-to-day activities, and the communication skills that lead to the development of intercultural competence will be a necessary part of people's personal and professional lives.

It should also be clear that intercultural communication is a complex and challenging activity. Intercultural competence, although certainly attainable in varying degrees, will elude everyone in at least some intercultural interactions. Nevertheless, we hope that, in addition to the challenges of intercultural interaction, this book also reminds you of the joys of discovery that can occur when interacting with people whose culture differs from your own.

In this closing chapter we turn our attention to some final thoughts about enhancing your intercultural competence. First we discuss some critical ethical issues that affect intercultural interactions. Next we offer a point of view about certain events that have been particularly newsworthy. By focusing on these events, we offer a glimpse into the ways that enormously powerful events and experiences can shape an entire generation's intercultural interactions—that is, how members of that generation are likely to perceive and engage people from other cultures. We also look at the apparent dichotomies that seem to shape individuals and nations in today's world. We conclude with an expression of optimism about the future of intercultural communication and with a renewed awareness of the need for a lifelong commitment to improving our multicultural world.

The Ethics of Intercultural Competence

Those who attempt to achieve intercultural competence must face a number of ethical dilemmas. It is imperative to explore the following issues to become aware of the choices that are made all too often without due consideration and reflection.

There are three key ethical dilemmas. The first is summarized in the adage "When in Rome, do as the Romans do." The second asks if it is possible to judge a particular belief, value, or norm as morally reprehensible. If so, when and under what circumstances? Stated in a slightly different way, if all cultures have differing beliefs, values, and norms, does that mean there are no true rights and wrongs? The third dilemma relates to the consequences of intercultural contacts. Are they necessarily positive for individuals and their societies? In other words, should all intercultural contacts be encouraged?[1]

CULTURE *connections*

In Maine, a refugee from Afghanistan was seen kissing the penis of his baby boy, a traditional expression of love by his father. To his neighbors and the police, it was child abuse, and his son was taken away. In Seattle, a hospital tried to invent a harmless female circumcision procedure to satisfy conservative Somali parents wanting to keep an African practice alive in their community. The idea got buried in criticism from an outraged public.

How do democratic, pluralistic societies like the United States, based on religious and cultural tolerance, respond to customs and rituals that may be repellent to the majority? As new groups of immigrants from Asia and Africa are added to the demographic mix in the United States, Canada and Europe, balancing cultural variety with mainstream values is becoming more and more tricky.

Many Americans confront the issue of whether any branch of government should have the power to intervene in the most intimate details of family life.

"I think we are torn," said Richard A. Shweder, an anthropologist at the University of Chicago and a leading advocate of the broadest tolerance for cultural differences. "It's a great dilemma right now that's coming up again about how we're going to deal with diversity in the United States and what it means to be an American."

—*Barbara Crossette*

When in Rome . . .

A fundamental issue confronting those who are in the midst of another culture is a decision about how much they should change their behaviors to fit the beliefs, values, and norms of those with whom they interact. Whose responsibility is it to attempt to take into account cultural differences in communication? Is it the responsibility of the visitors, newcomers, or sojourners to adjust their behaviors to the cultural framework of the host culture, or should members of the host culture adjust their communication and make allowances for the newcomers and strangers? Because English predominates in the United States, are all those who live in the United States required to use English? To what extent must individuals adapt their cultural beliefs, values, and norms to the dominant cultural patterns?

The old adage "When in Rome, do as the Romans do," which clearly places the responsibility for change on the newcomer, offers a great deal of wisdom, but it cannot be followed in all circumstances. In most cases, behaviors that conform to cultural expectations show respect for the other culture and its ways. Conformity with common cultural practices also allows the newcomer to interact with and to meet people from the host culture on some kind of genuine basis. Respecting differences in nonverbal and verbal codes means that the ethical intercultural communicator takes responsibility for learning as much about these codes as is possible and reasonable. Naturally, what is

This Russian Jewish immigrant uses a dictionary to translate between languages while doing his homework.

possible and reasonable will vary, depending on a range of circumstances. Sometimes, wholesale adoption of new cultural practices by a group of newcomers may be seen as disrespectful and can upset those from the host culture. In the 1960s, for example, U.S. and European students visiting India wore Indian clothes, didn't wear shoes, and lived in very poor circumstances. Many Indians regarded this "conforming" behavior as insulting and disrespectful of their cultures. The visitor to a culture cannot simply adopt the beliefs and practices of a new culture without also risking being perceived as insincere and superficial.

Sometimes it is difficult for people to change their behaviors to match cultural patterns that contradict their own beliefs and values. For example, many U.S. American women, who were taught to value freedom and equality, may find it difficult to respond positively to cultural practices that require women to wear veils in public and to use male drivers or chaperones. The ethical dilemma that intercultural communicators face is the decision about how far to go in adapting their behaviors to another culture. Should people engage in behaviors that they regard as personally wrong or difficult? At what point do people lose their own sense of self, their cultural identities, and their moral integrity? At what point does the adoption of new cultural behaviors offend and insult others? One of the challenges and delights of intercultural communication is in discovering the boundaries and touchstones of one's own moral perspective while simultaneously learning to display respect for other ways of dealing with human problems.

Another perspective from which to explore the ethical issues embedded in the adage is that of the "Romans." A common point of view, often expressed by U.S. Americans about those who have recently immigrated to the United States or who still retain many of the underlying patterns of their own culture, is that since these people now live in the United States, they should adjust to its cultural ways. The same comments are often made about students from other countries who come to the United States to study.

We ask you to consider the experiences of those people who immigrate to or study in another country. Perhaps you are such a person. Or perhaps your parents or grandparents did so. Not all immigrants or students have freely chosen the country where they now reside. Large numbers of people migrate from one country to another because political, military, and economic upheavals in their own country make living and learn-

CULTURE *connections*

Mr. Malchode moved then to sit beside me. Quietly he said, "I don't mean to insult, but for your own sake you should know as a white you're intruding here. This is *our* place. It's not a zoo for tourists to see how 'natives' live. Even now we can't drink in a Messina hotel bar—the prices are trebled to keep us out. But you take it for granted you can come and drink here—you're white, so you can drink wherever you choose. Do you know enough about South Africa to understand what I say?"

—Dervla Murphy

ing there nearly impossible. For many, the choice to leave is juxtaposed against a choice to die, to starve, or to be politically censored. We also ask you to consider how difficult it must be for people to give up their culture. Remember how fundamental your cultural framework is, how it provides the logic for your behavior and your view of the world. How easy would it be for you if you were forced into new modes of behavior? Adjustment to another culture is difficult.

Are Cultural Values Relative or Universal?

A second ethical issue confronting the intercultural communicator is whether it is ever acceptable to judge the people of a culture when their behaviors are based on a radically different set of beliefs, values, and norms. Are there any values that transcend the boundaries of cultural differences? Are there any universally right or wrong values?

A culturally relativistic point of view suggests that every culture has its own set of values and that judgments can be made only within the context of the particular culture. Most people do not completely subscribe to this view, partly because it would lead to a lack of any firm beliefs and values on which to build a sense of self-identity.

David Kale argues that there are two values that transcend all cultures. First, the human spirit requires that all people must struggle to improve their world and to maintain their own sense of dignity, always within the context of their own particular culture. Thus Kale suggests that "the guiding principle of any universal code of intercultural communication, therefore, should be to protect the worth and dignity of the human spirit."[2] The second universal value is a world at peace. Thus, all ethical codes must recognize the importance of working toward a world in which people can live at peace with themselves and one another.[3]

Ethical intercultural communicators continually struggle with the dilemmas presented by differences in cultural values. The tensions inherent in seeking to be tolerant of differences while holding firmly to one's own critical cultural values must always be reconciled. Kale's suggestions for responding ethically to cultural differences in values are excellent starting points for the internal dialogue that all competent intercultural communicators must conduct.

Do the Ends Justify the Means?

The final ethical dilemma we wish to raise concerns these questions: Should all intercultural contacts be encouraged? Are the outcomes of intercultural contacts positive? Are all circumstances appropriate for intercultural contact? In short, do the ends justify the means?

We have been shamelessly enthusiastic about the potential benefits and delights of intercultural interaction. Nevertheless, certain outcomes may not necessarily be justified by the means used to obtain them. Tourism, for example, can sometimes create an ethical dilemma. Although it often provides economic benefits for those living in the tourist destination and allows people from one culture to learn about another, it can also produce serious negative consequences. In some popular tourist destinations, for instance, the tourists actually outnumber the native population, and tourists may consume natural resources at a greater rate than they can be replaced.

Some of the following questions must be confronted:

CULTURE *connections*

An interesting problem surfaced at an educational conference yesterday. Thirty-five "foreign experts" and the headsirs from their assigned schools met to resolve apprehensions. A concern of several of the headsirs was that the foreigners in their villages would not observe proper etiquette in treatment of the lowest castes. What was supposed to be a meeting designed to help bridge cultural gaps got off to the wrong start, with some volunteers proselytizing about democracy.

This raises an interesting dilemma. What do you do as a culturally sensitive development worker when elements of the system you are trying to be sensitive to are basically abhorrent to your own values? People who are wonderfully tolerant when it comes to religion seem to have a little more trouble with the caste issue. The women in the group make no bones whatsoever about their intentions to enlighten Nepali women to the possibilities of change from their present subordinate status. It seems easy. We're right and they're wrong.

But what if the Nepalis came over to the U.S. and started telling Iowa beef farmers that it was wrong to kill cows? Or what if the Saudi Arabians came and told women in New York that it was wrong for them to drive cars? Is this what is meant by cultural imperialism? A "culturally sensitive" development worker is beginning to seem a contradiction in terms.

—*Barbara J. Scott*

> Is it ethical to go to another country, for whatever reason, if you are naive and unprepared for cultural contact?
> Should intercultural contacts be encouraged for those who speak no language but their own?
> Should those who are prejudiced seek out intercultural contacts?
> Is it ethical to send missionaries to other countries?
> Is it acceptable to provide medical assistance to help a culture resist a disease, when in providing the assistance you may destroy the very infrastructure and nature of the indigenous culture?
> Is it justifiable for the sojourner from one culture to encourage a person from another culture to disregard his or her own cultural values?

There are no simple answers to any of these questions, but the competent intercultural communicator must confront these ethical dilemmas.

Ethics—Your Choices

We have offered few specific answers to these ethical dilemmas because every person must provide his or her own response. In the context of your own experiences and your own intercultural interactions, therefore, you must resolve the ethical dilemmas that will inevitably occur in your life. Kale provides four principles to guide you as you develop your own personal code of ethics. Ethical communicators should do the following:

▶ Address people of other cultures with the same respect that they would like to receive themselves.

▶ Try to describe the world as they perceive it as accurately as possible.

▶ Encourage people of other cultures to express themselves in their unique natures.

▶ Strive for identification with people of other cultures.

The Perils and Prospects for Intercultural Competence

Today's world is buffeted by an enormously powerful set of forces. Some of these forces are not unique to this era but have existed at other times throughout the history of the world. Some, however, are wholly new, and they cause profound and, to some extent at least, unpredictable changes. The changes are set in motion by the speed with which global capital, information, goods, and the people who would trade in them can move across borders and throughout the world. Indeed, we are living through, yet do not fully understand, an unprecedented series of revolutions in communications, transportation, and technologies, which impose instantaneous interconnectedness upon most of the world's nations, their cultures, and their economies.

Impact of National and International Events on Intercultural Communication

Consider the following examples, each of which is drawn from the history of the United States and has had profound consequences throughout the world. As you reflect upon them, identify for yourself how these events were first shaped by global forces and, in turn, helped to shape subsequent global events.

October 24, 1929: a Thursday in early fall, and the day when the Roaring Twenties abruptly ended. The U.S. stock market crashed, a decade of unbelievable prosperity ended, and the Great Depression rapidly followed. Within three years, U.S. stock prices lost nearly 90 percent of their value, banks and other financial institutions collapsed, factories and businesses failed, unemployment soared by 700 percent, and ordinary working people were destitute, having lost both their jobs and their accumulated savings. Hunger was widespread, breadlines were commonplace, and medical care and durable goods were unaffordable. U.S. Americans of a certain age have been forever seared by these events, and their collective experiences have figured prominently in the subsequent financial, political, social, and vocational choices that were made.

December 7, 1941: a Sunday that, for many elderly U.S. Americans, will always be remembered as a day of infamy. The surprise was complete. The assault came that morning in two waves—the first at 7:53, the second an hour later. By ten o'clock it was over; more than 350 airplanes broke off the attack and left Oahu for their carriers, which returned them to Japan. Pearl Harbor, home of the U.S. Pacific Fleet, had been crippled: over two thousand dead, thousands more injured, eight battleships damaged or destroyed, and nearly 200 planes ruined. In the wake of this attack, both patriotism and fear followed; as the United States was drawn into World War II, courageous men and women marched off to defend their homeland and their loved ones, bravely facing

CULTURE *connections*

The encounter of worlds and worldviews is the shared experience of our times. We see it in the great movements of modern history, in colonialism and the rejection of colonialism, in the late-twentieth-century "politics of identity"—ethnic, racial, and religious. We experience our own personal versions of this encounter, all of us, whether Christian, Hindu, Jewish, or Muslim; whether Buddhist, Apache, or Kikuyu; whether religious, secular, or atheist. What do we make of the encounter with a different world, a different worldview? How will we think about the heterogeneity of our immediate world and our wider world? This is our question, our human question, at the end of the twentieth century.

—*Diana L. Eck*

death and the unfathomable horrors of war. Many who remained in the United States shared a newfound pride; U.S. flags were prominently displayed, slogans and posters to encourage patriotism were seemingly everywhere, and a desire to contribute to the national effort was palpable. Sadly, however, some U.S. Americans became the targets of unbridled fear, including those loyal U.S. citizens of Japanese ancestry who were required to abandon most of their belongings and were forced into detention camps for several years.

November 22, 1963: a warm Friday afternoon in Dallas. With an enthusiastic crowd cheering, President John F. Kennedy's motorcade passed through the streets in an open car. Suddenly at least three shots rang out, and the president was hit twice: in the base of the neck, and squarely in the head. By 1:00 P.M.— less than an hour later—he was declared dead at the age of forty-six. In remarks prepared for delivery later that day, Kennedy had intended to say,

> In a world of complex and continuing problems, in a world full of frustrations and irritations, America's leadership must be guided by the lights of learning and reason or else those who confuse rhetoric with reality and the plausible with the possible will gain the popular ascendancy with their seemingly swift and simple solutions to every world problem.[4]

Three days later, leaders from more than ninety nations attended Kennedy's funeral; a million people lined the route as a horse-drawn caisson bore his body to St. Matthew's Cathedral for a requiem mass. Then, as more than a hundred million people watched on television, the president was buried in Arlington National Cemetery, where an eternal flame still marks his grave. Now, some forty years later, U.S. Americans of a certain age remember vividly the tragedy of that assassination.

January 28, 1986: a cold Tuesday morning in Florida. At 11:38, a rocket left its launching pad for a seven-day mission. The countdown hadn't exactly gone smoothly, with weather and equipment problems plaguing the launch; but after seven delays spanning five days, liftoff finally occurred. From classrooms across the nation, excited schoolchildren watched the live coverage of the shuttle's launch. They were eagerly following the successes of Christa McAuliffe, the first "teacher in space," who was to speak to them the following day in a live telecast. Just seventy-three seconds into the flight, the unimaginable happened: the space shuttle Challenger exploded in a fiery blast, instantly killing all seven crew. The United States was stunned and shaken. The State of the Union address, scheduled for delivery by President Ronald Reagan that evening, was postponed. In its place, the president delivered a short but moving tribute to the fallen astronauts; three days later, a sorrowful nation participated via television in a memorial service in Houston, as the United States mourned the "Challenger Seven." Ask U.S. Americans of a certain age—particularly those who were schoolchildren then—and they will tell you that they vividly remember the day the Challenger exploded; nearly two decades later, many can recall precisely where they were and what they were doing when they learned of the disaster.

September 11, 2001: a clear Tuesday morning, with a hint of fall in the air. Abruptly, at 8:50 A.M., a hijacked commercial airplane smashed into the northern tower of New York's World Trade Center. Twenty-four minutes later, another hijacked plane struck the southern tower. Twenty-four minutes after that, at 9:38, a third hijacked plane struck the Pentagon, a portion of which collapsed. Pandemonium ensued. Within the hour, these jet-fueled fireballs had caused both of the 110-story towers of the World Trade Center to collapse. Fears of additional attacks were widespread: the Sears Tower in Chicago was evacuated, an anti-terrorism division was mobilized in Los Angeles, and Seattle's Space Needle was closed. Air traffic was halted, financial markets were

CULTURE *connections*

In Tokyo's Komazawa Park, a long-standing Japanese rite of spring has been *hanami*—"looking at cherry blossom"—parties. Families, friends, and corporate colleagues—along with their bicycles, blankets, dogs, scooters, skateboards, strollers, and lots of other paraphernalia—gather at local parks to celebrate, to take part in the merrymaking and laughter, and to enjoy the *sakura* blossoms with their delicate pink colors. Traditionally, many revelers brought extensive cooking equipment to the park and created elaborately prepared meals. Recently, however, using cell phones to place their orders and pinpoint their locations, many picnickers prefer to have pizza and other take-out foods delivered to them. Would-be customers phone the nearby Pizza Hut or Domino's tents and order their pizzas, which are topped with such delicacies as potato salad and bacon, tuna fish and mayonnaise, or pineapple and corn. Without cell phones, such a delivery system would be impossible; with them, business is booming for these mouth-watering treats.

shut down, troops were mobilized, life was more uncertain, U.S. flags were everywhere, patriotism was admired, and donations soared. And Arab Americans—indeed, peace-loving Muslims throughout the world—were a bit more fearful for the safety of their children.

What sense should we make of these experiences, particularly the most recent of them? Each of these experiences, and many others we could provide from around the world, creates an indelible memory for certain U.S. Americans, who then pass on the lessons learned from them. Each of these events fundamentally alters the basic and often unquestioned understandings that people have of their social world, and it raises issues such as the following:

▶ What does my culture and nation represent to others? That is, from the perspective of others who view us differently than we view ourselves, what does my culture and nation stand for?
▶ What are the beliefs, values, and norms that seem to guide my culture's actions?
▶ In what ways am I interconnected with other cultures and economies in the world?
▶ To what extent should I trust people who seem different from me? To what extent *must* I trust people who seem different from me, as a prerequisite for our mutual survival?

Events such as those described above, therefore, have profound effects upon many individuals, who subsequently shape the understandings of others in the generations that follow. The September 11 terrorist attacks, for example, have tested the very fabric of the United States as a multicultural nation. Fears and uncertainties have encouraged people to evaluate others negatively based solely on such attributes as their physical appearance, choice of religious observance, culture of origin, and the like. But they have also created a healthy reevaluation of national priorities, the values inherent in a multicultural nation, and the means to achieve these goals.

CULTURE *connections*

Diversity, of course, is not pluralism. Diversity is simply a fact, but what will we make of that fact, individually and as a culture? Will it arouse new forms of ethnic and religious chauvinism and isolation? Or might it lead to a genuine pluralism, a positive and interactive interpretation of plurality? These are critical questions for the future, as people decide whether they value a sense of identity that isolates and sets them apart from one another or whether they value a broader identity that brings them into real relationship with one another.

—*Diana L. Eck*

Forces That Pull Us Together and Apart

There are two powerful yet opposing forces that are tugging on the United States and its many cultures. Indeed, these forces are not exclusive to the United States; they affect every nation and culture on earth, often in significant ways.

The opposing forces could variously be described as engagement versus isolationism, globalism versus nationalism, secularism versus spiritualism, consumerism versus fundamentalism, or capitalism versus tribalism. That is, intercultural relationships among cultural groups throughout the world are simultaneously being pushed together and wrenched apart. Though the terminology to describe these potent forces may vary, and their influential consequences may fluctuate widely across cultures and regions of the world, they nevertheless provide us with powerful lenses through which to view the changing interrelationships among the world's cultures.

One such force—promoting engagement, globalism, secularism, and capitalism—is nurtured and sustained by the economic interdependence of today's world. Economic interdependence, in turn, is linked to the rapid communications systems that now connect people virtually in real time, as events are displayed instantaneously through a variety of powerful technological innovations—television, film, videos, music, and the Internet. Transportation systems, as well, can quickly take people from one part of the globe to another. Almost anywhere one travels, there will be familiar signs of the interdependent global economy: television shows such as *All in the Family, The Mary Tyler Moore Show, LA Law,* and *ER* all have burgeoning international audiences; film and musical performers, from rap to salsa, from Ricky Martin to the St. Petersburg Opera, are known internationally; and MTV is seen globally, with local shows adapting the U.S. format by tailoring it to their audiences' sensibilities. One can hear Peruvian musicians on a corner in Brussels, Beatles tunes in an elevator in Malaysia, reggae music on the streets of Guatemala City, and African rhythms at a park in San Francisco. In many parts of the world, the music played on the radio stations could be described, at least in part, as global, and not representative of that country's musical traditions.

Closely related to mass media's impact is the speed of communications that now link much of the world. Events that occur in one country are displayed, within minutes, to people tens of thousands of miles away. As a consequence, events in one part of the world have dramatic consequences in others. International telephone usage is on the rise; the Internet has drastically reduced the cost for such calls, and it has made it much easier to communicate over long distances.

Added to all of these forces is the stark reality of global economic interdependence. There are obvious signs of this "sharing" of the world's economy. The now-familiar KFC (Kentucky Fried Chicken), Pizza Hut, and McDonald's fast-food outlets are seemingly everywhere; Fords, Toyotas, and Volkswagens are driven the world over; and consumer products by Coca Cola, Sony, Nestles, and Bayer are marketed internationally. The world traveler could easily assume, incorrectly, that similarities in consumer products and media messages result from or will lead to a homogenization of world cultures.

A counterpoint to these forces for globalization is another, and equally powerful, set of constraints. These alternative influences—for isolationism, nationalism, spiritualism, and tribalism—derive from a desire to preserve, protect, and defend what is seen as unique but threatened: the culture's language, religion, values, or way of life. As an example of these forces, consider the frequent desires expressed among members of a culture to protect its language from the intrusions of other languages; France, for example, is very vigilant about keeping non-French words from the national language. Similarly, people may elect to safeguard their economies from foreign products; they may do this formally—with protectionist tariffs on goods from other nations, particularly if the foreign goods compete favorably with those locally grown or manufactured—or informally, by common consent—witness the dearth of Japanese-manufactured automobiles in Detroit, where major U.S. automakers are located. Cultures and nations may also attempt to protect their people from the deleterious effects of the beliefs, values, and norms imposed on them from the "outside," which might negatively influence people's

Global economic interdependence can produce a collage of symbols from multiple cultures. Would you have guessed that this building is located in New York City?

These immigrants aboard ship in 1902 are headed for a new life as U.S. Americans. Their great-grandchildren must live in a multicultural world that demands competent intercultural communication skills.

behaviors. Prohibitions of certain imported films, or videos of artistic performances, frequently occur in many places.

There is no doubt that these two sets of forces are powerful and dynamic, and they will likely shape much of the human experience in the twenty-first century. Discussions about these countervailing forces often come down to asking which forces are stronger: those promoting globalization and homogenization or those that encourage cultures to maintain their distinctiveness and unique ways of living?

We believe that what is missing from most discussions about the relative strengths of these forces is an understanding of the effects of culture on the human communication process. While these forces simultaneously push us together and pull us apart, what hasn't been acknowledged is that humans still bring their cultural backgrounds to their interpretations of these global events and symbols, which then shape the ways they make sense of them. That is, McDonald's arches, Jean Claude van Damm's films, Ice-T's music videos, internet chatroom messages, and acts of "humanitarianism" are all interpreted and analyzed through individuals' differing cultural and national structures.

The patina of familiarity and commonality does not necessarily produce a shared understanding of the nature of everyday events. In Chapter 1, we discussed the important distinction between understanding and agreement in communication outcomes. The goal of living in a multicultural world, therefore, may sometimes mean that we must attempt to achieve understanding while recognizing that agreement may not always be likely, or even possible. Perhaps, however, we can sometimes "agree to disagree," with respect, civility, and caring. Intergroup tensions have characterized human interaction since the beginning of time, and they are not likely to abate soon. Stereotyping, we have suggested, is a natural and inevitable human tendency to categorize groups of others and

Using personal experiences, the Resources section at the end of this book, or other means available to you, enjoy learning about intercultural communication with cultures that differ from your own. Do this periodically, for the rest of your life.

thereby make the world more predictable. Our challenge is to assess individuals on their own merits, rather than merely as members of groups or nations, while simultaneously recognizing that humans typically identify, and often react to their worlds, as members of a culture.

Cultures and their symbolic systems also can change over time. No culture is static. Even cultures that have minimal contact with the outside world are affected by changing ecological conditions and events, which in turn change how they experience and understand their own familiar world.

We suggest that both the forces promoting globalization and those encouraging individuation are mediated by the cultural patterns—the beliefs, values, and norms—of all peoples. Even identical messages, therefore, are interpreted differently by those whose codes and cultures differ. Thus, while we recognize the far-reaching effects of technological, societal, and economic forces, we must also remember that one's culture provides the meaning systems by which all messages are experienced and interpreted.

Summary

Ethical issues in the development of intercultural competence concern questions about whose responsibility it is to adjust to a different culture, issues about right and wrong, and the degree to which all intercultural contacts should be encouraged. Global forces, which bring people together, are met with equally strong forces that pull people apart. Always, however, people bring to every communicative interaction understandings that are filtered and framed by their own cultural patterns. Thus, one must interpret intercultural experiences within the context of national and international events.

Concluding Remarks

We began this book with a sense of optimism, but also with a deep concern about the pressing need for intercultural communication competence. Here in the twenty-first century, such competence is an essential attribute for personal survival, professional success, national harmony, and international peace. The challenge of living in a multicultural world is the need to transcend the unpredictability of intercultural interactions, to cope with the accompanying fears that such interactions often engender, and to feel joy and comfort in the discovery of cultural variability.

Our focus has been on the interpersonal hurdles—the person-to-person problems—that arise in coping with the realities of cultural diversity. We commend and encourage all who have struggled to adjust to the multicultural nature of the human landscape. Inclusion of others is the means to a better future, so we must "reconstitute the inner circle"[5] by celebrating and acknowledging cultural differences in all aspects of life.

The need for an intercultural mentality to match our multicultural world, the difficulties inherent in the quest of such a goal, the excitement of the challenges, and the rewards of the successes are summarized in the words of Troy Duster:

There is no longer a single racial or ethnic group with an overwhelming numerical and political majority. Pluralism is the reality, with no one group a dominant force. This is completely new; we are grappling with a phenomenon that is both puzzling and alarming, fraught with tensions and hostilities, and yet simultaneously brimming with potential and crackling with new energy. Consequently, we swing between hope and concern, optimism and pessimism about the prospects for social life among people from differing racial and cultural groups.[6]

We urge you to view this book and each intercultural experience as steps in a life-long commitment to competence in intercultural communication. Intercultural competence is, in many ways, an art rather than a science. Our hope is that you will use your artistic talents to make the world a better place in which people from all cultures can live and thrive.

For Discussion

1. What responsibility does a visitor from another culture have to the host culture's ways of living, thinking, and communicating? For example, should people visiting from another culture accept or engage in behaviors they find ethically wrong but which the culture sanctions as ethically correct?
2. What are some of the advantages and problems with cultural relativism?
3. Are there universal values that you believe are found in every culture? Explain.
4. What can we do—what can you do—to make the world a place where many cultures thrive?

For Further Reading

Kenneth Cushner and Richard W. Brislin, *Intercultural Interactions: A Practical Guide,* 2nd ed. (Thousand Oaks, CA: Sage, 1996). A compendium of case examples of interactions between individuals from diverse cultures in a variety of settings. Analysis of such intercultural experiences as being a tourist, a guest, or a host; functioning in the workplace, the family, and in educational settings; and adapting to one's home culture upon returning there.

Josina Makau and Ronald C. Arnett (eds.), *Communication Ethics in an Age of Diversity* (Urbana: University of Illinois Press, 1997). Offers insights into the personal ethical choices and issues that people face as they interact in personal and professional settings with those whose cultural backgrounds are different from their own. The book also explores the impact of the rapid and ubiquitous communication now possible through the use of many new technologies.

For additional information about intercultural films and about Web sites on specific cultures, turn to the Resources section at the back of this book.

Resources

Information about cultures and about intercultural communication can come from many different sources. In addition to the resource materials within each chapter, we provide here a list of many resources that you can use to increase your culture-specific knowledge about the beliefs, values, and norms of many cultures.

Intercultural Films

Here are some suggestions for films you might want to view. Many of these films may be available at your local video rental store. In addition, many schools have audiovisual departments that might carry some of these titles.

Each of the film titles is followed (in parentheses) by the culture(s) portrayed. Typically, the central characters in the films are from the indicated cultures, and the action of the film's story is usually set in those cultures as well.

As we have mentioned at numerous places throughout this book, a word of caution is warranted. The characters in these films, like all other individuals you might experience, are not "perfect representations" of their cultures. While some of the revealed beliefs, values, and norms may be "typical" of a majority of members of the portrayed cultures, others may be common only to a few cultural members, and some characteristics will undoubtedly be unique to the individuals in the films. We caution you, therefore, to guard against the presumption that *any* depiction of cultural members will be a completely accurate one.

In our judgment, each of the listed films portrays the members of a culture with complexity and integrity. Omitted from this list are Hollywood blockbuster films such as *The Joy Luck Club* and *Schindler's List*. While such films are often excellent (and, as is true with these two examples, are often must-see films), they are likely to be better known than those we list here. While our listing is by no means complete, it does contain some of our favorites. Enjoy!

Babette's Feast (Danish)
Beyond Rangoon (Burmese)
Bread and Chocolate (Swiss, Italian)
Cinema Paradiso (Italian)
The Circle (Iranian)
Cry, The Beloved Country (South African)
Eat Drink Man Woman (Chinese)
Eureka (Japanese)
Europa Europa (European)
Il Postino (The Postman) (Italian)
Indochine (Vietnamese)
The Last Emperor (Chinese)
Like Water for Chocolate (Mexican)
Little Buddha (Tibetan)
To Live (Chinese)
The Makioka Sisters (Japanese)

Mediterraneo (Italian, Greek)
Mi Familia (Latino)
Mississippi Massala (African American, Indian American)
My Life as a Dog (Swedish)
Picture Bride (Japanese)
Pushing Hands (Chinese, Chinese American)
Raise the Red Lantern (Chinese)
Red Firecracker, Green Firecracker (Chinese)
The Road Home (Chinese)
The Scent of Green Papaya (Vietnamese)
Shall We Dance? (Japanese)
The Story of Qui Ju (Chinese)
Tortilla Soup (Latino)
A Walk in the Clouds (Latino)

Online Resources

Web Sites about Multiple Countries and Their Cultures

Arab Net   http://www.arab.net
Links to information about the geography, history, and culture of more than twenty countries in or near the Middle East.

Asian Studies   http://coombs.anu.edu.au/WWWVL-AsianStudies.html
Asian Studies Virtual Library. Links to information about more than sixty countries.

Latin America   http://lanic.utexas.edu/subject/countries.html
Links to information about forty countries in Central and South America.

Library of Congress Country Studies   http://lcweb2.loc.gov/frd/cs
The Library of Congress provides in-depth information about the culture, geography, and history of more than one hundred countries around the world, from Albania to Zaire.

Lonely Planet: Travel Guides   http://www.lonelyplanet.com/destinations
Where in the world do you want to go? The Lonely Planet series of travel guides provide information about many of the world's countries and cultures.

Web of Culture   http://www.worldculture.com
Many resources that promote intercultural communication.

World Factbook   http://www.odci.gov/cia/publications/factbook/index.html
Information on the geography, people, government, and other information for hundreds of countries.

Web Sites about Specific Countries and Their Cultures

Albania   http://www.albanian.com
Angola   http://www.angola.org
Austria   http://www.austria-info.at
Australia   http://www.csu.edu.au/australia

Azerbaijan   http://www.friends-partners.org/oldfriends/azerbaijan/index.html
Bangladesh   http://www.virtualbangladesh.com
Belgium   http://belgium.fgov.be
Belize Online   http://www.belize.com
Belize Government Page   http://www.belize.gov.bz
Cambodia   http://www.cambodia.org
Canada   http://canada.gc.ca
Cape Verde   http://www.umassd.edu/specialprograms/caboverde/capeverdean.html
China, Republic of (Taiwan)   http://www.gio.gov.tw
Denmark   http://www.denmarkemb.org
Estonia: Institute of Baltic Studies   http://www.ibs.ee
Estonia: Country Guide   http://www.ciesin.ee/ESTCG
Finland   http://virtual.finland.fi
France: French Ministry of Foreign Affairs
      http://www.france.diplomatie.fr/index.gb.html
France: History   http://instruct1.cit.cornell.edu/Courses/french_history
Georgia   http://www.parliament.ge
Germany   http://www.government.de
Ghana   http://www.ghanaweb.com
Guyana   http://www.guyana.org
Hungary   http://www.fsz.bme.hu/hungary/homepage.html
Iceland   http://www.whatson.is
India   http://alfa.nic.in
Iran: Iranian Cultural Information Center   http://persia.org
Iran: PersiaNet   http://userwww.service.emory.edu/~sebrahi/PersiaNet.html
Iraq   http://www.iraqfoundation.org
Ireland: Central Statistics Office   http://www.cso.ie
Ireland: General   http://www.itw.ie//wwwlib.html
Ireland, Northern   http://www.interknowledge.com/northern-ireland/index.html
Israel   http://www.israel-mfa.gov.il/index.html
Italy: Dolce Vita   http://www.dolcevita.com
Italy: Embassy in U.S.   http://www.italyemb.org
Jamaica   http://www.jamaicans.com
Japan: Information Network   http://www.jinjapan.org
Japan: Window Project   http://www.jwindow.net
Jewish: Judaism 101   http://www.jewfaq.org
Jewish: Resources   http://shamash.org/trb/judaism.html
Kurdistan   http://www.xs4all.nl/~tank/kurdish/htdocs/index.html
Libya   http://ourworld.compuserve.com/homepages/dr_ibrahim_ighneiwa
Lithuania   http://www.litnet.lt/litinfo/litinfo.html
Luxembourg   http://www.luxembourg.lu/sip/english/wwwserveng.html
Malaysia   http://www.jaring.my
Maltese Islands   http://www.magnet.mt
Mexico: Reference Desk   http://lanic.utexas.edu/la/Mexico
Mexico: Tourism   http://mexico-travel.com/mexico/owa/sectur.inicio
Mexico: Art, Culture, History   http://www.arts-history.mx/index2.html

Nepal   http://www.info-nepal.com
Netherlands   http://www.nbt.nl
New Zealand   http://nz.com
Norway   http://www.norway.org
Papua New Guinea   http://www.niugini.com
Peru   http://ekeko.rcp.net.pe/rcp/rcp-peru.shtml
Poland   http://ciesin.ci.uw.edu.pl/poland/poland-home.html
Russia   http://www.learner.org/exhibits/russia
Samoa   http://public-www.pi.se/~orbit/samoa/welcome.html
Scotland   http://members.aol.com/sconemac/index.html
Singapore: National Museum   http://www.museum.org.sg
Singapore: InfoMap   http://www.sg
Singapore: Government   http://www.gov.sg
Slovakia   http://www.eunet.sk/slovakia/polit.html
South Africa   http://www.polity.org.za
Spain   http://www.docuweb.ca/SiSpain/english/index.html
Sweden   http://www.sverigeturism.se/smorgasbord
Tunisia   http://www.tunisiaonline.com
Turkey   http://www.turkey.org/turkey
Ukraine   http://www.physics.mcgill.ca/WWW/oleh/ukr-info.html
United Arab Emirates   http://www.uae.org.ae
United Kingdom: Travel Guide   http://www.uktravel.com/index.html
United Kingdom: UK Online   http://www.open.gov.uk
USA, African American: Universal Black Pages   http://www.ubp.com
USA, African American: Black Network   http://www.netnoir.com
USA, Asian American: Asian American Net   http://www.asianamerican.net
USA, Asian American: Internet Sites   http://latino.sscnet.ucla.edu/Asian.links.html
USA, Latino: Hispanic Online   http://www.hispaniconline.com
USA, Latino: Latino Culture   http://latinoculture.about.com/mbody.htm
USA, Latino: Latino Web   http://www.latinoweb.com
USA, Native Americans   http://www.indians.org/welker/nations1.htm
USA, Native American, Cherokee   http://www.uark.edu/depts/comminfo/UKB/
welcome.html
USA, Native American, Lakota   http://puffin.creighton.edu/lakota/index.html
USA, Native American, Seneca   http://www.sni.org
USA, Hawaiian   http://www.hawaii-nation.org

Notes

Chapter 1

1. Catharine R. Stimpson, "A Conversation, Not a Monologue," *Chronicle of Higher Education,* March 16, 1994, B1.
2. Mark E. Mendenhall, Edward Dunbar, and Gary R. Oddou, "Expatriate Selection, Training, and Career-Pathing: A Review and Critique," *Human Resource Management* 26 (1987): 331–345.
3. President's Commission on Foreign Language and International Studies (Washington, DC: Department of Health, Education and Welfare, 1979), 1.
4. Robert Shuter, "The Centrality of Culture," *Southern Communication Journal* 55 (1990): 241.
5. Pew Research Center for the People and the Press survey conducted by Princeton Survey Research Associates, April 6–May 6, 1999. Accessed online February 2, 2001. www.pollingreport.com/20th .htm
6. William A. Henry III, "Beyond the Melting Pot," *Time,* April 9, 1990, 28.
7. "United States Population Estimates by Age, Sex, Race, and Hispanic Origin, 1990 to 1996," U.S. Bureau of the Census, Population Division, Release PPL-57.
8. "Profiles of General Demographic Characteristics: 2000 Census of Population and Housing," U.S. Census Bureau, May 2001, Table DP-1.
9. U.S. Census Bureau, "Annual Projections of Total Resident Population: Middle, Low, and High Series, 1996 to 2050." Accessed online December 2, 1999. www.census.gov/population/ www/projections/natproj.html; Population Reference Bureau, "The Changing American Pie, 1999 and 2025." Accessed online August 8, 2001. www.ameristat.org
10. Bureau of the Census, *Statistical Abstract of the United States: 1996,* 116th ed. (Washington, DC, 1996).
11. "New Census Study Shows America's Changing Face," *San Francisco Chronicle,*" September 16, 1999, A26.
12. "Profiles of General Demographic Characteristics: 2000 Census of Population and Housing," U.S. Census Bureau, May 2001, Table DP-1.
13. Bureau of the Census, *Statistical Abstract of the United States: 1996,* 116th ed. (Washington, DC, 1996).
14. Angela Brittingham, "The Foreign-Born Population in the United States: Population Characteristics," U.S. Bureau of the Census, August 2000. See also "Coming to America: A Profile of the Nation's Foreign Born," U.S. Bureau of the Census, August 2000.
15. Randolph E. Schmid, "Nearly 1 in 10 U.S. Residents Born Abroad, Report Says," *Sacramento Bee,* September 19, 1999, A7.
16. Brittingham, "Profile of the Foreign-Born Population in the United States: 1997," U.S. Bureau of the Census, Population Division, Release P23-195, August 2000.
17. "Coming to America: A Profile of the Nation's Foreign Born," U.S. Bureau of the Census, August 1999.
18. "One Nation, One Language?" *U.S. News & World Report,* September 25, 1995, 40.
19. "One Nation, One Language?"

20. Steven A. Holmes, "Census Bureau Predicts Huge U.S. Ethnic Shift," *Sacramento Bee,* March 14, 1997, A1, A12.

21. Holmes; U.S. Bureau of the Census, *Statistical Abstract of the United States: 1996,* 116th ed. (Washington, DC, 1996).

22. Antonia Pantoja and Wilhelmina Perry, "Cultural Pluralism: A Goal to Be Realized," *Voices from the Battlefront,* ed. Marta Moreno Vega and Cheryll Y. Greene (Trenton, NJ: Africa World Press, 1993), 136.

23. "Classrooms of Babel," *Newsweek,* February 11, 1991, 56–57.

24. David Ferrell and Robert Lee Hotz, "Ethnic Pockets Amid a Vast Fabric of English," *Los Angeles Times,* January 23, 2000, A1, A16–18.

25. Ferrell and Hotz.

26. "Classrooms of Babel," 57.

27. Schools to Be One-Third Minority by 1995, Study Says," *Sacramento Bee,* September 13, 1991, A8.

28. "By '95, Minority Graduates to Be Majority in State, Study Says," *San Diego Union,* September 23, 1991, A42.

29. "The Nation," *Chronicle of Higher Education Almanac,* September 1, 2000, 12.

30. See Frank E. X. Dance, "The 'Concept' of Communication," *Journal of Communication* 20 (1970): 201–210; Frank E. X. Dance and Carl E. Larson, *The Functions of Human Communication* (New York: Holt, Rinehart and Winston, 1976), appendix A.

31. Dance.

32. Dance and Larson.

33. Claude E. Shannon and Warren Weaver, *The Mathematical Theory of Communication* (Urbana: University of Illinois Press, 1949).

34. Interactional models include David K. Berlo, *The Process of Communication* (New York: Holt, Rinehart and Winston, 1960); Wilbur Schramm, *The Process and Effects of Mass Communication* (Urbana: University of Illinois Press, 1954); and Bruce H. Westley and Malcolm S. MacLean, Jr., "A Conceptual Model for Communication Research," *Journalism Quarterly* 34 (1957): 31–38.

35. Dean Barnlund, *Interpersonal Communication: Survey and Studies* (Boston: Houghton Mifflin, 1968), 512.

36. Donald W. Klopf, *Intercultural Encounters: The Fundamentals of Intercultural Communications* (Englewood, CO: Morton, 1987), 23–24.

37. John C. Condon, *Good Neighbors: Communicating with the Mexicans* (Yarmouth, ME: Intercultural Press, 1985), 34.

38. Dwight Conquergood, "Rethinking Ethnography: Towards a Critical Cultural Politics," *Communication Monographs* 58 (1991): 186.

39. See, for example, Jessie Carroll Grearson and Lauren B. Smith, *Love in a Global Village: A Celebration of Intercultural Families in the Midwest* (Iowa City: University of Iowa Press, 2001).

40. Renato Rosaldo, *Culture and Truth: The Remaking of Social Analysis* (Boston: Beacon Press, 1989), 28.

Chapter 2

1. Alfred L. Kroeber and Clyde Kluckhohn, *Culture: A Critical Review of Concepts and Definitions* (Cambridge, MA: Harvard University Press, 1952).

2. Mary Jane Collier and Milt Thomas, "Cultural Identity: An Interpretive Approach," *Theories in Intercultural Communication,* ed. Young Yun Kim and William B. Gudykunst (Newbury Park, CA: Sage, 1988), 103.

3. William Wetherall, "Ethnic Ainu Seek Official Recognition," *Japan Times,* January 25–31, 1. Reprinted in *Ethnic Groups,* vol. 4, ed. Eleanor Goldstein (Boca Raton, FL: Social Issues Resources Ser., 1994), art. no. 62.

4. See, for example, Karen Brodkin, *How Jews Became White Folks and What That Says about Race in America* (New Brunswick, NJ: Rutgers University Press, 2000).

5. Brodkin, 74.

6. For an elaboration of this idea, see Brodkin; Richard Delgado and Jeanne Stefancic (eds.), *Critical White Studies: Looking Behind the Mirror* (Philadelphia: Temple University Press, 1997); Marc Edelman, "Devil, Not-Quite-White, Rootless Cosmopolitan: Tsuris in Latin America, the Bronx, and the USSR," *Composing Ethnography: Alternative Forms of Qualitative Writing,* ed. Carolyn Ellis and Arthur Bochner (Walnut Creek, CA: Altamira Press, 1996); Ruth Frankenberg, *White Women, Race Matters: The Social Construction of Whiteness* (Minneapolis: University of Minnesota Press, 1993); Ian F. Haney Lopez, *White by Law: The Legal Construction of Race* (New York: New York University Press, 1996); Noel Ignatiev, *How the Irish Became White*

(Cambridge, MA: Harvard University Press, 1995); David Stowe, "Uncolored People: The Rise of Whiteness Studies," *Lingua Franca* 6 (1996): 68–77.

7. Gustav Ichheiser, *Appearances and Realities: Misunderstanding in Human Relations* (San Francisco: Jossey-Bass, 1970), 8.

8. David McCullough, 1994 Commencement Address at the University of Pittsburgh, quoted in *Chronicle of Higher Education,* June 8, 1994, B2.

9. Geert Hofstede, *Culture's Consequences: International Differences in Work-Related Values* (Beverly Hills, CA: Sage, 1980).

10. Peter A. Andersen, "Cues of Culture: The Basis of Intercultural Differences in Nonverbal Communication," *Intercultural Communication: A Reader,* 8th ed., ed. Larry A. Samovar and Richard E. Porter (Belmont, CA: Wadsworth, 1997), 244–256; Edward T. Hall, *The Hidden Dimension* (New York: Doubleday, 1966); Miles L. Patterson, *Nonverbal Behavior: A Functional Perspective* (New York: Springer-Verlag, 1983); Carol Zinner Dolphin, "Variables in the Use of Personal Space in Intercultural Transactions," *Intercultural Communication: A Reader,* 8th ed., ed. Larry A. Samovar and Richard E. Porter (Belmont, CA: Wadsworth, 1997), 266–276.

11. Peter A. Andersen, Myron W. Lustig, and Janis F. Andersen, "Changes in Latitude, Changes in Attitude: The Relationship Between Climate and Interpersonal Communication Predispositions," *Communication Quarterly* 38 (1990): 291–311.

12. Charlotte Evans, "Barbed Wire, the Cutting Edge in Fencing," *Smithsonian* 22(4) (July 1991): 72–78, 80, 82–83.

13. See Clayton Jones, "Cultural Crosscurrents Buffet the Orient," *Christian Science Monitor,* December 8, 1993, 11, 13; Sheila Tefft, "Satellite Broadcasts Create Stir Among Asian Regimes," *Christian Science Monitor,* December 8, 1993, 12–13.

14. Daniel L. Hartl, *Our Uncertain Heritage: Genetics and Human Diversity,* 2nd ed. (New York: Harper and Row, 1985).

15. Sandra Scarr, A. J. Pakstis, S. H. Katz, and W. B. Barker, "Absence of Relationship between Degree of White Ancestry and Intellectual Skills within a Black Population," *Human Genetics* 39 (1977): 69–86; Sandra Scarr and Richard A. Weinberg, "I.Q. Test Performance of Black Children Adopted by White Families," *American Psychologist* 31 (1976): 726–739; Richard A. Weinberg, Sandra Scarr, and Irwin D. Waldman, "The Minnesota Transracial Adoption Study: A Follow-up of IQ Test Performance at Adolescence," *Intelligence* 16 (1992): 117–135. See also Thomas J. Bouchard, Jr., David T. Lykken, Matthew McGue, Nancy Segal, and Auke Tellegen, "Sources of Human Physiological Differences: The Minnesota Study of Twins Reared Apart," *Science* 250 (1990): 223–228.

15. Michael Winkelman, *Ethnic Relations in the U.S.: A Sociohistorical Cultural Systems Approach* (Minneapolis: West, 1993), 67–68.

17. Cary Quan Gelernter, "Racial Realities," *Seattle Times/Post-Intelligencer,* January 15, 1989, K1. Reprinted in *Ethnic Groups,* vol. 4., ed. Eleanor Goldstein (Boca Raton, FL: Social Issues Resources Ser., 1994), art. no. 83.

18. Linda Vigilant, Mark Stoneking, Henry Harpending, Kristen Hawkes, and Allan C. Wilson, "African Populations and the Evolution of Human Mitochondrial DNA," *Science* 253 (1991): 1503–1507.

19. For discussions of race and ethnicity as social and political distinctions rather than as a genetic one, see Richard D. Alba, *Ethnic Identity: The Transformation of White America* (New Haven: Yale University Press, 1990); Martha E. Bernal and George P. Knight, *Ethnic Identity: Formation and Transmission Among Hispanics and Other Minorities* (Albany: State University of New York Press, 1993); Stephen Cornell, *The Return of the Native: American Indian Political Resurgence* (New York: Oxford University Press, 1988); Ellis Cose, *A Nation of Strangers: Prejudice, Politics, and the Populating of America* (New York: Morrow, 1992); Yen Le Espiritu, *Asian American Panethnicity: Bridging Institutions and Identities* (Philadelphia: Temple University Press, 1992); Susan E. Keefe and Amado M. Padilla, *Chicano Ethnicity* (Albuquerque: University of New Mexico Press, 1987); Susan Olzak, *The Dynamics of Ethnic Competition and Conflict* (Stanford, CA: Stanford University Press, 1992); Michael Omi and Howard Winant, *Racial Formation in the United States: From the 1960s to the 1980s* (New York: Routledge and Kegan Paul, 1986); Felix M. Padilla, *Latino Ethnic Consciousness: The Case of Mexican Americans and Puerto Ricans in Chicago* (Notre Dame, IN: University of Notre Dame

Press, 1985); Mary C. Waters, *Ethnic Options: Choosing Identities in America* (Berkeley, CA: University of California Press, 1990).

20. Jonathan Tilove, "Racial Identity in U.S. Is a Mix of Politics, Fashion and Genetics," *Houston Chronicle,* April 26, 1992, 8A. Reprinted in *Ethnic Groups,* vol. 4, ed. Eleanor Goldstein (Boca Raton, FL: Social Issues Resources Ser., 1994), art. no. 48. See also Scott Thybony, "Against All Odds, Black Seminole Won Their Freedom," *Smithsonian,* August 1991, 90–101.

21. See, for instance, Richard J. Herrnstein and Charles Murray, *The Bell Curve: Intelligence and Class Structure in American Life* (New York: Free Press, 1994).

22. See Richard L. Worsnop, "Native Americans," *CQ [Congressional Quarterly] Researcher,* May 8, 1992, 387–403. Reprinted in *Ethnic Groups,* vol. 4, ed. Eleanor Goldstein (Boca Raton, FL: Social Issues Resources Ser., 1994), art. no. 52.

23. Marshall R. Singer, *Intercultural Communication: A Perceptual Approach* (Englewood Cliffs, NJ: Prentice Hall, 1987).

24. The idea that the degree of heterogeneity among participants distinguishes intercultural from intracultural communication, and thereby results in a continuum of "interculturalness" of the communication, was first introduced by L. E. Sarbaugh, *Intercultural Communication* (Rochelle Park, NJ: Hayden, 1979).

25. For a more detailed discussion of the relationships among these terms, see Molefi Kete Asante and William B. Gudykunst (eds.), *Handbook of Intercultural Communication* (Newbury Park, CA: Sage, 1989), 7–13.

Chapter 3

1. The melting pot metaphor for U.S. cultural diversity was popularized by Israel Zangwell's play of 1908, *The Melting Pot.* The idea was anticipated over a hundred years earlier in Crèvecoeur's description of America: "Here individuals of all nations are melted into a new race of men, whose labors and posterity will one day cause great changes in the world." See J. Hector St. John Crèvecoeur, *Letter from an American Farmer* (New York: Albert and Charles Boni, 1782/1925), 55; Israel Zangwell, *The Melting Pot. Drama in Four Acts* (New York: Arno Press, 1908/1975).

2. Judith N. Martin, Robert L. Krizek, Thomas K. Nakayama, and Lisa Bradford, "Exploring Whiteness: A Study of Self Labels for White Americans," *Communication Quarterly* 44 (1996): 125–144; Thomas K. Nakayama and Robert L. Krizek, "Whiteness: A Strategic Rhetoric," *Quarterly Journal of Speech* 81 (1995): 291–309.

3. See Rodolfo O. de la Garza, Louis DeSipio, F. Chris Garcia, John Garcia, and Angelo Falcon, *Latino Voices: Mexican, Puerto Rican, & Cuban Perspectives on American Politics* (Boulder, CO: Westview Press, 1992).

4. James Diego Vigil, *From Indians to Chicanos: The Dynamics of Mexican American Culture* (Prospect Heights, IL: Waveland Press, 1980), 1.

5. Mark Z. Barabak, "Differences Found Among U.S. Hispanics," *San Diego Union,* August 30, 1991, A2.

6. Juan L. Gonzales, Jr., *Racial and Ethnic Groups in America* (Dubuque, IA: Kendall/Hunt, 1990), 199.

7. Earl Shorris, "The Latino vs. Hispanic Controversy," *San Diego Union-Tribune,* October 29, 1992, B11. See also Earl Shorris, *Latinos: A Biography of the People* (New York: Norton, 1992); Earl Shorris, "Latinos: The Complexity of Identity," *Report on the Americas* 26 (1992): 19–26.

8. Michael L. Hecht and Sidney Ribeau, "Sociocultural Roots of Ethnic Identity: A Look at Black America," *Journal of Black Studies* 21 (1991): 501–513.

9. For a discussion of the concept and measurement of communicative competence, see Arthur P. Bochner and Clifford W. Kelly, "Interpersonal Competence: Rationale, Philosophy, and Implementation of a Conceptual Framework," *Speech Teacher* 23 (1974): 279–301; Myron W. Lustig and Brian H. Spitzberg, "Methodological Issues in the Study of Intercultural Communication Competence," *Intercultural Communication Competence,* ed. Richard L. Wiseman and Jolene Koester (Newbury Park, CA: Sage, 1993), 153–167; Charles Pavitt, "The Ideal Communicator as the Basis for Competence Judgments of Self and Friend," *Communication Reports* 3 (1990): 9–14; Brian H. Spitzberg, "Communication Competence as Knowledge, Skill, and Impression," *Communication Education* 32 (1983): 323–329; Brian H. Spitzberg, "Issues in the Study of Communicative Competence," *Progress in*

Communication Sciences (1987): 1–46; Brian H. Spitzberg, "Communication Competence: Measures of Perceived Effectiveness," *A Handbook for the Study of Human Communication,* ed. Charles H. Tardy (Norwood, NJ: Ablex, 1988), 67–105; Brian H. Spitzberg, "Issues in the Development of a Theory of Interpersonal Competence in the Intercultural Context," *International Journal of Intercultural Relations* 13 (1989): 241–268; Brian H. Spitzberg, "An Examination of Trait Measures of Interpersonal Competence," *Communication Research* 3 (1991): 22–29; Brian H. Spitzberg, "The Dark Side of (In)Competence," *The Dark Side of Interpersonal Communication,* ed. William R. Cupach and Brian H. Spitzberg (Hillsdale, NJ: Erlbaum, 1994), 25–49; Brian H. Spitzberg and Claire C. Brunner, "Toward a Theoretical Integration of Context and Competence Research," *Western Journal of Speech Communication* 55 (1991): 28–46; Brian H. Spitzberg and William R. Cupach, *Handbook of Interpersonal Competence Research* (New York: Springer-Verlag, 1989); Brian H. Spitzberg and William R. Cupach, *Interpersonal Communication Competence* (Beverly Hills, CA: Sage, 1984); Brian H. Spitzberg and Michael L. Hecht, "A Component Model of Relational Competence," *Human Communication Research* 10 (1984): 575–599; John Wiemann, "Explication and Test of a Model of Communicative Competence," *Human Communication Research* 3 (1977): 195–213; John M. Wiemann and Philip M. Backlund, "Current Theory and Research in Communicative Competence," *Review of Educational Research* 50 (1980): 185–199; John M. Wiemann and James J. Bradic, "Metatheoretical Issues in the Study of Communicative Competence," *Progress in Communication Sciences* 9 (1988): 261–284.

10. Brian H. Spitzberg, "Communication Competence: Measures of Perceived Effectiveness," *A Handbook for the Study of Human Communication,* ed. Charles H. Tardy (Norwood, NJ: Ablex, 1988), 67–105.

11. William R. Cupach and T. Todd Imahori, "Identity Management Theory: Communication Competence in Intercultural Episodes and Relationships," *Intercultural Communication Competence,* ed. Richard L. Wiseman and Jolene Koester (Newbury Park, CA: Sage, 1993), 112–131; T. Todd Imahori and Mary L. Lanigan, "Relational Model of Intercultural Communication Competence," *International Journal of Intercultural Relations* 13 (1989): 269–286.

12. Fathi S. Yousef, "Human Resource Management: Aspects of Intercultural Relations in U.S. Organizations," *Intercultural Communication: A Reader,* 5th ed., ed. Larry A. Samovar and Richard E. Porter (Belmont, CA: Wadsworth, 1988), 175–182.

13. See, for example, John T. Masterson, Norman H. Watson, and Elaine J. Cichon, "Cultural Differences in Public Speaking," *World Communication* 20 (1991): 39–47.

14. Jolene Koester and Margaret Olebe, "The Behavioral Assessment Scale for Intercultural Communication Effectiveness," *International Journal of Intercultural Relations* 12 (1988): 233–246; Margaret Olebe and Jolene Koester, "Exploring the Cross-Cultural Equivalence of the Behavioral Assessment Scale for Intercultural Communication," *International Journal of Intercultural Relations* 13 (1989): 333–347.

15. Brent D. Ruben, "Assessing Communication Competency for Intercultural Adaptation," *Group and Organization Studies* 1 (1976): 334–354; Brent D. Ruben, Lawrence R. Askling, and Daniel J. Kealey, "Cross-Cultural Effectiveness," *Overview of Intercultural Training, Education, and Research, Vol. I: Theory,* ed. David S. Hoopes, Paul B. Pedersen, and George W. Renwick (Washington, DC: Society for Intercultural Education, Training and Research, 1977), 92–105; Brent D. Ruben and Daniel J. Kealey, "Behavioral Assessment of Communication Competency and the Prediction of Cross-Cultural Adaptation," *International Journal of Intercultural Relations* 3 (1979): 15–48.

Chapter 4

1. Milton Rokeach, *Beliefs, Attitudes, and Values: A Theory of Organization and Change* (San Francisco: Jossey-Bass, 1969).

2. Elisabeth Bumiller, *May You Be the Mother of a Hundred Sons* (New York: Fawcett Columbine, 1990), 11.

3. Milton Rokeach, *The Nature of Human Values* (New York: Free Press, 1973); Milton Rokeach, "Value Theory and Communication Research: Review and Commentary," *Communication*

Yearbook 3, ed. Dan Nimmo (New Brunswick, NJ: Transaction, 1979), 7–28.

4. Shalom H. Schwartz, "Universals in the Content and Structure of Values: Theoretical Advances and Empirical Tests in 20 Countries," *Advances in Experimental Social Psychology,* vol. 25, ed. Mark P. Zanna (San Diego: Academic Press, 1992), 1–65; Shalom H. Schwartz, "Are There Universal Aspects in the Structure and Content of Values?" *Journal of Social Issues* 50 (1994): 19–45; Shalom H. Schwartz and Lilach Sagiv, "Identifying Culture-Specifics in the Content and Structure of Values," *Journal of Cross-Cultural Psychology* 26 (1995): 92–116; Shalom H. Schwartz, Markku Verasalo, Avishai Antonovsky, and Lilach Sagiv, "Value Priorities and Social Desirability: Much Substance, Some Style," *British Journal of Social Psychology* 36 (1997): 3–18. See also Paul R. Abrahamson and Ronald Inglehart, *Value Change in Global Perspective* (Ann Arbor: University of Michigan Press, 1995).

5. Florence Rockwood Kluckhohn and Fred L. Strodtbeck, *Variations in Value Orientations* (Evanston, IL: Row, Peterson, 1960).

6. Our primary sources for this section include John C. Condon and Fathi Yousef, *An Introduction to Intercultural Communication* (Indianapolis: Bobbs-Merrill, 1975); Edward C. Stewart, *American Cultural Patterns: A Cross-Cultural Perspective* (Pittsburgh: Regional Council for International Education, 1971); Edward C. Stewart and Milton J. Bennett, *American Cultural Patterns: A Cross-Cultural Perspective,* rev. ed. (Yarmouth, ME: Intercultural Press, 1991). Excellent resources with thorough descriptions of the cultural patterns of U.S. American cultural groups include Don C. Locke, *Increasing Multicultural Understanding: A Comprehensive Model* (Newbury Park, CA: Sage, 1992); Eleanor W. Lynch and Marci J. Hanson, *Developing Cross-Cultural Competence: A Guide for Working with Young Children and Their Families* (Baltimore: Paul Brookes, 1992); and Esther Wanning, *Culture Shock: USA* (Singapore: Times Books International, 1991).

7. See, for example, Ringo Ma, "The Role of Unofficial Intermediaries in Interpersonal Conflicts in the Chinese Culture," *Communication Quarterly* 40 (1992): 269–278.

8. Mary Jane Collier, Sidney A. Ribeau, and Michael L. Hecht, "Intracultural Communication Rules and Outcomes Within Three Domestic Cultures," *International Journal of Intercultural Relations* 10 (1986): 452. Also see Mary Jane Collier, "A Comparison of Conversations Among and Between Domestic Cultural Groups: How Intra- and Intercultural Competencies Vary," *Communication Quarterly* 36 (1988): 122–144.

9. Jack L. Daniel and Geneva Smitherman, "How I Got Over: Communication Dynamics in the Black Community," *Quarterly Journal of Speech* 62 (1976): 29.

10. Daniel and Smitherman, 31.

11. Jamake Highwater, *The Primal Mind* (New York: New American Library, 1981).

12. Melvin Delgado, "Hispanic Cultural Values: Implications for Groups," *Small Group Behavior* 12 (1981): 75.

13. Daniel and Smitherman, 29.

14. Daniel and Smitherman, 32.

Chapter 5

1. Edward T. Hall, *Beyond Culture* (Garden City, NY: Anchor, 1977).

2. Geert Hofstede, *Culture's Consequences: Comparing Values, Behaviors, Institutions, and Organizations across Nations,* 2nd ed. (Thousand Oaks, CA: Sage, 2001); Geert Hofstede, *Cultures and Organizations: Software of the Mind* (London: McGraw-Hill, 1991).

3. Hofstede, *Culture's Consequences*; Denise Rotondo Fernandez, Dawn S. Carlson, Lee P. Stepina, and Joel D. Nicholson, "Hofstede's Country Classification 25 Years Later," *Journal of Social Psychology* 137 (1997): 43–54.

4. Hui-Ching Chang and G. Richard Holt, "More Than Relationship: Chinese Interaction and the Principle of *Kuan-Hsi,*" *Communication Quarterly* 39 (1991): 268.

5. See Harry C. Triandis, *The Analysis of Subjective Culture* (New York: Wiley, 1972); C. Harry Hui and Harry C. Triandis, "Individualism-Collectivism: A Study of Cross-Cultural Researchers," *Journal of Cross-Cultural Psychology* 17 (1986): 225–248.

6. Data from twenty-two countries are reported in: Chinese Culture Connection, "Chinese Values

and the Search for Culture-Free Dimensions of Culture," *Journal of Cross-Cultural Psychology* 18 (1987): 143–164. Data on the People's Republic of China, which were added to the survey after the initial publication of results, can be found in Geert Hofstede, *Cultures and Organizations: Software of the Mind* (London: McGraw-Hill, 1991), 166. Data for the remaining four countries are from subsequent studies conducted by various researchers and reported in Hofstede, *Culture's Consequences*.

7. Hofstede, *Cultures and Organizations,* 164–166; *Culture's Consequences,* 360.

8. Hofstede, *Cultures and Organizations,* 164; *Culture's Consequences.*

9. We draw on the following sources for the ideas presented: Chang and Holt 251–271; Guo-Ming Chen and Jensen Chung, "The Impact of Confucianism on Organizational Communication," *Communication Quarterly* 42 (1994): 93–105; Raymond Dawson, *Confucius* (New York: Hill and Wang, 1982); Hofstede, *Culture's Consequences*; Geert Hofstede and Michael Harris Bond, "The Confucius Connection: From Cultural Roots to Economic Growth," *Organizational Dynamics* 16 (1988): 5–21; Sonja Vegdahl Hur and Ben Seungwa Hur, *Culture Shock! Korea* (Singapore: Times Books International, 1988), 34–45; June Ock Yum, "Korean Philosophy and Communication," *Communication Theory: Eastern and Western Perspectives,* ed. D. Lawrence Kincaid (San Diego: Academic Press, 1987), 71–86; June Ock Yum, "The Practice of *Uye-Ri* in Interpersonal Relationships," *Communication Theory: Eastern and Western Perspectives,* ed. D. Lawrence Kincaid (San Diego: Academic Press, 1987), 87–100; June Ock Yum, "The Impact of Confucianism on Interpersonal Relationships and Communication Patterns in East Asia," *Communication Monographs* 55 (1988): 374–388. For an alternative view on the centrality of Confucian values to East Asian cultures, see Hui-Ching Chang and G. Richard Holt, "The Concept of *Yuan* and Chinese Interpersonal Relationships," *Cross-Cultural Interpersonal Communication,* ed. Stella Ting-Toomey and Felipe Korzenny (Newbury Park, CA: Sage, 1991), 28–57.

10. Chang and Holt, 253–254.

11. Donald Dale Jackson, " 'Behave Like Your Actions Reflect on All Chinese,' " *Smithsonian*, February 1991, 115.

12. Yum, "The Practice of *Uye-Ri,*" 94.

Chapter 6

1. Marilyn Brewer and Donald T. Campbell, *Ethnocentrism and Intergroup Attitudes* (New York: Wiley, 1976).

2. Our labels are analogous to Triandis's tripartite distinction among one's collective self, public self, and private self. See Harry C. Triandis, "The Self and Social Behavior in Differing Cultural Contexts," *Psychological Review* 96 (1989): 506–520. See also Henri Tajfel, *Differentiation between Social Groups* (London: Academic Press, 1978); Henri Tajfel, *Human Groups and Social Categories: Studies in Social Psychology* (Cambridge: Cambridge University Press, 1981).

3. Our discussion of the stages of cultural identity draws heavily upon the works of Jean S. Phinney, particularly Jean S. Phinney, "A Three-Stage Model of Ethnic Identity Development in Adolescence," *Ethnic Identity: Formation and Transmission among Hispanics and Other Minorities,* ed. Martha E. Bernal and George P. Knight (Albany: State University of New York Press, 1993), 61–79. See also Jean S. Phinney, "Ethnic Identity in Adolescents and Adults: Review of Research," *Psychological Bulletin* 108 (1990): 499–514; Jean S. Phinney, "Ethnic Identity and Self-Esteem: A Review and Integration," *Hispanic Journal of Behavioral Sciences* 13 (1991): 193–208.

4. Frances E. Aboud, "Interest in Ethnic Information: A Cross-Cultural Developmental Study," *Journal of Cross-Cultural Psychology* 7 (1977): 289–300; Frances E. Aboud, "The Development of Ethnic Self-Identification and Attitudes," *Children's Ethnic Socialization,* ed. Jean S. Phinney and Mary Jane Rotheram (Newbury Park, CA: Sage, 1987), 32–55; Frances E. Aboud, *Children and Prejudice* (New York: Blackwell, 1988).

5. See, for example, Richard D. Alba, *Ethnic Identity: The Transformation of White America* (New Haven, CT: Yale University Press, 1990); Theodore W. Allen, *The Invention of the White Race: Racial Oppression and Social Control* (New York: Verso, 1994); Russell Ferguson, "Introduction: Invisible Center," *Out There: Marginaliza-*

tion and Contemporary Cultures, ed. Russell Ferguson, Martha Gever, T. M. Trinh, and C. West (Cambridge, MA: MIT Press, 1992), 9–14; Ruth Frankenburg, *White Women, Race Matters: The Social Construction of Whiteness* (Minneapolis: University of Minnesota Press, 1993); Judith N. Martin, Robert L. Krizek, Thomas K. Nakayama, and Lisa Bradford, "Exploring Whiteness: A Study of Self Labels for White Americans," *Communication Quarterly* 44 (1996): 125–144; Thomas K. Nakayama and Robert L. Krizek, "Whiteness: A Strategic Rhetoric," *Quarterly Journal of Speech* 81 (1995): 291–309.

6. Martin et al., 125.

7. Fernando P. Delgado, "Chicano Movement Rhetoric: An Ideographic Interpretation," *Communication Quarterly* 43 (1995): 446–454; Fernando P. Delgado, "Chicano Ideology Revisited: Rap Music and the (Re)Articulation of Chicanismo," *Western Journal of Communication* 62 (1998): 95–113; Fernando P. Delgado, "When the Silenced Speak: The Textualization and Complications of Latina/o Identity," *Western Journal of Communication* 62 (1998): 420–438; Fernando P. Delgado, "All Along the Border: Kid Frost and the Performance of Brown Masculinity," *Text and Performance Quarterly* 20 (2000): 388–401.

8. For interesting research on identity change among Asian Indians and Chinese Americans see, respectively, Jean Bacon, "Constructing Collective Ethnic Identities: The Case of Second Generation Asian Indians," *Qualitative Sociology* 22 (1999): 141–160; Zhuojun Joyce Chen, "Chinese-American Children's Ethnic Identity: Measurement and Implications," *Communication Studies* 51 (2000): 74–95.

9. Young Yun Kim, "Identity Development: From Cultural to Intercultural," *Interaction and Identity,* ed. Hartmut B. Mokros (New Brunswick, NJ: Transaction, 1996), 350.

10. Edward Dunbar, "The Personal Dimensions of Difference Scale: Measuring Multi-Group Identity with Four Ethnic Groups," *International Journal of Intercultural Relations* 21 (1997): 1–28.

11. William G. Sumner, *Folkways* (Boston: Ginn, 1940), 27.

12. Sumner.

13. Walter Lippmann, *Public Opinion* (New York: Harcourt, Brace, 1922), 25.

14. See Carl Friedrich Graumann and Margret Wintermantel, "Discriminatory Speech Acts: A Functional Approach," *Stereotyping and Prejudice: Changing Conceptions,* ed. Daniel Bar-Tal, Carl F. Graumann, Arie W. Kruglanski, and Wolfgang Stroebe (New York: Springer-Verlag, 1989), 183–204.

15. Henri Tajfel, *Differentiation Between Social Groups: Studies in the Social Psychology of Intergroup Relations* (New York: Academic Press, 1978).

15. Marilynn B. Brewer, "When Stereotypes Lead to Stereotyping: The Use of Stereotypes in Person Perception," *Stereotypes and Stereotyping,* ed. C. Neil Macrae, Charles Stangor, and Miles Hewstone (New York: Guilford, 1996), 254–275; Diane M. Mackie, David L. Hamilton, Joshua Susskind, and Francine Rosselli, "Social Psychological Foundations of Stereotype Formation," *Stereotypes and Stereotyping,* ed. C. Neil Macrae, Charles Stangor, and Miles Hewstone (New York: Guilford, 1996), 41–78; Charles Stangor and Mark Schaller, "Stereotypes as Individual and Collective Representations," *Stereotypes and Stereotyping,* ed. C. Neil Macrae, Charles Stangor, and Miles Hewstone (New York: Guilford, 1996), 3–37.

17. Micah S. Thompson, Charles M. Judd, and Bernadette Park, "The Consequences of Communicating Social Stereotypes," *Journal of Experimental Social Psychology* 36 (2000): 567–599; Vincent Y. Yzerbyt, Alastair Coull, and Steve J. Rocher, "Fencing Off the Deviant: The Role of Cognitive Resources in the Maintenance of Stereotypes," *Journal of Personality and Social Psychology* 77(3) (1999): 449–462.

18. See Charles M. Judd and Bernadette Park, "Definition and Assessment of Accuracy in Social Stereotypes," *Psychological Review* 100 (1993): 109–128; Carey S. Ryan, Bernadette Park, and Charles M. Judd, "Assessing Stereotype Accuracy: Implications for Understanding the Stereotyping Process," *Stereotypes and Stereotyping,* ed. C. Neil Macrae, Charles Stangor, and Miles Hewstone (New York: Guilford, 1996), 121–157.

19. Marilynn B. Brewer, "Social Identity, Distinctiveness, and In-Group Homogeneity," *Social Cognition* 11 (1993): 150–164; E. E. Jones, G. C. Wood, and G. A. Quattrone, "Perceived Variability of Personal Characteristics in In-Groups and Out-

Groups: The Role of Knowledge and Evaluation," *Personality and Social Psychology Bulletin* 7 (1981): 523–528; Charles M. Judd and Bernadette Park, "Out-Group Homogeneity: Judgments of Variability at the Individual and Group Levels," *Journal of Personality and Social Psychology* 54 (1988): 778–788; P. W. Linville and E. E. Jones, "Polarized Appraisals of Out-Group Members," *Journal of Personality and Social Psychology* 38 (1980): 689–703; Brian Mullen and L. Hu, "Perceptions of Ingroup and Outgroup Variability: A Meta-Analytic Integration," *Basic and Applied Social Psychology* 10 (1989): 233–252; Thomas M. Ostrom, Sandra L. Carpenter, Constantine Sedikides, and Fan Li, "Differential Processing of In-Group and Out-Group Information," *Journal of Personality and Social Psychology* 64 (1993): 21–34.

20. David Barsamian, "Albert Mokhiber: Cultural Images, Politics, and Arab Americans," *Z Magazine,* May 1993, 46–50. Reprinted in *Ethnic Groups,* vol. 4, ed. Eleanor Goldstein (Boca Raton, FL: Social Issues Resources Ser., 1994), art. no. 73.

21. Ziva Kunda and Bonnie Sherman-Williams, "Stereotypes and the Construal of Individuating Information," *Personality and Social Psychology Bulletin* 19 (1993): 97.

22. John J. Seta and Catherine E. Seta, "Stereotypes and the Generation of Compensatory and Noncompensatory Expectancies of Group Members," *Personality and Social Psychology Bulletin* 19 (1993): 722–731.

23. C. Neil Macrae, Alan B. Milne, and Galen V. Bodenhausen, "Stereotypes as Energy-Saving Devices: A Peek Inside the Cognitive Toolbox," *Journal of Personality and Social Psychology* 66 (1994): 37–47.

24. Judee K. Burgoon, Charles R. Berger, and Vincent Waldron, "Mindfulness and Interpersonal Communication," *Journal of Social Issues* 56 (2000): 105–127.

25. Gordon W. Allport, *The Nature of Prejudice* (New York: Macmillan, 1954).

26. John F. Dovidio, John C. Brigham, Blair T. Johnson, and Samuel L. Gaertner, "Stereotyping, Prejudice, and Discrimination: A Closer Look," *Stereotypes and Stereotyping,* ed. C. Neil Macrae, Charles Stangor, and Miles Hewstone (New York: Guilford, 1996), 276–319.

27. Richard W. Brislin, *Cross-Cultural Encounters: Face-to-Face Interaction* (New York: Pergamon Press, 1981), 42–49.

28. For a recent test of the ego-defensive functions of attitudes, see Maria Knight Lapinski and Franklin Boster, "Modeling the Ego-Defensive Function of Attitudes," *Communication Monographs* 68 (2001): 314–324.

29. Steven Fein and Steven J. Spencer, "Prejudice as Self-Image Maintenance: Affirming the Self Through Derogating Others," *Journal of Personality and Social Psychology* 73 (1997): 31–44.

30. Teun A. van Dijk, *Communicating Racism: Ethnic Prejudice in Thought and Talk* (Newbury Park, CA: Sage, 1987).

31. Marilynn B. Brewer, "The Psychology of Prejudice: Ingroup Love or Outgroup Hate?" *Journal of Social Issues* 55 (1999): 429–444. See also Marilynn B. Brewer and Wendi L. Gardner, "Who Is This 'We'? Levels of Collective Identity and Self Representations," *Journal of Personality and Social Psychology* 71 (1996): 83–93.

32. For a discussion of the causes and consequences of some forms of racism, see Joe R. Feagin and Hernán Vera, *White Racism: The Basics* (New York: Routledge, 1995).

33. Robert Blauner, *Racial Oppression in America* (New York: Harper and Row, 1972), 112.

34. Dalmas A. Taylor, "Race Prejudice, Discrimination, and Racism," *Social Psychology,* ed. A. Kahn, E. Donnerstein, and M. Donnerstein (Dubuque, IA: Wm. C. Brown, 1984); cited in Phyllis A. Katz and Dalmas A. Taylor, "Introduction," *Eliminating Racism: Profiles in Controversy,* ed. Phyllis A. Katz and Dalmas A. Taylor (New York: Plenum, 1988), 6.

35. Katz and Taylor, 7.

36. Blauner.

37. James M. Jones, "Racism in Black and White: A Bicultural Model of Reaction and Evolution," *Eliminating Racism: Profiles in Controversy,* ed. Phyllis A. Katz and Dalmas A. Taylor (New York: Plenum, 1988), 130–131.

38. S. Elizabeth Bird, "Gendered Construction of the American Indian in Popular Media," *Journal of Communication* 49 (1999): 78.

39. Bird 80. See also Richard Morris, "Educating Savages," *Quarterly Journal of Speech* 83 (1997): 152–171.

40. Jones, 118–126.

41. Katz and Taylor, 7.

42. Jenny Yamoto, "Something about the Subject Makes It Hard to Name," *Race, Class, and Gender in the United States: An Integrated Study,* 2nd ed., ed. Paula S. Rothenberg (New York: St. Martin's Press, 1992), 58.

43. For discussions of racism and prejudice, see Benjamin P. Bowser, Gale S. Auletta, and Terry Jones, *Confronting Diversity Issues on Campus* (Newbury Park, CA: Sage, 1994); John C. Brigham, "College Students' Racial Attitudes," *Journal of Applied Social Psychology* 23 (1993): 1933–1967; Richard W. Brislin, "Prejudice and Intergroup Communication," *Intergroup Communication,* ed. William B. Gudykunst (London: Arnold, 1986), 74–85; Brislin (1981): 42–49; Charles E. Case, Andrew M. Greeley, and Stephan Fuchs, "Social Determinants of Racial Prejudice," *Sociological Perspectives* 32 (1989): 469–483; Samuel L. Gaertner and John F. Dovidio, "The Aversive Form of Racism," *Prejudice, Discrimination and Racism: Theory and Research,* ed. John F. Dovidio and Samuel L. Gaertner (New York: Academic Press, 1986), 61–89; David Milner, "Racial Prejudice," *Intergroup Behavior,* ed. John C. Turner and Howard Giles (Chicago: University of Chicago Press, 1981), 102–143; Albert Ramirez, "Racism toward Hispanics: The Culturally Monolithic Society," *Eliminating Racism: Profiles in Controversy,* ed. Phyllis A. Katz and Dalmas A. Taylor (New York: Plenum, 1988), 137–157; David O. Sears, "Symbolic Racism," *Eliminating Racism: Profiles in Controversy,* ed. Phyllis A. Katz and Dalmas A. Taylor (New York: Plenum, 1988), 53–84; Key Sun, "Two Types of Prejudice and Their Causes," *American Psychologist* 48 (1993): 1152–1153; Ian Vine, "Inclusive Fitness and the Self-System: The Roles of Human Nature and Sociocultural Processes in Intergroup Discrimination," *The Sociobiology of Ethnocentrism: Evolutionary Dimensions of Xenophobia, Discrimination, Racism, and Nationalism,* ed. Vernon Reynolds, Vincent Falger, and Ian Vine (London: Croom Helm, 1987), 60–80; Bernd Wittenbrink, Charles M. Judd, and Bernadette Park, "Evidence for Racial Prejudice at the Implicit Level and Its Relationship with Questionnaire Measures," *Journal of Personality and Social Psychology* 72 (1997): 262–274.

44. Jacqueline N. Sawires and M. Jean Peacock, "Symbolic Racism and Voting Behavior on Proposition 209," *Journal of Applied Social Psychology* 30 (2000): 2092–2099.

45. Brigham, 1934.

46. For summaries of these studies, see William B. Gudykunst (ed.), *Intergroup Communication* (London: Arnold, 1986); Ellen Bouchard Ryan and Howard Giles (eds.), *Attitudes Toward Language Variation: Social and Applied Contexts* (London: Arnold, 1982).

47. Cynthia Gallois, Arlene Franklyn-Stokes, Howard Giles, and Nikolas Coupland, "Communication Accommodation in Intercultural Encounters," *Theories in Intercultural Communication,* ed. Young Yun Kim and William B. Gudykunst (Newbury Park, CA: Sage, 1988), 157–188.

48. Yehuda Amir, "Contact Hypothesis in Ethnic Relations," *Psychological Bulletin* 71 (1969): 319–343.

49. Gallois et al.

50. Miles Hewstone and Rupert Brown, "Contact Is Not Enough: An Intergroup Perspective on the 'Contact Hypothesis,'" *Contact and Conflict in Intergroup Encounters,* ed. Miles Hewstone and Rupert Brown (Oxford: Blackwell, 1986), 1–44.

51. Miles Hewstone and Howard Giles, "Social Groups and Social Stereotypes in Intergroup Communication: A Review and Model of Intergroup Communication Breakdown," *Intergroup Communication,* ed. William B. Gudykunst (London: Arnold, 1986), 10–26.

52. The definition is modified from one proposed by Young Yun Kim. See Young Yun Kim, "Adapting to an Unfamiliar Culture," *Handbook of International and Intercultural Communication,* 2nd ed., ed. William B. Gudykunst and Bella Mody (Thousand Oaks, CA: Sage, 2002), 260; Young Yun Kim, *Becoming Intercultural: An Integrative Theory of Communication and Cross-Cultural Adaptation* (Thousand Oaks, CA: Sage, 2001), 31.

53. John W. Berry, Uichol Kim, and Pawel Boski, "Psychological Acculturation of Immigrants," *Cross-Cultural Adaptation: Current Approaches,* ed. Young Yun Kim and William B. Gudykunst (Newbury Park, CA: Sage, 1988).

54. Kalvero Oberg, "Cultural Shock: Adjustment to New Cultural Environments," *Practical Anthropology* 7 (1960): 176.

55. Oberg.

56. Michael Brein and Kenneth H. David, "Intercultural Communication and the Adjustment of the Sojourner," *Psychological Bulletin* 76 (1971): 215–230; Kevin F. Gaw, "Reverse Culture Shock in Students Returning from Overseas," *International Journal of Intercultural Relations* 24 (2000): 83–104; J. Gullahorn and J. E. Gullahorn, "An Extension of the U-Curve Hypothesis," *Journal of Social Issues* 14 (1963): 33–47; Daniel J. Kealey, "A Study of Cross-Cultural Effectiveness: Theoretical Issues, Practical Applications," *International Journal of Intercultural Relations* 13 (1989): 387–428; Otto Klineberg and W. Frank Hull, *At a Foreign University: An International Study of Adaptation and Coping* (New York: Praeger, 1979); Jolene Koester, "Communication and the Intercultural Reentry: A Course Proposal," *Communication Education* 23 (1984): 251–256; Judith N. Martin, "The Intercultural Reentry: Conceptualizations and Suggestions for Future Research," *International Journal of Intercultural Relations* 8 (1984): 115–134.

57. See, for instance, Sarah Brabant, C. Eddie Palmer, and Robert Gramling, "Returning Home: An Empirical Investigation of Cross-Cultural Reentry," *International Journal of Intercultural Relations* 14 (1990): 387–404.

58. Walter Enloe and Philip Lewin, "Issues of Integration Abroad and Readjustment to Japan of Japanese Returnees," *International Journal of Intercultural Relations* 11 (1987): 223–248; Louise H. Kidder, "Requirements for Being 'Japanese': Stories of Returnees," *International Journal of Intercultural Relations* 16 (1992): 383–393.

59. Enloe and Lewin, 235.

60. Nancy Adler, "Re-Entry: Managing Cross-Cultural Transitions," *Group and Organization Studies* 6 (1981): 341–356; Austin Church, "Sojourner Adjustment," *Psychological Bulletin* 91 (1982): 540–572; Dennison Nash, "The Course of Sojourner Adaptation: A New Test of the U-Curve Hypothesis," *Human Organization* 50 (1991): 283–286.

61. See, for example, Young Yun Kim and Brent D. Ruben, "Intercultural Transformation: A Systems Theory," *Theories in Intercultural Communication,* ed. Young Yun Kim and William B. Gudykunst (Newbury Park, CA: Sage, 1988), 299–321.

62. Daniel J. Kealey, "A Study of Cross-Cultural Effectiveness: Theoretical Issues, Practical Applica-

tions," *International Journal of Intercultural Relations* 13 (1989): 387–428.

63. Andrew G. Ryder, Lynn E. Alden, and Delroy L. Paulhus. "Is Acculturation Unidimensional or Bidimensional? A Head-to-Head Comparison in the Prediction of Personality, Self-Identity, and Adjustment," *Journal of Personality and Social Psychology* 79 (2000): 49–65.

64. Mitchell R. Hammer, William B. Gudykunst, and Richard L. Wiseman, "Dimensions of Intercultural Effectiveness: An Exploratory Study," *International Journal of Intercultural Relations* 2 (1978): 382–393.

65. See Colleen Ward and Antony Kennedy, "Locus of Control, Mood Disturbance, and Social Difficulty During Cross-Cultural Transitions," *International Journal of Intercultural Relations* 2 (1992): 175–194; Colleen Ward and Antony Kennedy, "Acculturation and Cross-Cultural Adaptation of British Residents in Hong Kong," *Journal of Social Psychology* 133 (1993): 395–397; Colleen Ward and Antony Kennedy, "The Measurement of Sociocultural Adaptation," *International Journal of Intercultural Relations* 23 (1999): 659–677; Colleen Ward and Wendy Searle, "The Impact of Value Discrepancies and Cultural Identity on Psychological and Sociological Adjustment of Sojourners," *International Journal of Intercultural Relations* 15 (1991): 209–225.

66. Guo-Ming Chen, "Communication Adaptability and Interaction Involvement as Predictors of Cross-Cultural Adjustment," *Communication Research Reports* 9 (1992): 33–41.

67. Berry, Kim, and Boski, 66.

68. Berry, Kim, and Boski, 71.

69. Young Yun Kim and Brent D. Ruben, "Intercultural Transformation: A Systems Approach," *Theories in Intercultural Communication,* ed. Young Yun Kim and William B. Gudykunst (Newbury Park, CA: Sage, 1988), 313–314.

Chapter 7

1. Peter A. Andersen, "Consciousness, Cognition, and Communication," *Western Journal of Speech Communication* 50 (1986): 87–101; Peter A. Andersen, John P. Garrison, and Janis F. Andersen, "Implications of a Neurophysiological Approach for the Study of Nonverbal Communication," *Human Communication Research* 6 (1979): 74–89.

2. Albert E. Scheflen, "On Communication Processes," *Nonverbal Behavior: Applications and Cross-Cultural Implications,* ed. Aaron Wolfgang (New York: Academic Press, 1979), 1–16.

3. Sheila J. Ramsey, "Nonverbal Behavior: An Intercultural Perspective," *Handbook of Intercultural Communication,* ed. Molefi Kete Asante, Eileen Newmark, and Cecil A. Blake (Beverly Hills, CA: Sage, 1979), 111.

4. Edward T. Hall, *The Silent Language* (Garden City, NY: Doubleday, 1959).

5. Charles Darwin, *The Expression of Emotions in Man and Animals* (New York: Appleton, 1872).

6. Michael Argyle, *Bodily Communication* (New York: International Universities Press, 1975), 95.

7. Paul Ekman and Wallace V. Friesen, "Constants across Cultures in the Face and Emotion," *Journal of Personality and Social Psychology* 17 (1971): 124–129; Paul Ekman and Wallace V. Friesen, *Unmasking the Face* (Englewood Cliffs, NJ: Prentice-Hall, 1975); Alan J. Fridlund, Paul Ekman, and Harriet Oster, "Facial Expressions of Emotion: Review of Literature, 1970–1983," *Nonverbal Behavior and Communication,* 2nd ed., ed. Aron W. Siegman and Stanley Feldstein (Hillsdale, NJ: Erlbaum, 1987), 143–224.

8. Robert Ardrey, *The Territorial Imperative: A Personal Inquiry into the Animal Origins of Property and Nations* (New York: Atheneum, 1966).

9. Judith N. Martin, Mitchell R. Hammer, and Lisa Bradford, "The Influence of Cultural and Situational Contexts on Hispanic and Non-Hispanic Communication Competence Behaviors," *Communication Quarterly* 42 (1994): 160–179.

10. Robert G. Harper, Arthur N. Wiens, and Joseph D. Matarazzo, *Nonverbal Communication: The State of the Art* (New York: Wiley, 1978).

11. Sharon Ruhly, *Intercultural Communication,* 2nd ed. (Chicago: Science Research Associates, 1982), 23–26.

12. John C. Condon and Fathi S. Yousef, *Intercultural Communication* (Indianapolis: Bobbs-Merrill, 1975), 122.

13. Ray Birdwhistell, *Kinesics and Context: Essays on Body Motion Communication* (Philadelphia: University of Pennsylvania, 1970), 34.

14. Aaron Wolfgang, "The Teacher and Nonverbal Behavior in the Multicultural Classroom," *Nonverbal Behavior: Applications and Cultural Implications,* ed. Aaron Wolfgang (New York: Academic Press, 1979), 167.

15. Joseph A. DeVito, *Messages: Building Interpersonal Communication Skills* (New York: Harper and Row, 1990), 218.

15. Paul Ekman and Wallace V. Friesen, "The Repertoire of Nonverbal Behavior: Categories, Origins, Usage, and Coding," *Semiotica* 1 (1969): 49–98.

17. Tom Brosnahan, *Turkey: A Travel Survival Kit,* 2nd ed. (Victoria, Australia: Lonely Planet, 1988), 27.

18. Paul Ekman, Wallace V. Friesen, and Phoebe Ellsworth, *Emotion in the Human Face: Guidelines for Research and an Integration of Findings* (New York: Pergamon Press, 1972).

19. See Klaus R. Scherer and Harald G. Wallbott, "Evidence for Universality and Cultural Variation of Differential Emotion Response Patterning," *Journal of Personality and Social Psychology* 66 (1994): 310–328.

20. James A. Russell, "Is There Universal Recognition of Emotion from Facial Expression? A Review of the Cross-Cultural Studies," *Psychological Bulletin* 115 (1994): 102–141; James A. Russell, "Culture and the Categorization of Emotion," *Psychological Bulletin* 110 (1991): 426–450.

21. Michael Harris Bond, "Emotions and Their Expressions in Chinese Culture," *Journal of Nonverbal Behavior* 17 (1993): 245–262.

22. Marianne LaFrance and Clara Mayo, "Racial Differences in Gaze Behavior During Conversations: Two Systematic Observational Studies," *Journal of Personality and Social Psychology* 33 (1976): 547–552.

23. Edward T. Hall, *The Hidden Dimension* (Garden City, NY: Doubleday, 1966).

24. Edward T. Hall and Mildred Reed Hall, *Understanding Cultural Differences* (Yarmouth, ME: Intercultural Press, 1990), 12.

25. Hall and Hall, 180.

26. Hall and Hall, 10.

27. Stanley E. Jones and A. Elaine Yarbrough, "A Naturalistic Study of the Meanings of Touch," *Communication Monographs* 52 (1985): 19–56.

28. Nancy M. Henley, *Body Politics: Power, Sex, and Nonverbal Communication* (Englewood Cliffs, NJ: Prentice-Hall, 1977).

29. Hall and Hall, 11.

30. Dean Barnlund, "Communication Styles in Two Cultures: Japan and the United States," *Organi-*

zational Behavior in Face-to-Face Interaction, ed. Adam Kendon, Richard M. Harris, and Mary Ritchie Key (The Hague: Mouton, 1975), 427–456.

31. Sidney M. Jourard, "An Exploratory Study of Body Accessibility," *British Journal of Social and Clinical Psychology* 5 (1966): 221–231.

32. John Reader, *Man on Earth* (New York: Harper and Row, 1988), 91. Reader's ideas are based on Paul Spencer, *The Samburu: A Study in Gerontocracy in a Nomadic Tribe* (London: Routledge and Kegan Paul, 1968).

33. Reader, 163.

34. Edward T. Hall, "The Hidden Dimensions of Time and Space in Today's World," *Cross-Cultural Perspectives in Nonverbal Communication,* ed. Fernando Poyatos (Toronto: C. J. Hogrefe, 1988), 151.

35. Hall, *The Silent Language.*

36. Hall, *The Silent Language,* 178.

37. Alexander Gonzalez and Philip G. Zimbardo, "Time in Perspective," *Psychology Today* 19 (March 1985): 20–26.

38. Rosita Daskel Albert and Gayle L. Nelson, "Hispanic/Anglo-American Differences in Attributions to Paralinguistic Behavior," *International Journal of Intercultural Relations* 17 (1993): 19–40.

39. Mara B. Adelman and Myron W. Lustig, "Intercultural Communication Problems as Perceived by Saudi Arabian and American Managers," *International Journal of Intercultural Relations* 5 (1981): 349–364; Myron W. Lustig, "Cultural and Communication Patterns of Saudi Arabians," *Intercultural Communication: A Reader,* 5th ed., ed. Larry A. Samovar and Richard E. Porter (Belmont, CA: Wadsworth, 1988), 101–103.

40. William S. Condon, "Cultural Microrhythms," *Interaction Rhythms: Periodicity in Communicative Behavior,* ed. Martha Davis (New York: Human Sciences Press, 1982), 66.

41. Befu 1975; as quoted in Sheila J. Ramsey, "Nonverbal Behavior," 118.

42. Holley S. Hodgins and Richard Koestner, "The Origins of Nonverbal Sensitivity," *Personality and Social Psychology Bulletin* 19 (1993): 466–473.

43. Anna-Marie Dew and Colleen Ward, "The Effects of Ethnicity and Culturally Congruent and Incongruent Nonverbal Behaviors on Interpersonal Attraction," *Journal of Applied Social Psychology* 23 (1993): 1376–1389.

44. David Matsumoto and Tsutomu Kudoh, "American-Japanese Cultural Differences in Attributions of Personality Based on Smiles," *Journal of Nonverbal Behavior* 17 (1993): 231–243. See also Ann Bainbridge Frymier, Donald W. Klopf, and Satoshi Ishii, "Affect Orientation: Japanese Compared to Americans," *Communication Research Reports* 7 (1990): 63–66; Donald W. Klopf, "Japanese Communication Practices: Recent Comparative Research," *Communication Quarterly* 39 (1991): 130–143.

Chapter 8

1. Charles F. Hockett, "The Origin of Speech," *Human Communication: Language and Its Psychobiological Bases (Readings from Scientific American)* (San Francisco: Freeman, 1982), 5–12.

2. No, it isn't just that *tka* begins with two consonant sounds. *Spring* begins with three such sounds. For an interesting discussion of the rules of language, see Steven Pinker, *The Language Instinct: How the Mind Creates Language* (New York: HarperCollins, 1994).

3. Roger Brown, *Social Psychology* (New York: Free Press, 1965); quoted in Donald W. Klopf, *Intercultural Encounters: The Fundamentals of Intercultural Communication* (Englewood, CO: Morton, 1987), 137.

4. Wen Shu Lee, "In the Names of Chinese Women," *Quarterly Journal of Speech* 84 (1998): 283–302.

5. Wen Shu Lee, "On Not Missing the Boat: A Processual Method for Inter/cultural Understanding of Idioms and Lifeworld," *Journal of Applied Communication Research* 22 (1994): 141–161.

6. Christiane F. Gonzalez, "Translation," *Handbook of International and Intercultural Communication,* ed. Molefi Kete Asante and William B. Gudykunst (Newbury Park, CA: Sage, 1989), 484.

7. For an example of the kinds of translation problems that occur in organizations with a multilingual workforce, see Stephen E. Banks and Anna Banks, "Translation as Problematic Discourse in Organizations," *Journal of Applied Communication Research* 19 (1991): 223–241. See also Henriette W. Langdon, *The Interpreter Translator Process in the Educational Setting* (Sacramento, CA: Resources in Special Education, California State University with the California Department of Education, 1994).

8. Eugene A. Nida, *Toward a Science of Translating* (Leiden, Netherlands: E. J. Brill, 1964).

9. Lee Sechrest, Todd L. Fay, and S. M. Zaidi, "Problems of Translation in Cross-Cultural Communication," *Intercultural Communication: A Reader,* 5th ed., ed. Larry A. Samovar and Richard E. Porter (Belmont, CA: Wadsworth, 1988), 253–262.

10. There is some evidence that as early as the fifteenth century an Asian scholar named Bhartvhari, in a work entitled *Vahyapidan,* argued that speech patterns are determined by social contexts.

11. Edward Sapir, *Language: An Introduction to the Study of Speech* (New York: Harcourt Brace, 1921).

12. Edward Sapir; quoted in Benjamin Lee Whorf, "The Relation of Habitual Thought and Behavior to Language," *Language, Thought, and Reality: Selected Writings of Benjamin Lee Whorf,* ed. J. B. Carroll (Cambridge, MA: MIT Press, 1939/1956), 134.

13. For a thorough summary and discussion of the experimental research in psychology investigating the validity of the linguistic determinism hypothesis, see John J. Gumperz and Stephen C. Levison (eds.), *Rethinking Linguistic Relativity* (Cambridge: Cambridge University Press, 1996); Curtis Hardin and Mahzarin R. Banaji, "The Influence of Language on Thought," *Social Cognition* 11 (1993): 277–308; Earl Hunt and Franca Agnoli, "The Whorfian Hypothesis: A Cognitive Psychology Perspective," *Psychological Review* 98 (1991): 377–389.

14. Whorf suggested there may be about seven words for snow, though the actual number is closer to twelve. Over time and numerous retellings of this example, however, the number of words claimed to represent forms of snow has increased dramatically, typically to the seventeen to twenty-three range; the *New York Times* once cavalierly referred to one hundred different words. See Geoffrey K. Pullum, *The Great Eskimo Vocabulary Hoax, and Other Irreverent Essays on the Study of Language* (Chicago: University of Chicago Press, 1991); "The Melting of a Mighty Myth," *Newsweek,* July 22, 1991, 63.

15. Richard W. Brislin, Kenneth Cushner, Craig Cherrie, and Mahealani Yong, *Intercultural Interactions: A Practical Guide* (Beverly Hills, CA: Sage, 1986), 276.

15. John C. Condon and Fathi S. Yousef, *An Introduction to Intercultural Communication* (Yarmouth, ME: Intercultural Press, 1975), 182.

17. Michael Cole and Sylvia Scribner, *Culture and Thought: A Psychological Introduction* (New York: Wiley, 1974), 2.

18. Eleanor Rosch Heider and Donald C. Olivier, "The Structure of the Color Space in Naming and Memory for Two Languages," *Cognitive Psychology* 3 (1972): 337–354.

19. For a more complete discussion of the evidence on variations in vocabulary of the color spectrum, see Cole and Scribner, 45–50; Thomas M. Steinfatt, "Linguistic Relativity: Toward a Broader View," *Language, Communication, and Culture: Current Directions,* ed. Stella Ting-Toomey and Felipe Korzenny (Newbury Park, CA: Sage, 1989), 35–75.

20. Stephen W. Littlejohn, *Theories of Human Communication,* 4th ed. (Belmont, CA: Wadsworth, 1992), 209.

21. Li-Rong Lilly Cheng, *Assessing Asian Language Performance: Guidelines for Evaluating Limited-English-Language Proficient Students* (Rockville, MD: Aspen, 1987), 8.

22. For an interesting discussion of the difficulties that Mandarin speakers might have in using English pronouns appropriately, see Stephen P. Banks, "Power Pronouns and Intercultural Understanding," *Language, Communication, and Culture: Current Directions,* ed. Stella Ting-Toomey and Felipe Korzenny (Newbury Park, CA: Sage, 1989), 180–198.

23. Michael Dorris, *The Broken Cord* (New York: Harper and Row, 1989), 2.

24. See Earl Hunt and Franca Agnoli, "The Whorfian Hypothesis: A Cognitive Psychology Perspective," *Psychological Review* 98 (1991): 377–389.

25. Wilma M. Roger, *National Foreign Language Center Occasional Papers* (Washington, DC: Johns Hopkins University Press, February 1989).

26. Studies of the relationship of language and intercultural communication are often conducted under the rubric of "intergroup behavior" or "intergroup communication." See, for example, John C. Turner and Howard Giles (eds.), *Intergroup Behavior* (Chicago: University of Chicago Press, 1981).

27. Henri Tajfel, "Social Categorization, Social Identity, and Social Comparison," *Differentiation Between Social Groups,* ed. Henri Tajfel (London: Academic Press, 1978).

28. Aaron Castelan Cargile and Howard Giles, "Language Attitudes Toward Varieties of English: An American-Japanese Context." *Journal of Applied Communication Research* 26 (1998): 336–356; Howard Giles and Patricia Johnson, "The Role of Language in Ethnic Group Relations," *Intergroup Behavior,* ed. John C. Turner and Howard Giles (Chicago: University of Chicago Press, 1981), 199–243.

29. Joshua A. Fishman, "Language and Ethnicity," *Language, Ethnicity, and Intergroup Relations,* ed. Howard Giles (London: Academic Press, 1977), 15–58.

30. William B. Gudykunst, "Cultural Variability in Ethnolinguistic Identity," *Language, Communication, and Culture: Current Directions,* ed. Stella Ting-Toomey and Felipe Korzenney (Newbury Park, CA: Sage, 1989), 223.

31. Rèal Allard and Rodrique Landry, "Subjective Ethnolinguistic Vitality Viewed as a Belief System," *Journal of Multilingual and Multicultural Development* 7 (1986): 1–12. For a review of the vitality framework, see Jake Harwood, Howard Giles, and Richard Y. Bourhis, "The Genesis of Vitality Theory: Historical Patterns and Discourse Dimensions," *International Journal of the Sociology of Language* 108 (1994): 167–206.

32. Howard Giles and Arlene Franklyn-Stokes, "Communicator Characteristics," *Handbook of International and Intercultural Communication,* ed. Molefi Kete Asante and William B. Gudykunst (Newbury Park, CA: Sage, 1989), 117–144.

33. Nancy F. Burroughs and Vicki Marie, "Communication Orientations of Micronesian and American Students," *Communication Research Reports* 7 (1990): 139–146.

34. Cynthia Gallois, Howard Giles, Elizabeth Jones, Aaron C. Cargile, and Hiroshi Ota, "Accommodating Intercultural Encounters: Elaborations and Extensions," *Intercultural Communication Theory,* ed. Richard L. Wiseman (Thousand Oaks, CA: Sage, 1995), 115–147; Howard Giles and Nikolas Coupland, *Language: Contexts and Consequences* (Pacific Grove, CA: Brooks/Cole, 1991); Howard Giles and Kimberly A. Noels, "Communication Accommodation in Intercultural Encounters," *Readings in Cultural Contexts,* ed. Judith N. Martin, Thomas K. Nakayama, and Lisa A. Flores (Mountain View, CA: Mayfield, 1998), 139–149; Howard Giles and Patricia Johnson, "Ethnolinguistic Identity Theory: A Social Psychological Approach to Language Maintenance," *International Journal of the Sociology of Language* 68 (1987): 66–99; Howard Giles, Anthony Mulac, James J. Bradac, and Patricia Johnson, "Speech Accommodation Theory: The Next Decade and Beyond," *Communication Yearbook 10,* ed. Margaret McLaughlin (Newbury Park, CA: Sage, 1987), 13–48.

35. Ellen Bouchard Ryan, Howard Giles, and Richard J. Sebastian, "An Integrative Perspective for the Study of Attitudes Toward Language Variation," *Attitudes toward Language Variation: Social and Applied Contexts,* ed. Ellen Bouchard Ryan and Howard Giles (London: Arnold, 1982), 1.

36. Michael L. Hecht, Mary Jane Collier, and Sidney Ribeau, *African American Communication: Ethnic Identity and Cultural Interpretation* (Newbury Park, CA: Sage, 1993), 84–89.

37. John R. Edwards, *Language Attitudes and Their Implications Among English Speakers,* ed. Ellen Bouchard Ryan and Howard Giles (London: Arnold, 1982), 22.

38. Hope Bock and James H. Pitts, "The Effect of Three Levels of Black Dialect on Perceived Speaker Image," *Speech Teacher* 24 (1975): 218–225; James J. Bradac, "Language Attitudes and Impression Formation," *Handbook of Language and Social Psychology,* ed. Howard Giles and W. Peter Robinson (Chichester, England: Wiley, 1990), 387–412.

39. Geneva Smitherman, *Talkin That Talk: Language, Culture, and Education in African America* (New York: Routledge, 2000), 21–22.

40. For an excellent summary of research on the effect of accent and dialect variations among ethnic groups, see Giles and Franklyn-Stokes. See also Diane M. Badzinski, "The Impact of Accent and Status on Information Recall and Perception Information," *Communication* 5 (1992): 99–106.

41. Edwards, 22–27.

42. Richard Rodriguez, *Hunger of Memory: The Education of Richard Rodriguez* (Toronto: Bantam Books, 1982), 14–16. Italics in original.

43. Hecht, Collier, and Ribeau 90; U. Dagmar Scheu, "Cultural Constraints in Bilinguals' Codeswitching," *International Journal of Intercultural Relations* 24 (2000): 131–150.

44. Abdelala Bentahila, *Language Attitudes among Arabic-French Bilinguals in Morocco* (London: Multilingual Matters, 1983), 27–65.

Chapter 9

1. Robert B. Kaplan, "Cultural Thought Patterns in Intercultural Education," *Language Learning* 16 (1966): 15.

2. Laurie G. Kirszner and Stephen R. Mandell, *Writing: A College Rhetoric*, 2nd ed. (New York: Holt, Rinehart and Winston, 1988), 185, 188.

3. Kaplan.

4. Satoshi Ishii, "Thought Patterns as Modes of Rhetoric: The United States and Japan," *Intercultural Communication: A Reader,* 4th ed., ed. Larry A. Samovar and Richard E. Porter (Belmont, CA: Wadsworth, 1985), 97–102.

5. Ulla Connor, *Contrastive Rhetoric: Cross-Cultural Aspects of Second Language Writing* (Cambridge: Cambridge University Press, 1996).

6. Yamuna Kachru, "Writers in Hindi and English," *Writing Across Languages and Cultures: Issues in Contrastive Rhetoric,* ed. Alan C. Purvis (Newbury Park, CA: Sage, 1988), 109–137.

7. Arpita Misra, "Discovering Connections," *Language and Social Identity*, ed. John L. Gumperz (Cambridge: Cambridge University Press, 1982), 57–71.

8. Linda Wai Ling Young, "Inscrutability Revisited," *Language and Social Identity*, ed. John L. Gumperz (Cambridge: Cambridge University Press, 1982), 72–84.

9. Joy Reid, "A Computer Text Analysis of Four Cohesion Devices in English Discourse by Native and Nonnative Writers," *Journal of Second Language Writing* 1 (1992): 90.

10. Hinds, "Reader versus Writer Responsibility: A New Typology," *Writing Across Languages: Analysis of L2 Written Text*, ed. Ulla Connor and Robert B. Kaplan (Reading, MA: Addison-Wesley, 1986), 141–152.

11. Judith Sanders, Robert Gass, Richard Wiseman, and Jon Bruschke, "Ethnic Comparison and Measurement of Argumentativeness, Verbal Aggressiveness, and Need for Cognition," *Communication Reports* 5 (1992): 50–56.

12. James F. Hamill, *Ethno-Logic: The Anthropology of Human Reasoning* (Urbana: University of Illinois Press, 1990), 23.

13. Stephen Toulmin, *Human Understanding, Volume I: The Collective Use and Evolution of Concepts* (Princeton, NJ: Princeton University Press, 1972), 95.

14. Xiaosui Xiao, "From the Hierarchical *Ren* to Egalitarianism: A Case of Cross-Cultural Rhetorical Mediation," *Quarterly Journal of Speech* 82 (1996): 38–54.

15. Robert B. Kaplan, "Foreword: What in the World Is Contrastive Rhetoric?" *Contrastive Rhetoric Revisited and Redefined,* ed. Clayann Gillima Panetta (Mahwah, NJ: Erlbaum, 2001), vii–xx.

15. Michael Cole and Sylvia Scribner, *Culture and Thought: A Psychological Introduction* (New York: Wiley, 1974), 3.

17. "Surplus Squid Suggest El Niño," *San Diego Union-Tribune,* May 29, 1997, A3; Cheryl Clark, "Experts Say El Niño Rains May Batter Area," *San Diego Union-Tribune,* June 22, 1997, A1, A25.

18. Dina Kraft, "Debate over Red Heifer Takes Israeli Spotlight," *San Diego Union-Tribune,* May 29, 1997, A2.

19. Barbara Johnstone, "Linguistic Strategies for Persuasive Discourse," *Language, Communication, and Culture: Current Directions,* ed. Stella Ting-Toomey and Felipe Korzenny (Newbury Park, CA: Sage, 1989), 139–156.

20. Anne Bliss, "Rhetorical Structures for Multilingual and Multicultural Students," *Contrastive Rhetoric Revisited and Redefined,* ed. Clayann Gilliam Panetta (Mahwah, NJ: Erlbaum, 2001), 19.

21. John C. Condon, *Good Neighbors: Communicating with the Mexicans* (Yarmouth, ME: Intercultural Press, 1985).

22. Robert Shuter, "The Culture of Rhetoric," *Rhetoric in Intercultural Contexts,* ed. Alberto Gonzalez and Dolores V. Tanno (Thousands Oaks, CA: Sage, 2000), 12–13.

23. Stanley B. Lubman, "Negotiations in China: Observations of a Lawyer Communicating with China," *Communicating with China,* ed. Robert A. Kapp (Chicago: Intercultural Press, 1983). See also Stanley B. Lubman (ed.), *China's Legal Reforms* (Oxford: Oxford University Press, 1996).

24. Johnstone.

25. Connor, 167.

26. Daniel Dolan, "Conditional Respect and Criminal Identity: The Use of Personal Address Terms in Japanese Mass Media," *Western Journal of Communication* 64 (1998): 459–473.

27. Patricia A. Sullivan, "Signification and African-American Rhetoric: A Case Study of Jesse Jackson's 'Common Ground and Common Sense' Speech," *Communication Quarterly* 41 (1993): 1–15.

28. Howard Giles, Nikolas Coupland, and John Wiemann, " 'Talk Is Cheap . . .' but 'My Word Is My Bond': Beliefs about Talk." *Sociolinguistics Today: International Perspectives,* ed. Kingsley Bolton and Helen Kwok (New York: Routledge, 1992), 218–243.

29. Lawrence Kincaid, "Communication East and West: Points of Departure," *Communication Theory: Eastern and Western Perspectives,* ed. D. Lawrence Kincaid (San Diego: Academic Press, 1987), 337.

30. See Giles, Coupland, and Wiemann.

31. Donald W. Klopf, *Intercultural Encounters: The Fundamentals of Intercultural Communication,* 2nd ed. (Englewood Cliffs, NJ: Morgan, 1991), 181.

32. June Ock Yum, "Korean Philosophy and Communication," *Communication Theory: Eastern and Western Perspectives,* ed. D. Lawrence Kincaid (San Diego: Academic Press, 1987), 79.

33. Yum, 83.

34. Peter Nwosu, "Negotiating with the Swazis," *Howard Journal of Communication* 1 (1988): 148.

35. Aino Sallinen-Kuparinen, James C. McCroskey, and Virginia P. Richmond, "Willingness to Communicate, Communication Apprehension, Introversion, and Self-Reported Communication Competence: Finnish and American Comparisons," *Communication Research Reports* 8 (1991): 55–64.

36. Keith H. Basso, " 'To Give Up on Words': Silence in Western Apache Culture," *Cultural Communication and Intercultural Contact,* ed. Donal L. Carbaugh (Hillsdale, NJ: Erlbaum, 1990), 303–320.

37. Basso, 308.

38. See, for example, Donal L. Carbaugh, ed., *Cultural Communication and Intercultural Contact* (Hillsdale, NJ: Erlbaum, 1990).

39. Klopf.

40. William B. Gudykunst and Stella Ting-Toomey, *Culture and Interpersonal Communication* (Newbury Park, CA: Sage, 1988), 99–116.

41. Min-Sun Kim, "Culture-Based Interactive Constraints in Explaining Intercultural Strategic Competence," *Intercultural Communication Competence,* ed. Richard L. Wiseman and Jolene Koester (Newbury Park, CA: Sage, 1993), 132–150; Min-Sun Kim, "Cross-Cultural Comparisons of the Perceived Importance of Conversational Constraints," *Human Communication Research* 21 (1994): 128–151; Min-Sun Kim, "Toward a Theory of Conversational Constraints: Focusing on Individual-Level Dimensions of Culture," *Intercultural Communication Theory,* ed. Richard L. Wiseman (Thousand Oaks, CA: Sage, 1995), 148–169; Min-Sun Kim and Mary Bresnahan, "Cognitive Basis of Gender Communication: A Cross-Cultural Investigation of Perceived Constraints in Requesting," *Communication Quarterly* 44 (1996): 53–69; Min-Sun Kim, John E. Hunter, Akira Miyahara, Ann-Marie Horvath, Mary Bresnahan, and Hye-Jin Yoon, "Individual- vs. Culture-Level Dimensions of Individualism and Collectivism: Effects on Preferred Conversational Styles," *Communication Monographs* 63 (1996): 29–49; Min-Sun Kim, Renee Storm Klingle, William F. Sharkey; Hee Sun Park, David H. Smith, and Deborah Cai, "A Test of a Cultural Model of Patients' Motivation for Verbal Communication in Patient-Doctor Interactions," *Communication Monographs* 67 (2000): 262–283; Min-Sun Kim and William F. Sharkey, "Independent and Interdependent Construals of Self: Explaining Cultural Patterns of Interpersonal Communication in Multi-Cultural Organizational Settings," *Communication Quarterly* 43 (1995): 20–38; Min-Sun Kim, William F. Sharkey, and Theodore M. Singelis, "The Relationship of Individuals' Self-Construals and Perceived Importance of Interactive Constraints," *International Journal of Intercultural Relations* 18 (1994): 117–140; Min-Sun Kim, Ho-Chang Shin, and Deborah Cai, "Cultural Influences on the Preferred Forms of Requesting and Re-Requesting," *Communication Monographs* 65 (1998): 47–66; Min-Sun Kim and Steven R. Wilson, "A Cross-Cultural Comparison of Implicit Theories of

Requesting," *Communication Monographs* 61 (1994): 210–235; Akira Miyahara, Min-Sun Kim, Ho-Chang Shin, and Kak Yoon, *International Journal of Intercultural Relations* 22 (1998): 505–525.

42. Thomas Kochman, "Force Fields in Black and White," *Cultural Communication and Intercultural Contact,* ed. Donal Carbaugh (Hillsdale, NJ: Erlbaum, 1990), 193–194.

43. Melanie Booth-Butterfield and Felecia Jordan, "Communication Adaptation Among Racially Homogeneous and Heterogeneous Groups," *Southern Communication Journal* 54 (1989): 265.

44. Ronald Scollon and Suzanne Wong-Scollon, "Athabaskan-English Interethnic Communication," *Cultural Communication and Intercultural Contact,* ed. Donal Carbaugh (Hillsdale, NJ: Erlbaum, 1990), 270.

45. Scollon and Wong-Scollon, 273.

Chapter 10

1. John Paul Feig, *A Common Core: Thais and Americans,* rev. Elizabeth Mortlock (Yarmouth, ME: Intercultural Press, 1989), 50.

2. John C. Condon, *Good Neighbors: Communicating with the Mexicans* (Yarmouth, ME: Intercultural Press, 1985).

3. Mary Jane Collier and Elirea Bornman, "Core Symbols in South African Intercultural Friendships," *International Journal of Intercultural Relations* 23 (1999): 133–156; Daniel Perlman and Beverley Fehr, "The Development of Intimate Relationships," *Intimate Relationships: Development, Dynamics, and Deterioration,* ed. Daniel Perlman and Steven Duck (Newbury Park, CA: Sage, 1987), 13–42.

4. Michael L. Hecht, Mary Jane Collier, and Sidney A. Ribeau, *African American Communication: Ethnic Identity and Cultural Interpretation* (Newbury Park, CA: Sage, 1993).

5. Mary Jane Collier, "Cultural Background and the Culture of Friendships: Normative Patterns," paper presented at the annual conference of the International Communication Association, San Francisco, May 1989. See also Mary Jane Collier, "Conflict Competence within African, Mexican, and Anglo American Friendships," *Cross-Cultural Interpersonal Communication,* ed. Stella Ting-Toomey and Felipe Korzenny (Newbury Park, CA: Sage, 1991), 132–154.

6. Stanley O. Gaines, Jr., "Communalism and the Reciprocity of Affection and Respect among Interethnic Married Couples," *Journal of Black Studies* 27 (1997): 352–364; Stanley O. Gaines, Jr., et al., "Patterns of Attachment and Responses to Accommodative Dilemmas Among Interethnic/ Interracial Couples," *Journal of Social and Personal Relationships* 16 (1999): 275–285; Stanley O. Gaines, Jr., et al., "Links between Race/ Ethnicity and Cultural Values as Mediated by Racial/Ethnic Identity and Moderated by Gender," *Journal of Personality and Social Psychology* 72 (1997): 1460–1476; Stanley O. Gaines, Jr., with Raymond Buriel, James H. Liu, and Diana I. Ríos, *Culture, Ethnicity, and Personal Relationship Processes* (New York: Routledge, 1997). See also Stella D. Garcia and Semilla M. Rivera, "Perceptions of Hispanic and African-American Couples at the Friendship or Engagement Stage of a Relationship," *Journal of Social and Personal Relationships* 16 (1999): 65–86; Regan A. R. Gurung and Tenor Duong, "Mixing and Matching: Assessing the Concomitants of Mixed-Ethnic Relationships," *Journal of Social and Personal Relationships* 16 (1999): 639–657.

7. Irene I. Blea, *Toward a Chicano Social Science* (New York: Praeger, 1988); Richard Lewis, Jr., George Yancy, and Siri S. Bletzer. "Racial and Nonracial Factors That Influence Spouse Choice in Black/White Marriages," *Journal of Black Studies* 28 (1997): 60–78.

8. Don C. Locke, *Increasing Multicultural Understanding: A Comprehensive Model* (Newbury Park, CA: Sage, 1992), 55.

9. Lin Yutang, *The Chinese Way of Life* (New York: World, 1972), 78.

10. We have synthesized a variety of sources to provide this generalization.

11. William D. Wilder, *Communication, Social Structure and Development in Rural Malaysia: A Study of Kampung Kuala Bera* (London: Athlone Press, 1982), 107.

12. Joe Cummings, Susan Forsyth, John Noble, Alan Samagalski, and Tony Wheelan, *Indonesia: A Travel Survival Guide* (Berkeley, CA: Lonely Planet Publications, 1990), 321.

13. Albert Mehrabian, *Silent Messages* (Belmont, CA: Wadsworth, 1971).

14. Edward T. Hall, *The Hidden Dimension* (Garden City, NY: Doubleday, 1966).

15. Peter A. Andersen, Myron W. Lustig, and Janis F. Andersen, "Changes in Latitude, Changes in Attitude: The Relationship Between Climate and Interpersonal Communication Predispositions," *Communication Quarterly* 38 (1990): 291–311.

15. Wilder, 105.

17. Feig, 41.

18. William O. Beeman, *Language, Status, and Power in Iran* (Bloomington: Indiana University Press, 1986), 86.

19. Harvey Taylor, "Misunderstood Japanese Nonverbal Communication," *Gengo Seikatsu* (Language Life), 1974; quoted in Helmut Morsbach, "The Importance of Silence and Stillness in Japanese Nonverbal Communication: A Cross-Cultural Approach," *Cross-Cultural Perspectives in Nonverbal Communication,* ed. Fernando Poyatos (Toronto: C. J. Hogrefe, 1988), 206.

20. We rely primarily on Leslie A. Baxter, "A Dialectical Perspective on Communication Strategies in Relationship Development," *Handbook of Personal Relationships: Theory, Research, and Interventions,* ed. Stephen W. Duck (New York: Wiley, 1988), 257–273; Leslie A. Baxter, "Dialectical Contradictions in Relationship Development," *Journal of Social and Personal Relationships* 7 (1990): 69–88; Leslie A. Baxter and Barbara M. Montgomery, *Relating: Dialogues and Dialectics* (New York: Guilford Press, 1996). See also Irwin Altman, "Dialectics, Physical Environments, and Personal Relationships," *Communication Monographs* 60 (1993): 26–34; Irwin Altman, Anne Vinsel, and Barbara B. Brown, "Dialectic Conceptions in Social Psychology: An Application to Social Penetration and Privacy Regulation," *Advances in Experimental Social Psychology,* vol. 14, ed. Leonard Berkowitz (New York: Academic Press, 1981), 107–160; Carl W. Backman, "The Self: A Dialectical Approach," *Advances in Experimental Social Psychology,* vol. 21, ed. Leonard Berkowitz (New York: Academic Press, 1988), 229–260; Daena Goldsmith, "A Dialectic Perspective on the Expression of Autonomy and Connection in Romantic Relationships," *Western Journal of Speech Communication* 54 (1990): 537–556.

21. See Erving Goffman, *Interaction Ritual: Essays on Face-to-Face Behavior* (Garden City, NY: Anchor Books, 1967).

22. David Yau-fai Ho, "On the Concept of Face," *American Journal of Sociology* 81 (1976): 867–884.

23. Penelope Brown and Stephen Levinson, "Universals in Language Use: Politeness Phenomena," *Questions and Politeness: Strategies in Social Interaction,* ed. Esther N. Goody (Cambridge: Cambridge University Press, 1978), 56–289; Penelope Brown and Stephen Levinson, *Politeness: Some Universals in Language Use* (Cambridge: Cambridge University Press, 1987). Though Brown and Levinson's ideas have been criticized on several points, the portions of their ideas expressed here are generally accepted. For a summary of the criticisms, see Karen Tracy and Sheryl Baratz, "The Case for Case Studies of Facework," *The Challenge of Facework: Cross-Cultural and Interpersonal Issues,* ed. Stella Ting-Toomey (Albany: State University of New York Press, 1994), 287–305.

24. Greg Leichty and James L. Applegate, "Social-Cognitive and Situational Influences on the Use of Face-Saving Persuasive Strategies," *Human Communication Research* 17 (1991): 451–484.

25. We have modified Lim's terminology and concepts somewhat but draw on his overall conception. See Tae-Seop Lim, "Politeness Behavior in Social Influence Situations," *Seeking Compliance: The Production of Interpersonal Influence Messages,* ed. James Price Dillard (Scottsdale, AZ: Gorsuch Scarisbrick, 1990), 75–86; Tae-Seop Lim, "Facework and Interpersonal Relationships," *The Challenge of Facework: Cross-Cultural and Interpersonal Issues,* ed. Stella Ting-Toomey (Albany: State University of New York Press, 1994), 209–229; Tae-Seop Lim and John Waite Bowers, "Facework: Solidarity, Approbation, and Tact," *Human Communication Research* 17 (1991): 415–450.

26. Lim, 211.

27. The Wade–Giles system for the Romanization of Chinese words is used, rather than the newer *pin-yin* system, in order to maintain consistency with the terms used in the quotes by Hu and by Hsu. Terms that the Wade–Giles system would render as *lien* and *mien-tzu* are written in the *pin-yin* system as, respectively, *lian* and *mian zi.*

28. Hsien Chin Hu, "The Chinese Concepts of 'Face,'" *American Anthropologist* 46 (1944): 45–64.

29. Francis L. K. Hsu, "The Self in Cross-Cultural Perspective," *Culture and Self: Asian and Western Perspectives,* ed. Anthony J. Marsella, George DeVos, and Francis L. K. Hsu (New York: Tavistock, 1985), 33.

30. Leo Rosten, *The Joys of Yiddish* (New York: Mc-Graw-Hill, 1968), 234.

31. Hu, 61–62.

32. Brown and Levinson, 66.

33. Brown and Levinson; see also Robert T. Craig, Karen Tracy, and Frances Spisak, "The Discourse of Requests: Assessment of a Politeness Approach," *Human Communication Research* 12 (1986): 437–468.

34. Ron Scollon and Suzie Wong-Scollon, "Face Parameters in East-West Discourse," *The Challenge of Facework: Cross-Cultural and Interpersonal Issues,* ed. Stella Ting-Toomey (Albany: State University of New York Press, 1994), 133–157.

35. Scollon and Wong-Scollon, 137.

36. Lijuan Stahl, "Face-Negotiation," unpublished manuscript (San Diego: San Diego State University, 1993), 12–13.

37. See John G. Oetzel, "The Effects of Ethnicity and Self-Construals on Self-Reported Conflict Styles," *Communication Reports,* 11 (1998): 133–144; John G. Oetzel, "The Influence of Situational Features on Perceived Conflict Styles and Self-Construals in Work Groups," *International Journal of Intercultural Relations,* 23 (1999): 679–695; John G. Oetzel, Stella Ting-Toomey, Tomoko Masumoto, Yumiko Yokochi, Xiaohui Pan, Jiro Takai, and Richard Wilcox, "Face and Facework in Conflict: A Cross-Cultural Comparison of China, Germany, Japan, and the United States," *Communication Monographs* 68 (2001): 235–258; Stella Ting-Toomey, "Toward a Theory of Conflict and Culture," *Communication, Culture, and Organizational Processes,* ed. William B. Gudykunst, Lea P. Stewart, and Stella Ting-Toomey (Beverly Hills, CA: Sage, 1985), 71–86; Stella Ting-Toomey, "Intercultural Conflict Styles: A Face-Negotiation Theory," *Theories in Intercultural Communication,* ed. Young Yun Kim and William B. Gudykunst (Newbury Park, CA: Sage, 1988), 213–235; Stella Ting-Toomey, "Intergroup Diplomatic Communication: A Face-Negotiation Perspective," *Communicating for Peace,* ed. Felipe Korzenny and Stella Ting-Toomey (Newbury Park: Sage, 1990), 75–95; Stella Ting-Toomey, "Intercultural Conflict Competence," *Competence in Interpersonal Conflict,* ed. William R. Cupach and Daniel J. Canary (New York: McGraw-Hill, 1997), 120–147; Stella Ting-Toomey and Beth-Ann Cocroft, "Face and Facework: Theoretical and Research Issues," *The Challenge of Facework: Cross-Cultural and Interpersonal Issues,* ed. Stella Ting-Toomey (Albany: State University of New York Press, 1994), 307–340; Stella Ting-Toomey and John G. Oetzel, *Managing Intercultural Conflict Effectively* (Thousand Oaks, CA: Sage, 2001).

38. Min-Sun Kim, "Culture-Based Interactive Constraints in Explaining Intercultural Strategic Competence," *Intercultural Communication Competence,* ed. Richard L. Wiseman and Jolene Koester (Newbury Park, CA: Sage, 1993), 132–150; Min-Sun Kim, "Cross-Cultural Comparisons of the Perceived Importance of Conversational Constraints," *Human Communication Research* 21 (1994): 128–151; Min-Sun Kim, "Toward a Theory of Conversational Constraints: Focusing on Individual-Level Dimensions of Culture," *Intercultural Communication Theory,* ed. Richard L. Wiseman (Thousand Oaks, CA: Sage, 1995), 148–169; Min-Sun Kim, John E. Hunter, Akira Miyahara, Ann-Marie Horvath, Mary Bresnahan, and Hye-Jin Yoon, "Individual- vs. Culture-Level Dimensions of Individualism and Collectivism: Effects on Preferred Conversational Styles," *Communication Monographs* 63 (1996): 29–49; Min-Sun Kim and William F. Sharkey, "Independent and Interdependent Construals of Self: Explaining Cultural Patterns of Interpersonal Communication in Multi-Cultural Organizational Settings," *Communication Quarterly* 43 (1995): 20–38; Min-Sun Kim, William F. Sharkey, and Theodore M. Singelis, "The Relationship of Individuals' Self-Construals and Perceived Importance of Interactive Constraints," *International Journal of Intercultural Relations* 18 (1994): 117–140; Min-Sun Kim and Steven R. Wilson, "A Cross-Cultural Comparison of Implicit Theories of Requesting," *Communication Monographs* 61 (1994): 210–235; Akira Miyahara, Min-Sun Kim, Ho-Chang Shin, and Kak Yoon, "Conflict Resolution Styles Among 'Collectivist' Cultures: A Comparison between Japanese and Koreans," *International Journal of Intercultural Relations* 22 (1998): 505–525.

39. Dean C. Barnlund, "Apologies: Japanese and American Styles," *International Journal of Intercultural Relations* 14 (1990): 193–206; William R. Cupach and T. Todd Imahori, "Managing Social

Predicaments Created by Others: A Comparison of Japanese and American Facework," *Western Journal of Communication* 57 (1993): 431–444; William R. Cupach and T. Todd Imahori, "A Cross-Cultural Comparison of the Interpretation and Management of Face: U.S. American and Japanese Responses to Embarrassing Predicaments," *International Journal of Intercultural Relations* 18 (1994): 193–219; Naoki Nomura and Dean Barnlund, "Patterns of Interpersonal Criticism in Japan and the United States," *International Journal of Intercultural Relations* 7 (1983): 1–18; Kiyoko Sueda and Richard L. Wiseman, "Embarrassment Remediation in Japan and the United States," *International Journal of Intercultural Relations* 16 (1992): 159–173.

40. Stahl, 14.

41. Robyn Penman, "Facework in Communication: Conceptual and Moral Challenges," *The Challenge of Facework: Cross-Cultural and Interpersonal Issues,* ed. Stella Ting-Toomey (Albany: State University of New York Press, 1994), 21.

42. For an elaboration of uncertainty reduction theory, see Charles R. Berger, "Communicating Under Uncertainty," *Interpersonal Processes: New Directions in Communication Research,* ed. Michael E. Roloff and Gerald R. Miller (Newbury Park, CA: Sage, 1987), 39–62; Charles R. Berger and James J. Bradac, *Language and Social Knowledge: Uncertainty in Interpersonal Relations* (London: Arnold, 1982); Charles R. Berger and Richard J. Calabrese, "Some Explorations in Initial Interaction and Beyond: Toward a Developmental Theory of Interpersonal Communication," *Human Communication Research* 1 (1975): 99–112; Glen W. Clatterbuck, "Attributional Confidence and Uncertainty in Initial Interaction," *Human Communication Research* 5 (1979): 147–157; William Douglas, "Uncertainty, Information-Seeking, and Liking During Initial Interaction, *Western Journal of Speech Communication* 54 (1990): 66–81; William B. Gudykunst, "The Influence of Cultural Similarity, Type of Relationship, and Self-Monitoring on Uncertainty Reduction Processes," *Communication Monographs* 52 (1985): 203–217; William B. Gudykunst, Elizabeth Chua, and Alisa J. Gray, "Cultural Dissimilarities and Uncertainty Reduction Processes," *Communication Yearbook 10,* ed. Margaret McLaughlin (Beverly Hills, CA:

Sage, 1984), 456–469; William B. Gudykunst and Tsukasa Nishida, "Individual and Cultural Influences on Uncertainty Reduction," *Communication Monographs* 51 (1984): 23–36; William B. Gudykunst, Seung-Mock Yang, and Tsukasa Nishida, "A Cross-Cultural Test of Uncertainty Reduction Theory: Comparisons of Acquaintances, Friends, and Dating Relationships in Japan, Korea, and the United States," *Human Communication Research* 11 (1985): 407–455; Kathy Kellermann and Rodney Reynolds, "When Ignorance Is Bliss: The Role of Motivation to Reduce Uncertainty in Uncertainty Reduction Theory," *Human Communication Research* 17 (1990): 5–75; Sally Planalp and James M. Honeycutt, "Events That Increase Uncertainty in Personal Relationships," *Human Communication Research* 11 (1985): 593–604; Sally Planalp, Diane K. Rutherford, and James M. Honeycutt, "Events That Increase Uncertainty in Personal Relationships II: Replication and Extension," *Human Communication Research* 14 (1988): 516–547; Michael Sunnafrank, "Predicted Outcome Value During Initial Interactions: A Reformulation of Uncertainty Reduction Theory," *Human Communication Research* 13 (1986): 3–33.

43. Kimberly N. Hubbert, William B. Gudykunst, and Sherrie L. Guerrero, "Intergroup Communication Over Time," *International Journal of Intercultural Relations* 23 (1999): 13–46; William B. Gudykunst, "Toward a Theory of Effective Interpersonal and Intergroup Communication: An Anxiety/Uncertainty Management (AUM) Perspective," *Intercultural Communication Competence,* ed. Richard L. Wiseman and Jolene Koester (Newbury Park, CA: Sage, 1994), 33–71; William B. Gudykunst, "Anxiety/Uncertainty Management Theory: Current Status," *Intercultural Communication Theory,* ed. Richard L. Wiseman (Thousand Oaks, CA: Sage, 1995), 8–58; William B. Gudykunst, "Intercultural Communication Theories," *Handbook of International and Intercultural Communication,* 2nd ed., ed. William B. Gudykunst and Bella Mody (Thousand Oaks, CA: Sage, 2002), 183–205; William B. Gudykunst and Carmen M. Lee, "Cross-Cultural Communication Theories," *Handbook of International and Intercultural Communication,* 2nd ed., ed. William B. Gudykunst and Bella Mody (Thousand Oaks, CA: Sage,

2002), 25–50; Walter G. Stephan, Cookie White Stephan, and William B. Gudykunst, "Anxiety in Intergroup Relations: A Comparison of Anxiety/Uncertainty Management Theory and Integrated Threat Theory," *International Journal of Intercultural Relations* 23 (1999): 613–628.

44. Edna B. Foa and Uriel G. Foa, "Resource Theory: Interpersonal Behavior as Exchange," *Social Exchange: Advances in Theory and Research,* ed. Kenneth Gergen, Martin S. Greenberg, and Richard H. Willis (New York: Plenum Press, 1980), 77–101.

45. Judee K. Burgoon, "Nonverbal Violation of Expectations," *Nonverbal Interaction,* ed. John M. Wiemann and Randall P. Harrison (Beverly Hills, CA: Sage, 1983), 77–111; Judee K. Burgoon, "Interpersonal Expectations, Expectancy Violations, and Emotional Communication," *Journal of Language and Social Psychology* 12 (1993): 30–48; Judee K. Burgoon, "Cross-Cultural and Intercultural Applications of Expectancy Violations Theory," *Intercultural Communication Theory,* ed. Richard L. Wiseman (Thousand Oaks, CA: Sage, 1995), 194–214.

46. Berger, 41.

47. Gudykunst and Nishida.

48. Tsukasa Nishida, "Sequence Patterns of Self-Disclosure Among Japanese and North American Students," paper presented at the Conference on Communication in Japan and the United States, Fullerton, CA, March 1991.

49. Judith A. Sanders, Richard L. Wiseman, and S. Irene Matz, "A Cross-Cultural Comparison of Uncertainty Reduction Theory: The Cases of Ghana and the United States," paper presented at the annual conference of the International Communication Association, San Francisco, May 1989.

50. Changsheng Xi, "Individualism and Collectivism in American and Chinese Societies," *Our Voices: Essays in Culture, Ethnicity, and Communication,* ed. Alberto González, Marsha Houston, and Victoria Chen (Los Angeles: Roxbury, 1994), 155.

51. Robert Littlefield, "Self-Disclosure Among Some Negro, White, and Mexican-American Adolescents," *Journal of Counseling Psychology* 21 (1974): 133–136.

52. Sidney Jourard, "Self-Disclosure Patterns in British and American College Females, *Journal of Social Psychology* 54 (1961): 315–320.

53. Stella Ting-Toomey, "Intimacy Expressions in Three Cultures: France, Japan, and the United States," *International Journal of Intercultural Relations* 15 (1991): 29–46.

54. Dean Barnlund, *Public and Private Self in Japan and the United States: Communicative Styles of Two Cultures* (Tokyo: Simul Press, 1975); Ting-Toomey, "Intimacy Expressions."

55. Sidney Jourard, *Self-Disclosure: An Experimental Analysis of the Transparent Self* (New York: Wiley, 1971).

56. George Levinger and David J. Senn, "Disclosure of Feelings in Marriage," *Merrill Palmer Quarterly* 13 (1987): 237–249.

57. See Stella Ting-Toomey and John G. Oetzel, *Managing Intercultural Conflict Effectively* (Thousand Oaks, CA: Sage, 2001); Stella Ting-Toomey and John G. Oetzel, "Cross-Cultural Face Concerns and Conflict Styles: Current Status and Future Directions," *Handbook of International and Intercultural Communication,* 2nd ed., ed. William B. Gudykunst and Bella Mody (Thousand Oaks, CA: Sage, 2002): 143–163. Our discussion of managing conflict also draws on a number of works, including John G. Oetzel, "The Effects of Self-Construals and Ethnicity on Self-Reported Conflict Styles," *Communication Reports* 11 (1998): 133–144; John G. Oetzel, "The Influence of Situational Features on Perceived Conflict Styles and Self-Construals in Work Groups," *International Journal of Intercultural Relations* 23 (1999): 679–695; John Oetzel, Stella Ting-Toomey, Tomoko Masumoto, Yumiko Yokochi, Xiaohui Pan, Jiro Takai, and Richard Wilcox, "Face and Facework in Conflict: A Cross-Cultural Comparison of China, Germany, Japan, and the United States," *Communication Monographs* 68 (2001): 235–258; Stella Ting-Toomey, "Managing Conflict in Intimate Intercultural Relationships," *Conflict in Personal Relationships,* ed. Dudley D. Cahn. (Hillsdale, NJ: Erlbaum, 1994), 47–77; Stella Ting-Toomey, Kimberlie K. Yee-Jung, Robin B. Shapiro, Wintilo Garcia, Trina J. Wright, and John G. Oetzel, "Ethnic/Cultural Identity Salience and Conflict Styles in Four US Ethnic Groups," *International Journal of Intercultural Relations* 24 (2000): 47–81; Ting-Toomey, "Conflict and Culture"; Stella Ting-Toomey, "Conflict Styles in Black and White Subjective Cultures," *Current Re-*

search in Interethnic Communication, ed. Young Yun Kim (Beverly Hills, CA: Sage, 1986); Ting-Toomey, "Face Negotiation Theory" (see note 37).

58. Deborah A. Cai, Steven R. Wilson, and Laura E. Drake, "Culture in the Context of Intercultural Negotiation: Individualism-Collectivism and Paths to Integrative Agreements," *Human Communication Research* 26 (2000): 591–617; Ge Gao, "An Initial Analysis of the Effects of Face and Concern for 'Other' in Chinese Interpersonal Communication," *International Journal of Intercultural Relations* 22 (1998): 467–482.

59. Ringo Ma, "The Role of Unofficial Intermediaries in Interpersonal Conflicts in the Chinese Culture," *Communication Quarterly* 40 (1992): 269–278.

60. Ting-Toomey, "Face Negotiation Theory" (see note 37).

61. Susan Cross and Robert Rosenthal, "Three Models of Conflict Resolution: Effects on Intergroup Expectancies and Attitudes," *Journal of Social Issues* 55(3) (1999): 561–580.

Chapter 11

1. Tamar Katriel, *Communal Webs: Communication and Culture in Contemporary Israel* (Albany: State University of New York Press, 1991), 35–49.

2. Joseph P. Forgas and Michael H. Bond, "Cultural Influences on the Perception of Interaction Episodes," *Journal of Cross-Cultural Psychology* 11 (1985): 75–88.

3. Robert T. Craig and Karen Tracy, *Conversational Coherence: Form, Structure, and Strategy* (Beverly Hills, CA: Sage, 1983); Susan B. Shimanoff, *Communication Rules: Theory and Research* (Beverly Hills, CA: Sage, 1980).

4. Aubrey Fisher, *Interpersonal Communication: Pragmatics of Human Relationships* (New York: Random House, 1987), 59.

5. Kellermann calls these interaction scenes "Memory Organization Packets" (MOPs). Our description of her research is based on the following: Kathy Kellermann, "The Conversation MOP II: Progression Through Scenes in Discourse," *Human Communication Research* 17 (1991): 385–414; Kathy Kellermann, "The Conversation MOP: A Model of Pliable Behavior," *The Cognitive Bases of Interpersonal Communication,* ed. Dean E. Hewes (Hillsdale, NJ: Erlbaum, 1995);

Kathy Kellerman and Tae-Seop Lim, "The Conversation MOP III: Timing of Scenes in Discourse," *Journal of Personality and Psychology* 54 (1990): 1163–1179.

6. See Gary L. Kreps and Elizabeth N. Kunimoto, *Effective Communication in Multicultural Health Care Settings* (Thousand Oaks, CA: Sage, 1994); Kim Witte and Kelly Morrison, "Intercultural and Cross-Cultural Health Communication," *Intercultural Communication Theory,* ed. Richard L. Wiseman (Thousand Oaks, CA: Sage, 1995), 216–246; Joan Luckmann, *Transcultural Communication in Health Care* (Albany, NY: Delmar-Thomson Learning, 2000).

7. For a detailed discussion of professional opportunities in transcultural nursing, see Margaret M. Andrews, "Cultural Perspectives on Nursing in the 21st Century," *Journal of Professional Nursing* 8 (1992): 7–15.

8. See, for example, Joyceen S. Boyle and Margaret M. Andrews, *Transcultural Concepts in Nursing Care,* 2nd ed. (Philadelphia: Lippincott, 1995); Susan M. Dobson, *Transcultural Nursing: A Contemporary Imperative* (London: Scutari Press, 1991); Geri-Ann Galanti, *Caring for Patients from Different Cultures: Case Studies from American Hospitals,* 2nd ed. (Philadelphia: University of Pennsylvania Press, 1991); Joyce Newman Giger and Ruth Elaine Davidhizar (eds.), *Transcultural Nursing: Assessment and Intervention,* 2nd ed. (St. Louis: Mosby Year Book, 1995); Janice M. Morse (ed.), *Issues in Cross-Cultural Nursing* (New York: Churchill Livingstone, 1988); Janice M. Morse (ed.), *Cross-Cultural Nursing: Anthropological Approaches to Nursing Research* (Philadelphia: Gordon and Breach, 1989); Cheryl L. Reynolds and Madeleine Leininger; *Cultural Care Diversity and Universality Theory* (Newbury Park, CA: Sage, 1993); Jean Uhl (ed.), *Application of Cultural Concepts to Nursing Care: Proceedings of the Ninth Annual Transcultural Nursing Conference,* Scottsdale, AZ, September 1993 (Salt Lake City: Transcultural Nursing Society, 1984).

9. See, for example, Larry D. Purnell and Betty J. Paulanka, *Transcultural Health Care: A Culturally Competent Approach* (Philadelphia: F. A. Davis, 1998).

10. Kathryn Hopkins Kavanagh and Patricia H. Kennedy, *Promoting Cultural Diversity Strategies*

for Health Care Professionals (Newbury Park, CA: Sage, 1992), 28.

11. Boyle and Andrews, 26–36; Witte and Morrison, 221–222.

12. Rachel E. Spector, *Cultural Diversity in Health and Illness,* 4th ed. (Norwalk, CT: Appleton-Lange, 1996), 193.

13. Sam Chan, "Families with Asian Roots," *Developing Cross-Cultural Competence: A Guide for Working with Young Children and Their Families,* ed. Eleanor W. Lynch and Marci J. Hanson (Baltimore: Paul Brookes, 1992), 223.

14. Richard H. Dana, "The Cultural Self as Locus for Assessment and Intervention with American Indians/Alaska Natives," *Journal of Multicultural Counseling and Development* 28 (2000): 66–82.

15. Chan, 222.

15. For a discussion of these issues, see Kavanagh and Kennedy, 22–24.

17. Ursula M. Wilson, "Nursing Care of American Indian Patients," *Ethnic Nursing Care: A Multicultural Approach,* ed. Modesta Soberano Orque, Bobbie Bloch, and Lidia S. Ahumada Monroy (St. Louis: Mosby, 1983), 277.

18. Joan Kuipers, "Mexican Americans," *Transcultural Nursing: Assessment and Intervention,* 2nd ed., ed. Joyce Newman Giger and Ruth Elaine Davidhizar (St. Louis: Mosby Year Book, 1995), 205–234.

19. Boyle and Andrews, 151–155.

20. Noreen Mokuau and Pemerika Tauili'ili, "Families with Native Hawaiian and Pacific Island Roots," *Developing Cross-Cultural Competence: A Guide for Working with Young Children and Their Families,* ed. Eleanor W. Lynch and Marci J. Hanson (Baltimore: Paul Brookes, 1992), 313.

21. Witte and Morrison, 224.

22. Kavanagh and Kennedy, 37. See also Kuipers.

23. See Kuipers, 209 and 212.

24. Kuipers, 209. See also Kavanagh and Kennedy; Wilson, 277.

25. Chan, 241.

26. Witte and Morrison, 227.

27. See for example, Luckmann, 61.

28. Min-Sun Kim, Renee Storm Klingle, William F. Sharkey, Hee Sun Park, David H. Smith, and Deborah Cai, "A Test of a Cultural Model of Patients' Motivation for Verbal Communication in Patient-Doctor Interactions," *Communication Monographs* 67 (2000): 262–283.

29. Boyle and Andrews, 55.

30. Haffner, "Translation Is Not Enough: Interpreting in a Medical Setting," *Western Journal of Medicine* 157 (1992): 255–260.

31. Luckmann, 191.

32. Luckmann, 56–57.

33. Jeffrey Trawick-Smith, *Early Childhood Development: A Multicultural Perspective,* 2nd ed. (Upper Saddle River, NJ: Merrill, 2000).

34. Lisa Delpit, *Other People's Children: Cultural Conflict in the Classroom* (New York: New Press, 1995); C. Raeff, Patricia M. Greenfield, and Blanca Quiroz, "Conceptualizing Interpersonal Relationships in the Cultural Contexts of Individualism and Collectivism," *Variability in the Social Construction of the Child,* ed. S. Harkness, C. Raeff, and C. Super, New Directions in Child Development, no. 87 (San Francisco: Jossey-Bass, 2000).

35. Patricia Phelan, Ann Locke Davidson, and Hanh Cao Yu, "Students' Multiple Worlds: Navigating the Borders of Family, Peer, and School Cultures," *Renegotiating Cultural Diversity in American Schools,* ed. Patricia Phelan and Ann Locke Davidson (New York: College Press, 1993), 52–88.

36. For an interesting ethnographic description of how Navajo philosophy permeates curriculum and classroom behaviors in a Navajo community college, see Charles A. Braithwaite, "Sa'ah Naagháí Bik'eh Hózhóón: An Ethnography of Navajo Educational Communication Practices," *Communication Education* 46 (1997): 219–233.

37. K. David Roach and Paul R. Byrne, "A Cross-Cultural Comparison of Instructor Communication in American and German Classrooms," *Communication Education* 50 (2001): 1–14.

38. Shumung Lu, "Culture and Compliance Gaining in the Classroom: A Preliminary Investigation of Chinese College Teachers' Use of Behavior Alteration Techniques," *Communication Education* 46 (1997): 20–21.

39. Cristy Lee, Timothy Levine, and Ronald Cambra, "Resisting Compliance in the Multicultural Classroom," *Communication Education* 46 (1997): 29–43; Lu, 10–28.

40. Lu, 24–25.

41. Elise Trumbull, Carrie Rothstein-Fisch, Patricia M. Greenfield, and Blanca Quiroz, *Bridging Cultures between Home and School: A Guide for Teachers* (Mahwah, NJ: Erlbaum, 2001), 10.

42. Jennie R. Joe and Randi Suzanne Malach, "Families with Native American Roots," *Developing Cross-Cultural Competence: A Guide for Working with Young Children and Their Families,* ed. Eleanor W. Lynch and Marci J. Hanson (Baltimore: Paul Brookes, 1992), 110.

43. Eunkyong L. Yook and Rosita Albert, "Perceptions of the Appropriateness of Negotiation in Education Settings: A Cross-Cultural Comparison among Koreans and Americans," *Communication Education* 47 (1998): 18–29.

44. Jolene Koester and Myron W. Lustig, "Communication Curricula in the Multicultural University," *Communication Education* 40 (1991): 250–254.

45. Paul David Bolls, Alex Tan, and Erica Austin, "An Exploratory Comparison of Native American and Caucasian Students' Attitudes toward Teacher Communicative Behavior and toward School," *Communication Education* 46 (1997): 198–202. See also Paul David Bolls and Alex Tan, "Communication Anxiety and Teacher Communication Competence Among Native American and Caucasian Students," *Communication Research Reports* 13 (1996): 205–213.

46. Barbara J. Shade and Clara A. New, "Cultural Influences on Learning: Teaching Implications," *Multicultural Education: Issues and Perspectives,* 2nd ed., ed. James A. Banks and Cherry A. McGee Banks (Boston: Allyn and Bacon, 1993), 320.

47. Maria E. Zuniga, "Families with Latino Roots," *Developing Cross-Cultural Competence: A Guide for Working with Young Children and Their Families,* ed. Eleanor W. Lynch and Marci J. Hanson (Baltimore: Paul Brookes, 1992), 151–179.

48. Joe and Malach, 108; Cornel Pewewardy, "Toward Defining a Culturally Responsive Pedagogy for American Indian Children: The American Indian Magnet School," *Multicultural Education for the Twenty-First Century, Proceedings of the Second Annual Meeting, National Association for Multicultural Education, February 13–16th, 1992,* ed. Carl A. Grant (Morristown, NJ: Paramount, 1992), 218.

49. See Sam Chan, "Families with Pilipino Roots," *Developing Cross-Cultural Competence: A Guide for Working with Young Children and Their Families,* ed. Eleanor W. Lynch and Marci J. Hanson (Baltimore: Paul Brookes, 1992), 276.

50. Leonard Davidman with Patricia T. Davidman, *Teaching with a Multicultural Perspective: A Practical Guide* (New York: Longman, 1994), 43; Trumbull, Rothstein-Fisch, Greenfield, and Quiroz, 55–74.

51. Virginia Shirin Sharifzadeh, "Families with Middle Eastern Roots," *Developing Cross-Cultural Competence: A Guide for Working with Young Children and Their Families,* ed. Eleanor W. Lynch and Marci J. Hanson (Baltimore: Paul Brookes, 1992), 341.

52. Jerry McClelland and Chen Chen, "Standing up for a Son: School Experiences of a Mexican Immigrant Mother," *Hispanic Journal of Behavioral Science* 19 (1997): 281–300.

53. McClelland and Chen, 291.

54. Josina Macau, *Embracing Diversity in the Classroom: Communication Ethics in an Age of Diversity,* ed. Josina Makau and Ronald C. Arnett (Urbana: University of Illinois Press, 1997), 48–67.

55. Joe and Malach, 109.

56. See, for example, James Calvert Scott, "Developing Cultural Fluency: The Goal of International Business Communication Instruction in the 21st Century," *Journal of Education for Business* 74 (1999): 140–143.

57. See, for example, John A. S. Abecasis-Phillips, *Doing Business with the Japanese* (Lincolnwood, IL: NTC Business Books, 1994); Roger E. Axtell, *The Do's and Taboos of Hosting International Visitors* (New York: Wiley, 1990); Gerald F. Cavanagh, *American Business Values,* 3rd ed. (Englewood Cliffs, NJ: Prentice-Hall, 1990); Chin-Ning Chu, *The Asian Mind Game: Unlocking the Hidden Agenda of the Asian Business Culture: A Westerner's Survival Manual* (New York: Rawson Associates, 1991); Boye Lafayette De Mente, *How to Do Business with the Japanese,* 2nd ed. (Lincolnwood, IL: NTC Business Books, 1993); Farid Elashmawi and Philip R. Harris, *Multicultural Management: New Skills for Global Success* (Houston: Gulf, 1993); Christopher Engholm, *When Business East Meets Business West: The Guide to Practice and Protocol in the Pacific Rim* (New York: Wiley, 1991); Edward T. Hall and Mildred Reed Hall, *Hidden Differences: Doing Business with the Japanese* (Garden City, NY: Anchor Press, 1987); Timothy Harper, *Cracking the New European Markets* (New York: Wiley, 1992); Philip R. Harris and Robert T. Moran, *Managing Cultural Differences,* 3rd ed. (Houston: Gulf, 1991); Michael Johnson and

Robert T. Moran, *Robert T. Moran's Cultural Guide to Doing Business in Europe,* 2nd ed. (Oxford: Butterworth-Heinemann, 1992); Christer Jonsson, *Communication in International Bargaining* (London: Pinter, 1990); Dennis Laurie, *Yankee Samurai: American Managers Speak Out About What It's Like to Work for Japanese Companies in the U.S.* (New York: HarperCollins, 1992); Candace Bancroft McKinniss and Arthur Natella, Jr., *Business in Mexico: Managerial Behavior, Protocol, and Etiquette* (New York: Haworth Press, 1994); Robert T. Moran, *Getting Your Yen'$ Worth: How to Negotiate with Japan, Inc.* (Houston: Gulf, 1985); Robert T. Moran, Philip R. Harris, and William G. Stripp, *Developing the Global Organization: Strategies for Human Resource Professionals* (Houston: Gulf, 1993); Robert T. Moran and William G. Stripp, *Dynamics of Successful International Business Negotiations* (Houston: Gulf, 1991); Mary O'Hara-Devereaux and Robert Johansen, *Globalwork: Bridging Distance, Culture, and Time* (San Francisco: Jossey-Bass, 1994); Sondra Snowdon, *The Global Edge: How Your Company Can Win in the International Marketplace* (New York: Simon and Schuster, 1986); Sondra B. Thiederman, *Profiting in America's Multicultural Marketplace: How to Do Business Across Cultural Lines* (New York: Lexington Books, 1991); I. William Zartman (ed.), *International Multilateral Negotiation: Approaches to the Management of Complexity* (San Francisco: Jossey-Bass, 1994).

58. Rosalie L. Tung, "Expatriate Assignments: Enhancing Success and Minimizing Failure," *Academy of Management Executive* 1 (1987): 117–126.

59. Gary Oddou and Mark Mendenhall, "Expatriate Performance Appraisal: Problems and Solutions," *International Human Resource Management,* ed. Mark Mendenhall and Gary Oddou (Boston: PWS-Kent, 1991), 364–374; Rosalie Tung and Edwin L. Miller, "Managing in the Twenty-First Century: The Need for Global Orientation," *Management International Review* 30 (1990): 5–18.

60. Harris and Moran.

61. Harris and Moran.

62. De Mente; Engholm.

63. Masami Nishishiba and David Ritchie, "The Concept of Trustworthiness: A Cross-Cultural Comparison Between Japanese and U.S. Business People," *Journal of Applied Communication Research* 28 (2000): 347–367.

64. Fons Trompenaars, *Riding the Waves of Culture: Understanding Diversity in Global Business* (Burr Ridge, IL: Irwin, 1994). See also J. C. Bruno Teboul, Ling Chen, and Lynn M. Fritz, "Intercultural Organizational Communication Research in Multinational Organizations," *Communicating in Multinational Organizations,* ed. Richard L. Wiseman and Robert Shuter (Thousand Oaks, CA: Sage, 1994), 12–29.

65. William B. Gudykunst and Yuko Matsumoto, "Cross-Cultural Variability of Communication in Personal Relationships," *Communication in Personal Relationships Across Cultures,* ed. William B. Gudykunst, Stella Ting-Toomey, and Tsukasa Nishida (Thousand Oaks: Sage, 1996), 19–56.

66. Cindy P. Lindsay and Bobby L. Dempsey, "Ten Painfully Learned Lessons about Working in China: The Insights of Two American Behavioral Scientists," *Journal of Applied Behavioral Science* 19 (1983): 265–276.

67. Alex Blackwell, "Negotiating in Europe," *Hemispheres,* July 1994, 43.

68. Jo Ann G. Heydenfeldt, "The Influence of Individualism/Collectivism on Mexican and US Business Negotiation," *International Journal of Intercultural Relations,* 24 (2000): 383–407.

69. Alan Goldman, "Communication in Japanese Multinational Organizations," *Communicating in Multinational Organizations,* ed. Richard L. Wiseman and Robert Shuter (Thousand Oaks, CA: Sage, 1994), 49–59.

70. Lecia Archer and Kristine L. Fitch, "Communication in Latin American Multinational Organizations," *Communicating in Multinational Organizations,* ed. Richard L. Wiseman and Robert Shuter (Thousand Oaks, CA: Sage, 1994), 75–93.

71. Myria Watkins Allen, Patricia Amason, and Susan Holmes, "Social Support, Hispanic Emotional Acculturative Stress and Gender," *Communication Studies* 49 (1998): 139–157; Patricia Amason, Myria Watkins Allen, and Susan A. Holmes, "Social Support and Acculturative Stress in the Multicultural Workplace," *Journal of Applied Communication Research* 27 (1999): 310–334.

72. Lindsay and Dempsey.

73. Harris and Moran.
74. William I. Gordon, "Organizational Imperatives and Cultural Modifiers," *Business Horizons* 27 (1984): 81.
75. See, for example, Christalyn Branner and Tracey Wilson, *Doing Business with Japanese Men: A Woman's Handbook* (Berkeley, CA: Stone Bridge Press, 1993).
76. Farid Elashmawi and Philip R. Harris, *Multicultural Management 2000: Essential Cultural Insights for Global Business Success* (Houston: Gulf, 1998), 118–125.
77. Richard H. Reeves-Ellington, "Using Cultural Skills for Cooperative Advantage in Japan," *Human Organization* 52 (1993): 203–215.
78. Young Yun Kim and Sheryl Paulk, "Interpersonal Challenges and Personal Adjustments: A Qualitative Analysis of the Experiences of American and Japanese Co-Workers," *Communicating in Multinational Organizations,* ed. Richard L. Wiseman and Robert Shuter (Thousand Oaks, CA: Sage, 1994), 117–140. See also Alan E. Omens, Stephen R. Jenner, and James R. Beatty, "Intercultural Perceptions in United States Subsidiaries of Japanese Companies," *International Journal of Intercultural Relations* 11 (1987): 249–264; David W. Shwalb, Barbara J. Shwalb, Delwyn L. Harnisch, Martin L. Maehr, and Kiyoshi Akabane, "Personal Investment in Japan and the U.S.A.: A Study of Worker Motivation," *International Journal of Intercultural Relations* 16 (1992): 107–124.
79. Harris and Moran, 418.
80. Sonja Vegdahl Hur and Ben Seunghwa Hur, *Culture Shock! Korea* (Singapore: Times Books International, 1988), 34.
81. Nongluck Sriussadaporn-Charoenngam and Fredric M Jablin, "An Exploratory Study of Communication Competence in Thai Organizations," *Journal of Business Communication* 36 (1999): 382–418.
82. See, for example, Monir H. Tayeb, *The Management of a Multicultural Workforce* (New York: Wiley, 1996); R. Roosevelt Thomas, Jr., *Redefining Diversity* (New York: AMACOM, 1996); Lewis Brown Griggs and Lente Louise Louw (eds.), *Valuing Diversity* (New York: McGraw-Hill, 1995).
83. Steven H. Cady and Joanie Valentine, "Team Innovation and Perceptions of Consideration: What Difference Does Diversity Make?" *Small Group Research* 30 (1999): 730–750. See also Georges Buzaglo and Susan A. Wheelan, "Facilitating Work Team Effectiveness: Case Studies from Central America," *Small Group Research* 30 (1999): 108–129; Graeme L Harrison, Jill L. McKinnon, Anne Wu, and Chee W. Chow, "Cultural Influences on Adaptation to Fluid Workgroups and Teams," *Journal of International Business Studies* 31 (2000): 489–505.
84. Lisa Millhous, "The Experience of Culture in Multicultural Groups: Case Studies of Russian-American Collaboration in Business," *Small Group Research* 30(3) (1999): 280–308.
85. Percy W. Thomas, "A Cultural Rapport Model," *Valuing Diversity,* ed. Lewis Brown Griggs and Lente Louise Louw (New York: McGraw-Hill, 1995), 136–137.
86. Thomas, 137.
87. Charles R. Bantz, "Cultural Diversity and Group Cross-Cultural Team Research," *Journal of Applied Communication Research* 21 (1993): 1–20.

Chapter 12

1. For reviews of the vast literature on ethics and intercultural communication, see Fred L. Casmir (ed.), *Ethics in Intercultural and International Communication* (Mahwah, NJ: Erlbaum, 1997); J. Vernon Jensen, *Ethical Issues in the Communication Process* (Mahweh, NJ: Erlbaum, 1997).
2. David W. Kale, "Ethics in Intercultural Communication," *Intercultural Communication: A Reader,* 6th ed., ed. Larry A. Samovar and Richard E. Porter (Belmont, CA: Wadsworth, 1991), 423.
3. Kale.
4. John F. Kennedy, "Remarks Intended for Delivery to the Texas Democratic State Committee in the Municipal Auditorium in Austin," November 22, 1963. Accessed online October 10, 2001. www.cs.umb.edu/jfklibrary/j112263a.htm.
5. Gale S. Auletta and Terry Jones, "Reconstituting the Inner Circle," *American Behavioral Scientist* 34 (1990): 137–152.
6. Troy Duster, "Understanding Self-Segregation on the Campus," *Chronicle of Higher Education,* September 25, 1991, B2.

Author Index

Abecasis-Phillips, John A. S., 371
Aboud, Frances E., 353
Abrahamson, Paul R., 352
Adelman, Mara B., 359
Adler, Nancy, 357
Agnoli, Franca, 360
Akabane, Kiyoshi, 373
Alba, Richard D., 349, 353
Albert, Rosita Daskel, 359, 371
Aldne, Lynn E., 357
Allard, Rèal, 361
Allen, Myria Watkins, 372
Allen, Theodore W., 353
Allport, Gordon W., 154, 173, 355
Altchech, Marie, 326
Altman, Irwin, 365
Alvarado, Diana, 32
Amason, Patricia, 372
Amir, Yehuda, 162, 356
Andersen, Janis F., 349, 357, 365
Andersen, Peter A., 202, 349, 357, 365
Andrews, Margaret M., 369, 370
Angelou, Maya, 91
Antonovsky, Avishai, 89, 90, 352
Anzaldúa, Gloria, 73
Applegate, James L., 365
Archer, Lecia, 372
Ardrey, Robert, 179, 358
Argyle, Michael, 179, 358
Arnett, Ronald C., 341, 371

Asante, Molefi Kete, 358, 359, 361
Askling, Lawrence, R., 351
Auletta, Gale S., 356, 373
Austin, Erica, 371
Axtell, Roger E., 371

Backlund, Philip M., 351
Backman, Carl W., 365
Bacon, Jean, 354
Badzinski, Diane M., 361
Banaji, Mahzarin R., 360
Banks, Anna, 359
Banks, Cherry A. McGee, 371
Banks, James A., 371
Banks, Stephen E., 359
Banks, Stephen P., 360
Bantz, Charles R., 324, 373
Bar-Tal, Daniel, 354
Barabak, Mark Z., 350
Baratz, Sheryl, 365
Barge, J. Kevin, 81
Barker, Larry L., 24
Barker, W. B., 349
Barnlund, Dean C., 16, 191, 286, 348, 358, 366, 367, 368
Barr, Cameron, W., 318
Barsamian, David, 355
Basso, Keith H., 255, 363
Bateson, Mary Catherine, 75, 308
Baxter, Leslie A., 273, 365
Beatty, James R., 373
Beeman, William O., 365
Bennett, Milton J., 93, 108, 352
Bentahila, Abdelala, 362

Berger, Charles R., 154, 284, 355, 367, 368
Berkowitz, Leonard, 365
Berlo, David K., 348
Bernal, Martha E., 349, 353
Berry, John W., 169, 356, 357
Bird, S. Elizabeth, 158, 355
Birdwhistell, Ray, 182, 358
Bizjak, Tony, 131
Blackwell, Alex, 372
Blake, Cecil A., 358
Blauner, Robert, 157, 355
Blea, Irene I., 364
Bletzer, Siri S., 364
Bliss, Anne, 249, 362
Bochner, Arthur P., 348, 350
Bock, Hope, 361
Bodenhausen, Galen V., 355
Bolls, Paul David, 371
Bolton, Kingsley, 363
Bond, Michael H., 130, 295, 353, 358, 369
Boni, Albert and Charles, 350
Booth-Butterfield, Melanie, 257, 364
Bornman, Elirea, 364
Boski, Pawel, 169, 356, 357
Boster, Franklin, 355
Bouchard, Thomas J., Jr., 349
Bourhis, Richard Y., 361
Bowers, John Waite, 365
Bowser, Benjamin P., 356
Boyle, Joyceen S., 369, 370
Brabant, Sarah, 357
Bradac, James J., 361, 367
Bradford, Lisa, 142, 180, 354, 358

Bradac, James J., 351
Braithwaite, Charles, 325, 370
Branner, Christalyn, 373
Breger, Rosemary, 291
Brein, Michael, 357
Bresnahan, Mary, 363, 366
Brewer, Marilyn B., 353, 355
Brigham, John C., 355
Brislin, Richard W., 154, 341, 355, 356, 360
Brittingham, Angela, 347
Brodkin, Karen, 348
Brooles, Geraldine, 200
Brosnahan, Tom, 358
Brown, Penelope, 275, 277, 365, 366
Brown, Roger, 359
Brown, Rupert, 356
Brunner, Claire C., 351
Bruschke, Jon, 362
Bumiller, Elisabeth, 108, 270, 351
Burgoon, Judee K., 154, 283, 355, 368
Buriel, Raymond, 364
Burrough, Nancy F., 361
Buzaglo, Georges, 373
Byrne, Paul R., 370

Cady, Steven H., 373
Cai, Deborah A., 363, 369, 370
Calabrese, Richard H., 367
Campbell, Donald T., 353
Canary, Daniel J., 366
Carbaugh, Donal L., 363
Cargile, Aaron Castelan, 361
Carlson, Dawn S., 352

Carpenter, Sandra L., 355
Carroll, Jessie, 188
Carroll, Raymonde, 282, 324
Case, Charles E., 356
Casmir, Fred L., 373
Cavanagh, Gerald F., 371
Chan, Sam, 370, 371
Chang, Hui-Ching, 124, 134, 279, 352, 353
Chang, Leslie, 297
Chen, Chen, 313, 371
Chen, Guo-Ming, 168, 353, 357
Chen, Ling, 372
Chen, Victoria, 368
Chen, Zhuojun Joyce, 354
Cheng, Li-Rong Lilly, 360
Cherrie, Craig, 360
Choi, Jung-Wook, 202
Chow, Chee W., 373
Chu, Chin-Ning, 371
Chua, Elizabeth, 367
Chung, Jensen, 353
Church, Austin, 357
Churchill, Winston, 11, 184, 209
Cichon, Elaine J., 351
Clark, Cheryl, 362
Clatterbuck, Glen W., 367
Cluckhohn, Clyde, 25
Cocroft, Beth-Ann, 366
Cody, Liza, 164
Cole, Michael, 246, 360, 362
Coles, Robert, 248
Collier, Mary Jane, 31, 100, 348, 352, 361, 362, 364
Condon, John C., 17, 93, 181, 247, 249, 266, 348, 352, 358, 360, 362
Condon, William S., 359
Confucius, 132
Connor, Ulla, 260, 362, 363
Conquergood, Dwight, 21, 348
Cornell, Stephen, 349
Cose, Ellis, 349
Coskran, Kathleen, 215
Coull, Alastair, 354
Coupland, Nikolas, 356, 361, 363
Craig, Robert T., 369
Crevecoeur, J. Hector St. John, 350
Cross, Susan, 369
Crossette, Barbara, 328

Cummings, Joe, 364
Cupach, William R., 351, 366, 367
Cushner, Kenneth, 325, 341, 360

Daley, Catherine, 326
Daloz Parks, Sharon, 45
Dana, Richard H., 304, 370
Dance, Frank E. X., 9, 348
Daniel, Jack L., 102, 104, 352
Darwin, Charles, 179, 358
David, Kenneth H., 357
Davidhizar, Ruth Elaine, 369, 370
Davidman, Leonard, 371
Davidman, Patricia T., 371
Davidson, Ann Locke, 370
Davidson, Cathy N., 173
Davis, Lennard J., 204
Davis, Martha, 359
Dawson, Raymond, 353
de Courtivron, Isabelle, 232
de la Garza, Rodolfo O., 350
De Mente, Boye Lafayette, 371, 372
Delgado, Fernando, 145, 354
Delgado, Melvin, 352
Delgado, Richard, 348
Delpit, Lisa, 370
Dembling, Sophia, 266
Dempsey, Bobby L., 372
DeSipio, Louis, 350
DeVito, Joseph A., 24, 358
DeVos, George, 365
Dew, Anna-Marie, 359
Dillard, James Price, 365
Dirie, Waris, 112, 244
Dobson, Susan M., 369
Dog, Mary Crow, 120
Dolan, Daniel, 251, 363
Dolphin, Carol Zinner, 349
Donnerstein, E., 355
Donnerstein, M., 355
Dorris, Michael, 107, 223, 360
Douglas, William, 367
Dovidio, John F., 355, 356
Drake, Laura E., 369
Duck, Stephen W., 365
Dunbar, Edward, 347, 354
Duong, Tenor, 364
Duster, Troy, 340, 373

Eck, Diana, 5, 219, 334, 336
Edwards, John R., 229, 361
Ekman, Paul, 179, 183, 186, 358
Elashmawi, Farid, 319, 320, 325, 371, 373
Ellis, Carolyn, 348
Ellsworth, Phoebe, 358
Engholm, Christopher, 371, 372
Enloe, Walter, 357
Espiritu, Yen Le, 349
Estrada, Maria J., 312
Evans, Charlotte, 349
Eyler, Kathryn, 326

Fadiman, Anne, 326
Falcon, Angelo, 350
Fay, Todd L., 360
Feagin, Joe R., 355
Fehr, Beverly, 364
Feig, John Paul, 272, 364, 365
Fein, Steven, 355
Ferguson, Russell, 353, 354
Fernandez, Denise Rotondo, 352
Ferrell, David, 348
Fisher, B. Aubrey, 298, 369
Fishman, Joshua A., 361
Fitch, Kristine L., 372
Flores, Lisa A., 361
Foa, Edna B., 368
Foa, Uriel G., 368
Forgas, Joseph P., 295, 369
Forsyth, Susan, 364
Frankenberg, Ruth, 348
Franklin, Brenda, 202
Franklyn-Stokes, Arelen, 356, 361
Fridlund, Alan J., 358
Friesen, Wallace V., 183, 358
Fritz, Lynn M., 372
Frymier, Ann Bainbridge, 359
Fuchs, Stephan, 356

Gaertner, Samuel L., 355, 356
Gaines, Stanley O., Jr., 364
Galanti, Geri-Ann, 369
Gallois, Cynthia, 356, 361
Gao, Ge, 81, 369
Garcia, F. Chris, 350
Garcia, John, 350
Garcia, Stella D., 364
Garcia, Wintilo, 368, 369

Gardner, Wendi L., 355
Garrison, John P., 357
Gass, Robert, 362
Gaut, Deborah A., 24
Gaw, Kevin F., 357
Gelernter, Car Quan, 349
Gergen, Kenneth, 368
Gever, Martha, 354
Giger, Joyce Newman, 369, 370
Giles, Howard, 163, 226–|228, 356, 360, 361, 363
Goffman, Erving, 274, 365
Golden, Kristen, 142
Goldman, Alan, 372
Goldstein, Eleanor, 348, 349, 350, 355
González, Alberto, 173, 260, 362, 368
Gonzalez, Alexander, 359
Gonzalez, Christiane F., 359
Goody, Esther N., 365
Gordon, William I., 373
Gramling, Robert, 357
Grant, Carl A., 371
Graumann, Carl Friedrich, 354
Gray, Alisa J., 367
Grearson, Jessie Carroll, 86, 104, 177, 188, 287, 289, 348
Greeley, Andrew M., 356
Greenberg, Martin S., 368
Greenfield, Patricia M., 326, 370, 371
Griggs, Lewis Brown, 373
Gudykunst, William B., 168, 202, 256, 280, 284, 291, 316, 348, 350, 356, 357, 359, 361, 363, 366, 367, 368, 372
Guerrero, Sherrie L., 367
Gullahorn, J. E., 357
Gumperz, John J., 237, 360, 362
Gurung, Regan A. R., 364

Haizlip, Shirley Taylor, 19
Hall, Edward T., 111–114, 138, 187, 189, 191, 194, 202, 271, 349, 352, 358, 359, 364, 371
Hall, Mildred Reed, 189, 191, 358, 371
Hamill, James F., 362

Hamilton, Charles V., 252
Hamilton, David L., 354
Hammer, Mitchell R., 168, 180, 357, 358
Hanson, Marci J., 352, 370, 371
Hardin, Curtis, 360
Harkness, S., 370
Harnisch, Delwyn L., 373
Harpending, Henry, 349
Harper, Robert G., 358
Harper, Timothy, 371
Harris, Eddy L., 90
Harris, Philip, 319, 320, 325, 371, 372, 373
Harris, Richard M., 359
Harrison, Graeme L., 373
Harrison, Randall P., 368
Hartl, Daniel L., 349
Harwood, Jake, 361
Hawkes, Kristen, 349
Hecht, Michael L., 63, 100, 202, 350, 351, 352, 361, 362, 364
Heider, Eleanor Rosch, 360
Henley, Nancy M., 358
Henry, William A. III, 347
Hernandez, Elvia, 326
Hernstein, Richard J., 350
Hewes, Dean E., 369
Hewstone, Miles, 163, 354, 355, 356
Heydenfeldt, Jo Ann G., 372
Highwater, Jamake, 138, 352
Hill, Rosanna, 291
Hillerman, Tony, 183
Ho, David Yau-fai, 365
Hockett, Charles F., 205, 359
Hodge, Norman, 303
Hodgins, Holley S., 359
Hofstede, Geert, 115–133, 138, 349, 352, 353
Holmes, Steven A., 348
Holmes, Susan A., 372
Holt, G. Richard, 124, 134, 279, 352, 353
Honeycutt, James M., 367
Hong Kingston, Maxine, 53
Hoobler, Gregory D., 202
Hoopes, David S., 351
Horvath, Ann-Marie, 363, 366
Hotz, Robert Lee, 348

Houston, Marsha, 368
Hsu, Francis L. K., 277, 365
Hu, Hsien Chin, 276, 365, 366
Hu, L., 355
Hubbert, Kimberly N., 367
Hull, W. Frank, 357
Hunt, Earl, 360
Hunter, John E., 363, 366
Huntington, Sharon, 231
Hur, Ben Seunghwa, 275, 353, 373
Hur, Sonja Vegdahl, 275, 353, 373

Ichheiser, Gustav, 349
Ignatiev, Noel, 348
Imahori, T. Todd, 351, 366, 367
Inglehart, Ronald, 352
Ishii, Satoshi, 242, 359, 362

Jablin, Fredric M., 373
Jackson, Donald Dale, 353
Jackson, Jesse, 252–253
Jenner, Stephen R., 373
Jensen, J. Vernon, 373
Joe, Jennie R., 371
Johansen, Robert, 372
Johnson, Blair T., 355
Johnson, Fern L., 237
Johnson, Patricia, 361
Johnstone, Barbara, 250, 362
Jones, E. E., 354, 355
Jones, Elizabeth, 361
Jones, James M., 355
Jones, Stanley E., 358
Jones, Terry, 356, 373
Jonsson, Christer, 372
Jordan, Felicia, 257, 364
Jourard, Sidney M., 359, 368
Judd, Charles M., 354, 355, 356

Kachru, Yamuna, 242, 243, 362
Kahn, A., 355
Kale, David, 331, 332, 373
Kaplan, Robert, 239, 242, 362
Kapp, Robert A., 362
Katriel, Tamar, 295, 369
Katz, Phyllis A., 355, 356
Katz, S. H., 349

Kavanagh, Kathryn Hopkins, 369, 370
Kealey, Daniel J., 167, 351, 357
Keefe, Susan E., 349
Keen, Cheryl, H., 45
Keen, James P., 45
Kellerman, Kathy, 298, 299
Kelly, Clifford W., 350
Kendon, Adam, 359
Kennedy, Antony, 357
Kennedy, John F., 35, 334, 373
Kennedy, Patricia H., 369, 370
Key, Mary Ritchie, 359
Kidder, Louise H., 357
Kim, Min-Sun, 257, 278, 363, 364, 366, 370
Kim, Uichol, 169, 356, 357
Kim, Young Yun, 145, 170, 173, 321, 348, 354, 356, 357, 366, 369
Kincaid, D. Lawrence, 253, 353, 363
King, Martin Luther, Jr., 35
King, Rodney, 139
Kingsolver, Barbara, 33
Kipling, Rudyard, 77
Kirszner, Laurie G., 362
Klineberg, Otto, 357
Klingle, Renee Storm, 363, 370
Klopf, Donald W., 16, 254, 348, 359, 363
Kluckhohn, Clyde, 54, 105, 348
Kluckhohn, Florence, 91–94, 352
Knight, George P., 349, 353
Kochman, Thomas, 257, 364
Koester, Jolene, 54, 72, 81, 350, 351, 363, 366, 367, 371
Koestner, Richard, 359
Korzenny, Felipe, 232, 353, 360, 361, 362, 364, 366
Kraft, Dina, 362
Krebs, Nina Boyd, 81
Kreps, Gary L., 369
Krizek, Robert, 142, 350, 354
Kroeber, Alfred L., 25, 54, 348

Kudoh, Tsutomu, 359
Kuipers, Joan, 370
Kunda, Ziva, 153
Kunimoto, Elizabeth N., 369
Kwok, Helen, 363

LaFrance, Marianne, 187, 358
Landers, Ann, 123
Landry, Rodrique, 361
Langdon, Henriette W., 359
Lanigan, Mary L., 351
Lapinski, Maria Knight, 355
Larson, Carl E., 9, 348
Laurie, Dennis, 372
Lawrence-Lightfoot, Sara, 156
Lee, Carmen M., 367
Lee, Chang-rae, 116, 207
Lee, Cristy, 370
Lee, Wen Shu, 212, 359
Leichty, Greg, 365
Leininger, Madeleine, 369
Lennon, John, 35
Levinger, George, 368
Levinson, Stephen C., 237, 275, 277, 360, 365, 366
Lewin, Philip, 357
Lewis, Richard, Jr., 364
Li, Fan, 355
Lim, Tae-Seop, 275, 365, 369
Lindsay, Cindy P., 372
Linville, P. W., 355
Lippmann, Walter, 151, 354
Littlefield, Robert, 368
Littlejohn, Stephen, 222, 360
Liu, James H., 364
Locke, Don C., 352, 364
Lopez, Ian F. Haney, 348
Louw, Lente Louise, 373
Lovato, Roberto, 62
Lu, Shumung, 370
Lubman, Stanley B., 249, 362
Luckman, Joan, 369, 370
Lustig, Myron W., 26, 54, 81, 349, 350, 359, 365, 371
Lykken, David T., 349
Lynch, Eleanor W., 352, 370, 371

Ma, Ringo, 289, 352, 369
Mackie, Diane M., 354
MacLean, Malcolm S., Jr., 348
Macrae, C. Neil, 354, 355
Maehr, Martin L., 373
Magnier, Mark, 293
Mah, Adeline Yen, 140
Mahony, Rosemary, 192
Makau, Josina, 313, 341, 371
Malach, Randi Suzanne, 371
Mandell, Stephen R., 362
Marie, Vicki, 361
Marsella, Anthony J., 365
Martin, Judith N., 142, 180, 350, 354, 357, 358, 361
Masterson, John T., 351
Masumoto, Tomoko, 366, 368
Matarazzo, Jospeh D., 358
Matsumoto, David, 202, 359
Matsumoto, Yuko, 316, 372
Matz, S. Irene, 368
Mayo, Clara, 187, 358
McAuliffe, Christa, 335
McCroskey, James C., 363
McCullough, David, 36, 349
McGue, Matthew, 349
McKinniss, Candace Bancroft, 372
McKinnon, Jill L., 373
McLaughlin, Margaret, 367
McLelland, Averil, 325
McLelland, Jerry, 313, 371
McLuhan, Marshall, 4
Meer, Ameena, 196
Mehrabian, Albert, 271, 364
Mendenhall, Mark E., 347, 372
Mercado, Giancario, 326
Mercer, Joyce, 185
Miller, Cathleen, 112, 244
Miller, Edwin L., 372
Miller, Gerald R., 367
Millhous, Lisa, 373
Milne, Alan B., 355
Milner, David, 356
Misra, Arpita, 362
Miyabe, Miyuki, 126
Miyahara, Akira, 363, 364, 366
Mody, Bella, 202, 356, 367, 368
Mokhiber, Albert, 152

Mokros, Hartmut B., 354
Mokuau, Noreen, 370
Montgomery, Barbara M., 365
Moran, Robert T., 371, 372, 373
Morreale, Sherwyn P., 81
Morrison, Kelly, 369, 370
Morsbach, Helmut, 365
Morse, Janice M., 369
Mortlock, Elizabeth, 364
Mulac, Anthony, 361
Mullen, Brian, 355
Murphy, Dervla, 100, 128, 245, 330
Murray, Charles, 350

Nakayama, Thomas K., 142, 350, 354, 361
Nash, Dennison, 357
Natella, Arthur, Jr., 372
Nelson, Gayle L., 359
New, Clara A., 371
Newmark, Eileen, 358
Nicholson, Joel D., 352
Nida, Eugene A., 360
Nishida, Tsukasa, 284, 291, 367, 368, 372
Nishishiba, Masami, 372
Noble, John, 364
Noels, Kimberly A., 361
Nomura, Naoki, 367
Nwosu, Peter, 254, 363

O'Hara-Devereaux, Mary, 372
Oberg, Kalvero, 165, 356, 357
Oddou, Gary R., 347, 372
Oetzel, John G., 287, 289, 291, 366, 368
Olebe, Margaret, 72, 351
Olivier, Donald C., 360
Olzak, Susan, 349
Omens, Alan E., 373
Omi, Michael, 349
Opstad, Paul, 185
Orque, Modesta Soberano, 370
Oskamp, Stuart, 173
Oster, Harriet, 358
Ostrom, Thomas M., 355
Ota, Hiroshi, 361
Ottesen, Carol Clark, 21

Padilla, Amado M., 349
Padilla, Felix M., 349
Pakstis, A. J., 349
Palmer, C. Eddie, 357
Pan, Xiaohui, 366, 368
Panetta, Clayann Gilliam, 260, 362
Pantoja, Antonia, 8, 348
Park, Bernadette, 354, 355, 356
Park, Hee Sun, 363, 370
Parks Daloz, Laurent A., 45
Paulanka, Betty J., 326, 369
Paulhus, Delroy L., 357
Paulk, Sheryl, 321, 371
Pavitt, Charles, 350
Paz, Octavio, 21
Peacock, M. Jean, 356
Pedersen, Paul B., 351
Penman, Robyn, 280, 367
Pérez, Amada Irma, 326
Perlman, Daniel, 364
Perry, Wilhemina, 8, 348
Phelan, Patricia, 370
Phinney, Jean S., 144, 353
Pinker, Steven, 237, 359
Pitts, James H., 361
Planalp, Sally, 367
Porter, Richard E., 349, 359, 360, 362, 373
Powell, Colin, 6
Pullum, Geoffrey K., 360
Purnell, Larry D., 326, 369
Purvis, Alan C., 362

Quattrone, G. A., 354
Quindlen, Anna, 148
Quiroz, Blanca, 326, 370, 371

Raeff, C., 370
Ramirez, Albert, 356
Ramsey, Sheila J., 358
Reader, John, 359
Reagan, Ronald, 335
Reeves-Ellington, Richard H., 322, 373
Reid, Joy, 362
Renwick, George W., 351
Reynolds, Cheryl L., 369
Reynolds, Rodney, 367
Ribeau, Sidney A., 63, 100, 350 352, 361, 362, 364
Richmond, Virginia P., 363
Ríos, Diana I., 364

Ritchie, David, 372
Rivera, Semilla M., 364
Roach, K. David, 370
Robinson, W. Peter, 361
Rocher, Steve J., 354
Rodriguez, Richard, 232, 237, 361
Roger, Wilma M., 224, 360
Rogers, David, 202
Rokeach, Milton, 351
Roloff, Michael E., 367
Rosaldo, Renato, 21, 348
Rosenthal, Robert, 369
Rosselli, Francine, 354
Rosten, Leo, 277
Rothenberg, Paula S., 356
Rotheram, Mary Jane, 353
Rothstein-Fisch, Carrie, 326, 370, 371
Ruben, Brent D., 170, 351, 357
Ruhly, Sharon, 358
Russell, James A., 186, 358
Rutherford, Diane K., 367
Rutten, Tim, 56
Ryan, Carey S., 354
Ryan, Ellen Bouchard, 356, 361
Ryder, Andrew G., 357

Safford, Philip, 325
Sagiv, Lilach, 89, 90, 352
Saiyzyk, Pearl, 326
Sallinen-Kuparinen, Aino, 363
Salzman, Mark, 259
Samagalski, Alan, 364
Samovar, Larry A., 349, 359, 360, 362, 373
Sanders, Judith A., 362, 368
Sapir, Edward, 217, 360
Sarbaugh, L. E., 350
Sawires, Jacqueline N., 356
Scarr, Sandra, 349
Scheflen, Albert E., 358
Scherer, Klaus R., 358
Scheu, U. Dagmar, 362
Schmid, Randolph E., 347
Schoenberger, Chana, 70
Schramm, Wilbur, 348
Schrest, Lee, 360
Schwartz, Shalom H., 88, 89, 90, 352
Scollon, Ron, 241, 257, 260, 278, 364, 366

Scollon, Suzie Wong, 278
Scott, Barbara J., 198, 332
Scott, James Calvert, 213, 371
Scribner, Sylvia, 246, 360, 362
Searle, Wendy, 357
Sebastian, Richard J., 361
Sedikides, Constantine, 355
Segal, Nancy, 349
Senn, David J., 368
Seta, Catherine E., 355
Seta, John J., 355
Shade, Barbara J., 371
Shakespeare, William, 327
Shane, Scott, 258
Shannon, Claude E., 348
Shapiro, Robin B., 368, 369
Sharifzadeh, Virginia Shirin, 371
Sharkey, William F., 363, 366, 370
Sherman-Williams, Bonnie, 153, 355
Shin, Ho-Chang, 363, 364, 366
Shorris, Earl, 62, 350
Shuter, Robert, 6, 347, 362, 372, 373
Shwalb, Barbara J., 373
Shwalb, David W., 373
Singelis, Theodore M., 363, 366
Singer, Marshall R., 350
Smallwood, Marya, 202
Smith, David H., 363, 370
Smith, Lauren B., 86, 104, 177, 188, 287, 289, 348
Smitherman, Geneva, 102, 104, 229, 237, 352, 361
Snowdon, Sondra, 372
Spector, Rachel E., 370
Spencer, Paul, 359
Spencer, Steven J., 355
Spitzberg, Brian, 64, 81, 350, 351
Sriussadaporn-Charoennga m, Nongluck, 373
Stabenow, Dana, 161, 254
Stahl, Lijuan, 366, 367
Stangor, Charles, 354, 355
Stavans, Ilan, 170, 223
Stefancic, Jeanne, 348
Steinfatt, Thomas M., 360
Stephan, Cookie White, 368

Stephan, Walter G., 368
Stepina, Lee P., 352
Stewart, Edward C., 93, 108, 352
Stewart, Lea P., 366
Stimpson, Catharine R., 2, 347
Stoneking, Mark, 349
Storti, Craig, 54
Stowe, David, 349
Stripp, William G., 372
Strodbeck, Fred, 91–94, 105, 352
Sueda, Kiyoko, 367
Sullivan, Patricia A., 363
Sumner, William G., 149, 354
Sunnafrank, Michael, 367
Sunwolf, 251
Super, C., 370
Susskind, Joshua, 354
Sylva, Bob, 307

Tajfel, Henri, 225, 353, 354, 361
Takai, Jiro, 366, 368
Takaki, Ronald, 24
Tan, Alex, 371
Tan, Amy, 50, 59
Tanno, Dolores V., 260, 260, 362
Tardy, Charles H., 351
Tatni, Haruyo, 202
Tauili'ili, Pemerika, 370
Tayeb, Monir H., 373
Taylor, Dalmas A., 158, 355, 356
Taylor, Harvey, 272, 365
Teboul, J. C. Bruno, 372
Tellegen, Auke, 349
Thiederman, Sondra B., 372
Thomas, Milt, 31, 348
Thomas, Percy W., 323, 373
Thomas, R. Roosevelt, Jr., 373
Thompson, Micah S., 354
Thybony, Scott, 350
Tilove, Jonathan, 350
Ting-Toomey, Stella, 81, 237, 256, 278, 287, 289, 291, 353, 360, 361, 362, 363, 364, 365, 366, 367, 368, 369, 372

Torres, Ben Fong, 276
Toulmin, Stephen, 244, 362
Tracy, Karen, 365, 369
Trawick-Smith, Jeffrey, 370
Trenholm, Sarah, 24
Triandis, Harry C., 127, 352, 353
Trinh, T. M., 354
Trompenaars, Fons, 316, 372
Trumbull, Elise, 326, 370, 371
Tung, Rosalie L., 372
Turner, John C., 356, 360, 361

Ugwu-oju, Dympna, 28
Uhl, Jean, 369

Valentine, Joanie, 373
van Dijk, Teun A., 156, 355
Vera, Hernán, 355
Verkasalo, Markkku, 89, 90, 352
Vigil, James Diego, 350
Vigilant, Linda, 349
Vine, Ian, 356
Volkman, Toby A., 18

Waldman, Irwin D., 349
Waldron, Vincent, 154, 355
Wallbott, Harald G., 358
Wallender, David, 166
Wanning, Esther, 108, 352
Ward, Colleen, 168, 357, 359
Ward, Ted, 36, 67
Waters, Mary C., 350
Watson, Norman H., 351
Weaver, Warren, 348
Weinberg, Richard A., 349
West, C., 354
Westley, Bruce H., 348
Wetherall, William, 348
Wheelan, Susan A., 373
Wheelan, Tony, 364
Whorf, Benjamin, 217, 221, 360
Wiemann, John M., 351, 363, 368
Wiens, Arthur N., 358
Wilcox, Richard, 366
Wilder, William D., 364, 365
Willis, Richard H., 368
Wilson, Allan C., 349

Wilson, Barbara, 234
Wilson, Steven R., 363, 366, 369
Wilson, Tracey, 373
Wilson, Ursula, 370
Winant, Howard, 349
Winkleman, Michael, 40, 349
Wintermantel, Margret, 354
Wiseman, Richard L., 81, 168, 350, 351, 357, 361, 362, 363, 366, 367, 368, 369, 372, 373
Witte, Kim, 369, 370
Wolfgang, Aaron, 182, 358
Wong, Jeannie, 131
Wong-Scollon, Suzanne, 241, 257, 260, 364, 366
Wood, G. C., 354
Worsnop, Richard L., 350
Wright, Trina J., 368, 369
Wu, Anne, 373

Xi, Changsheng, 368
Xiao, Xiaosui, 362

Yamoto, Jenny, 356
Yancy, George, 364
Yang, Seung-Mock, 367
Yarbrough, A. Elaine, 190, 358
Ye, Ting-Xing, 264
Yokochi, Yumiko, 366, 368
Yong, Mahealani, 360
Yook, Eunkyong L., 371
Yoon, Hye-Jin, 363, 366
Yoon, Kak, 364, 366
Young, Linda Wai Ling, 362
Yousef, Fathi, 93, 181, 247, 351, 358, 360
Yu, Hanh Cao, 370
Yum, June Ock, 135, 254, 353, 363
Yutang, Lin, 364
Yzerbyt, Vincent Y., 354

Zaidi, S. M., 360
Zangwell, Israel, 350
Zanna, Mark P., 352
Zartman, I. William, 372
Zimbardo, Philip G., 359
Zuniga, Maria E., 371

Subject Index

Accents, 230
Acculturation, 169
Accuracy, 13
Achievement, 89
Acquaintances, 263–264
Actional view of communication, 14
Actions, 71
Activation, 272–273
Activities. *See* Try This
Activity orientation, 94–96
Adaptation, 164–170
Adaptors, 187
Adjustment, 164
Adjustment function, 154
Admiration face, 277
Affect blends, 186
Affect displays, 185–186
Affective style, 257
Affiliation, 271–272
African American Vernacular English, 229
African Americans
   activity orientation, 94
   blood type, 40
   body movements, 187
   census figures, 7–9
   Kwanzaa, 143
   racism, 158, 159, 160
   self-orientation, 100
   social relations orientation, 97, 98
   time orientation, 104
Agreement, 13
Algeria, 268, 300
Ambiguity, 76
Amish, 304
Analogical style, 250–251

Anxiety, 281
Anxiety/uncertainty management
   theory, 280–284
Apache tribe, 255
Appropriateness, 64, 68–69
Approval face, 276–277
Arab Americans, 152
Arab countries, 320
Argentina
   dating, 268
   family, 269
   time orientation, 104
Argot, 232
Artifactual code system, 197
Asian Americans
   blood type, 40
   census figures, 7
   defined, 63
   racism, 160
   self-orientation, 101
Assimilation, 164, 168–169
Athabaskan, 257
Autonomy-connection dialectic, 273
Aversive racism, 160

BASIC skills, 72–76
Becoming cultures, 94, 95
Behavioral Assessment Scale for
   Intercultural Competence
   (BASIC), 72–76
Being cultures, 94–96
Belgium, 300
Beliefs, 87–88
Benevolence, 89
Bias. *See* Cultural biases
Biology, 39–41

Biomedical approach, 304
Black English, 229
Black Standard English, 229
Blacks. *See* African Americans
Blood type, 40
Body language, 183
Body movements, 183–187
British English, 216
Browning of America, 7–8
Business context, 314–324
Business negotiations, 318–320

Census figures, 7–8
Central beliefs, 87
Challenge of communication, 19–23
Challenger space shuttle disaster,
   335–336
Chemical code system, 197
Chicano, 62. *See also* Latinos, Mexican
   Americans
Chile, 300
China
   affect displays, 186
   business decisions, 319
   classroom interaction, 310
   contracts, 317
   facework, 278, 279
   family, 269
   report cards, 279
   rhetorical tradition, 249
   social relations orientation, 97
   touch, 191
Chronemics, 192
Classroom interaction, 309–312
Climate, 117, 126
Clocks, 216

Co-culture, 34
Code switching, 232–233
Code usage, 238–260
    conversational rules, 255–258
    intercultural competence, 258–259
    organizational preferences, 239–243
    persuasion, 243–253
    talk/silence, 253–255
    U.S. English, 239–242
Communication
    actional view, 14
    characteristics, 10–17
    contextual, as, 16–17
    defined, 9–10
    interactional view, 15
    intercultural, 50–53
    interpersonal, 18–19
    interpretive, as, 12–14
    process, as, 17
    shared meaning, 17
    symbolic, as, 10–12
    transactional view, 15
Communication accommodation
        theory, 227
Competence, 64–80
    actions, 71
    appropriateness/effectiveness, 68–69
    BASIC skills, 72–76
    context, 65–67
    description, interpretation,
        evaluation, 76–80
    intercultural. See Intercultural
        competence
    intracultural communication, 64
    knowledge, 69–71
    motivations, 71
Conceptual equivalence, 217
Conformity, 89, 329–330
Confucian cultural values, 132–135
Confucianism, 132
Connotative meanings, 209–210
Contact. See Intercultural contact
Context, 16–17, 65–67
Contexts. See Social contexts
Contextual style, 257
Continuum of interculturalness, 49, 50
Control, 270–271
Control face, 275–276
Conversational expressiveness, 272–273
Conversational rules, 255–258
Conversational styles, 256–257
Coping, 164
Cross-cultural communication, 52
Cultural biases, 145–160
    discrimination, 156–157

ethnocentrism, 148–151
prejudice, 154–155
racism, 157–160
social categorizing, 147–148
stereotyping, 151–154
Cultural conversational styles, 256–257
Cultural identity
    characteristics, 144–145
    formation, 142–144
    nature of identity, 140–142
Cultural identity achievement, 144
Cultural identity search, 143, 144
Cultural patterns, 84–138, 146
    activity orientation, 94–96
    beliefs, 87–88
    defined, 85–87
    functions, 91–93
    Hall's high-/low-context cultures,
        111–114
    Hofstede's dimensions, 115–132. See
        also Hofstede's cultural patterns
    intercultural competence, 105–108
    norms, 91
    self-orientation, 99–101
    social episode, as, 294–295
    social relations orientation, 96–99
    time orientation, 104–105
    values, 88–90
    world orientation, 102–103
Cultural racism, 158
Cultural taxonomies, 135–137
Culturally shared beliefs, 87
Culture, 25–54
    behaviors, and, 30
    beliefs/values/norms, 30
    defined, 27
    differences in, 34–43
    intercultural communication, 50–53
    interrelatedness of cultural forces, 44
    large groups of people, 30–31
    learned, as, 27–29
    shared interpretations, 29–30
Culture shock, 165–167

D-I-E framework, 76–80
Dances with Wolves, 41
Dani, 220
Dating, 267–268
Degree of deviance, 282–283
Degree of unfamiliarity, 160
Denmark, 300
Denotative meanings, 209
Dermal code system, 197
Description interpretation, evaluation,
    76–80

Deviant behaviors, 282–283
Dialectics, 273–274
Dialects, 229–230
Direct style, 256
Discrimination, 156–157
Display of respect, 72–73
Display rules, 180–182
Doing cultures, 94–96
Dominant, 162
Dynamic equivalence, 214

Ear wax, 40
Ebonics, 229–230
Ecology, 36–38
Economic development, 126
Ecuador, 300
Educational context, 307–314
Effectiveness, 68–69
Ego-defensive function, 154
Elaborate style, 257
Emblems, 11, 183–184
Empathy, 74–75
Endnotes, 343–373
English as a second language (ESL), 239
Equivalence, 214–217
Eskimo language, 220
ESL, 239
Ethnic group, 33
Ethnicity, 33–34
Ethnocentrism, 148–151
European Americans
    activity orientation, 94
    beliefs, 87, 88
    body movements, 187
    cultural identity, 142
    defined, 62, 63
    directness, 137
    display rules, 181
    ethnocentrism, 150
    individualism, 127
    orientation to knowledge, 73
    racism, 158
    self-orientation, 100, 101
    social relations orientation, 97, 98
    territoriality, 189
    time orientation, 104, 193
    touch, 191
    world orientation, 103
Evaluation, 78–80
Examples of intercultural interactions,
    45–49
Exercises. See Try This
Expectations about future interactions,
    281–282
Experiential equivalence, 216

Face, 274–280
Face needs, 275–277
Face-threat potential, 278–279
Facework, 277–280
Family, 268–270
Feedback, 14
Feelings, 71
Finland, 254
Forces that pull us together/apart,
    337–340
Formal time systems, 193–194
France
    intercultural contact, 170
    negotiations, 318
    non-French words, 338
    status, 271
    talk about work (dinner party), 298
Friendships, 264–267
Future-oriented cultures, 193

Garden salad metaphor, 58
Genetic variations, 39–40
Genuine likes and dislikes, 160
Germany
    negotiations, 318
    status, 271
    territoriality, 189
Ghana, 269, 285
Globalization, 337
Gone with the Wind, 150
Grammatical-syntactical equivalence,
    215–216
Great Depression, 333
Greece, 94
Guatemala, 252

Hall's high-/low-context cultures,
    111–114
Haragei, 254
Hawaiians, 304
Health care context, 301–307
Hedonism, 89
Hereditary differences, 39–40
High-context cultures, 111–114
Hispanic, 62. See also Latinos, Mexican
    Americans
Historical precedent, 251
History, 35–36
Hmong people, 207, 216
Hofstede's cultural patterns, 115–133
    individualism-collectivism
        dimension, 122–127
    masculinity-femininity dimension,
        127–129
    power distance, 116–120

time-orientation dimension, 130,
    131
uncertainty avoidance, 120–122
Holistic approach, 303
Hong Kong, 300
Hopi language, 221

Identity, 140. See also Cultural identity
Idiomatic equivalence, 215
Idioms, 215
Idiosyncratic interpretation, 181
IDV, 123
Igbos, 285
Illustrators, 185
Incentive value, 282
India
    dating, 268
    family, 268
    languages, 227
    namaste gesture, 186
    time orientation, 104
Indirect style, 256
Individual racism, 158
Individualism-collectivism dimension,
    122–127, 315
Individualism index (IDV), 123
Indonesia, 271
Informal time systems, 194
Ingroups, 114, 140
Institutional networks, 41–43
Institutional racism, 158
Instrumental style, 257
Integration, 169
Intensity, 89
Intentions, 71
Interaction contexts, 301
Interaction management, 75
Interaction posture, 76
Interaction scenes, 298–301
Interactional views of communication,
    15
Intercultural competence, 2–9
Intercultural communication, 44–45,
    50–51
Intercultural competence
    business context, 323–324
    code usage, 258–259
    components, 65–71
    cultural patterns, 105–108
    cultural taxonomies, 135–137
    educational context, 313–314
    episodes/contexts, 324–325
    ethics, 328–333
    health care context, 307
    interpersonal relationships, 290

national/international events,
    333–336
nonverbal communication, 199–201
    tools for improving, 72–80
    verbal codes, 233–235
Intercultural contact, 161–170
    attitudes among cultural members,
        162–163
    dominance/subordination between
        groups, 161–162
    outcomes of, 163–170
Intercultural films, 343–344
Intercultural interactions, 45–49
Intercultural transformation, 170
Interculturally competent
    communicator, 170–172
Interculturalness scale, 49
Interethnic communication, 52
International communication, 53
Internet web sites, 344–346
Interpersonal communication, 18–19
Interpersonal communication patterns,
    43
Interpersonal context, 17
Interpersonal relationships, 262–291
    activation, 272–273
    affiliation, 271–272
    control, 270–271
    disagreements, 287–289
    dynamics of, 273–274
    face, 274–280
    improving, 280–289
    intercultural competence, 290
    types, 262–270
Interpretation, 78–80, 213, 214
Interracial communication, 52
Interrelatedness of cultural forces, 44
Intimate space, 188
Intracultural communication, 52
Intracultural communication
    competence, 64
Inuktitut, 220
Inupit, 220
IQ scores, 40
Iran, 272
Iranian Americans, 230
Isolationism, 337–339
Israel
    evidence/reasonableness, 249
    social episodes, 295

Japan
    bowing, 198
    collectivism, 127
    self-orientation, 101

Japan (*cont.*)
  social relations orientation, 97
  values, 89
Jargon, 231
Jen, 277

Kalaallisut, 220
Kamayrua Indians, 220
Kennedy assassination, 334
Kenya, 104
Kibun, 321–322
Kinesics, 183
Kinship relationships, 268
Knowledge, 69–71
Knowledge function, 154
Korea
  business cards, 68
  classroom interaction, 310
  kibun, 321–322
  oldest males relative, 43
  social relations orientation, 97
  status, 271
  stranger, 263
  talk, 254
  values, 89
Kwanzaa, 143

Lakota speakers, 249
Language. *See* Verbal communication
Latinos/latinas
  census figures, 7, 8
  display rules, 181
  family, 268
  friendships, 267
  health, 304, 305
  self-orientation, 100
Liberia, 246
Lien, 277, 278
Linguistic grammars, 221–224
Linguistic relativity, 217, 224
Lone Ranger, The, 150
Los Angeles Unified School District, 8
Low-context cultures, 111–114

Magico-religious personalistic
  approach, 303
Malaysia
  chemical codes, 197
  conversational expressiveness,
    272
  social status, 270
Marginalization, 169
MAS, 127
Masculinity index (MAS), 127

Masculinity-femininity dimension,
  127–129
Meaning, 10–11
Media, 38–39, 337
Melting pot metaphor, 56
Memorial services, 102
Mensh, 277
Mesibot kiturim, 295
Message, 11
Metaphors of U.S. cultural diversity,
  56–58
Mexican Americans
  defined, 62
  display rules, 181
  racism, 160
  self-orientation, 100
Mexico
  business relationships, 319
  college students, 43
  friends, 266
  persuasion, 249
  reward systems, 316
  values, 89
Micronesia, 227
Mien-tzu, 277
Minority majorities, 7
Mitochondrial DNA, 41
Modern racism, 160
Monochronic time system, 194
Morocco
  code switching, 233
  friendship, 265
Morphemes, 208, 209
Morphology, 208–209
Motivations, 71

Namaste gesture, 186
Nation, 31–32
Nationalism, 337–339
Native Americans
  census figures, 7, 41
  defined, 62–63
  ear wax, 40
  racism, 158
  time systems, 193
Naturalistic approach, 303
Negative valence inaccuracy, 152
New Zealand, 264
Nonverbal communication,
  176–202
  body movements, 183–187
  characteristics, 178
  cultural universals, 179
  cultural variations, 180–182

  intercultural competence, and,
    199–201
  multichanneled, as, 182
  other nonverbal code systems,
    197
  space, 187–190
  synchrony of, 198
  time, 192–195
  touch, 190–192
  verbal communication, compared,
    178–179
  voice, 195–197
Norms, 91
Notes, 343–373
Novelty-predictability dialectic, 273

Old-fashioned racism, 159
Online resources, 344–346
Openness-closedness dialectic, 274
Oppression, 159
Orientation knowledge, 73–74
Outgroup homogeneity effect, 152
Outgroups, 114, 140

Pacific Islanders, 304
Pakistan, 264
Parthenon, 35
Particularistic cultures, 316
Past-oriented cultures, 192
PDI, 117
Pearl Harbor, 333–334
Perceived ethnolinguistic vitality,
  226
Perceived threat, 163
Peripheral beliefs, 87
Personal identity, 141
Personal space, 187–189
Personal style, 257
Personality traits, 67
Persuasion, 243–253
  cultural differences in style, 249–253
  evidence, 245–246
  intercultural encounters,
    243–245
  reasonableness, 246–249
Phonemes, 208
Phonology, 208
Physical code system, 197
Physical context, 16
Playfulness, 190
Polychronic time system, 195
Population size, 117
Positive valence inaccuracy, 152
Power, 89

Power distance, 116–120
Power distance index (PDI), 117
Pragmatics, 212
Prejudice, 154–155
Present-oriented cultures, 193
Presentational style, 250
President's Commission on Foreign Languages and International Studies, 5
Primary affect displays, 186
Process, 17
Pronouns, 223–224
Proxemics, 187
Public space, 188

Quasilogical style, 250

Race, 32–33, 39
Racial distinctions, 40–41
Racism, 157–160
Re-entry shock, 166
Regulators, 186–187
Relational dynamics, 273–274
Relational role behavior, 76
Relationships. See Interpersonal relationships
Religion, 42–43
Resources, 343–346
Respect, 72, 222–223
Rh-negative blood, 40
Rhetorical traditions, 249
Romantic partners, 267–268
Rules of interaction, 297–298

Samburu, 193
Sapir-Whorf hypothesis, 217–219
Scandinavia, 318
Seclusion, 169
Security, 89
Segregation, 169
Self-concept, 140
Self-direction, 89
Self-disclosure, 284–286
Self-orientation, 99–101
Semantics, 209–211
Separation, 169
September 11 terrorist attacks, 335–336
Shared interpretation, 146
Shared interpretations, 29–30
Shared meanings, 17
Shared perceptions, 84
Silence, 253, 255
Similarity-attraction hypothesis, 282
Singapore, 227

Sister city programs, 161
Social categorizing, 147–148
Social context, 16–17
Social contexts, 301–324
    business context, 314–324
    educational context, 307–314
    health care context, 301–307
Social dominance, 270–271
Social episodes, 292–301
    cultural patterns, 294–295
    interaction contexts, 301
    interaction scenes, 298–301
    nature of, 292–294
    rules of interaction, 297–298
    social roles, 295–296
Social hierarchy, 222–223
Social identity, 141
Social relations orientation, 96–99
Social role, 295–296
Social space, 188
South Sea islands, 220
Southern Californians, 221
Space, 187–190
Spain
    dating, 268
    time systems, 195
Spanglish, 211
Spiritualism, 337–339
Standard American English, 229, 230
Statement of description, 78, 79
Statement of evaluation, 78–80
Statement of interpretation, 78–80
Status, 270–271
Stereotype inaccuracy, 152–153
Stereotyping, 151–154
Stimulation, 89
Stock market collapse (1929), 333
Storybook pattern, 250
Strangers, 263
Subculture, 34
Succinct style, 257
Swaziland
    social relations orientation, 98
    talk, 254
Symbolic racism, 160
Symbols, 10–12
Syntactics, 211

Talk, 253–255
Tapestry metaphor, 58
Task role behavior, 75–76
Taxonomies, 135–137
Technical time systems, 193
Technology, 38–39

Television, 337
Terminology, 61–63
Territoriality, 189–190
Thailand
    beliefs, 88
    Buddhist monks, 95
    business, 323
    friendships, 265
Theory of linguistic determinism, 217
Time, 192–195, 221–222
Time orientation, 104–105, 192–193
Time-orientation dimension, 130, 131
Time systems, 193–195
Timing, 285
Tokenism, 160
Tolerance for ambiguity, 76
Touch, 190–192
Tradition, 89
Trait approaches, 67
Transactional view of communication, 15
Transcultural nursing, 302
Translation, 213
Tribalism, 337–339
Tributaries metaphor, 56–58
Try This
    accents, 230
    BASIC skills, 72
    belief/value/norm, 30, 142
    competent communicator, 65
    criticism, 93
    cultural background, 7
    cultural characteristics, 87, 107
    cultural diversity, 20
    cultural patterns, 132
    cultural reasoning, 247
    cultural views, 127
    D-I-E framework, 78
    demographic profile, 11
    different words, 208
    disagreements, 290
    enjoyment of learning, 340
    everyday activities, 167
    foreign speakers, 220
    friends/acquaintances, etc., 264, 266, 272
    Hofstede's five dimensions, 115
    intercultural interactions, 44
    interview with professional, 314
    metaphor of cultural diversity, 58
    nonverbal communication, 181, 186
    ordinary/strange behavior, 147
    origin of words, 214
    personal space, 189

Try This (*cont.*)
  public/private topics, 286
  slang, 226
  stereotype, 152
  strangers, 298
  telephone conversation openings, 253
  telephone/e-mail, 38
  visit to doctor, 306
  wedding, 300
Turkey, 184
Type B blood, 40
Typicality, 163

U-curve hypothesis, 166
UAI, 120
Uncertainty, 280
Uncertainty avoidance, 120–122
Uncertainty avoidance index (UAI), 120
Uncertainty reduction theory, 280
Understanding, 12, 13
Unexamined cultural identity, 142, 144
United Arab Emirates, 264
United States
  climate, 37
  college students, 43
  cultural groups, 61–63
  cultural mixing, 7, 13
  English language, 227, 228
  high school report cards, 279
  historical forces, 35
  intercultural community, as, 55–58

  negotiations, 319
  persuasion, 248–249
  racial tensions, 162
  second language learners, 234
  status, 271
  strangers, 263
U.S. Americans
  defined, 60–61
  emblems, 183
  ethnocentrism, 149, 150
  history, 35
  touch, 191
  values, 89
U.S. English, 216, 239–242
Universalism, 89
Universalism-particularism, 316
Utilitarian function, 154

Valence, 89, 285
Value-expressive function, 154
Values, 88–90
Verbal codes. *See* Code usage
Verbal communication, 203–237
  alternate versions of language,
    229–233
  equivalence, 214–217
  ethnic group identity/dominance,
    225–229
  features of language, 206–208
  intercultural competence, 233–235
  interpretation, 213–214

  linguistic grammars, 221–224
  linguistic relativity, 224
  morphology, 208–209
  phonology, 208
  power of language, 203–205
  pragmatics, 212
  pronouns, 223–224
  respect/social hierarchy, 222–223
  rule systems, 208–212
  Sapir-Whorf hypothesis, 217–219
  semantics, 209–211
  syntactics, 211
  time, 221–222
  vocabulary, 220–221
Vietnamese Americans, 100
Vocabulary, 220–221
Vocabulary equivalence, 215
Vocalics, 195
Voice, 193–195

W-curve hypothesis, 166
Wealth, 119
Web sites, 344–346
Weddings, 296
Western approach, 304
Whorfian hypothesis, 217
Wisdom teeth, 40
World orientation, 102–103

Yin and yang, 304
Yugoslavia, 162